Colonial America

COLONIAL

FROM THE FIRST SETTLEMENTS TO THE

AMERICA

CLOSE OF THE AMERICAN REVOLUTION

By the Editors of the

Album of American History

(OF WHICH IT IS THE FIRST VOLUME)

CHARLES SCRIBNER'S SONS · New York

NOTE ON THE BINDING DESIGN

The view at the top is the Carwitham view of Boston and shows that city as it appeared in the middle 1730's. Peter Cooper's painting of Philadelphia, *circa* 1720, is displayed across the middle of the binding, and at the bottom is the Roberts view of Charleston, South Carolina, in 1739. The top and bottom engravings are used by courtesy of the Stokes Collection, New York Public Library; Cooper's painting is by courtesy of The Library Company of Philadelphia.

PREFACE

JUST before the outbreak of the Second World War, the late James Truslow Adams projected and began the *Album of American History*, which he intended to be a faithful, far-ranging and objective study of the American people in carefully chosen pictures of tested historical value and authority. No picture was to be included for the sake of its subject alone, or for its importance as an artistic rendering; the sole criterion was its value as a document, as a true representation of past reality. The emphasis in the work was to be on the whole people of America—on what they were, how they lived, what they made, what they thought—without any tincture of special pleading, sectional narrowness, or editorial bias.

Successive boards of editors have carried on the project in the spirit of its projector, so that the *Album of American History* is presently established as the most complete and trustworthy source of pictorial Americana available and the six-volume set is to be found on the reference shelves of most libraries.

As we approach the two-hundredth anniversary of American Independence, a renewal of interest in the origins of the United States is becoming manifest and the publishers have received numerous requests for a separate publication of that part of the *Album* which deals with the first settlements, the founding of the colonies, and their constitution as a nation—one which can be purchased or borrowed for home study and leisured reading. *Colonial America*, a unit complete in itself and with its own Index, is offered for that purpose. The pictures and text are exactly as they appear in the latest revised edition of the reference set. All elements of American colonial history and society are presented here in graphic form, from the period of exploration down through the successful conclusion of the revolt against British rule.

J.G.E.H.

ACKNOWLEDGMENT

WITHOUT the advice and assistance of the museums, libraries and individuals in whose possession were the originals of the pictures and objects reproduced in this work, its preparation and publication would have been impossible. Throughout we have aimed to give proper credit in each case, but particular acknowledgment of the aid given us is herewith made to the following:

Albany Institute of History and Art, Albany, N. Y., American Antiquarian Society, Worcester, Mass., American Geographical Society, New York, N. Y., The Museum of the American Numismatic Society, New York, N. Y., American Scenic and Historic Preservation Society, New York, N. Y., American Swedish Historical Museum, Philadelphia, Pa., The American-Swedish News Exchange, Inc., New York, N. Y., Ancient and Honourable Artillery Company, Boston, Mass., Mrs. Imogene Anderson, New York, N. Y., The Magazine *Antiques*, New York, N. Y., The Atwater Kent Museum, Philadelphia, Pa., The Baltimore Museum of Art, Baltimore, Md., Bowdoin College Museum of Fine Arts, Brunswick, Me., Prof. Marion J. Bradshaw, Bangor, Me., The Brooklyn Museum, Brooklyn, N. Y., The Bucks County Historical Society, Doylestown, Pa., Major Charles T. Cahill, Boston, Mass., Mrs. Louise W. Carmichael, Fredericksburg, Va., Carolina Art Association, Gibbes Memorial Art Gallery, Charleston, S. C., The Charleston Museum, Charleston, N. C., The Cincinnati Art Museum, Cincinnati, Ohio, Columbia University in the City of New York, N. Y., Cooper Union for the Advancement of Science and Art, Museum for the Arts of Decoration, New York, N. Y., Enoch Pratt Free Library, Baltimore, Md., The Essex Institute, Salem, Mass., Dr. Henry Chandlee Forman, Macon, Ga., Frick Art Reference Library, New York, N. Y., Harvard College Library, Cambridge, Mass., The Hispanic Society of America, New York, N. Y., Historic American Buildings Survey, National Park Service, U. S. Department of the Interior, Washington, D. C., The John Carter Brown Library,

Providence, R. I., Mr. J. Frederick Kelly, New Haven, Conn., Mrs. Bella C. Landauer, New York, N. Y., Landis Valley Museum, Lancaster, Pa., Library of Congress, Washington, D. C., Litchfield Historical Society, Litchfield, Conn., Maine Historical Society, Portland, Me., Maryland Historical Society, Baltimore, Md., Mr. George Carrington Mason, Newport News, Va., Massachusetts Historical Society, Boston, Mass., The Metropolitan Museum of Art, New York, N. Y., William L. Clements Library, University of Michigan, Ann Arbor, Mich., The Moravian Historical Society, Nazareth, Pa., Museum of the American Indian, Heye Foundation, New York, N. Y., Museum of the City of New York, N. Y., Museum of Fine Arts, Boston, Mass., National Park Service, U. S. Department of the Interior, Washington, D. C., New Castle Historical Society, New Castle, Del., New Hampshire Antiquarian Society, Hopkinton, N. H., New Hampshire Historical Society, Concord, N. H., New Haven Colony Historical Society, New Haven, Conn., New York Academy of Medicine, New York, N. Y., The New-York Historical Society, New York, N. Y., The New York Public Library, New York, N. Y., New York State Library, The University of the State of New York, Albany, N. Y., North Carolina Department of Conservation and Development, Raleigh, N. C., The North Carolina Historical Historical Commission, Raleigh, N. C., The Archives of the University of Notre Dame, Notre Dame, Ind., Old Quinabaug Village, Sturbridge, Mass., Onondaga Historical Association, Syracuse, N. Y., Pennsylvania German Society, Norristown, Pa., Philadelphia Museum of Art, Philadelphia, Pa., Pilgrim Society, Plymouth, Mass., Dr. J. Hall Pleasants, Baltimore, Md., Pocumtuck Valley Memorial Association of Deerfield, Mass., Rhode Island Historical Society, Providence, R. I., The Society for the Preservation of New England Antiquities, Inc., Boston, Mass., Mr. Harry Stone, New York, N. Y., The Valentine Museum, Richmond, Va., Vermont Historical Society, Montpelier, Vt., Mr. Philip B. Wallace, Philadelphia, Pa., Wells Historical Museum, Southbridge, Mass., Colonial Williamsburg, Inc., Williamsburg, Va., Wilmington Institute Free Library, Wilmington, Del., Miss Alice Winchester, New York, N. Y., Yale University Art Gallery, New Haven, Conn., The Historical Society of York County, York, Pa.

CONTENTS

PREFACE v

FROM COLUMBUS TO JAMESTOWN 1

FISHERMEN, PILGRIMS AND "DOWN-EASTERS" 31

THE PURITANS 72

THE HUDSON AND THE DELAWARE 136

MARYLAND 176

THE CAROLINAS AND GEORGIA 196

PENNSYLVANIA 228

THE FIRST HALF OF THE EIGHTEENTH CENTURY . . . 252

THE SELF-CONSCIOUS ERA 293

THE AMERICAN REVOLUTION 358

INDEX 413

Colonial America

1
FROM COLUMBUS TO JAMESTOWN

America Has Been a Land of Dreams

from the beginning. Viking sea-rovers and nameless fishermen may have sighted its shores before the days of Christopher Columbus, but fact and fiction are hopelessly confused. As the Fifteenth Century neared its close the search for a direct route to rich Cathay occupied the minds of men, stimulating the imagination. Whether this route lay East or West was a matter of conjecture.

Columbus Sailed West . . .

Woodcut. 1493. A contemporary interpretation of what Columbus found.

And in 1492 Discovered America . . .

but was deeply disappointed in not finding Cathay. Legend would have us believe that he found a region full of cannibals and monsters.

Cannibals

Woodcut made at Augsburg ca. 1505.

Monsters

Pieter Van der Aa *Voyagien*. 1706-07.

Mystery . . .

A map from Münster's edition of Ptolemy. 1540

Note the name "Americam." Here is shown a fair understanding of the New World, although Japan (Zipangri) and China (Cathay) are placed across a narrow sea from our west coast. The New World perils are shown—giants (Gigantum) and Cannibals (Canibali).

And Glory . . .

Amerigo Vespucci. Date depicted 1497. Date issued ca. 1585

Courtesy, Stokes Collection. The New York Public Library.

When rumors of gold unleashed the "Age of Discovery," among the many voyages was the somewhat vague but well publicized ones by an Italian, Amerigo Vespucci, whose name was attached to the New Continent in 1507 by a German geographer, Waldseemüller. In the early days of our Republic there was much sentiment in favor of calling it Columbia in honor of Columbus.

. . . and Gold

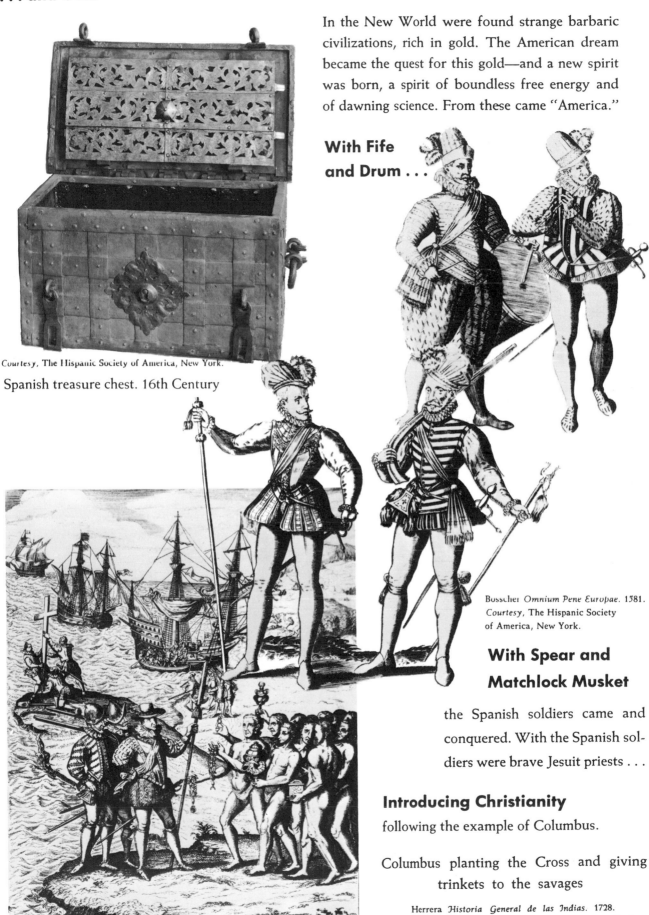

In the New World were found strange barbaric civilizations, rich in gold. The American dream became the quest for this gold—and a new spirit was born, a spirit of boundless free energy and of dawning science. From these came "America."

With Fife and Drum . . .

Courtesy, The Hispanic Society of America, New York.

Spanish treasure chest. 16th Century

Busscher *Omnium Pene Europae.* 1581.
Courtesy, The Hispanic Society of America, New York.

With Spear and Matchlock Musket

the Spanish soldiers came and conquered. With the Spanish soldiers were brave Jesuit priests . . .

Introducing Christianity

following the example of Columbus.

Columbus planting the Cross and giving trinkets to the savages

Herrera *Historia General de las Indias.* 1728.
Courtesy, The Hispanic Society of America, New York.

Florida (Land of Flowers)

became a land of bloodshed. The Spanish built the fortified city of St. Augustine in 1565.

St. Augustine, Florida

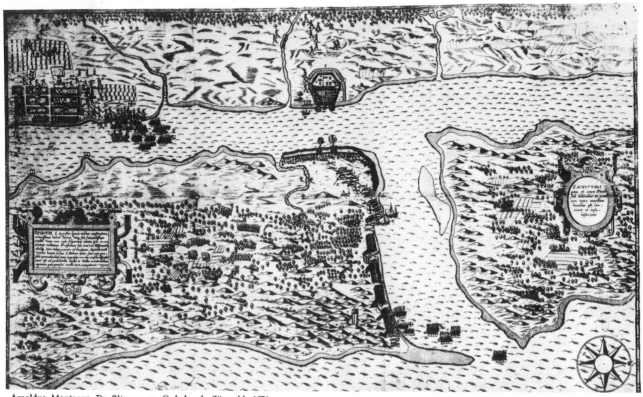

Arnoldus Montanus *De Nieuwe en Onbekende Weereld.* 1671.

Fleur de Lis

The French, a year earlier, had built Fort Caroline at the mouth of the St. Johns River. Jacques Le Moyne, an artist with the expedition, has left us these pictures of the fort, with its moat and bastions, cannon, and flag with its *Fleur de Lis*, the lilies of France.

Fort Caroline completed   The beginnings of Fort Caroline in Florida

Drawings by Jacques Le Moyne in De Bry *Grands Voyages.* 1592.

Roanoke

In 1584 a new name appeared on the maps. It was Roanoke. Sir Walter Raleigh tried to found a colony on Albemarle Sound in what is now North Carolina. When his expedition brought reports of the new region Queen Elizabeth named it Virginia in honor of herself.

Sir Walter Raleigh

Ship such as the ones sent out by Sir Walter Raleigh

Elizabethan coin, showing a ship

Hollar *Navium Variae Figurae et Formae.*
1647.

We see the Indian palisades, the fishermen, the English landing party, and the sunken ships off the barrier of Hatteras, then, as now, a graveyard of ships. We see again what Sixteenth Century ships looked like.

Map of Roanoc. Engraved by Theodore De Bry, 1590, after the original by John White.

In this larger map we see the rivers of Florida and Carolina (named after the great rivers of France) in their geographic relation to Roanoke.

Map by John White ca. 1585. *Courtesy,* William L. Clements Library, Ann Arbor, Mich.

Before the White Man Was the Indian

Note the corn in various stages of growth. A scarecrow on the platform in the upper cornfield kept the birds from eating the crop. *At the bottom* are the place of prayer and the ceremonial dance.

Indian chief   Indian woman

Close-up view of the palisade

All illustrations are water colors by John White ca. 1585. *Courtesy*, The William L. Clements Library, Ann Arbor, Mich.

Indians fishing . . . note the dugout

15   315   213

eating . . .

Water colors by John White ca. 1585. *Courtesy,* The
William L. Clements Library, Ann Arbor, Mich.

At the left is the Indian
method of making a dug-
out. The trees were felled
with fire, the wood was
burned out, and the dug-
out finished by scraping
with shells and stones.

Engraved by Theodore De Bry. 1590

Homesick

The Roanoke colonists were soon hungry and homesick. They lived in constant fear of being wiped out by the Spaniards. In 1586 the discouraged settlers saw a fleet of twenty-three sail. Were the Spaniards approaching? A joyful shout went up. It was Sir Francis Drake, fresh from the sacking of Spanish-held Santo Domingo, Cartagena, and St. Augustine.

Drake's fleet. Detail of an engraving from *Expeditio Francisci Draki equitis angli in Indias Occidentalis.* 1588.

Drake, who had visited California in 1579 and had taken possession of it in the name of Queen Elizabeth, was now a greater hero than ever in the eyes of his countrymen at Roanoke Island. Most of them accepted his offer to take them back to England.

An English Ship

A water color by John White. 1585.

Van der Aa *Voyagien.* 1706-07.

Note the formal act of annexation. Drake named California New Albion.

The brass plate at the left was nailed to a "firm poste" by Drake in California in 1579. It was found in 1936 on the western shore of San Francisco Bay. The inscription reads:

Bee it knowne unto all men by these presents Iune 17 1579 by the grace of God and in the name of herr maiesty Queen Elizabeth of England and herr successors forever I take possession of this kingdome whose King and people freely resigne their right and title in the whole land unto herr maiesties keeping now named by me an to bee knowne unto all men as Nova Albion.

Francis Drake

The Lost Colony

Scarcely had Drake departed when a relief expedition under Grenville arrived, and finding Roanoke deserted, left fifteen men to hold the place until more settlers could be brought. These came in 1587 under John White, he who made the pictures we have just seen. They did not find the fifteen men, nor did White's own colony, including his granddaughter, Virginia Dare, the first white child born in America, survive except in a never-dying legend built around three letters CRO engraved on a tree and the word CROATON engraved on a doorpost.

Courtesy, Department of Conservation and Development, Raleigh, N. C.
Roanoke Island as it appears today. What an unhappy site this was for a colony! It had practically no advantages to recommend it.

The Folly of It All

To reach Roanoke all vessels had to risk the hazards of the treacherous reef off Hatteras, which, as has already been pointed out, was a graveyard of ships. It was much more dangerous to sail from Boston to Charleston throughout the whole Colonial Era than to cross the Atlantic Ocean.

Courtesy, Department of Conservation and Development, Raleigh, N. C.
Shipwreck on Hatteras beach

Time and Tide

Courtesy, Department of Conservation and Development, Raleigh, N. C.

Sand dunes near Roanoke Island.

The Vine That Forgot to Die

Courtesy, Department of Conservation and Development, Raleigh, N. C.

One of the ancient scuppernong grapevines in the Mother Vineyard at Roanoke Island. It was growing when the first white men landed at Roanoke. Surviving the storms and blights of more than three centuries it antedates the beginning of our nation and is both a witness to our youth and a promise of our strength.

Shifting Sands

Courtesy, Department of Conservation and Development, Raleigh, N. C.

Shore line of Roanoke Sound, near where the first colonists landed.

JAMESTOWN

The fate of the Roanoke settlement did not deter the English from colonizing America. In 1606 James, "by the grace of God, King of England, Scotland, France, and Ireland, Defender of the Faith, &c." issued a charter under which a group of "Adventurers," shortly to be known as the Virginia Company of London, were authorized to plant a colony in "that part of America, commonly called Virginia."

In 1607 the ships *Susan Constant*, under Captain Christopher Newport, the *Goodspeed*, under Captain Bartholomew Gosnold, and the *Discovery*, under Captain John Ratcliffe, dropped anchor at the entrance of Chesapeake Bay. Exploration disclosed a broad river which was named the James in honor of the King, and a site on its low shores was chosen for a settlement which was called Jamestown (*below*, a modern view).

Courtesy, National Park Service.

Pieter Van der Aa *Voyagien*. 1706-07.

The English in Virginia: an early 18th century rendering.

One of the first structures erected at Jamestown was a so-called fort, probably little more than a wooden structure enclosed in a palisade. The first houses may have resembled these.

Defense and Shelter

Fludd *Tractatus Secundus.* 1618.

Herrera *Historia General de las Indias.* 1728.

Note the method of building a ship (caravel).
Spanish houses in the West Indies. 16th Century.

Greate Gunns . . .

Fludd *Tractatus Secundus* 1618

Cannon, called "greate gunns," defended Jamestown

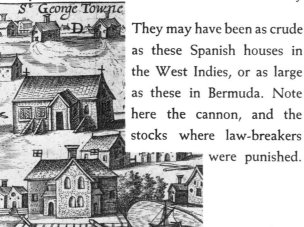

They may have been as crude as these Spanish houses in the West Indies, or as large as these in Bermuda. Note here the cannon, and the stocks where law-breakers were punished.

John Smith *Generall Historie.* 1624.

. . . and Drums

Fludd *Tractatus Secundus.* 1618.

The rat-a-tat-tat or the roll of the drum was frequently heard and with many meanings: the arrival of a ship, the call to arms; the opening of the assembly, or—all too often—a requiem for the dead.

Among the settlers at Jamestown was John Smith, who wrote a history of the colony. The prime explorer of Virginia, his map shown *below* is so accurate that it is still referred to in boundary disputes.

From John Smith's *Generall Historie.* 1624.

From *Generall Historie.* 1632.

John Smith

Smith was captured by the Indians and brought before their chief, Powhatan. (See his dwelling in Smith's map *above*, upperleft hand corner.) Powhatan's comely daughter, legend says, saved Smith from death by pleading with her father to show clemency. In 1614 she married John Rolfe, one of the English colonists at Jamestown, who took her to England in 1616, where the portrait to the *right* was painted. The following year as she was preparing to return to Virginia she died of smallpox.

Courtesy, National Gallery of Art, Washington, D. C.

Pocahontas

English readers of the Seventeenth Century were thrilled by John Smith's romantic account of his adventures. These are the very pictures they looked at as they turned the pages of his book. This, for them, was America.

John Smith captured by the Indians. 1607.

Indian conjuration about Captain Smith. 1607.

Smith taking King Pamaunkee prisoner. 1608.

Pocahontas saving John Smith's life.

Illustrations from John Smith's *Generall Historie.* 1624.

The Jamestown colonists were sent over to develop trade, and were instructed to look for new agricultural and drug products, precious minerals, and furs.

They found ginseng which had a ready market in Europe where it was used as a drug.

They found the sweet-smelling sassafras, also used widely as a drug

Mark Catesby *The Natural History of Carolina.* 1754.

Ginseng

Potatoes

They found both the Spanish potato and the Virginia potato

Mark Catesby *The Natural History of Carolina.* 1754.

Sassafras

John Parkinson *Paradisi in Sole.* 1629.

Spanish, or Sweet potatoes

Virginia, or Irish potatoes

John Parkinson *Paradisi in Sole.* 1629.

The persimmon tree was everywhere, its ripe fruit was eaten, and persimmon beer, recommended to the Jamestown colonists by the Indians was sometimes substituted for more palatable drinks if these were not obtainable.

Silk

They found mulberry trees in abundance, the leaves of which were used as a food for silk worms. They had high hopes of manufacturing silk at Jamestown, but this dream was soon shattered.

John Parkinson *Paradisi in Sole.* 1629.
Persimmon

John Parkinson *Paradisi in Sole.* 1629.
The Mulberry

They Found No Gold

Gold was not found, and a shipload of yellow soil, which seemed to contain gold dust, when tested in England, proved to be worthless. The mighty forests which surrounded them supplied thousands of staves, and these were cut and shipped to England.

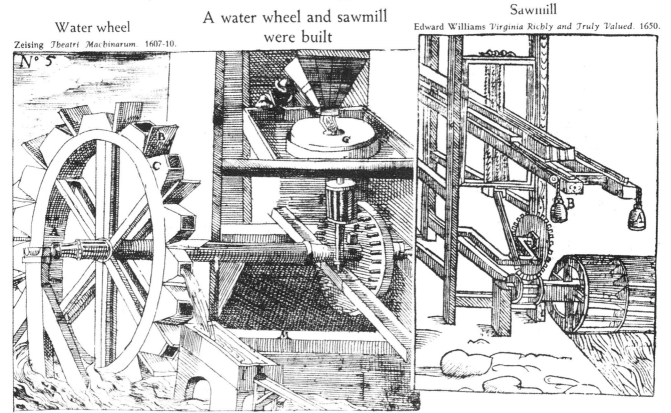

Water wheel

Zeising *Theatri Machinarum.* 1607-10.

A water wheel and sawmill were built

Sawmill

Edward Williams *Virginia Richly and Truly Valued.* 1650.

The Venetian Art of Glassmaking

Glassmakers were among those who settled at Jamestown in 1607. Fuel, potash, and glass sands were plentiful. The art of making glass was a secret confined to a small guild, and a few Venetian families were the greatest artisans.

Kunckel *Ars Vitraria Experimentalis.* 1679.

Tools used in glass manufacture

Kunckel *Ars Vitraria Experimentalis.* 1679.

Glass blower

Diderot and D'Alembert *Encyclopedie.*

Glassmaking

Diderot and D'Alembert *Encyclopedie. Recueil des Planches.* 1762-72.

Glass furnace

Money

Glass beads were made at Jamestown. They were used as a medium of exchange, the Indians placing a high value upon them.

Wampum, made of shells, was the standard medium of exchange among the Indians.

Courtesy, National Park Service.

Glass beads found at Jamestown

Courtesy, Museum of the American Indian, Heye Foundation, New York.

Wampum

There were very few English coins at Jamestown. There was no need for them. Now and then a coin has been found by the excavators of Jamestown.

Double Crown
James I. Period

Until tobacco farms were planted the Jamestown colony languished. Its promoters were discouraged. They resorted to a publicity campaign in an attempt to glorify Virginia, hoping to find gullible investors and settlers. The title-page of *Nova Britannia* is an example of this advertising. Tobacco became the most important medium of exchange in Virginia. John Rolfe, the husband of Pocahontas, discovered a new method of curing tobacco in 1612 which immediately made it a profitable item of export.

The picture of the ship is interesting for it gives us an idea of the kind of craft the Jamestown settlers had come over in two years earlier.

Nova Britannia.

OFFERING MOST

Excellent fruites by Planting in
VIRGINIA.

Exciting all such as be well affected
to further the same.

LONDON
Printed for SAMVEL MACHAM, and are to be fold at
his Shop in Pauls Church-yard, at the
Signe of the Bul-head.
1 6 0 9.

Tobacco . . .

Recent excavations at Jamestown have unearthed hundreds of clay pipes. King James I protested against the tobacco habit in vain. Sir Walter Raleigh, who was largely responsible for the founding of Roanoke and Jamestown, was an ardent champion of tobacco and is credited with introducing it to England.

The medicinal value of tobacco rose in popular estimation, and its praises were sung in numerous books. Among them was Gilles Everard's *Panacea. Below* we see Gilles enjoying a good smoke.

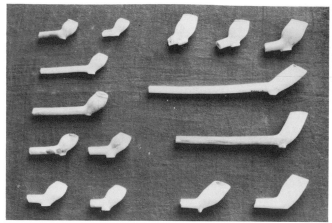

Courtesy, National Park Service.

Clay pipes found at Jamestown

Gilles Everard *Panacea.* 1659.

Slaves . . .

The successful cultivation of tobacco opened up possibilities for mass production, lacking only one thing—cheap labor. Slavery was the ultimate answer. As far back as 1562 John Hawkins had discovered that money was to be made by calling on the West Coast of Africa, picking up shiploads of Negroes and selling them in the slave marts of the West Indies. Queen Elizabeth in fact granted Hawkins a coat-of-arms with a captive Negro as its crest. The first cargo of Negroes arrived at Jamestown in 1619, although there is some question as to whether these first arrivals were sold as slaves for life or only for a term of years as were the white indentured servants.

A New General Collection of Voyages. 1745-47.

Although tobacco was much the most important export from Virginia there were many other products as this price list for the year 1621 will show. Here also is a glowing account of Virginia.

(44)

this Countrey ; I shall with his pardon believe him , distrustfull of Gods providence ; or if he be so vitiously disposed as to hope after a Land where he may enjoy an undisturbed plenty without the sweat of his browes , the Maps are so extreamely deficient in the description of such a Countrey , that I must desire him to looke for a new World and Kingdome, for such an easie accommodation.

If any make an Objection why this Countrey stored with all these Riches , furnished with all these Staples , hath so long held downe her head in the lownesse of a desperate condition ? Why being capable to crowne her browes with Garlands of Roses and plenty , she sate desolate amongst the Willowes of neglect and poverty ? Let them but recall their Memory , how by the prevailency of *Gondamore* the Corporation was dissolved , their patent cancelled, to which if wee adde the cooperation of the Indian treachery in their first massacre , they will cease their wonder at its languishing condition , and convert it to a full admiration, how that Colony could ever raise her endangered head out of those Gulfes of distraction, in which the Gold of Spaine , the disincouragement of the Court, the discontent of the better sort of Planters, and the desperate negligence of the more inconsiderable had in humane opinion irrecoverably involved her.

But the incomparable Virgin hath raised her dejected head, cleared her enclouded reputation, and now like the Eldest Daughter of Nature expresseth a priority in her Dowry ; her browes encircled with opulency to be believed by no other triall , but that of experience, her unwounded wombe full of all those Treasuries which indeere Provinces to respect of glory, and may with as great justice as any Countrey the Sunne honours with his eye-beames, intitle her selfe to an affinity with Eden , to an absolute perfection above all but Paradize.

And this those Gentlemen to whom she vouchsafes the honour of her Embraces, when by the blessings of God upon their labours sated with the beauty of their Cornefield, they shall retire into their Groves checkered with Vines , Olives, Mirtles, from thence dilate themselves into their Walkes covered in a manner , paved with Orenges and Lemmons, whence surfeited with variety , they incline to repose in their Gardens upon nothing lesse perfumed then Roses and Gilly-flowers. When they shall see their numerous Heards wanton

(45)

wanton with the luxury of their Pasture, confesse a narrownesse in their Barnes to receive their Corne , in bosomes to expresse fully their thankefulnesse to the Almighty Authour of these blessings , will chearefully confesse : Whilst the Incomparable Roanoak like a Queene of the Ocean, encircled with an hundred attendant Islands , and the most Majestick Carolana shall in such an ample and noble gratitude by her improvement repay her Adventurers and Creditors with an Interest so far transcending the Principall.

♦♦♦♦♦♦♦♦♦♦♦♦♦♦♦♦♦♦♦♦♦♦♦♦♦♦♦♦♦♦♦♦♦♦♦

A valuation of the Commodities growing and to be had in *Virginia*: valued in the year, 1621.

And since those Times improved in all more or lesse, in some ⅓, in others ⅔, in many double, and in some treble.

Iron, ten pounds the Tun.
Silke Coddes, two shillings six pence the pound.
Raw silk, 1 3s. 4d. the pound, now at 2 5s. and 28. *per* pound.
Silke grasse to be used for Cordage, 6d. the pound : but we hope it will serve for many better uses , and so yeeld a far greater rate, wherof there can never be too much planted. Of this Q. *Elizabeth* had a silke Gowne made.
Hemp, from 10s. to 22s. the hundred.
Flax, from 22s. to 30s. the hundred.
Cordage, from 20s. to 24s. the hundred.
Cotton wooll, 8d. the pound.
Hard pitch, 5s. the hundred.
Tarre, 5s. the hundred.
Turpentine, 12s. the hundred.
Rozen, 5s. the hundred.
Madder crop, 4 s. the hundred : course madder, 25s. the hundred.
Woad, from 12s. to 20 the hundred.
Annice seeds, 40s. the hundred.
Powder Sugar, Panels, Muscavadoes and whites, 25s. 40. and 3l. the hundred.   H 3   Sturgeon,

Sumac
Sumac was used for tanning leather

(46)

Sturgeon, and Caveare, as it is in goodnesse.
Salt, 30s. the weight.
Mastick, 3s. the pound.
Salsa Perilla wild, 5l. the hundred.
Salsa Perilla domestick, 10l. the hundred.
Red earth Allenagra, 3s. the hundred.
Red Allum, called Carthagena Alum, 10s. the hundred.
Roach Allum, called Romish Allum, 10s. the hundred.
Berry graine, 2s. 6d. the pound : the powder of graine, 9s. the pound : it groweth on trees like Holly berries.
Masts for shipping, from 12s. to 3l. a peece.
Pot-ashes, from 12s. the hundred, to 14. now 40. and 35s. the hundred.
Sope-ashes, from 6s. to 8s. the hundred.
Clapboord watered, 30s. the hundred.
Pipe staves, 4l. the thousand.
Rape-seed oyle, 10l. the tun, the cakes of it feed Kine fat in the Winter.
Oyle of Walnuts, 12l. the tun.
Linseed oyle 10l. the tun.
Saffron, 20s. the pound.
Honey, 2s. the gallon.
Waxe, 4l. the hundred.
Shomacke, 7s. the hundred , whereof great plenty in Virginia, and good quantity will be vented in England.
Fustick yong, 8s. the hundred.
Fustick old, 6s. the hundred, according to the sample.
Sweet Gums, Roots, Woods, Berries for Dies and Drugs, send of all sorts as much as you can , every sort by it selfe , there being great quantities of those things in Virginia, which after proof made, may be heere valued to their worth. And particularly, we have great hope of the Pocoon root, that it will prove better then Madder.
Sables, from 8s. the payre, to 20s. a payre.
Otter skins, from 3s. to 5s. a piece.
Luzernes, from 2s. to 10 a piece.
Martins the best, 4s. a piece.
Wild Cats, 8d. a piece.
Fox skins, 6d. a piece.

(47)

Muske Rats skins, 2s. a dozen : the cods of them will serve for good perfumes.
Bever skins that are full growne, in season, are worth 7s. a piece.
Bever skins, not in season, to allow two skins for one, and of the lesser, three for one.
Old Bever skins in Mantles, gloves or caps, the more worne, the better, so they be full of fur, the pound weight is 6s.
The new Bevers skins are not to bee bought by the pound , because they are thicke and heavy Leather , and not so good for use as the old.
Pearles of all sorts that ye can find : Ambergreece as much as you can get : Cristall Rocke : send as much as you can , and any sort of Minerall stones, or earth that weighs very heavy.
Preserve the Walnut trees to make oile of, & cut them not downe : so also preserve your Mulberry and Chestnut trees very carefully.
In the month of June, bore holes in divers sorts of Trees, wherby you shall see what gums they yield , and let them bee well dried in the Sun every day, and send them home in very dry caske.

Woad
A blue dye was made from woad

Iron

Even iron ore was found in Virginia, not in mines but fished out of ponds and swamps (*left*). It was called bog iron.

Diderot and D'Alembert *Encyclopedie. Recueil des Planches.* 1762-72.

Indian Massacre

In 1622 occurred a setback of a sort which was to plague Americans on their frontiers for two hundred and fifty years—an Indian massacre (*below*). In this case it was planned by Powhatan's brother and all but wiped out the English settlements beyond fortified Jamestown.

An engraving by Theodore De Bry. 1590.

Bricks

Wooden huts at Jamestown were gradually replaced by brick houses. The bricks were made at Jamestown as excavations on the site by the National Park Service conclusively prove. To the *right* is an old brick kiln excavated at Jamestown. Note the partially fired bricks still in place.

Courtesy, National Park Service.

Zeising *Theatri Machinarum*. 1607-10.

The bricks were of different sizes. The average dimension would be about 9 x 3⅜ x 2⅜ inches. In color they ranged from light orange, through salmon and red, to a dark brownish red. They were comparatively soft. At the *left* we see bricklaying as practiced in Europe in 1607.

To the *right* are the foundations of the first State House at Jamestown. South of the ruin is the James River.

Courtesy, National Park Service.

Jamestown Lives Again

Hardly a trace of this first permanent English settlement in America remained among the ruins of Jamestown until the National Park Service began its excavations. Below we see the foundations of the "Country House," built around 1640 (*left*). Upon its foundations the remains of two other houses were found, the William Sherwood House, built some forty years later and the Ambler House (ruins at *right*), built between 1710 and 1721.

Courtesy, National Park Service.

Courtesy, National Park Service.

Fortunately a few Seventeenth Century houses still stand in the neighborhood of Jamestown. Among them are Bacon's Castle (*below, left*), built around 1650 and the Adam Thoroughgood House (*below, right*), built about 1640.

Courtesy, Library of Congress.

Courtesy, Library of Congress.

The first Virginia mansion of great size was Greenspring, built three miles above Jamestown by Governor William Berkeley, around 1642. It stood until 1796 when William Ludwell Lee replaced it with a house designed by Benjamin Latrobe, who made this drawing of the older house.

The Old Brick Church in Isle of Wight County gives us a good idea of 17th Century church architecture in Virginia.

The House of God

One of the first buildings erected at Jamestown was a church. It was replaced by a fine brick edifice. The ruined tower shown below was attached to the fifth Jamestown church, 1639-44.

Courtesy, National Park Service.

Views of the old church at Jamestown

Old Brick Church, Isle of Wight County, Va. 17th Century. Also known as St. Luke's Church, or Newport Parish Church.

Interior of Old Brick Church, Isle of Wight County, showing methods of construction. This picture was taken shortly before the roof fell in during a storm in 1887. The church was restored in 1894.

Magic Casement

Let us visit a Seventeenth Century Jamestown house and get acquainted with the life of the people. Through a leaded casement window the occupant of the house sees us approach. Battered though it is, one can almost hear, across the centuries, the faint squeak of the latch as an English hand reaches through a lace cuff to open the window and wave to us.

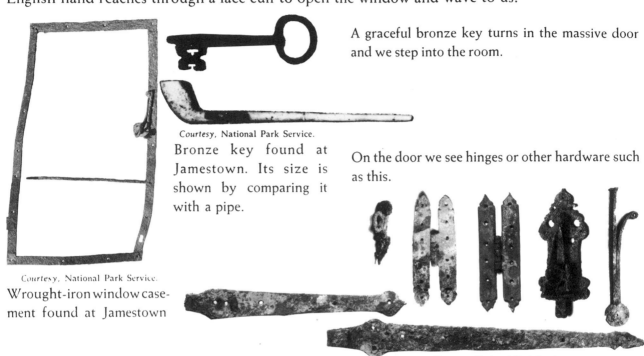

Courtesy, National Park Service.

Bronze key found at Jamestown. Its size is shown by comparing it with a pipe.

A graceful bronze key turns in the massive door and we step into the room.

On the door we see hinges or other hardware such as this.

Courtesy, National Park Service.

Wrought-iron window casement found at Jamestown

Courtesy, National Park Service.

Hinges and other hardware found at Jamestown

We are greeted by a Virginia gentleman and his wife —and it may be thus that we see them.

Cavalier

The gentleman may have looked like this

Naturally he wore spurs. Here is all that remains of one found at Jamestown.

Jaquemin Iconographie du Costume.

If our host does not have on his jack-boots and spurs he may wear low shoes with buckles like these.

Shoe buckle found at Jamestown

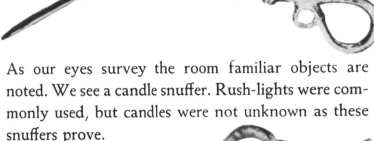

As our eyes survey the room familiar objects are noted. We see a candle snuffer. Rush-lights were commonly used, but candles were not unknown as these snuffers prove.

A spigot, dagger hilt, ring, and other objects

We see a jew's harp

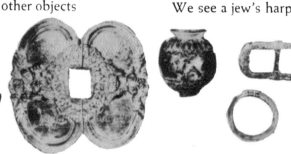

On the shelves we see flasks, jugs, bottles, plates, and other beautiful objects. The Jamestown men were heavy drinkers. Beer mugs and wine bottles were conspicuous.

Drinking
Wine bottle found at Jamestown

Bottles excavated at Jamestown

Note how the caps were held on the bottle top by wire. Screw tops were not used at Jamestown.

Bottle tops found at Jamestown

One of the features of a Jamestown dinner was a German wine imported in a glazed stone-ware jug bearing a crest. One of these jugs (*below, left*) was found at Jamestown. In the crest can be seen the date 1661. A similar 17th Century jug (*below, right*), called a "Bellarmine" jug, was found in New England.

Courtesy, National Park Service.

Courtesy, Old Sturbridge Village, Sturbridge, Mass.

Courtesy, National Park Service.

Decorated pottery objects found in excavations at Jamestown.

Eating

The knives, forks, and spoons used at Jamestown were of lovely workmanship, offering a surprising contrast to the rough-and-tumble life of this outpost of civilization, a life beset with hardships of all kinds.

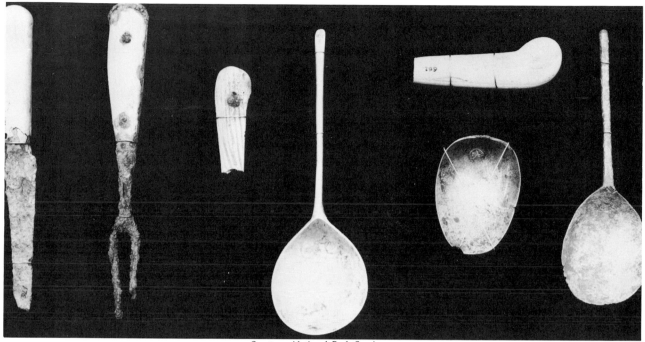

Courtesy, National Park Service.

Spoons knives and forks unearthed at Jamestown

Courtesy, National Park Service.

"Chuckatuck" spoon

Here was found the first bit of pewter bearing the "touch" of an American maker, the so-called "Chuckatuck" spoon made by Joseph Copeland in 1675.

Somewhere on the wall hung a strange mask. Whose face did it represent?

The fireplace was ornamented with delftware tiles like this one

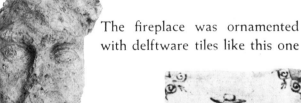

Courtesy, National Park Service.

Courtesy, National Park Service.

Linen Chest still used in Lower Chapel, Middlesex County, Va. 17th Century.

Courtesy, Mr. George C. Mason, Newport News, Va.

In the corner was an adz, reminder that there was work to be done

Courtesy, National Park Service.

"Ye Englyshe Nation"

The founders of little Jamestown lie buried, but their spirit lives. What they planted became not only the "Old Dominion" of history and legend, the Virginia of Washington, Jefferson and Lee, but the cradle of our nation. Had they like their predecessors failed in trying to realize Sir Walter Raleigh's dream of an "Englyshe nation" in the New World, the Pilgrims and Puritans might never have come to the wilderness which had proved so baffling. Jamestown itself, the center of the young colony, was destroyed in Bacon's Rebellion, 1675-76, but the seat of government was moved to Williamsburg, a better site, and the colonists marched on.

The Dead

Courtesy, National Park Service.

View of the Travis graveyard at Jamestown Island

The Living

At Williamsburg was founded the College of William and Mary in 1693; which still lives, a hallowed link with the past.

Courtesy, Colonial Williamsburg, Inc. Photo by Richard Garrison.

Wren Building. College of William and Mary, Williamsburg, Va. 1695. Designed by Sir Christopher Wren, the architect who built St. Paul's Cathedral in London.

II
FISHERMEN, PILGRIMS AND "DOWN-EASTERS"

Fog

In the fog-bound North Atlantic, fishermen from Western Europe, long before Columbus, discovered another part of America. That this land furnished a place on which to sort and dry their catch of fish was all that mattered to them. With the taciturnity of deep-sea fishermen, they probably did not talk about it.

Courtesy, American Geographic Society, New York.

North Atlantic Seascape

Cod

Bretons, Basques, Spaniards, Portuguese, and Englishmen, in boats such as these, fished for cod on the Grand Banks. The methods have changed but little through the centuries.

Fishing for cod on the Grand Banks

Duhamel du Monceau *Traité générale des pesches.* 1769-1777.

On the submerged tablelands called "banks" the prolific codfish provided an inexhaustible supply of food for the European markets. The Catholic countries, with a church calendar containing many fast days, looked forward to the arrival of the fishing fleets.

"Green" cod was dressed on the fishing vessels, salted down in barrels and taken home for immediate consumption. At the *top* we see the fishermen packing "green" cod. In the *center* is an engraving of the cod. To the *left* is the drying of the cod. "Dried" cod was prepared in fishing stages. These stages were erected on the shores of those parts of North America now known as Newfoundland, Nova Scotia, and Maine.

Illustrations from Duhamel du Monceau *Traité générale des pesches.* 1769-77.

Cold and Desolate

Here we catch our first glimpse of that part of America bathed by the Labrador current. It was a bleak, forbidding region, but teemed with fur-bearing animals and marine life, sources of potential wealth greater than the gold of the Incas.

In these two views of fishing stages, note the fish being dressed, salted, and laid out to dry, and the stumps of trees along the shore where a partial clearing has been made.

Illustrations from Duhamel du Monceau *Traité générale des pesches.* 1769-77.

Northwest Passage

The lure of the East with its silks and spices was not wholly lacking even in these Northern waters. Between 1497 and 1542 attempts were made by the Cabots, acting under the King of England, and by Jacques Cartier, acting for the King of France, to seek a Northwest Passage to Japan and India. When they failed to get through, interest lapsed, but the fishermen kept on fishing.

Sebastian Cabot

Jacques Cartier

Samuel de Champlain

With the opening of the Seventeenth Century came a new era, that of settlement. Samuel de Champlain, again for the King of France, explored the St. Lawrence country, and on June 7, 1613, accidentally lost his astrolabe (an instrument used to make astronomical observations). It was found in the Province of Ontario, Canada, in 1867, is now in the museum at Fort Ticonderoga, New York, and is shown at *left*.

Champlain explored the Bay of Fundy and attempted to found a settlement at St. Croix Island. At *right* is a plan of the town according to Champlain's narrative published 1613. As the book was calculated to inspire Frenchmen to settle in America, the illustrations may have been exaggerated.

Champlain *Voyages*. 1613.

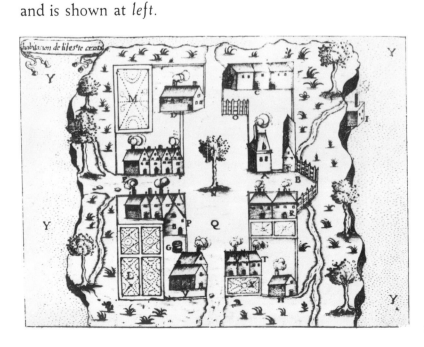

"Salvages"

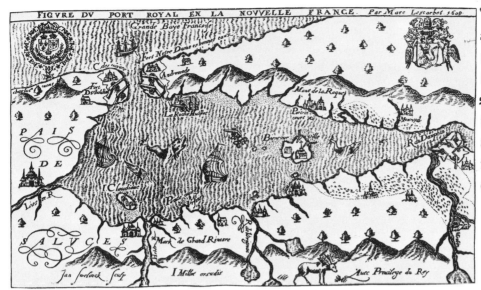

Lescarbot *Histoire de la Nouvelle France.* 1609.

Port Royal

The French soon moved across the Bay of Fundy and started a new settlement at Port Royal, shown here. Note that there were "salvages" about, not to mention moose. Note also the church and the cannon.

Prayers

Side by side with discovery and settlement went the conversion of the Indians by the Jesuit priests, and here we see Father Le Clercq attempting to teach the Indians a Christian prayer, and Father Jumeau conducting a mass for the Miramichi. Note the moose and the dance of the Miramichi.

Courtesy, The Champlain Society, and the University of Toronto Press, Toronto, Canada.

Illustration inserted in a copy of Father Le Clercq's *Nouvelle Relation de la Gaspesie*

Dreams

The urge to create settlements in this new land was not confined to the French. The merchants of Bristol, England, had long profited from fisheries in the North Atlantic. In Bristol lived Sir Ferdinando Gorges, an influential man of great wealth and vision. He dreamed of establishing a feudal domain across the sea.

The wharfs at Bristol. England

Barrett, *History and Antiquities of Bristol.* 1789.

Sagadahoc

At the same time that the Virginia Company of London was organizing, Gorges and others formed the Virginia Company of Plymouth, which sent an expedition to found a settlement at the mouth of the Sagadahoc (Kennebec) River on the coast of Maine. The settlement was made in the summer of 1607, some three months after the founding of Jamestown, in Virginia.

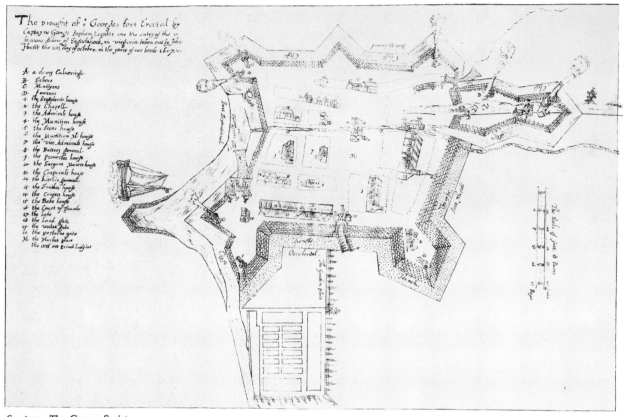

Courtesy, The Gorges Society.

Contemporary map of Sagadahoc

Courtesy, Marion J. Bradshaw The Maine Land.
1941.
Maine Birches

In this crude drawing we see houses and fortifications that most likely did not exist, but like Champlain's drawings were meant to arouse colonizing zeal at home. The truth is that Sagadahoc was abandoned the following year, its English garrison sailed back home and the settlement was forfeited to the wilderness. The birch trees marched in again.

*Courtesy, Federal Works Agency,
Washington, D. C.*
Maine Birches

The Coast of Maine

It seemed for the moment that the Maine coast was to be left to the French, who, in 1613, established a little settlement at Somes Sound, near Mount Desert. However, the English from Jamestown made short work of this settlement, Samuel Argall chasing the French out in no uncertain manner.

Somes Sound

George E. Street *Mount Desert*.

Courtesy. Federal Works Agency, Washington, D. C.

Thunder Hole. Mount Desert Island

The following year Captain John Smith made a detailed drawing of the New England coast, on which young Prince Charles, son of James I, placed English names, some of which stuck, although not in the same places. The area from the Penobscot River southward was thus established as a prospective region for English settlement.

John Smith's Map of New England 1614

Meanwhile the title from the English King to this stretch of coast underwent some changes. The Virginia Company of Plymouth expired and was superseded by a grant to another group of proprietors known as the Council for New England, prominent in which was Sir Ferdinando Gorges, still intent on establishing a feudal regime in America.

Scrooby

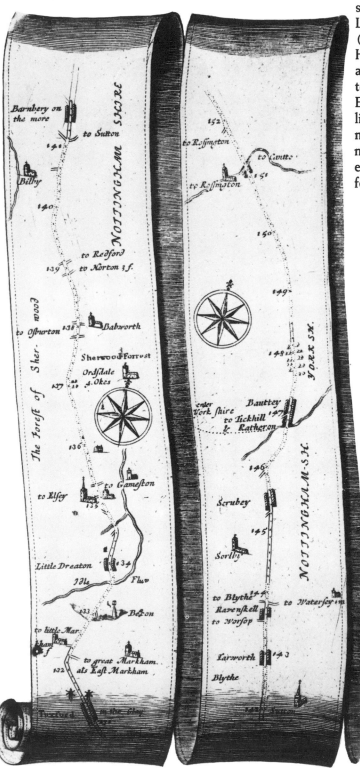

The English background of the first permanent settlement is interesting. On the road from London to York was the little village of Scrooby (spelled Scrubey on this map by John Ogilby). Here, as in other places all over England, was a group of nonconformists, those who refused to conform to the practices of the Church of England. The group at Scrooby, including William Brewster and John Robinson, the preacher, made plans to escape with their followers to more liberal Holland, Religious thinking in this era of bitter feelings was tinctured with the fear of persecution.

Seyer *Memoirs Historical and Topographical of Bristol.* 1823.

Two contemporary examples of the English mode of punishment

John Ogilby *Britannia.* 1698.

Road map showing the location of Scrooby

Leyden

Finally, in 1608, they reached Amsterdam and shortly thereafter took up residence in the city of Leyden, center of the textile industry in which many of them found employment.

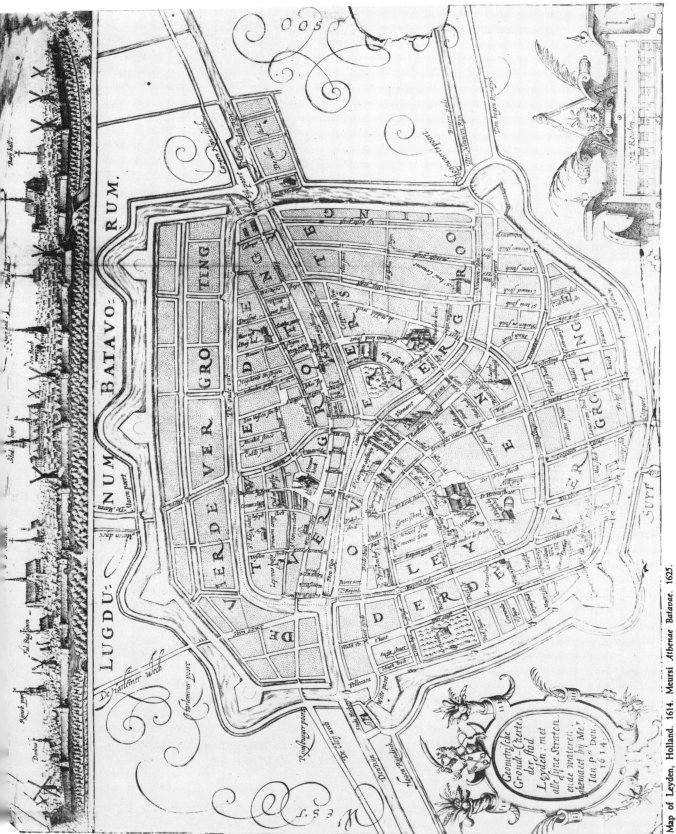

Map of Leyden, Holland. 1614. Meursi *Athenae Batavae*. 1625. John Robinson's house was on Clock Street, near St. Peter's cathedral (shown within the circle on the map)

William Bradford, whose journal is our main source of information about Plymouth Colony was a member of the non-conformist group at Leyden, and called himself a fustianworker which means cloth worker. At Leyden he married Dorothy May, who was destined to fall overboard and drown when the *Mayflower* reached Cape Cod.

At *right* is their marriage record.

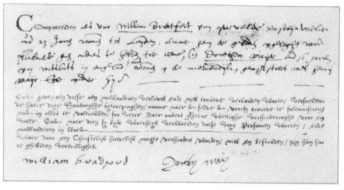

Courtesy, Pilgrim Hall, Plymouth, Mass.

But these exiled Englishmen were not happy in Holland. They yearned for a permanent sanctuary where their children could grow up in the pure faith and retain their native English language. The new land of America appealed to them and when a group of London merchants, thinking of opportunities for trade, offered to finance their removal to the new world, they accepted.

One group embarked at the Dutch town of Delftshaven in 1620 in the *Speedwell*, which was to carry them to England, where they were to join the new colony for America.

The Pilgrims embarking at Delftshaven. This 17th Century painting has been attributed to the Dutch painter Albert Cuyp.

John Fiske *The Beginnings of New England.* 1898.

Bound for America

The separation of friends and relatives was a heartbreaking moment—for not all were equal to the pilgrimage—and the contemporary picture at *right*, although not identified as an actual portrayal of the Pilgrims, suggests the pathos of a similar scene.

Herckmans *Der Zee-Vaert Lof*. 1634.

On the Mayflower

At Southampton the *Speedwell* was joined by a larger vessel of 180 tons, the *Mayflower*, sailing with a group of laborers and other colonists gathered up in London by the merchants. The *Speedwell* having proved unseaworthy, both vessels put back into Plymouth whence, in the month of September, 1620, the *Mayflower*, with 87 passengers and 14 servants (including both the Leyden and the London people), together with a crew of 48, started westward across the Atlantic. The modern replica *below*, was sailed over the same course in 1957 by Capt. Alan Villiers.

Courtesy, Socony Mobil Oil Co., Inc., New York City.

Mayflower Compact

As the *Mayflower* neared the shores of America, it became evident that, unless some form of government was established, the ungodly among the colonists (meaning those from the London group) would not only wreck the dream of founding a new Kingdom of God in America, but would wreck the whole colony as well. Accordingly, the famous Mayflower Compact (*below, left*) was drawn up and signed by the male passengers. Among the names on this document were those of William Bradford, William Brewster, and Myles Standish. See the autographs of the *Mayflower* Pilgrims *below, right*.

From Bradford's *History of Plymouth Plantation*.

Winsor Narrative and Critical History of America. v. 3. 1884.

The Pilgrim's First View of America

The *Mayflower* dropped anchor at Cape Cod in November 1620. The sand dunes offered little hope of sustenance. *Below*, a modern view of the dunes approximately as the Pilgrims might have seen them.

Courtesy, Massachusetts Department of Commerce, Boston, Mass.

Plymouth

The Pilgrims explored Cape Cod, under the leadership of Captain Myles Standish, had a brief skirmish with Indians, and finally chose a spot for settlement which they named Plymouth. Here on a bleak December day they set foot, as legend would have it, on the rock which has become enshrined in our history.

Plymouth Rock

On the edge of the wilderness they erected a rude shelter. They heard the howl of the timber wolf.

Hexham *Principles of the Art Military.* 1637.

Military costume of the Pilgrim Period

Deer tracks were seen

They smelled the skunk

Mark Catesby *The Natural History of Carolina.* 1754.

Engraved by Sartain after a painting by Doughty.
Cabinet of Natural History. 1830.

The First Winter

Crude wigwams and shacks were built or cellars covered over. Bark, thatch and wattles daubed with beach mud were the materials at hand. The Pioneer Village, reconstructed at Salem, Mass., attempts to re-create the first buildings of the Pilgrims and Puritans. It can be definitely stated that cabins made of horizontal logs were not used in these early English settlements.

English wigwams

Framework of an English wigwam

Framework of
a colonial house

Courtesy, The President and
Fellows of Harvard College.

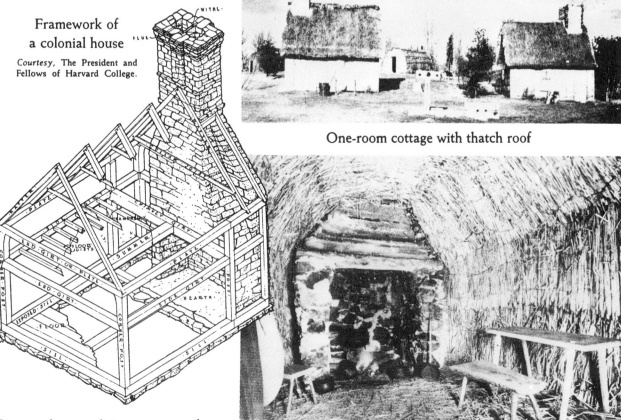

One-room cottage with thatch roof

Later, when conditions warranted more permanent dwellings, frame houses were erected.

Courtesy, Society for the Preservation of New England Antiquities, Boston.

Interior of an English wigwam

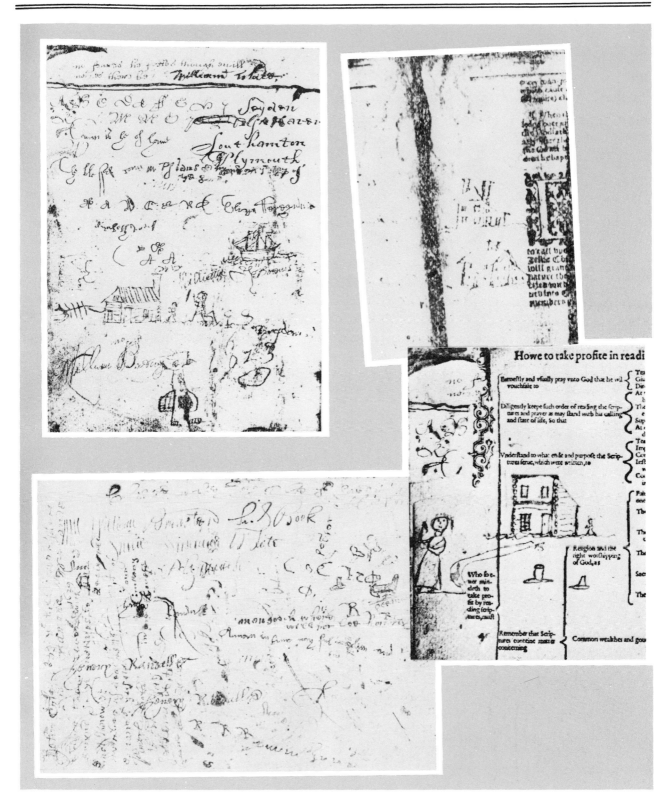

Marginal notes and drawings believed to have been made by Pilgrim hands. These crude notes and sketches were found in a *Bible* dated 1588, bound with *The Book of Common Prayer* and Sternhold and Hopkins' *Psalms and Hymns.* Note the type of houses. One is a distinct salt box house, and immediately above it is a type of 17th Century house with two chimneys, found in Virginia. The rough lean-to seems to be constructed of horizontal logs, which might cast some doubt on the authenticity of the drawings, since it is now generally believed that the Swedes on the Delaware were the first to build log cabins.

Corn and Sugar

De Bry *Grandes Voyage.* 1590.

The Pilgrims made friends with the Indians, remnants of once powerful tribes, but now weakened by war and disease. The White Men and the Red Men exchanged tools and utensils, wearing apparel and other objects, thus instituting a system of barter.

The Indians taught the Pilgrims how to plant corn (*left*), and how to make maple sugar.

Below is a painting of an Indian sugar camp by Capt. S. Eastman which, though of a much later date, catches the true atmosphere of the New England woods.

Schoolcraft *Archives of Aboriginal Knowledge.* 1860.

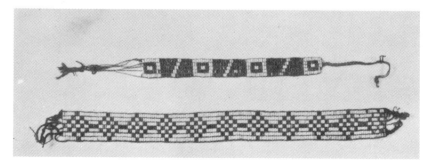

Courtesy, Museum of the American Indian. Heye Foundation, New York City.

Wampum

The Indian medium of exchange was wampum, beads or shells strung together in definite patterns, the color and quantity of these establishing the value of the belt of wampum. The belts (*left*) are from the Passamaquoddy (*top*) and Seneca (*bottom*) tribes.

Musket and Pike

Myles Standish was the military leader of the Pilgrims. He was probably equipped in the manner of this musketeer of the period. The heavy matchlock musket had to be rested on a forked rod in firing. Pikes were also used, and as Myles Standish put his men through their military exercises they went through the motions shown here, taken from a contemporary manual of arms for the use of the pike. Only sixteen of the thirty-three motions are reproduced below.

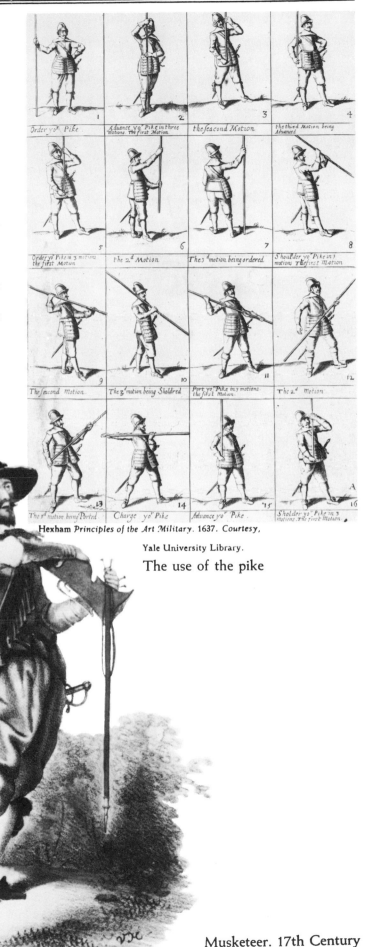

Hexham *Principles of the Art Military.* 1637. Courtesy, Yale University Library.

The use of the pike

Musketeer. 17th Century

Pioneer groups soon explored and settled Cape Cod and the region near Plymouth, establishing towns at Duxbury, Scituate, Sandwich, Bourne, Dennis, Barnstable, Yarmouth, and other localities. Their houses were built around huge chimneys, as the illustration on page 44 shows, and in the beginning many of them caught fire, the flames eating through the mud daub of the chimney and igniting the wattles.

At the *top* we see the John Alden House, Duxbury, Mass., 1653. In the *center* is the Standish House, Duxbury, built by Alexander Standish, the son of Myles Standish. The *bottom* illustration shows the Allerton or Cobb House, Kingston, Mass., ca. 1640.

All illustrations are from Whitefield *The Homes of Our Forefathers*. 3 v. 1880-86.

Howland House. Plymouth, Mass.

The Major John Bradford House. Kingston, Mass.

Whitefield *The Homes of Our Forefathers.* 3 v. 1880-86.

Bradford House. Before restoration

Welcome Stranger

The pious Pilgrim Fathers would have opened their doors to us in true Christian hospitality had we visited Plymouth, and they would have shared their simple meal with us and given us a bed for the night. We might have entered a room like this.

Thomas Hart House. Ipswich, Mass. ca. 1640

"Give Us This Day Our Daily Bread"

Opening the Bible shown on the table in the Hart House we would have seen this title-page, so familiar to the Pilgrims. The table itself, a carved oak wainscot chair-table, could be used as a chair when the table top was lifted and swung backwards.

Courtesy, Massachusetts Historical Society, Boston.

Genevan Bible. 1599

Courtesy, Pilgrim Hall, Plymouth, Mass.

Iron pot belonging to Captain Myles Standish

In the fireplace would be found an iron pot like the above.

The court-cupboard against the wall held a variety of objects, including drinking vessels, the day's food supply, table linens, etc. Some houses had press-cupboards, with the lower part enclosed, such as we see here.

In Pilgrim Hall in Plymouth is Peregrine White's cradle. Peregrine was born on the *Mayflower*, the first Pilgrim child of the New World.

Press-cupboard. 17th Century

Courtesy, Pilgrim Hall, Plymouth, Mass.

Chairs

When little Peregrine White was old enough to sit in a high-chair it was no doubt similar to the one brought over by the Mather family to Massachusetts Bay in 1630.

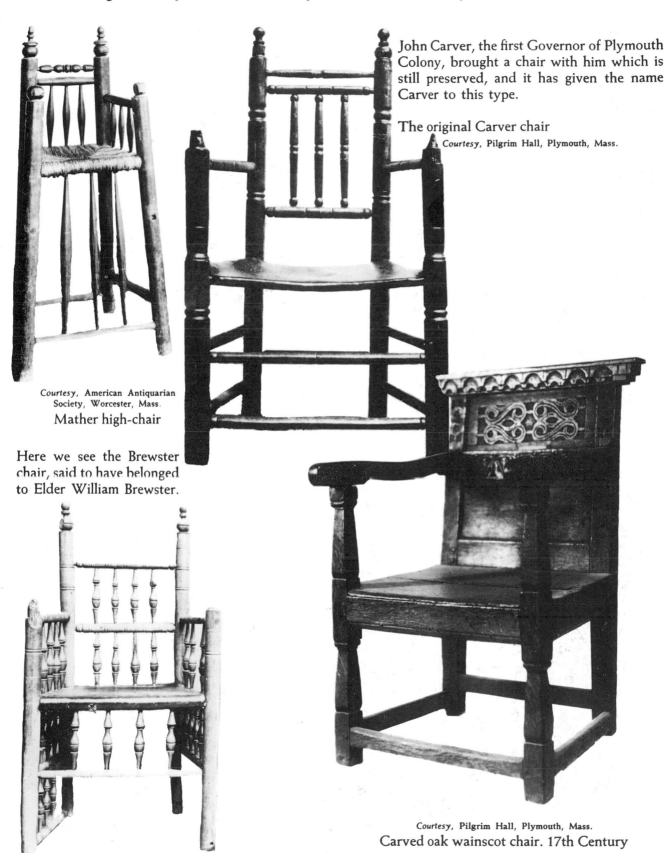

John Carver, the first Governor of Plymouth Colony, brought a chair with him which is still preserved, and it has given the name Carver to this type.

The original Carver chair

Courtesy, Pilgrim Hall, Plymouth, Mass.

Courtesy, American Antiquarian Society, Worcester, Mass.

Mather high-chair

Here we see the Brewster chair, said to have belonged to Elder William Brewster.

Courtesy, Pilgrim Hall, Plymouth, Mass.

Carved oak wainscot chair. 17th Century

Courtesy, Pilgrim Hall, Plymouth, Mass.

The Kitchen Was the Center of Family Life

Entering the restored kitchen of the Harlow House in Plymouth (*below*) we see this scene. The Pilgrims most likely used rush lights for illumination. Dry rushes were gathered, soaked in grease, and fastened in an iron holder (*bottom, left*). These rushes burned unevenly and made a flickering light. Note the bake oven in the chimney. The wooden bench or settle could be placed in front of the fireplace. Its high back served as a protection against cold air coming from the back of the room.

Another fireplace in the Harlow House (*below*) shows a bake oven in the chimney and the long wooden shovel used for putting things in the oven. A three-legged pot is set on an iron trivet. The chair is a turned slat-back chair.

Courtesy, Pilgrim Hall, Plymouth, Mass. Photo by The Dicksons.

Rush light holders

Courtesy, Mrs. J. Insley Blair Collection, Cooper Union Museum for the Arts of Decoration, New York.

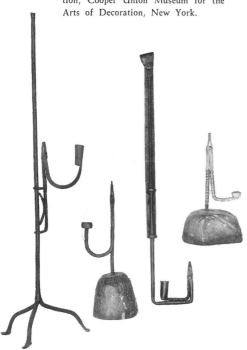

Courtesy, Plymouth Antiquarian Society, Plymouth, Mass.

Women Plain . . .

The women of Plymouth made their own clothing from wool and linen, wool carded and spun by hand, and linen from homegrown flax.

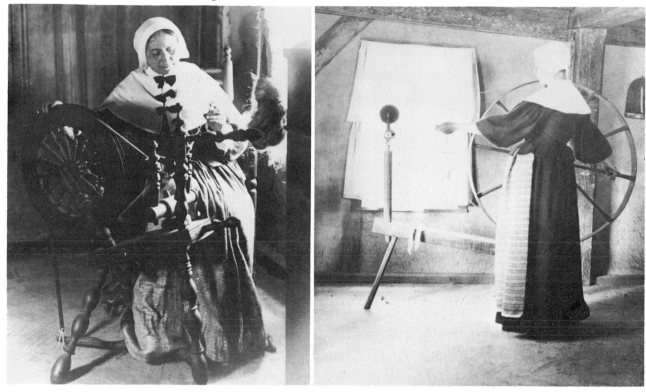

Photographs by E. P. Laughlin. *Courtesy*, Pilgrim Hall, Plymouth, Mass.

Flax wheel   Spinning wheel

The costumes shown above reveal a charming simplicity. More elaborate clothing was worn on Sundays and special occasions, as these contemporary English fashion plates will show.

. . . And Women Vain

Hollar *Ornatus Muliebris Anglicanus*. London, 1640. *Courtesy*, The New York Public Library.

"Woman's Work Is Never Done"

Harlow House. Plymouth, Mass.

Here is a Pilgrim woman at a colonial loom. Her right hand holds a wooden shuttle containing a strand of yarn, called the woof, which is thrown between the shed of lengthwise yarn, called the warp. The left hand pulls the batten towards the weaver, pushing the woof tightly against the woven edge. This is called battening. The heddles, immediately back of the batten and reed, separate the warp threads in such a manner that the shuttle, in passing through the shed, goes under one warp thread and over the next, and vice versa the next time the shuttle is thrown, thus tying the strands firmly together.

Here we see Pilgrim women at the churn. The large shallow stone is a primitive drain board and shows the Dutch influence.

Interior. Harlow House

Close-up of stone drain board

Wooden scales

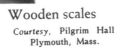

Courtesy, The Metropolitan Museum of Art, Gift of Mrs. J. Insley Blair, 1945.

Courtesy, The Metropolitan Museum of Art, Gift of Mrs. J. Insley Blair, 1951.

Napkins, bed linen and clothing were kept in chests. *Above* is an example of a late 17th Century panelled pine chest, probably from Massachusetts. To the *left* is another product of 17th Century craftsmanship, a curious style oak and maple folding table from Essex County, Mass. At the *bottom* is a trestle table. It was the most common table in Plymouth, around which the entire family sat during meals. Usually of an oak frame and pine top, it was made on the spot, there being an abundance of timber.

Courtesy, The Metropolitan Museum of Art, Gift of Mrs. Russell Sage, 1909.

Wooden Trenchers . . .

Most of the tableware at Plymouth was made of wood. Two people or more ate from the same wooden plate or trencher. They ate with their fingers, there being no forks and very few spoons. Saffron-stained fingers were wiped on napkins, of which there were plenty.

Courtesy, Pocumtuck Valley Memorial Association of Deerfield, Mass.

Wooden tableware

. . . and Wooden Tankards

The Pilgrims drank huge quantities of beer and ale, and when their first orchards came to maturity, even greater quantities of cider.

Burl

From Indian corn the Pilgrims made mush, or "hasty pudding," hoe cakes, and hominy, or samp as the Indians called it. Samp was eaten from bowls made of burl, knotty growths on old trees which were carved into useful shapes by the Indians.

Below, Utensils made of burl
Courtesy, Old Quinabaug Village, Sturbridge, Mass.

Courtesy, The Essex Institute, Salem, Mass.
Wooden tankards

Many a meal was prepared in what we now call a Dutch oven, which could be placed in the fireplace and covered with hot coals.

Courtesy, United States National Museum, Washington, D. C.
Dutch oven

Pounding Corn

Schoolcraft *Indian Tribes.* 1854.

Indian woman pounding corn with mortar and pestle

Peirce *Indian History.* 1878.

Zerviah G. Mitchell, direct descendant of Massasoit, Chief of the Wampanoags

Courtesy, American Museum of Natural History, New York. Painting by Arthur A. Jansson.

Old windmill at Eastham. Cape Cod, Mass.

Trees

Below Peregrine White's pear tree. Plymouth, Mass.

Russell *Guide. to Plymouth.* 1846.

Courtesy, Essex Institute, Salem, Mass.

Ancient Oak Tree. Peabody, Mass.

"Yarbs"

The women planted herb gardens, and all foods were seasoned with herbs, which were also used for medicinal purposes.

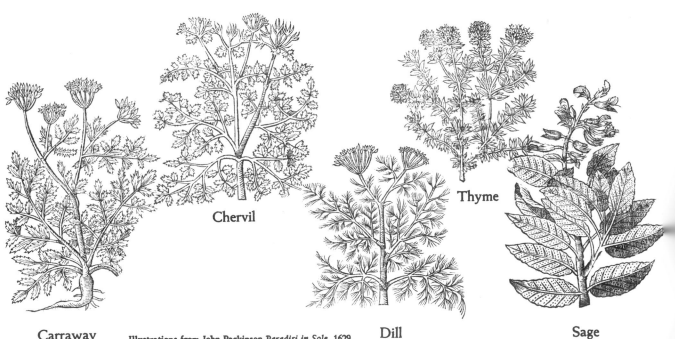

Chervil

Thyme

Carraway   Illustrations from John Parkinson *Paradisi in Sole.* 1629.   Dill   Sage

"Thy Kingdom Come . . ."

We will now leave the homes of the Pilgrims and accompany them to church. This painting is enshrined in the hearts of Americans, and it seems fitting to reproduce it. The men carried their muskets to church, placing them on a gun rack. In the center of the picture is the preacher with his Bible. Note the costume of the period.

Painting by George H. Boughton, 1867. *Courtesy,* New-York Historical Society, New York City.
From the Robert L. Stuart Collection.

Below, left, is a portrait of Governor Edward Winslow, one of the founders of Plymouth Colony. *Below, right,* is a drawing of unknown date which shows the Second Meeting House in Plymouth, built in 1683.

Courtesy, Pilgrim Hall, Plymouth, Mass.

Courtesy, Colonial Society of Massachusetts, Boston.

Here are the christening mitts and shirt of Governor William Bradford.

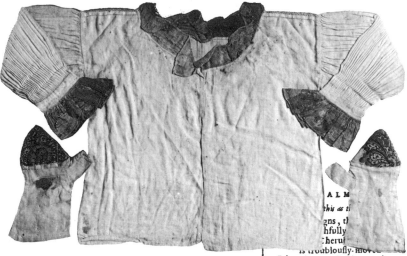

Courtesy, The Essex Institute, Salem, Mass.

"Old Hundred"

The Pilgrims used Ainsworth's *The Book of Psalmes*. The favorite hymn tune in it was "Old Hundred." New England hills echoed with this hymn for generations.

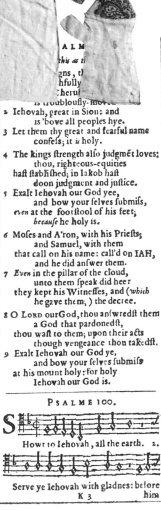

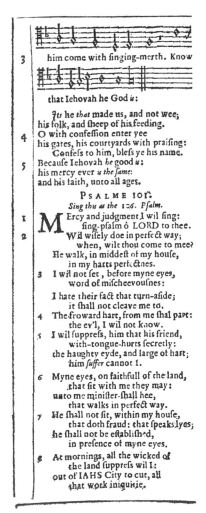

Ainsworth *The Book of Psalmes*. 1618. *Courtesy, The New York Public Library.*
Psalms 99, 100, and 101

Here They Buried Their Dead

W. H. Bartlett *The Pilgrim Fathers*. 1853.
Burial hill. Plymouth, Mass.

Children

Pilgrim children had to work hard. Idle hands were sinful. The girls embroidered samplers. They were allowed to play with dolls, rag dolls for the most part, such as the one shown here, but the Indian girls taught them how to make corn-husk dolls. The features of the rag doll were drawn with charcoal, or painted with poke-berry juice. This is the real folk doll of America.

Rag doll

Courtesy, The Doll Museum, Wenham, Mass.

Corn-husk dolls

Courtesy, The Doll Museum, Wenham, Mass.

Courtesy, The Essex Institute, Salem, Mass.

Sampler made by Mary Hollingworth before 1675

High Street

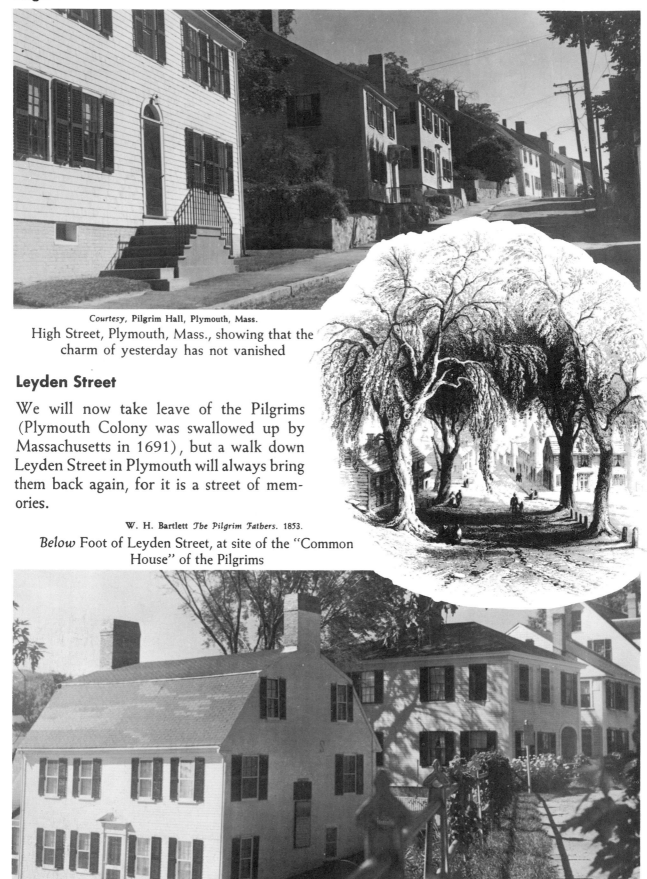

Courtesy, Pilgrim Hall, Plymouth, Mass.

High Street, Plymouth, Mass., showing that the charm of yesterday has not vanished

Leyden Street

We will now take leave of the Pilgrims (Plymouth Colony was swallowed up by Massachusetts in 1691), but a walk down Leyden Street in Plymouth will always bring them back again, for it is a street of memories.

W. H. Bartlett *The Pilgrim Fathers.* 1853.

Below Foot of Leyden Street, at site of the "Common House" of the Pilgrims

Courtesy, Pilgrim Hall, Plymouth, Mass.

"Down-Easters"

The Pilgrims were not the only early settlers on the New England coast. Various merchants and traders were developing grants which they had obtained from the Council for New England.

On the lower side of Boston Bay, Wessagusset (Weymouth) had a more or less continuous existence from 1622 onward. John Mason and others settled Strawberry Bank on the Piscataqua River, now Portsmouth, N. H.

Farther up the coast were fishing and trading colonies centering around Richmond's Island (Cape Elizabeth). Directly *below* are coins unearthed at Richmond's Island.

Courtesy, Maine Historical Society, Portland, Maine.

At *right* are Seventeenth Century coins (obverse and reverse) from the Castine Hoard, discovered in 1840 on the banks of the Bagaduce River, near Penobscot, Me. (*Upper left*) Lima, Peru. Philip IV. 8 Reales. 1659. (*Upper right*) France. Louis XIII. Ecu blanc. 1652. (*Center*) Netherlands. Leewen Daalder (Lion dollar). 1641. (*Lower left*) Massachusetts Pine Tree Shilling. 1652. (*Lower right*) Potosi (now Bolivia). Charles II. 8 Reales. 1678.

Courtesy, The Maine Historical Society, Portland, Me.
and the American Numismatic Society, New York.

Monhegan

In Maine, at and off the mouth of the Kennebec (then called the Sagadahoc), were the trading and fishing posts of Pemaquid and Monhegan Island. The latter was the favorite rendezvous of British mariners. Even today its bleak rocks present a scene not vastly different from the one that met the eyes of the first white men.

Marion J. Bradshaw *The Maine Land*. 1941.

Monhegan Island

Pemaquid

At Pemaquid was once a flourishing settlement. Ancient cellars and pavements have been excavated on the site which may go back as far as the Fifteenth Century.

Section of ancient pavings at Pemaquid, Maine

Seventeenth Century felling axe found in Maine

Courtesy, Bucks County Historical Society, Doylestown, Pa.

Maine

In the Northeasterly part of Maine was a debatable land where the English and French were to fight it out for 140 years. Fort Pentegoet was soon to be established as a French frontier post on the Penobscot, to which place came Frenchmen from Quebec by canoe or on snowshoes, and from whence the Jesuit priests carried forward their Christianization of the Indian.

Bacquerie de la Potherie *Histoire de l'Amerique Septentrionale*. 1753.
Canadian on snowshoes

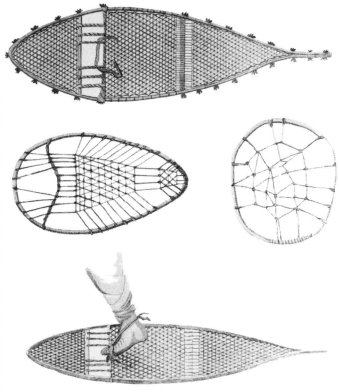

Schoolcraft *Indian Tribes*. Pt. III. 1853.
Snowshoes

Indian convert
Bacquerie de la Potherie, *Histoire de l'Amerique Septentrionale*. 1753.

Along the rivers and bays and by the wooded lakes of Maine embryo settlements began which were to become Bar Harbor, Augusta, Portland, York, and other towns of today.

Courtesy, Federal Works Agency,
Washington, D. C.
Scene on shore of Great Pond, Acadia National Park, Mount Desert, Me.

The Crown Collection, in the British Museum.
The fort at Saco, Maine

Fur Trade

The English and French traders fought for fur trading rights in these wilderness outposts. Beaver skins were much in demand. In Europe fur was the fashion.

Here we have a rather quaint conception of the beaver and beavers building their huts.

The World Displayed. 1759

New Hampshire

Isles of Shoals. New Hampshire. These pictures show the bleak and rocky terrain

Harper's Magazine. Oct. 1874.

There were early settlements at the Isles of Shoals (which were divided between Mason and Gorges), and along the banks of the Piscataqua. Besides the furs and fisheries there was the lucrative lumbering industry to attract bold "adventurers" like John Mason. New Hampshire timber was used in the building of British ships. Each ship from England brought supplies for hardy settlers.

"A pass . . . granted for the Neptune of Bristol to go for New England and from thence to Newfoundland and so to Spain for wines to bring for Bristol. The 125 passengers are to take the Oaths at Crocan Pill, and the cargo list comprises:

150 Barrells of Beefe
40 Hogsheads of Mault
40 Hogsheads of Meale
150 dozen of Stockins
2 Tons of Wine
100 Gallons of Oyle
10000 Nayles.
1 Tonn and halfe of Strong water
150 dozen of Shoes
150 suits of clothes
150 dozen of Shirts
150 dozen of Drawers
20 dozen of Monmouth Caps
10 dozen of Hatts
4 barrells of powder
20 Musketts
500 weight of small shot
15 hogsheads of Oatmeale
200 ells of Cloth to make shirts
20 pounds worth of Iron Tooles
1000 weight of Candles
20 dozen of Bootes
10 hogsheads of pease
250 weight of pewter
500 weight of Soape
2 Tonns of Vinegar."[1]

Courtesy, Bristol Record Society.

List of goods on the *Neptune,* sailing for New England from Bristol, England, Jan. 17, 1640

Map showing one of the New Hampshire timber areas set aside for the use of the Royal Navy

The Crown Collection in the British Museum.

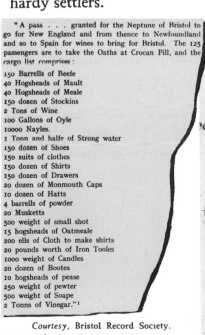

The King's Wood of White Pines Preserved for the Use of the Royal Navy.

Winnipifeoha Pond

The King's Wood of White Pines Preserved for The Use of the Royal Na...

North Boundary Line run

Home made shovel made in one piece from a white oak plank

Courtesy, New Hampshire Historical Society, Concord, N. H.

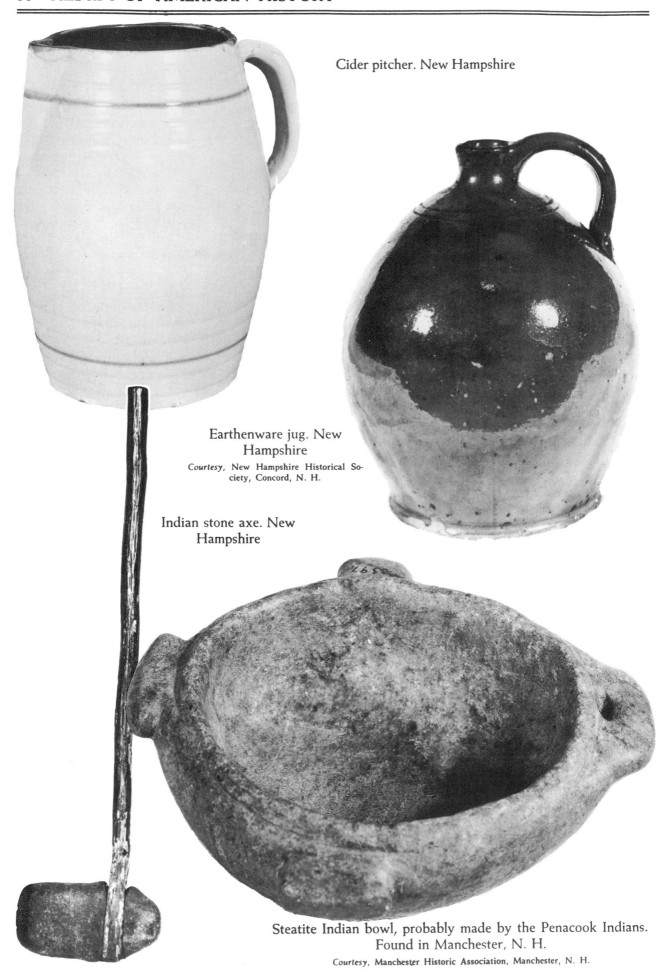

Cider pitcher. New Hampshire

Earthenware jug. New
Hampshire

Courtesy, New Hampshire Historical Society, Concord, N. H.

Indian stone axe. New
Hampshire

Steatite Indian bowl, probably made by the Penacook Indians.
Found in Manchester, N. H.

Courtesy, Manchester Historic Association, Manchester, N. H.

Further examples of New Hampshire craftsmanship are the doll's cradle (*below, left*) and the 17th Century cane chair (*below, right*).

Courtesy, New Hampshire Historical Society, Concord, N. H.

Photo by Swenson.

Courtesy, New Hampshire Historical Society, Concord, N. H.

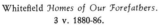

Whitefield *Homes of Our Forefathers.*
3 v. 1880-86.

Above is the Wentworth-Vaughn House, Portsmouth, N. H., built around 1670 and occupied by three of the state's Governors, two of whom were Wentworths.

To the *right* is an illustration of the Old Man of the Mountain. Trappers and woodsmen returning from the White Mountains told of this great stone face.

Charlton *New Hampshire As It Is.* 1857.

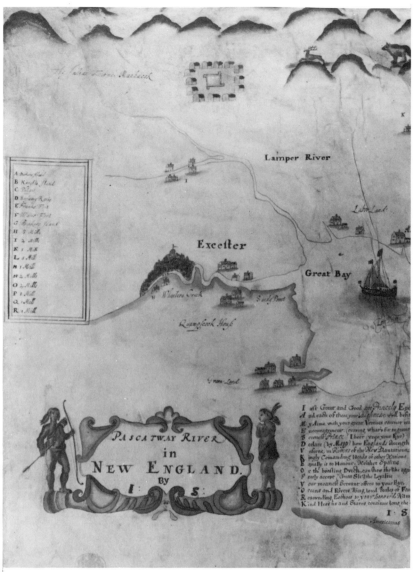

Right

Undated map showing the location of Strawberry Bank and other New Hampshire settlements

Courtesy, The Crown Collection in The British Museum.

As Strawberry Bank grew in importance, forts were erected at the mouth of the Piscataqua River. By the end of the Seventeenth Century these forts presented a formidable appearance.

Below

Fort William and Mary, on the Piscataqua River

Courtesy, Public Archives of Canada. Ottawa, Canada.

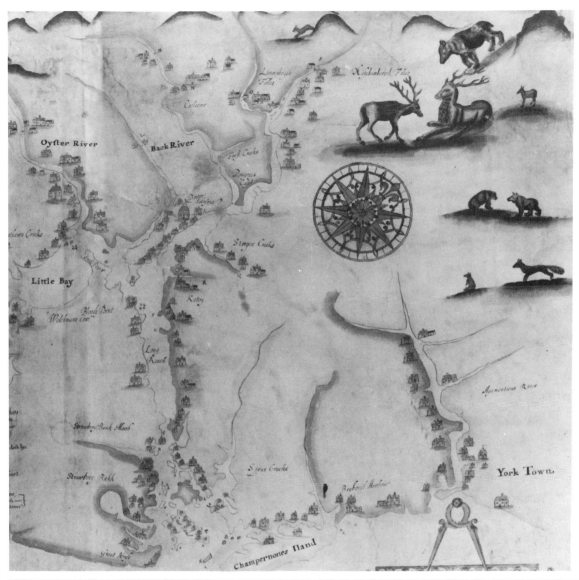

3

THE PURITANS

Among the many small fishing ventures along the New England coast was one at Cape Anne, established by a stock company of Dorchester, England, in about 1625. Three years later this settlement was moved to Naumkeag (Salem), and under a reorganized management (the New England Company) John Endecott was sent over as Governor.

Courtesy, Frick Art Reference Library, New York City. Collection of State House, Boston.

By still another reorganization of this company the region about Massachusetts Bay was, by royal charter in 1629, granted to the Massachusetts Bay Company, and in 1630 came the Great Migration of the so-called Puritans.

At the *left* is a portrait of John Endecott, first governor of the Massachusetts Bay Company.

To the *right* is Gov. Endecott's sundial, the oldest timepiece in New England. It was made by William Bowyer in 1630, the year the Puritans founded the Massachusetts Bay Colony.

Courtesy, Essex Institute, Salem, Mass.

Charter of the Massachusetts Bay Colony.

The preliminary hardships over, this new colony flourished as had no previous English colony in the New World. From it were soon settled the new colonies of Connecticut, Rhode Island and New Haven, including the eastern end of Long Island; while it dominated the life of Plymouth and New Hampshire, and even annexed Maine. It was the seed pot from which grew New England.

Stern Faces

John Winthrop, first governor under the Charter.

Rev. Richard Mather
Wood engraving by John Foster.

William Pynchon
Courtesy, Essex Institute, Salem, Mass.

Puritans

The Puritans were those members of the Church of England who wished to hold to the gains of the Protestant Reformation. They were opposed to the retention of a ritual and an episcopacy not unlike that of the Church of Rome. The Puritans leaned towards congregationalism, which permitted each congregation the freedom of regulating its own affairs. Unlike the Pilgrims, the Puritan leaders were relatively wealthy. John Winthrop's memorandum giving his reasons for emigrating show mixed motives. Political and economic considerations as well as religious ones animated the Puritans. They glimpsed a church-state which would make the leaders important, and to effect this they would have to be as independent of England as possible.

Forsaking the Old . . .

Thompson *History and Antiquities of Boston.* 1856.
The Old Vicarage, Boston, England, where John Cotton resided

To Embrace the New

Church used by Roger Williams at Salem, Mass. (Restored)

T. Allen *The History of the County of Lincoln.* 1833-34.
St. Botolph's Church. Boston, England, where John Cotton was vicar

Place Names

The settlement at Shawmut was also called Tremontaine, or Tri-mountain, on account of its three hills, and on one of the hills was placed a beacon. From these historical associations come the names Tremont Street and Beacon Hill, in Boston

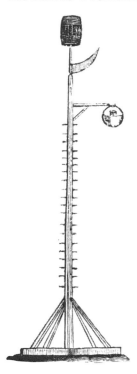

Courtesy, Essex Institute, Salem, Mass. Photo by Eric Muller.

Reconstructed Pioneer Village at Naumkeag, or Salem, Mass., showing the ship *Arbella* and houses of the Puritan period

Early beacon on Beacon Hill. The barrel of pitch was to be lighted in case of a threatened invasion

As soon as rude shelters—often mere covered cellars—were ready, the Puritans took their belongings from the ships in trunks such as this.

Trunk covered with cowhide, owned by Jonathan Corwin of Salem

Courtesy, Essex Institute, Salem, Mass.

They Felled the Trees

The sound of the axe was heard as the men felled trees to make clearings and to secure timber for houses.

Colonial axes

Courtesy, Essex Institute, Salem. Mass.

Broad axes

Courtesy, Society for the Preservation of New England Antiquities, Boston.

Hewing hatchets

The blacksmith set up his forge and anvil, made and mended tools, and beat out iron hinges. Later he would make shoes for oxen. Horses were not brought to America in the beginning.

They Sawed Planks

The carpenters sawed planks and made staves.

Cats Wercken. 1658.

Garzoni Allegemeine Schawplatz. 1641.

Courtesy, Essex Institute, Salem, Mass.
17th Century saw

Made Shingles

Courtesy, Society for the Preservation of New England Antiquities, Boston.
Draw knives

This shows the method of using a shaving horse.

Shaving horse, on which shingles, clapboards, and barrel staves were shaved
Courtesy, Society for the Preservation of New England Antiquities, Boston.

They Had to Be Good Carpenters . . .

Shingles were also split from blocks of wood by means of the frow and frow club, and boards were squared and planed.

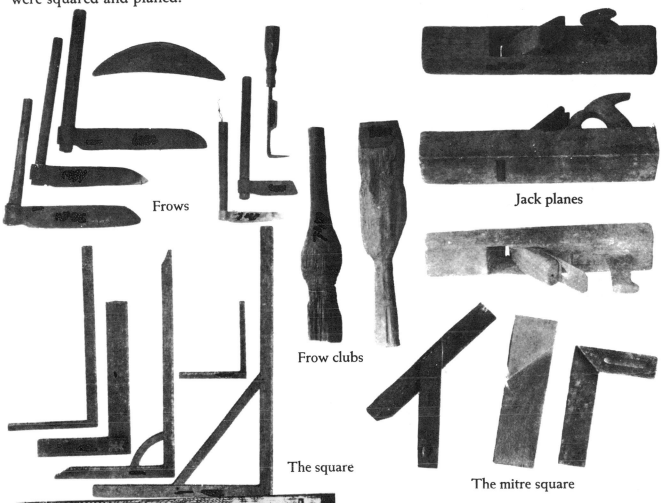

Frows

Frow clubs

The square

Jack planes

The mitre square

Nails were not generally available and wooden pegs or dowels were used instead, and beams were dovetailed by means of mortise and tenon. Here we see a carpenter chipping out a mortise. A tenon is shown on the end of the beam upon which he is at work.

Carpenter at work

Van der Lys and Luyken *Spiegel van het menselyk bedryf.* 1718.

. . . To Build Houses Like These

Note in this old house the huge chimney, the casement windows and the sturdy door.

The Old House. Cutchogue, Long Island, N. Y 17th Century. The early houses at Salem were very similar to this Puritan house on Long Island

Courtesy, The Magazine *Antiques*, and Mr. James Van Alst.

"Scotch-Boardman House." Saugus, Mass. Built 1651

The Abraham Browne, Jr. House. Watertown, Mass. ca. 1663

Some of the Puritan houses had a medieval look with their many gables and their second-story overhang.

Courtesy, Essex Institute, Salem, Mass.
John Ward House. Salem, Mass. Built 1684

Whitefield *The Homes of Our Forefathers.* 3 v. 1880-86.

Saltonstall House. Ipswich, Mass. ca. 1635

Iron works house. Saugus, Mass. 1643

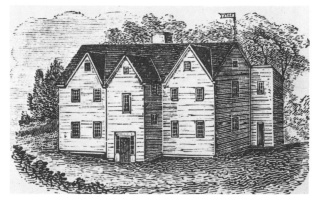

Whitefield *The Homes of Our Forefathers.* 3 v. 1880-86.

Lynde House. Melrose, Mass. 17th Century

Pierce-Little House. Newbury, Mass.

There were a few brick mansions such as the Pierce-Little House *above.*

Barber *Historical Collections of Massachusetts.* 1841.

Leonard House. Raynham, Mass. 17th Cent.

Whitefield *The Homes of Our Forefathers.* 3 v. 1880-86.

Sutton House. Ipswich, Mass. 17th Cent.

Old Boston and New

The houses in Boston, England, had some influence on the architecture of its young namesake in New England. All of these old houses were standing when the Puritans left for America.

Pishey Thompson *History and Antiquities of Boston.* 1856.
The Old Three Tuns, Boston, England

Old house in Archer Lane, Boston, England
Pishey Thompson *History and Antiquities of Boston.* 1856.

Bowen's *Boston News-Letter and City Record.* 1825.
House in Boston, Mass., said to have been the birthplace of Benjamin Franklin

Pishey Thompson *Collections for a Topographical and Historical Account of Boston.* 1820.
Old house in Boston, England, showing overhang

We will enter a Puritan house and see how its occupants lived during the course of a New England day. From a bedroom like this the mother and father awoke early and dressed by the faint gleams of rush lights or betty lamps.

Thomas Hart House. Ipswich, Mass. ca. 1640

By the Light of Betty Lamps

Note the "Betty lamp" on the wall, suspended on a trammel. A rush light is seen on the oak chest beside the Bible. The casement windows were kept closed at night, for the Puritans thought that fresh night air was injurious to health.

Trammel, with betty lamp

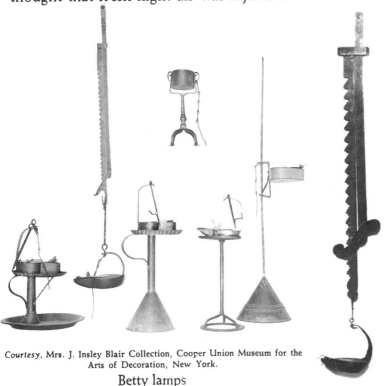

Rush light

Betty lamps

The wealthier Puritans arose from beds like these, in paneled rooms, and dressed by the light of candles, which were not so common in those days, and which were comparatively expensive unless made at home in a candle mould.

Room from the Shaw House, Hampton, N. H.

Courtesy, The American Wing, The Metropolitan Museum of Art, New York.

Candle mould

When the sun came up the casement windows would be swung open to let in light and sunshine if it were a summer's day. In poorer houses oiled paper was used instead of window glass, but many a Puritan house was adorned with leaded casements such as those pictured here.

They Flung Open Casement Windows

Courtesy, Society for the Preservation of New England Antiquities, Boston.
Original casement windows
Abraham Browne, Jr. House, Watertown, Mass. ca. 1663

Courtesy, The Essex Institute, Salem, Mass.
Casement window. 17th Century

Chests

Clothes were taken from carved oak chests like these, or from wooden pegs in the wall timbers.

Carved oak chests. Late 17th Century

Left, blanket chest. Hartford, Conn.
Late 17th Century
Courtesy, Old Quinabaug Village, Sturbridge, Mass.

**"Bofet, Thre
Fotyd Stole"**

Courtesy, Wells Museum, Southbridge, Mass.
Hadley Chest. Connecticut

Three-legged or Boffet chair. 16th Century
Courtesy, Harvard University, Cambridge, Mass.

The Puritan pulled on his hose or hosen, as breeches were then called.

Turned slat-back chair.
ca. 1650

Wainscot chair. ca. 1600

Gov. John Endecott's
chair

Courtesy, Commonwealth of Massachusetts State Library, Boston.

He sat in chairs like these while he pulled on his jackboots.

He then put on his doublet, and reached for his coat.

(17th Century costumes, Victoria and Albert Museum, London)

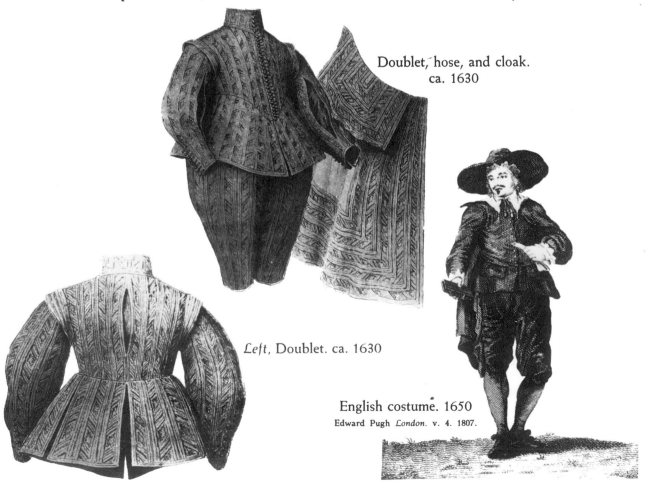

Doublet, hose, and cloak.
ca. 1630

Left, Doublet. ca. 1630

English costume. 1650

Edward Pugh *London*. v. 4. 1807.

"Obed! Josiah! Come Down!"

Thus shouted the Puritan father to his sons sleeping in the attic. They bore Biblical names chosen from John Speed's *Genealogy of the Bible* which was usually appended to the Genevan version of the *Holy Bible* (1611), the one the Puritans used in preference to the King James version. *Below* are two pages from the *Genealogy*.

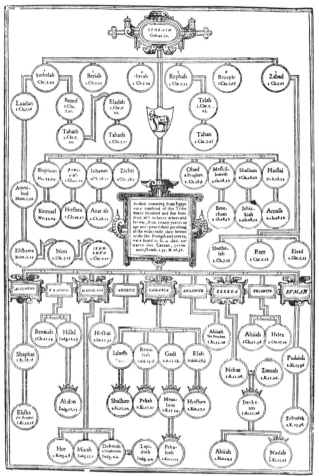
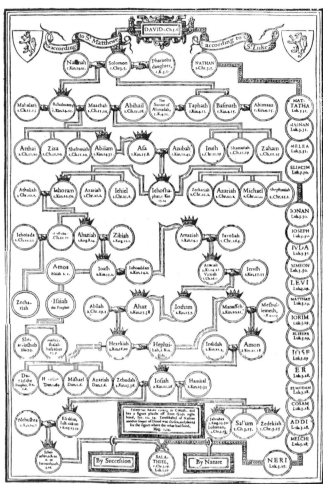

To the *right* is the attic of the Eleazer Arnold House, Lincoln, R. I., ca. 1681. The boys slept in an attic like this. The icy attics were sometimes tempered by heat from a huge chimney.

Courtesy, Society for the Preservation of New England Antiquities, Boston, Mass.

The chimney of the Eleazer Arnold House (*below, left, as restored*) occupied the whole end of the house, a typical feature of early New England dwellings. If the fire had gone out, one of the boys would be sent to a neighbor's house to borrow some live coals in a fire scoop (*below, right*), for there were no matches in those days.

Courtesy, New-York Historical Society,
New York City.

Courtesy, Society for the Preservation of New England Antiquities, Boston, Mass.

Stairways

Obed and Josiah and their younger brothers came tumbling down stairs such as those shown *below, right,* of The Old House, Cutchogue, Long Island, N. Y., for their father's strict command was one to be promptly obeyed. Contrast the stairway (*left*) of the Samuel Wentworth House, Portsmouth, N. H.

Courtesy, The Metropolitan Museum of Art, New York City.

Courtesy, *Antiques* Magazine.

The mother or grandmother, the latter often only in her thirties, was up early to start the breakfast. Life centered in the kitchen, and its warmth, cosiness, and appetizing odors made it doubly attractive on a frosty morning. Families were large, despite the fact that infant mortality was high.

Women . . .

Hollar *Ornatus Muliebris Anglicanus.* 1640.
Female attire. 17th Century

And Many Babies

Artist unknown. *Courtesy,* Mrs. William Scofield and Mr. Andrew W. Sigourney.
Mrs. Elizabeth Clarke Freake and baby Mary. 1674

Photo by Roy.
Firing the brick oven
Ocean-Born-Mary House, Henniker, N. H.

Utensils with legs which kept them the proper distance
from the hot coals in the fireplace
Courtesy, The Metropolitan Museum of Art, New York.

Kitchens

The kitchen fireplace could not have looked like this, but almost every article in this picture is an authentic Colonial kitchen utensil. Note the trivets above the settle, and the Dutch ovens and roasting kitchen on the hearth. The roasting kitchen was open in the back and the heat from the fire roasted meats to a turn. A spit, operated by a handle, was attached to one end.

Kitchen exhibit

Courtesy, Pocumtuck Valley Memorial Association of Deerfield, Mass.

Below Kitchen Parson Capen House, Topsfield, Mass.

Courtesy, The Metropolitan Museum of Art, New York.

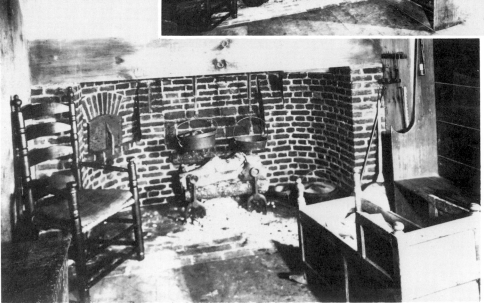

Another view of the Parson Capen kitchen, showing the pine settle, the chamber or lantern clock, and the press cupboard and Carver chair near it, and the slat-back chair by the fireplace.

Wood and Pewter

Meals were commonly served on wooden trenchers, but some families boasted pewter plates. See example at far *right*. Porringers of pewter, such as the one at *right*, were used for porridge.

Corn meal for mush was pounded with mortar and pestle (*below* in the Abraham Browne, Jr., kitchen, to the left of the fireplace). The Browne House, Watertown, Mass., was built about 1663.

Courtesy, Mrs. J. Insley Blair Collection, The Metropolitan Museum of Art, New York City.

Courtesy, Society for the Preservation of New England Antiquities, Boston, Mass.

Burl

These utensils are made of burl, the knotted growths on trees. From *left to right* they are scoop, piggin, and soap dish. Bowls of different sizes and shapes were made by the Indians from burl.

Courtesy, Old Sturbridge Village, Sturbridge, Mass.

Division of Labor

After breakfast the whole family busied itself with the day's occupations. One of the boys yoked the ox team to the cart and went to gather hay from the meadows, if it were summer, or to the woods to gather sap from sugar maples if it were spring.

Courtesy, Old Quinabaug Village, Sturbridge, Mass.

Sap buckets

Ox team

Drawn by F. O. C. Darley. Engraved by K. Huber.

Ox team. Cape Cod. A throw back to the olden time

The women and girls worked in the herb and vegetable gardens. In wet weather the women wore pattens on their feet in lieu of rubbers.

Courtesy, Philadelphia Museum of Art, Philadelphia.

Wooden patten. Wooden sole, iron ring, leather strap

Woman with vegetable basket. Note the pattens

Hollar *Ornatus Muliebris Anglicanus.* 1640.

Snow-bound

The New England winter had its hardships, but it had its beauties.

> "All day the hoary meteor fell;
> And when the second morning shone,
> We looked upon a world unknown."
> —*Whittier*

Courtesy, Maine Department of Economic Development, Augusta, Me.

Fish and Fowl

The housewife may have exchanged some article she had made with her own hands for a couple of chickens.

Sometimes skunks invaded the chicken pen and killed a fat hen or rooster.

Braun Civitates Urbis Terrarum. *1618.*

Cabinet of Natural History. 1830-34.

The women cleaned the fish.

Braun Civitates Urbis Terrarum. *1618.*

Clams were abundant along the beaches, and they kept many a family from starving, according to early colonial records.

Clam rake

Courtesy, New Haven Colony Historical Society, New Haven, Conn.

Vegetables and Herbs

Every Puritan woman knew the virtues of all the common herbs. Foods were seasoned with them, and many family remedies were concocted from herbs.

Beans   Peas

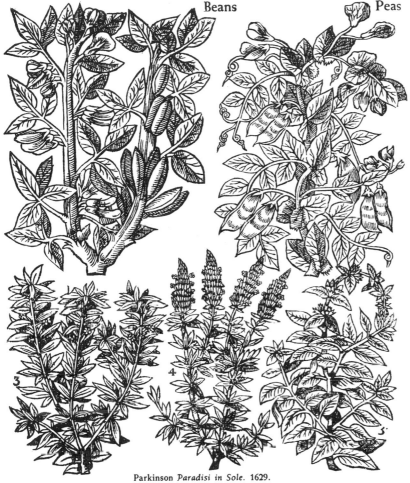

Racqueville de la Potherie *Histoire de l' Amerique Septentrionale.* 1753.

Seneca or snakeroot

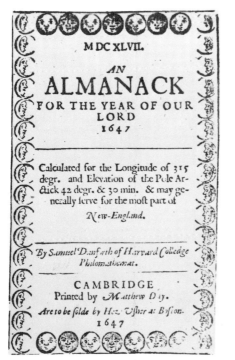

Parkinson *Paradisi in Sole.* 1629.

Savory (3) Hyssop (4) and Pennyroyal (5)

From the Indians the Puritans learned the medicinal value of snakeroot, or seneca as it was sometimes called.

There were no seed catalogues, but John Parkinson's *Paradisi in Sole* was an encyclopedia of gardening information. Then there was the almanac, dear to our forefathers. They planted everything according to the phases of the moon.

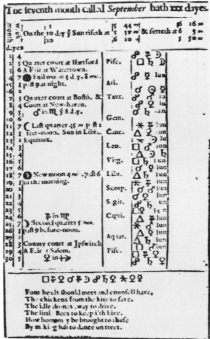

Title-page and sample pages from Samuel Danforth's *Almanack.* 1647

The Salem and Watertown fairs are mentioned

Red Men

Indians there were, and they occasionally committed mischief, but they were not a serious threat in the beginning. Some were converted to Christianity by John Eliot and other missionaries, but these "Praying Indians" were few in number and generally reverted to savagery.

Courtesy, Maryland Historical Society, Baltimore, Md.

John Eliot preaching to the Indians

The Train Band

Because of the Indian menace men and boys were compelled by law to devote a certain number of hours to militia drill. The militia was called the train band. The sound of fife and drum brought the train band post haste to the town common. Seventeenth century musical instruments, including the fife and drum, are shown here.

A man like Governor John Leverett of the Massachusetts Bay Colony made a handsome figure in his military uniform.

By an unknown artist. *Courtesy*, The Essex Institute, Salem, Mass.

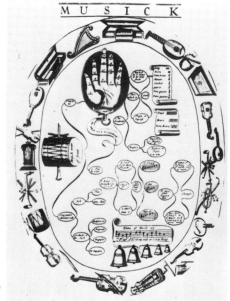

Richard Blome *The Gentleman's Recreation.* 1686.

Captain John Underhill, the professional soldier hired by the Massachusetts Bay Colony to train its militia, was a swashbuckling person. We can almost hear him barking the commands: "Rest your musket! Draw out your match!"

Courtesy, Yale University Library.
Hexham *Principles of the Art Military.* 1637.
Manual of arms used by Captain Underhill

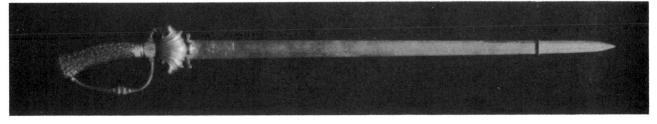

Courtesy, The Commonwealth of Massachusetts State Library.
Gov. John Endecott's sword

"Give Fire!"

Hexham *Principles of the Art Military.* 1637.
Courtesy, Yale University Library.

The matchlock musket used by the Puritans was a cumbersome weapon which had to be rested on a forchette (forked stick) stuck in the ground. One wonders how the soldiers ever shot an Indian with a weapon which took so long to fire. Extra ammunition was carried in the bandoleer thrown over the left shoulder, to which a powder flask was attached on the right side.

The First Frontier

By 1635 most of the good land about Massachusetts Bay had been taken, and our first "Westward Movement" occurred—to the Connecticut Valley.

From the new River Towns of Windsor, Hartford and Wethersfield, Roger Ludlow, writing to "the Governor and brethren of the Massachusetts Bay", voiced the spirit both of Puritanism and of many succeeding American Frontiers.

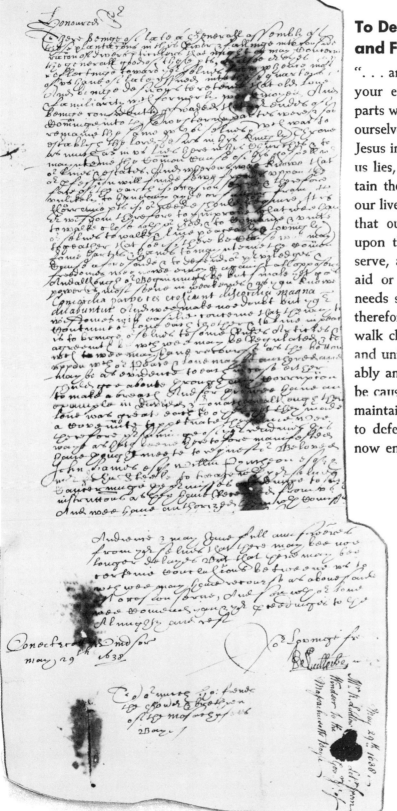

To Defend Our Privileges and Freedoms

". . . and being confidently persuaded that your ends of coming into these western parts were, and so remained, the same with ourselves, which was to establish the Lord Jesus in his Kingly Throne, as much as in us lies, here in his churches, and to maintain the common cause of his gospel with our lives and estates; and whereas we know that our profession will find few friends upon the face of the world, if occasion serve, and therefore unlikely to have any aid or succour from foreign parts if our needs should so require, it is our wisdom therefore to improve what we have and to walk close with our God, and to combine and unite ourselves to walk and live peaceably and lovingly together, that so, if there be cause, we may join hearts and hands to maintain the common cause aforesaid, and to defend our privileges and freedoms we now enjoy against all opposers."

Roger Ludlow's letter

Courtesy, Massachusetts Historical Society, Boston.

Connecticut Colony

Courtesy, Connecticut Development Commission, Hartford, Conn. Photo by Josef Scaylee.

Whitefield *The Homes of Our Forefathers.* 3 v. 1880-86.

At the *top* of the page we see the Connecticut River and the surrounding countryside. Directly below, on the *left,* is the Old Stone Fort at Windsor, Conn., built around 1666; to the *right* is the Hartford, Conn., Meeting House, the first church building erected in Connecticut. At *bottom* is the house of the Rev. Thomas Hooker, Hartford's first religious leader.

Illustrations from Barber
Connecticut Historical Collections. 1838.

Pendants

The Connecticut settlers built sturdy frame houses, and the second-story overhang, with pendants, was a distinctive feature.

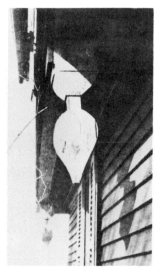

J. Frederick Kelly *The Early Domestic Architecture of Connecticut.* 1924.
Courtesy, The Yale University Press.

Upper left, Gleason House, Farmington; upper right, Caldwell House, Guilford; lower left, Hyland-Wildman House, Guilford; lower right, Hollister House, South Glastonbury.

Upper left, Whitman House, Farmington; upper right, the Older Cowles House, Farmington; lower left, from a demolished house, Farmington; lower right, Moore House, Windsor.

Peace and Plenty

Whitefield *The Homes of Our Forefathers*. 3 v. 1880-86.

Whitman House. Farmington, Conn. ca. 1660

Hempstead House. New London, Conn. 1643

Whitefield *The Homes of Our Forefathers*. 3 v. 1880-86.

Mill at New London, Conn., built by John Winthrop, son of Gov. John Winthrop of Massachusetts. ca. 1650

Kelly *Early Domestic Architecture of Connecticut. Courtesy,* The Yale University Press.

Stairway. Brockway House. Hamburg, Conn.

Above Clark House. Stratford, Conn.

To the left Whitfield House or Old Stone House. Guilford, Conn. ca. 1640

Whitefield *The Homes of Our Forefathers*. 3 v. 1880-86.

Saybrook

At the mouth of the Connecticut River still another group had built a fort to keep out the Dutch. George Fenwick was sent from England to govern this settlement, and with him came his young wife, whose tombstone, still standing a stone's throw from the old fort, is perhaps a symbol of the rude life which a delicate lady endured far from friends at home.

Courtesy, Mrs. Gilman C. Gates.
Grave of Lady Fenwick at Saybrook. She died there in 1645

Rhode Island

Almost at the same time that Connecticut was coming into being, Roger Williams, disagreeing with his fellow ministers of Boston on matters of doctrine and law, fled into the Narragansett country and became the father of Rhode Island as well as the Baptist Church in America. To escape the Puritan wrath, many other men and women fled to the sanctuary of Rhode Island.

Picturesque America. 1872-74.
Indian Rock. Narragansett, R. I.

Williams House. Providence, R. I. Built by Joseph Williams, son of Roger Williams

Whitefield, *The Homes of Our Forefathers.* 3 v. 1880-86.

Baptist Shrine

Downing *Early Homes of Rhode Island.* 1937.
Courtesy, Garrett and Massie, Richmond, Va.
Interior of Elder Ballou meeting house

To the left Elder Ballou meeting house. Cumberland, R. I.
Built before 1749

Whitefield *The Homes of Our Forefathers.* 3 v. 1880-86.

Below left Coddington House.
Newport, R. I. 1641

Below right Gorton House. Providence, R. I. 17th Century. One part of the house was built by Samuel Gorton

Whitefield *The Homes of Our Forefathers.*
3 v. 1880-86.

To the left Fenner House. Johnston, R. I. 17th Century

Whitefield *The Homes of Our Forefathers.* 3 v. 1880-86.

Below, at right, is Roger Mowry's "Ordinarie" or Inn, Providence, R. I., built about 1653 and claimed to be Rhode Island's oldest building. At *left* is an 18th Century American painting of Sachem Ninigret, a Narragansett Indian of Rhode Island. He visited Boston in 1637.

Courtesy, Museum of Art, Rhode Island
School of Design, Providence, R. I.

Whitefield *The Homes of Our Forefathers.* 3 v. 1880-86.

Among those who found Rhode Island a haven of tolerance was William Blackstone, the first white settler (1623) on the land where Boston now stands. Being a Church of England man,

he did not get along with the Puritans. He moved to Rhode Island in 1634 and died there in 1675. To the *left* is Blackstone's deserted grave near Lonsdale, R. I.

Whitefield *The Homes of Our Forefathers.* 3 v. 1880-86.

What Was It?

Was this old tower at Newport there when Rhode Island was settled, or was it built subsequently? Was it an old mill? Was it some pre-Columbian structure?

Schoolcraft *Indian Tribes.* 1851-57.

Pequots—on the War Path

Whether it was due to these new settlements, or simply to the perversity—white as well as red —of human nature, the year 1637 found the Pequot Indians actively engaged against the whites. The new colony of Connecticut joined with Massachusetts in a war of extermination. The first real battle took place easterly of the present Thames River in eastern Connecticut, where the colonial forces under Captains John Mason and John Underhill set fire to the Pequot forts, burning alive some 500 Indian men, women and children. Those who tried to escape were shot. From a book which Underhill wrote, we get this picture of what took place.

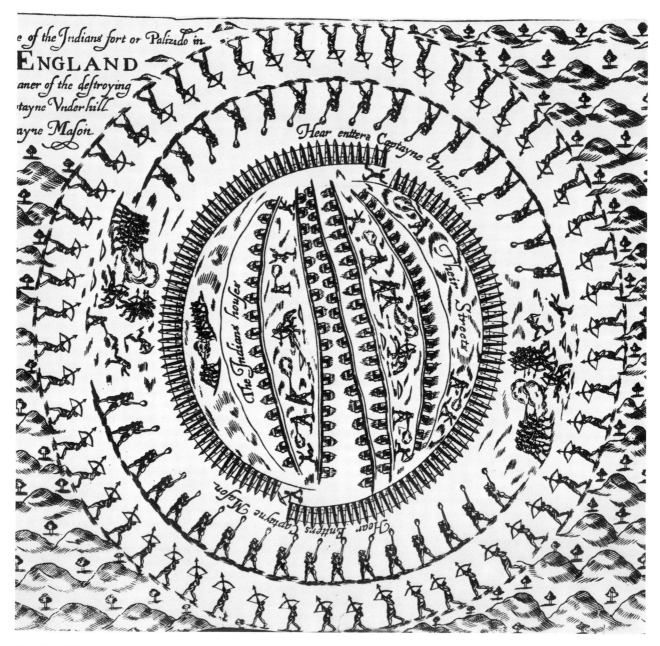

John Underhill *News from America.* 1638.

The defeat of the Pequots

And Still Another New Colony

The defeat of the Pequots was probably only one factor in the establishment, under the guidance of Theophilus Eaton, of a new colony at the mouth of the Quinnipiac River, known as New Haven Colony.

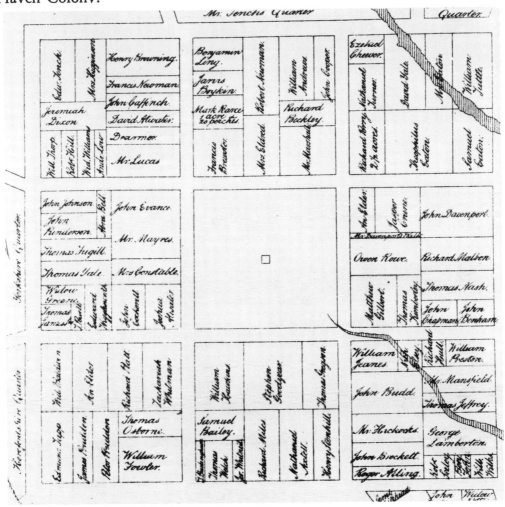

Plan of New Haven, Conn. 1641, showing the nine squares, the names of the first property owners, and the church in the center of the town. This is a notable example of New England town planning, and the original nine squares still make up the heart of present day New Haven and Yale University.

Above Theophilus Eaton House. New Haven
Right Signatures of John Davenport and Theophilus
Eaton, and First Meeting House in New Haven

West Rock

A prominent feature of the landscape around New Haven was West Rock.

An early house in Norwalk
Whitefield, *The Homes of Our Forefathers.* 3 v. 1880-86.

West Rock   Courtesy, *Connecticut Magazine.*

Settlements at Fairfield and Norwalk soon followed the one at New Haven.

Interior of Ogden House. Fairfield, Conn.
Note the size of the fireplace
and the wooden beams

Courtesy, Miss Mary Allis.

Ogden House. Fairfield, Conn.   Shingled salt box type   Courtesy, Miss Mary Allis.

Long Island

The men of Connecticut crossed Long Island Sound and established a settlement at Southampton in 1640. Others from Massachusetts founded Southold at about the same time. These towns in Eastern Long Island resisted the Dutch influence in the western part of the island.

Sayre House. Southampton, L. I.

J. T. Adams, *History of the Town of Southampton.* 1918.

Below, View of Southold, L. I. The house at the extreme left was built in the 17th Century

Lambert, *History of the Colony of New Haven.* 1838.

Indian. Engraved on
a Powder Horn

Courtesy, Mr. Stewart Culin.

Saw Mill. Long
Island

J. T. Adams, *History of the
Town of Southampton.* 1918.

Above, Mill. Bridgehampton, L. I.

J. T. Adams, *History of the Town of Southampton.* 1918.

And Still the Indian

From 1637 to 1675 the Indian made little trouble, but in the latter year "King Philip" gave the colonists a real struggle.

King Philip. Engraving by Paul Revere

Defense

These block houses to the north indicate the direction from which the Indian threat was next to come.

Detail of the Gilman Garrison House, Exeter, N. H. Alleged date ca. 1650

William Damme Garrison House, Dover, N. H. ca. 1698

Left, above is the McIntire Garrison House, York, Maine, built about 1640. *Right, above,* is the Jenkins Garrison House, also in York, Maine. To the *right,* Peter Tufts House or "Old Fort," also known as the Craddock House, Medford, Mass. 1677–80. The occupants fired at Indians through the portholes.

Tavern Tales

Rumors of French and Indian forays in the northern settlements were carried from town to town, and in the taverns each stranger was questioned by eager listeners and treated to flip, a drink made by thrusting a hot poker or loggerhead into a mug of sweetened beer flavored with a dash of rum. *Below (left)* is the Wayside Inn, Sudbury, Mass., built about 1686. To the *right* is the Poore House, Old Newbury, Mass., built around 1650.

All illustrations from Whitefield *The Homes of Our Forefathers.* 1880-86.

America's Oldest Military Company

To foster a military spirit John Underhill and others founded the Ancient and Honourable Artillery Company in Boston, in 1638. It is still in existence, and has its headquarters in Faneuil Hall.

Facsimile of the original charter of the Ancient and Honourable Artillery Company. This charter was signed by Gov. John Winthrop

Courtesy, Major Charles T. Cahill, Boston.

The flag of the Cross of St. George, the first flag used by the Ancient and Honourable Artillery Company

Courtesy, Major Charles T. Cahill, Boston.

Gov. John Endicott, whose sundial is shown at the head of this chapter, once cut the Cross of St. George from the British flag at Salem, because he held that it was a symbol of Popery. Such fanaticism was not uncommon in the annals of the early Puritans.

Ships

Returning from Indian skirmishes the men and older boys put down their muskets and went back to work. Some joined the cod fishing expeditions to the Maine coast. The abundance of timber made shipbuilding a profitable venture, and the shipyards of New England were soon building ships for the British fleet. The maritime importance of Massachusetts was apparent from the very beginning. As early as 1631, John Winthrop launched his "Blessing of the Bay" a thirty ton bark, at Mistick, now Medford, Mass.

Carver *History of Boston.* 1834.

A 19th Century conception of the "Blessing of the Bay"

Van der Aa *Voyagien.* 1606-07.

Shipbuilding. 17th Century

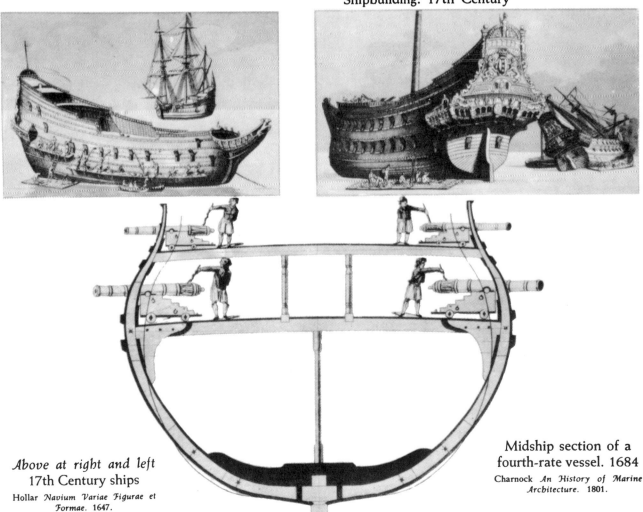

Midship section of a fourth-rate vessel. 1684

Charnock *An History of Marine Architecture.* 1801.

Above at right and left 17th Century ships

Hollar *Navium Variae Figurae et Formae.* 1647.

Excitement

Sometimes a whale was washed ashore and this was an exciting episode. The men cut up the whale and rendered the blubber in large iron kettles placed over fires built on the beach, obtaining valuable whale oil.

Pomet *A Compleat History of Druggs.* 1725.
The male and female whale

"Whale Ashore!"

"Fire! Fire!"

Next to finding a whale or a school of black-fish washed ashore, a big fire was the most exciting event in a Puritan village, whether the flames were put out by bucket brigades or by crude fire engines imported from Europe. The whole town and countryside came running to the scene of the conflagration.

Pelham *God's Power and Providence.* 1631
Whaling scenes. 16th Century

Zeising *Theatri Machinarum.* 1607-10.

All Men Were Not Free and Equal

Well-to-do Puritans brought indentured servants to America. These men and women were bound by contract to from five to seven years, as a rule, before they were free to own land or to start a business of their own. In the crafts one had to work as an apprentice for seven years before becoming a master craftsman.

Reverend Cotton Mather (*below*), vain, irascible, powerful, wrote books and is remembered; the Puritan shoemakers, scissors grinders, farmers, furriers, fishermen, carpenters, coopers, and blacksmiths are forgotten.

Courtesy, American Antiquarian Society, Worcester, Mass.

Judge Samuel Sewall (*left*) helped to burn witches, made public repentance, and wrote a chatty diary.

Photo by George M. Cushing, Jr., *Courtesy*, Massachusetts Historical Society, Boston, Mass.

Spinning and Weaving

We have seen John Doe's family going forth in the morning—the son with the ox cart, the women with their vegetable baskets—the men drilling and fighting, building ships and cutting up a whale. Let us return to them and watch them at other tasks.

Most of the rugs, carpets, linens, and clothes were made by hand in the home. The women carded wool, after it had been washed and dried. The teeth of the wool-cards combed out the matted fibres. These fibres were then put on a spindle and twisted into yarn. This was done by means of the spinning wheel. The spinning was usually done in the warm kitchen. The stool on which the spinner sat was called a linset.

Wool-cards

Spinning wheel. Single spindle

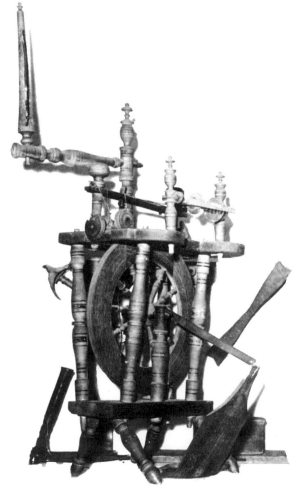

Spinning wheel. Multiple spindle

The Birth of New England Industry

The spun yarn was wound into skeins on reels like these found in Connecticut.

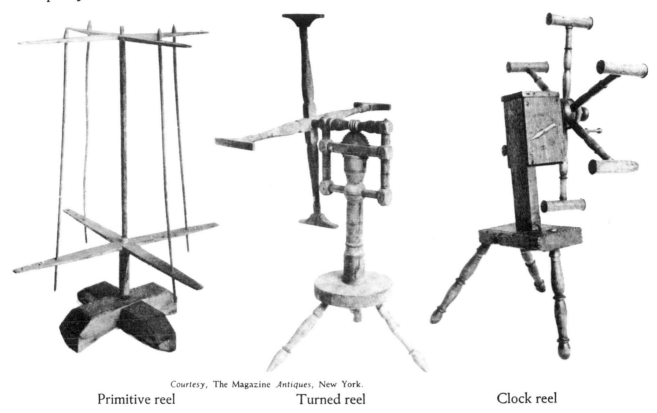

Courtesy, The Magazine Antiques, New York.

Primitive reel　　　　Turned reel　　　　Clock reel

The skeins of yarn were then ready for the loom.

Colonial loom

Courtesy, Pocumtuck Valley Memorial Association of Deerfield, Mass.

17th Century weavers at work

Cats Wercken. 1658.

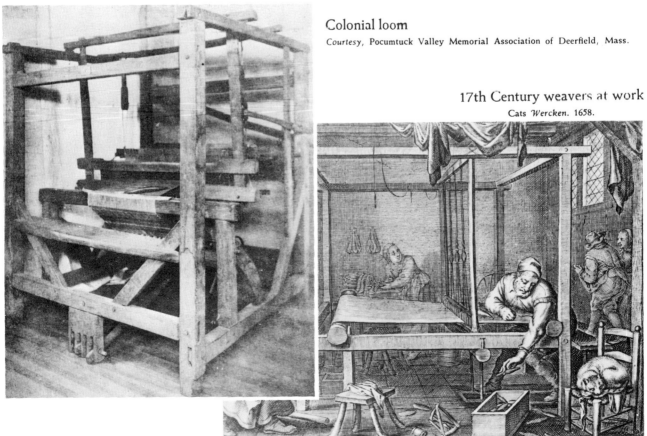

Flax

Linen was made from flax which was grown in New England from seed. The flax plant was from twenty to forty inches high. The round seed pod contained ten flat seed from which linseed oil was made. When its bright blue flower fell the flax was uprooted and when dry was drawn into thin fibres by the flax brakes and hatchels, the same tools used in dressing hemp.

Flax brake

Drawing hemp fibres through hatchels
Universal Magazine. 1756.

Hemp

Heckling hemp. Note the similarity between the flax brake and the hemp brake in this picture
Universal Magazine. 1756.

To the left Hemp plant
Universal Magazine. 1756.

Rope was made from hemp, and almost every New England town had a rope walk where rope was manufactured.

Twisting rope
Diderot and D'Alembert *Encyclopedie. Recueil des Planches.* 1762-72.

Domestic room, show-ing reel, spinning wheel, flax brake, hatchel, and skeins of wool and flax

Courtesy, Pocumtuck Valley Memorial Association, Greenfield, Mass.

Leather

Hides were tanned with tannic acid, leached by being passed through a series of vats, the hair was removed, the hides stretched and shaved, etc. It took a year to prepare hide for shoe leather.

Tan bark mill. New Hampshire

Granite Monthly. Sept. 1880.

Oak bark used in tanning leather had to be ground with a stone wheel operated by an ox or horse.

Tanners

Garzoni Allgemeine Schawplatz. 1641.

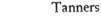

Diderot and D'Alembert *Encyclopedie. Recueil des Planches.* 1762-72.

Tanners at work

Bayberry Candles

The women boiled the berries of the prolific bayberry bush and obtained a wax from which sweet-smelling candles were made.

The Bayberry

Catesby *Natural History of Carolina.* 1754.

Skins and Furs

Beaver skins were not only used for money but were made into hats. Other skins and furs were used for rugs and coats. The raccoon, the bear, the deer and the opossum supplied the Puritans with warm clothing—as well as an article of trade much desired in Europe.

Room from West Boxford, Mass. ca. 1675-1704.
Note the furniture

Courtesy, Museum of Fine Arts, Boston.

Furrier

Garzoni *Allgemeine Schawplatz.* 1641.

Tools

Below
Cabinet-maker

Garzoni *Allgemeine Schawplatz.* 1641.

Furniture

The Puritan was handy with tools of all kinds. He made simple benches, tables and chairs. Sometimes the local turner or cabinet-maker was given the task of making the more elegant pieces of furniture.

Coopers and wheelwrights made barrels and wagon wheels.

Cooper's shave and wheelwright's spoke shave

Courtesy, Bucks County Historical Society, Doylestown, Pa.

At right The Turner. 17th Century

Etching by Jan Joris Van Vliet.

Windmills

There were a number of windmills in early New England. The Puritan took his corn and wheat to the grist mill and had them ground into meal and flour—if there was a good wind blowing.

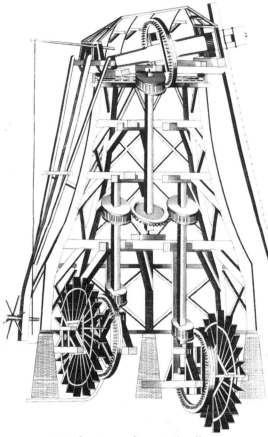

Mechanism of a windmill

Natius *Groot Volkomen Moolenboeck.* 1734.

Tide Mills

Other mills were built in inlets where the incoming and outgoing tides turned the wheels that ground the corn. There was never a lack of power. Some of these old tide mills still stand.

Tide mill. Hingham, Mass. Built 1643

Courtesy, *Old-Time New England.* Apr. 1935.

Spice . . .

Tea and coffee were unknown to the Puritans in the early days, but spices were used, and almost every family owned a spice mill. What a pleasant odor filled the kitchen where spice was being ground or bayberry wax was being boiled!

Spice mill

Courtesy, Pocumtuck Valley Memorial Association, of Deerfield, Mass.

and Milk

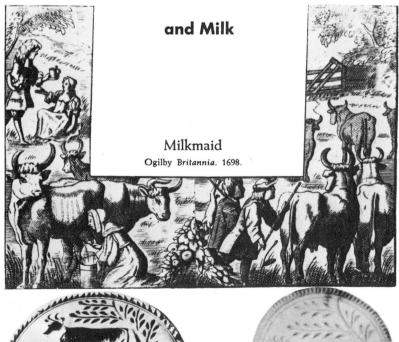

Milkmaid

Ogilby *Britannia.* 1698.

Butter molds

Courtesy, Landis Valley Museum, Landis Valley, Pa.

There Were No Professional Doctors

Many Puritans, young and old, were killed by contagious diseases, occupational injuries, and by superstitions and taboos. The minister was usually a quack doctor, and the old women prescribed herb remedies. Midwives were kept busy, and there were few ways to ease the pains of child-birth. The crude surgery of the time was performed without benefit of anesthesia. Scultetus was the advanced authority on surgery during the Puritan Era, and here we see his methods demonstrated.

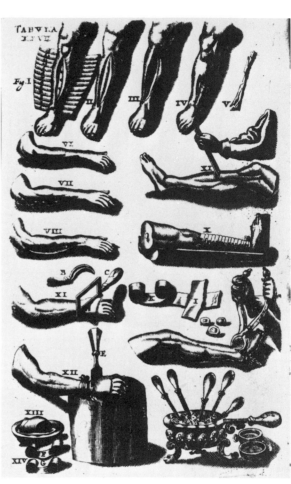

Scultetus *Chyrurgeons Store-House*. 1674.

Ear, nose and throat operations. 17th Century   Amputation. 17th Century

At the beginning of the Eighteenth Century a few barbers came to America. The itinerant barber was frequently a surgeon. In the early days some member of the family usually cut the hair of the men and boys.

To the left
Barber shop. 17th Century
Garzoni *Allgemeine Schawplatz*. 1641.

To the right
Method of cutting hair in Connecticut. A pumpkin shell was placed over the head and the hair was trimmed around the rim of the shell. From this custom came the phrase "pumpkin head"
S. Peters *A General History of Connecticut*. 1829.

The Children

Robert Gibbs   *Courtesy*, Museum of Fine Arts, Boston.   John Quincy

Puritan children were dressed as we see above. Like all other children they played with stick horses, toys, and dolls.

Elizabethan doll

De Bry *Grandes Voyages*. 1590.

Compare this rag doll with the Elizabethan one (*left*) given to an Indian child by the English settlers at Roanoke Colony. A doll was called a babe or baby in colonial times.

Courtesy, Doll Museum, Wenham, Mass.

The Horn-Book

Schools were few and far between in the Puritan Era. The alphabet was taught to the children by means of a horn-book, made from a piece of wood and a thin covering of horn.

Learning the ABC's

Hornbye's Horn-book. 1622.

Miss Campion, with horn-book. 1661

Tuer *History of the Horn-Book*. 1896.

"Young Obadias,
David, Josias,
All Were Pious"

The celebrated *New England Primer*, first printed at Boston in 1690, ran through dozens of editions. Generations of Puritan children wore out the pages.

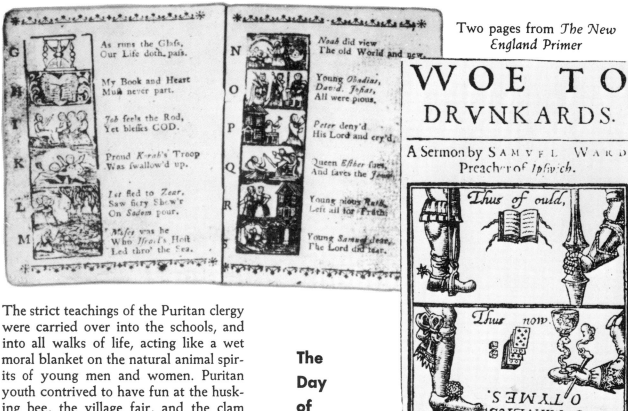

Two pages from *The New England Primer*

Title-page of *Woe to Drunkards.* 1622

The strict teachings of the Puritan clergy were carried over into the schools, and into all walks of life, acting like a wet moral blanket on the natural animal spirits of young men and women. Puritan youth contrived to have fun at the husking bee, the village fair, and the clam bake in spite of this spirit of "Thou shalt not." Frequently they made too many trips to the hard-cider barrel.

The average Puritan was a perfectly normal human being once he was out of earshot of the sermons which consigned him to eternal punishment. Life went on despite the awful pronouncements in *The Day of Doom*, by the lugubrious poet, Michael Wigglesworth of Malden.

**The
Day
of
Doom**

Pages from *The Day of Doom* (1673 edition), a best-seller of its day

Sunday Dress

Let us go to church with the Puritans. Here we see the women in their Sunday best. They wore masks to protect themselves from wind and sun, and wore chicken skin gloves in bed to keep their hands white.

Hollar *Ornatus Muliebris Anglicanus.* 1640.

Here is Anne Pollard with her Bible.

Anne Pollard. Portrait painted in 1721 when she was 100 years old

Courtesy, Massachusetts Historical Society, Boston.

She no doubt carried a foot stove filled with hot coals, for there was no heat in the church.

Foot stove

Courtesy, Onondaga Historical Association, Syracuse, N. Y.

Cold Feet

Beds were warmed at night by moving a warming pan, filled with hot coals, between the cold sheets.

Warming pan

Courtesy, Metropolitan Museum of Art, New York.

Man of God

Rev. John Davenport
Portrait by an unknown artist. 1670

The Puritan minister was dressed like the Reverend John Davenport, of New Haven.

The congregation knew the poem and prayer in front of their Genevan version of the *Bible* by heart.

They sang from the "The Bay Psalm Book," the first book in English printed in America.

¶ Of the incomparable Treasure of
the holy Scriptures, with a Prayer
for the true vse of the same.

Efai.12.3 & 49 10.reue.21.16. and 12.17. Ierem.33.15. pfal.119 160. reue.2.7.and 22.2.pfal.119. 142,144. Iohn 6.35.	HEre is the Spring where waters flow, to quench our heat of finne : Here is the Tree where trueth doth grow, to leade our liues therein : Here is the Iudge that ftints the ftrife, when mens deuices faile : Here is the Bread that feeds the life, that death can not affaile.
Luke 2.10.	The tidings of Saluation deere, comes to our eares from hence :
Ephef.6.16.	The fortreffe of our Faith is heere, and fhield of our defence.
Matth.7.6.	Then be not like the hogge, that hath a pearle at his defire,
2.Pet.2.22.	And takes more pleafure of the trough and wallowing in the mire.
Matth.6.22.	Reade not this booke, in any cafe, but with a fingle eye :
Pfal.119.27, 73.	Reade not, but firft defire Gods grace, to vnderftand thereby.
Iude 20.	Pray ftill in faith, with this refpect, to fructifie therein,
Pfal.119.11.	That knowledge may bring this effect, to mortifie thy finne.
Iofhua 1.8.	Then happy thou, in all thy life,
Pfal.1.1,2.	whatfo to thee befalles :
Pfal.94 12,13.	Yea, double happy fhalt thou be, when God by death thee calles,

O Gracious God and moft mercifull Father, which haft vouchfafed vs the rich and precious iewell of thy holy Word, affift vs with thy Spirit, that it may be written in our hearts to our euerlafting comfort, to reforme vs, to renew vs according to thine owne image, to build vs vp, and edifie vs into the perfect building of thy Chrift fanctifying and increafing in vs all heauenly vertues. Grant this, O heauenly Father, for Iefus Chriftes fake. Amen.

Poem and prayer in front matter of the *Holy Bible*.
Genevan version. 1606

The First Book . . .

and the Press on Which it was Printed

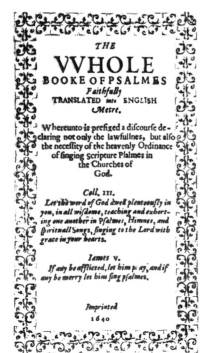

THE
VVHOLE
BOOKE OF PSALMES
Faithfully
TRANSLATED *into* ENGLISH
Metre.

Whereunto is prefixed a difcourfe de-
claring not only the lawfullnes, but alfo
the neceffity of the heauenly Ordinance
of finging Scripture Pfalmes in
the Churches of
God.

Coll. III.
*Let the word of God dwell plenteoufly in
you, in all wifdome, teaching and exhort-
ing one another in Pfalmes, Hymnes, and
fpirituall Songs, finging to the Lord with
grace in your hearts.*

Iames V.
*If any be afflicted, let him pray, and if
any be merry let him fing pfalmes.*

Imprinted
1640

Title-page of "The Bay Psalm Book". Printed by Stephen Daye, Cambridge, Mass. 1640

Printing press used by Stephen Daye in printing "The Bay Psalm Book"

The Meeting House

"Old Ship" Meeting House, Hingham, Mass. 1681

Some of the timbers of the "Old Ship" Meeting House, from a duplication of them in The Metropolitan Museum of Art, New York, showing the influence of the Gothic style in Puritan architecture.

There was nothing democratic in the seating of the Puritan congregation. Each church had its rented pews, and the seating committee allotted pews according to official rank, social prestige, and wealth. Feelings were injured right and left by this unpopular committee.

Building the church roof and steeple

Institut de France. Academie Royale des Sciences. Description des Arts et Metiers. 1761-80.

Art was Satan's Work

The pewter or silver communion service in the Puritan churches was invariably elegant, and this was about the only concession to art these ascetic iconoclasts were willing to make. The Puritan church banned instrumental music, as well as murals, stained glass, tapestries, and statuary. Stark simplicity, within and without the church, was the rule.

Coin was Scarce

Very little coin was dropped in the collection box, for there was very little in circulation. Most of the members paid their church dues in corn, fruits, furs and skins, and other commodities. The church attic was frequently used as a store-house.

Massachusetts issued its famous "Pine Tree Shilling" in 1652. The mint was closed in 1683.

Silver communion cup. First church in Boston. Given by John Winthrop

The "Pine tree shilling"

Bibles, coins, and other valuables, were often kept in a desk box.

American oak desk box. 1671. Found in Greenfield, Mass.

David Rejoiceth

The Puritans had been brought up on the resounding psalms of Sternhold and Hopkins appended to the Genevan version of the *Bible*.

Thomas Sternhold and John Hopkins
The Whole Book of Psalmes. 1606

In the *Book of Exodus* in this same Genevan version they found a justification for the punishment of witches.

"Thou Shalt Not Suffer a Witch to Live"

Page from the *Book of Exodus* in *The Holy Bible*. Genevan version, 1611, showing the moral precepts which the Puritans followed to the letter. Note paragraph eighteen.

Witch cicatrix. A scar or wound on a tree, which, in healing, took the form of a witch

Courtesy, The Essex
Institute, Salem, Mass.

"For Covenanting with the Devil"

Fanatical witch hunts spread throughout New England, culminating in the infamous witchcraft trials in Salem, Massachusetts in 1692, in which eighteen innocent and harmless men and women were hanged, and one old man, Giles Corey, was pressed to death. Judge Samuel Sewall and the Reverend Cotton Mather were leaders in the effort to discover and punish persons suspected of witchcraft. They repented of their parts in this shocking episode at Salem, but repentance came too late to stay the hangman's hand.

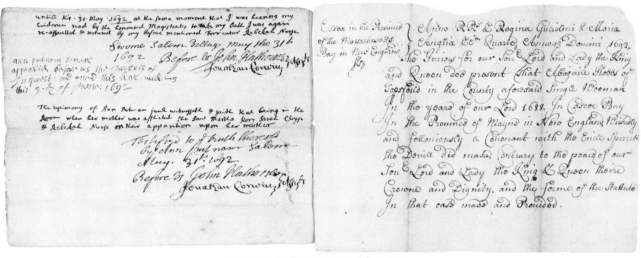

Courtesy, The Essex Institute, Salem, Mass.

Depositions of Mrs. Ann Putnam and Ann Putnam, Jr. before magistrates Hathorne and Corwin, Salem, May 31, 1692

Indictment against Abigail Hobbs of Topsfield "For Covenanting with the Devil." 1692

"I Know Not the Least Thinge of Witchcraft"

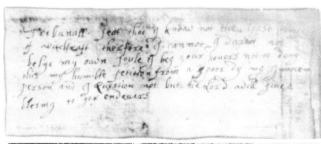

Excerpt from the petition of Mary Easty, from the court files of Essex County, Salem, Mass.

Rebecca Nurse, an aged woman of Danvers, Massachusetts was hanged for witchcraft. Her house still stands, and is called the "Witch House."

Rebecca Nurse House, Danvers, Mass. 1678

Courtesy, Society for the Preservation of New England Antiquities. Boston.

In spite of the exhortations of the Puritan divines the "Old Adam" got in his work and fit punishment was meted out by the magistrates.

Public Humiliation

Stocks

Puritans in the Stocks. A satirical drawing by Hogarth to illustrate a scene from Butler's *Hudibras*

Gaol

Old gaol. York, Maine

Courtesy, Historic American Buildings Survey, Washington, D. C.

Gossips and scolds were placed on the ducking stool and ducked in the local pond, or were forced to wear a barbaric contraption known as a brank, or scolding bridle.

Brank, or scolding bridle

Courtesy, New Haven Colony Historical Society, New Haven, Conn.

The Scarlet Letter

One harsh Puritan custom was exemplified by the so-called Scarlet Letter Law, which compelled persons convicted of adultery to wear the letter "A" sewed to their upper garments. Nathaniel Hawthorne's masterpiece *The Scarlet Letter*, was inspired by this law.

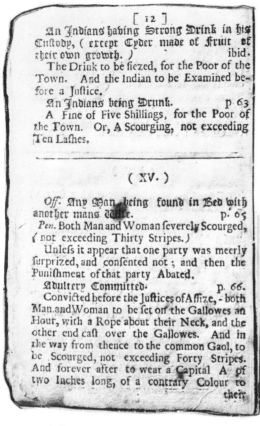 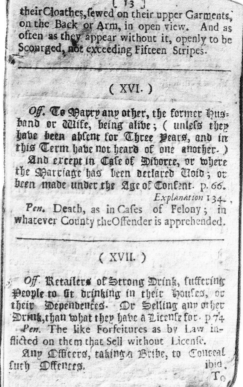

Abstract of the Lawes, showing the Scarlet Lettter clause

Courtesy, Essex Institute, Salem, Mass.

Regicides

These same Puritans were ready to defy their own King by harboring the "Regicides," who had caused Charles I. to be beheaded, and who fled to America from England after the Restoration. The Reverend John Davenport, Governor Leete, and William Jones hid two of the Regicides, William Goffe and Edward Whalley in a cave on West Rock near New Haven, Conn.

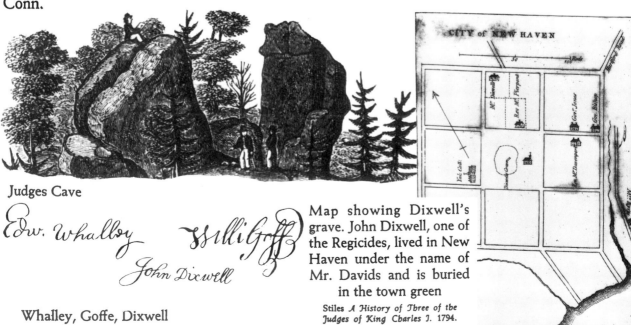

Judges Cave

Whalley, Goffe, Dixwell

Map showing Dixwell's grave. John Dixwell, one of the Regicides, lived in New Haven under the name of Mr. Davids and is buried in the town green

Stiles *A History of Three of the Judges of King Charles I.* 1794.

"Go Back to England! Leave Us Alone!"

The Puritans wanted to govern themselves without too much interference from the Royal Governors sent over from England. One of the more unpopular governors was Sir Edmond Andros. Church doors were used as bulletin boards and one day in 1689 this broadside was seen posted on church doors and other public places.

Governor Andros had infuriated the people of Connecticut in 1687 by appearing in Hartford and demanding that the Connecticut Charter of 1662 be surrendered to him. To avoid this ignominy the charter was hidden in an old oak tree, known thereafter as the "Charter Oak." It fell to the ground Aug. 21, 1856.

Warning to Gov. Andros
Apr. 18, 1689

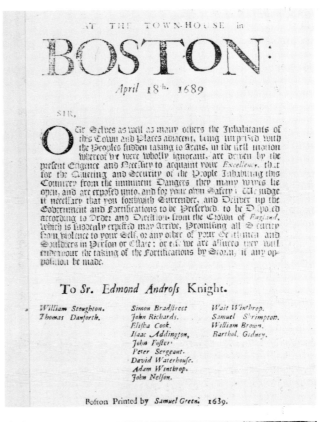

The Connecticut Charter. 1662

Communications and Travel

Hartford was the midway station in the first postal route in New England in 1672. Governor Lovelace of New York (when the English took New Amsterdam from the Dutch in 1664 they changed the name to New York in honor of the Duke of York), wrote to Governor Winthrop of Connecticut explaining the new postal route from New York to Boston. Part of this route is still known as the Boston Post Road.

Letter dated Dec. 27, 1672, from Gov. Lovelace of New York to Gov. Winthrop of Connecticut

Stokes *Iconography of Manhattan Island*.

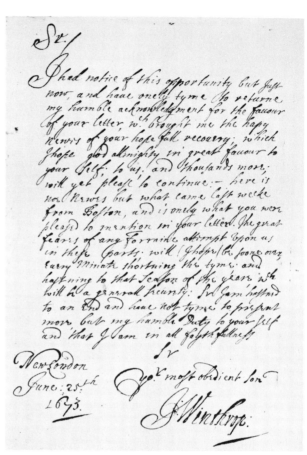

Letter by John Winthrop the Younger, Governor of Connecticut

Courtesy, Harvard University Library.

Letters like this were carried in the postman's pouch. They were written with a goose quill, and blotted with black sand, which was kept in a receptacle called a standish.

How letters were folded and sealed

Courtesy, Harvard University Library.

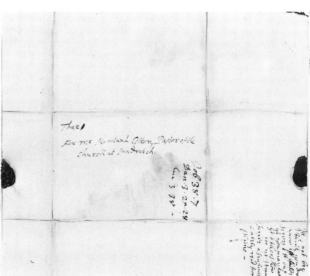

New England Charm . . .

The stern, sometimes fanatical, words and deeds of the Puritans may blind us to their integrity, sincerity, and simplicity. The old houses they lived in, now mellowed by time, have a charm that increases with the years. The men and women who built houses like these have left us a precious heritage.

Fairbanks House, Dedham, Mass. ca. 1636, with later additions

Courtesy, Society for the Preservation of New England Antiquities, Boston.

The Parson Capen House, Topsfield, Mass. 1683

Courtesy, Historic American Buildings Survey, Washington, D. C.

. . . And Romance

The House of the Seven Gables, Salem, Mass. 1662. Restored. Note the medieval style of gables. Nathaniel Hawthorne has immortalized this house in his novel *The House of the Seven Gables.* 1851.

Courtesy, The Essex Institute, Salem, Mass.

They Were Naïve in Art . . .

Province House,
Boston. ca. 1676
Drake Old Landmarks
of Boston. 1873.

Gravestone. Charter Street Burying
Ground, Salem, Mass.
Courtesy, The Essex Institute, Salem, Mass.

Upper left
Shem Drowne's weathervane, ca. 1720,
which once adorned Province House in
Boston. Another of Drowne's weathervanes, in the form of a grasshopper, may
still be seen on Faneuil Hall, Boston
Courtesy, Massachusetts Historical Society, Boston.

But They Knew How to Lay Out a Town

Model of Old Quinabaug Village, Sturbridge,
Mass., a restoration of a typical New
England village
Courtesy, Old Quinabaug Village, Sturbridge, Mass.

They Founded at Boston and Cambridge a Center of American Culture

In 1636, at New Towne, now Cambridge, Massachusetts, they founded
Harvard College.

Right Harvard Hall, built 1672-82,
Stoughton Hall, 1698-1700, and
Massachusetts Hall, 1718-20
Engraving by William Burgis. 1726.

Puritan Poet

Anne Bradstreet, wife of Governor Simon Bradstreet, was New England's first poet. Her volume of poetry, *The Tenth Muse*, was published in 1650.

Bradstreet House, North Andover, Mass. Home of Anne Bradstreet

Whitefield *The Homes of Our Forefathers.* 3 v. 1880-86.

Right Simon Bradstreet, Governor of Massachusetts 1679-86, 1689-92

Courtesy, The Commonwealth of Massachusetts, State Library.

Puritan Land

John Seller *Atlas Maritimus.* 1675.

Map of New England

4

THE HUDSON AND THE DELAWARE

Henry Hudson . . .

In 1609 Henry Hudson, an English navigator in the employ of the Dutch, sailed between the wooded palisades of a picturesque river in America in search of the Northwest Passage to India. His yacht, or vlie-boat, a vessel of eighty tons burden called the *Half Moon*, finally dropped anchor at a spot which is now Albany, New York. Hudson's name was given to the river.

Courtesy, The New-York Historical Society, New York.
Model of the Half Moon

Pontanus *Rerum et Urbis Amstelodamensium Historia.* 1611.
Dutch ships of Henry Hudson's day

And His Beautiful River

Aquatint view of the Hudson River. 1802
Courtesy, Stokes Collection,
The New York Public Library

The Shot That Lost An Empire

In this same year of 1609, Champlain, the Frenchman, pushing south from the St. Lawrence country, met and massacred a body of Iroquois Indians at the present site of Fort Ticonderoga. Champlain dropped the Iroquois chief with a single shot from his arquebus. The Indians had never heard the sound of a gun before, and this unequal contest aroused their undying hatred, a fact which was to play a crucial part in the future of America. While Champlain was making implacable enemies for the French, Henry Hudson, a few miles to the southwest, was making friends for the Dutch.

Champlain *Voyages*. 1613.

The Dutch West India Company

Hudson's report on the beauties of the Hudson River scenery did not impress the merchants of Amsterdam nearly so much as the beaver skins he showed them. Furs were the fashion in Europe, and American pelts were in great demand. The Dutch West India Company was formally chartered in 1621 to exploit the New World.

Courtesy, Vinkhuizen Collection, The New York Public Library.

French soldier. 1608

Dapper *Historische Beschryvinghe van Amsterdam*. 1663.

The West India House. Amsterdam

The West India Company was backed by the wealth and power of Holland. Its Director-General in New Amsterdam, as the little Dutch settlement on the tip of Manhattan Island was called, was a person of considerable importance. Manhattan Island had been purchased from the Indians by Peter Minuit in 1626 for the equivalent of twenty-four dollars. A few Dutch settlers had lived on the island from 1613-14.

t' Fort nieuw Amsterdam op de Manhatans

Joost Hartgers *Beschryvinghe van Virginia. Nieuw Nederlandt.* 1651.

Carolus Allard *Orbis Habitabilis.* 1700-10.

Above is the earliest known view of New Amsterdam. To the *left* is a later view of New Amsterdam in which the fur trade is symbolized.

Illustrations *Courtesy,* Stokes Collection, The New York Public Library.

"Old Wooden Leg"

Peter Stuyvesant arrived in New Amsterdam with his famous wooden leg in 1646, and things began to hum. It was his task as Director-General to restore the prestige of the Dutch West India Company, which had been lowered by the weak administration of Wouter Van Twiller.

At the *right* is a contemporary portrait of Peter Stuyvesant. The artist is unknown. *Below* (*right*) is armor such as Stuyvesant's pikemen wore. Accompanied by his bodyguard, the Director-General was a picturesque figure.

In the picture *below* (*left*) of a 17th Century Dutch soldier we see a matchlock musket, a powder flask, and a rope of match which was used to ignite the powder.

Courtesy, The New-York Historical Society, New York City.

Courtesy, Vinkhuizen Collection, The New York Public Library.

Courtesy, Museum of the City of New York.

When Broadway Was Young

We know what New Amsterdam looked like in 1660 thanks to the Castello Plan, and a careful topographical model based upon it. Let us stroll through its quaint streets.

Courtesy, Museum of the City of New York.

Model of New Amsterdam. Based on the Castello Plan. 1660

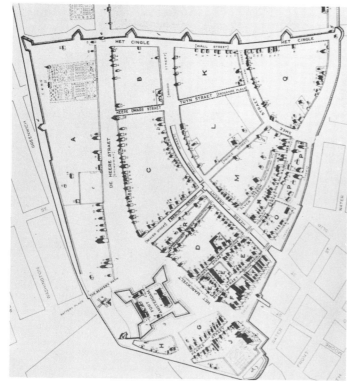

Courtesy, Museum of the City of New York.

At left Key to the above model

From the fort in the foreground we go up De Heere Straet or Breede Wegh (Broadway) until we come to the city limits at Het Cingle (Wall Street). In Section A, to our left are the gardens of the Dutch West India Company. In Section B, across from the gardens, is Peter Stuyvesant's orchard. In Section E, is the storehouse of the Company, with quarters for employees. Jacob Steendam, the poet, lived at no. 2 in Section G. Peter Stuyvesant's house is at no. 1 in Section J. The City Hall or Stadthuys is at nos. 8-9 in Section O. Other houses in this picture have been identified by I. N. Phelps Stokes in his *Iconography of Manhattan Island*.

That New Amsterdam was a small-scale imitation of Old Amsterdam in the Mother Country, this map will show.

Left A small section of a map of Amsterdam, Holland

Braun *Civitates Orbis Terrarum.* 1618.

New Amsterdam had a fine harbor, and under Peter Stuyvesant its wharfs were busy. Stuyvesant established a weigh house and market, which no longer exist, but this picture (*below*) of the weigh house in Amsterdam may suggest a parallel.

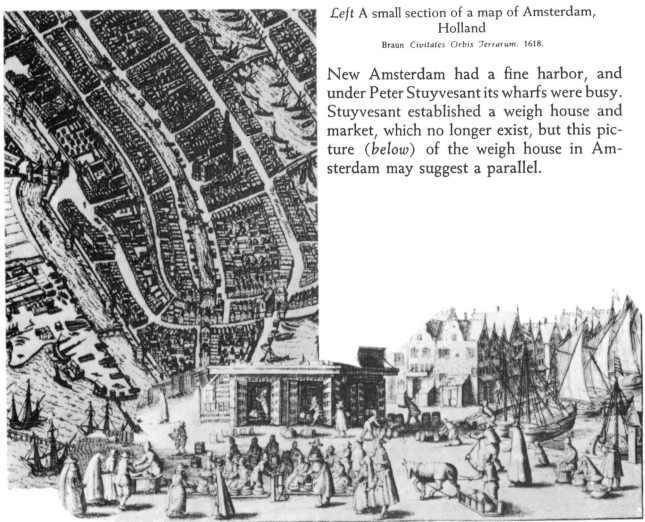

Pontanus *Rerum et Urbis Amstelodamensium Historia.* 1611.

Stadthuys

Official business was transacted at the Government House, or Stadthuys.

Left Stadthuys. New Amsterdam, in 1679

Valentine's Manual.

This weathervane was once on the Stadthuys. Washington Irving acquired it and placed it on his house at "Sunnyside". He gave it to the Saint Nicholas Society of New York in 1848.

Weathervane

Courtesy, The Saint Nicholas Society of New York, New York City.

Dutch Houses

The Dutch style of architecture was distinct from the English. Built mostly of brick and stone their houses were high and narrow, with steep, stair-step gables. The windows were protected by swinging wooden shutters or storm windows. Here are a few of the old houses in New Amsterdam.

Valentine's Manual. 1853.

Dutch Cottage. Beaver Street. 1679

Note the Dutch door was made in two sections, the top part could be swung open independently of the lower part.

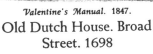

Valentine's Manual. 1847.

Old Dutch House. Broad Street. 1698

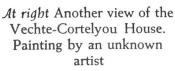

Valentine's Manual. 1858.

The Vechte-Cortelyou House at Gowanus (now in Brooklyn). 1699

Valentine's Manual. 1847.

Old Dutch House. Pearl Street. 1626. Rebuilt 1697

At right Another view of the Vechte-Cortelyou House. Painting by an unknown artist

Courtesy, The New-York Historical Society, New York.

Farms

A few blocks from Fort Amsterdam one came to the farms or "boweries" of the Dutch squires, and beyond the clearings were the primeval woods.

Bogardus farm looking southwards towards New Amsterdam. ca. 1679

Note the windmills in the picture. Note also the similarity between the above view and this scene below, which shows the country around Amsterdam, Holland.

Dutch landscape   Van der Heide *Bescbryving . . . Slang-Brand-Spuiten . . .* 1690.

Windmills

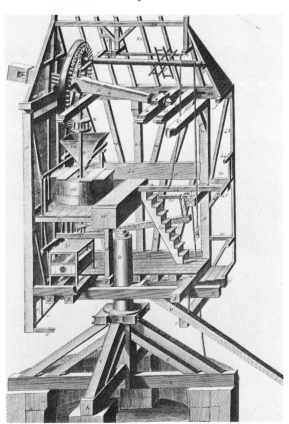

Mechanism of a windmill

Diderot and D'Alembert
*Encyclopedie. Recueil des
Planches.* 1762-72.

Where The Dutch Went . . .

Probably many of the tools, utensils, articles of dress, furniture, etc., shown in these animated scenes from a contemporary Dutch book by a popular author, could be duplicated in New Amsterdam.

Tailor   Dentist   Barber

. . . There Was Holland

Blacksmith   Farmer   The market

Domestic scene   Milady's toilet   Gentleman being undressed for bed

Illustrations from Cats *Wercken*. 1658.

Pots and Pans

Cats *Wercken*. 1658.

Cats *Wercken*. 1658.

Courtesy, The Magazine
Antiques, New York

Dutch cruet bottles

Packing meat. Allegorical piece by Peter Breughel the Elder

Let No One Starve

Silver

Left Silver cordial cup by Gerrit Onkelbag

Courtesy, The Mabel Brady Garvan Collection, Yale University Art Gallery.

Right Silver caudle cup by Gerrit Onkelbag

Courtesy, Museum of the City of New York.

The Eternal Feminine

Dutch merchant's wife

Cats *Wercken.* 1658.

At right Old print in
Musée du Costume,
Paris

Courtesy, The New-York Historical Society,
New York.

Linen press

Linen press
Courtesy, Brooklyn Museum, Brooklyn, N. Y.

Courtesy, French & Company, Inc., New York.

Dutch cushion cover

Dutch Interiors

Let us step inside some of the old houses of New Netherland.

New Amsterdam setting

Dining room of Schenck House, Canarsie Park, Brooklyn

Delftware plate. 17th Century

Schenck House

Dutch Dwellings: Brick and Stone

The De Bries House, East Greenbush, New York

Courtesy, C. V. D. Hubbard

Morris Graham House, Pine Plains, New York

Courtesy, C. V. D. Hubbard

The later Dutch influence is shown in this reconstructed room in the American wing of the Metropolitan Museum of Art in New York. The fireplace is from the Benjamin Hasbrouck House, High Falls, N. Y., and the Dutch door is from the Stephen Thors House, New Hackensack, N. Y.

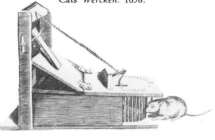

Every house had its mouse
Cats *Wercken*. 1658.

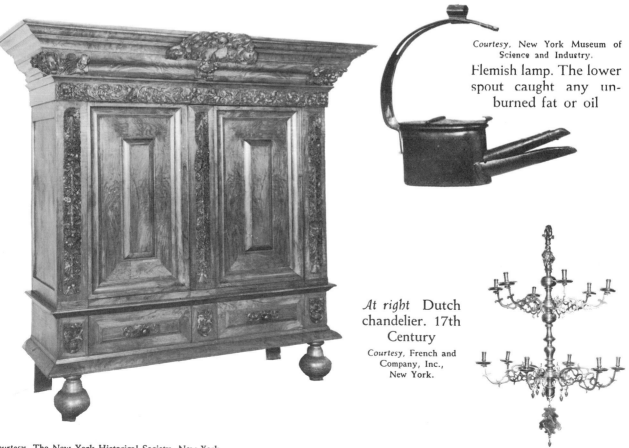

Courtesy, New York Museum of Science and Industry.

Flemish lamp. The lower spout caught any un-burned fat or oil

At right Dutch chandelier. 17th Century

Courtesy, French and Company, Inc., New York.

Courtesy, The New York Historical Society, New York.

Kas made in Holland. 17th Century. It belonged to James Beekman (1732-1807) of New York

Amusements

In the summer the men enjoyed bowling on the green. A section of lower Manhattan is still called Bowling Green.

Braun *Civitates Orbis Terrarum*. 1618.

The happiest event in New Amsterdam was the annual kermiss, or fair. No picture of the New Amsterdam kermiss exists, but contemporary Dutch paintings will give a fair idea of their joyous nature.

Kermiss of St. George. By Peter Breughel the Elder

Kermiss of Hoboken, in Holland. By Peter Breughel the Elder

Dutch Children

Children's games, the heritage of centuries of folkways, were the same in New Netherland as they were in Holland.

Children at play. By Peter Breughel the Elder

Cats *Wercken.* 1658.

Dutch toys. Probably New York
Courtesy, Metropolitan Museum of Art, New York.

Cats *Wercken.* 1658.
The game of marbles

Toyland

Cats *Wercken*. 1658.
Toy shop

Courtesy, Mr. Joseph B. Brenauer, New York
and the Museum of the City of New York.

Child's kas

Dutch boy. Primitive
painting by unknown artist.
New Amsterdam.

Courtesy, Mr. Harry Stone, New York.

Wooden Shoes

Diderot and D'Alembert *Encyclopedie.*

The manufacture of wooden shoes as worn by the children of New Amsterdam

. . . And Water

Down at the busy wharves were ships and sailors.   Dutch ships. 17th Century

Kruisdaalder (Cross dollar). 1655.
Brabant. Philip IV of Spain

Gulden. 1698. United
Provinces. Gelderland
and Zeeland

Pistole or two escudos. Charles II
of Spain. 1655-1700

Courtesy, The American Numismatic Society, New York.

Dutch Faces

Let us look at some typical Dutch faces as recorded by the early painters in New York.

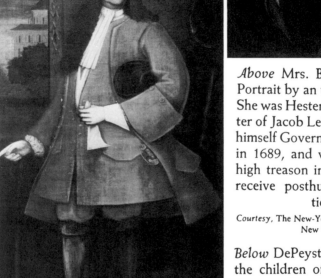

Above Barent Rynders, merchant. Portrait by an unknown artist

Courtesy, The New-York Historical Society, New York.

To the right Peter Schuyler (1657-1724), the first mayor of Albany. He was a friend of the Iroquois Indians, who called him "Quidor" This portrait hangs in the mayor's office at Albany, N. Y.

Below Mrs. Gerret Duyckinck. Portrait by Gerret Duyckinck. The Duyckincks were married in 1683

Above Mrs. Barent Rynders. Portrait by an unknown artist. She was Hester Leisler, daughter of Jacob Leisler, who made himself Governor of New York in 1689, and was hanged for high treason in 1691, only to receive posthumous vindication

Courtesy, The New-York Historical Society, New York.

Below DePeyster Boy. One of the children of Abraham De Peyster, Jr.
Portrait by an unknown artist

Courtesy, The New-York Historical Society, New York.

Fort Orange

For many years the Dutch settlement at Fort Orange (Albany, New York) was fully as important as New Amsterdam. It was the center of the fur trade, and was near the great Mohawk Trail, gateway to the rich lands of the Five Nations. Here is a layout of Fort Orange.

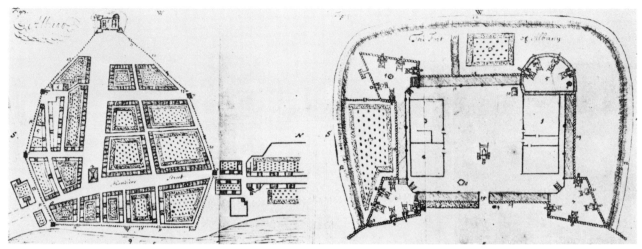

John Miller *New York Considered and Improved.* 1695.

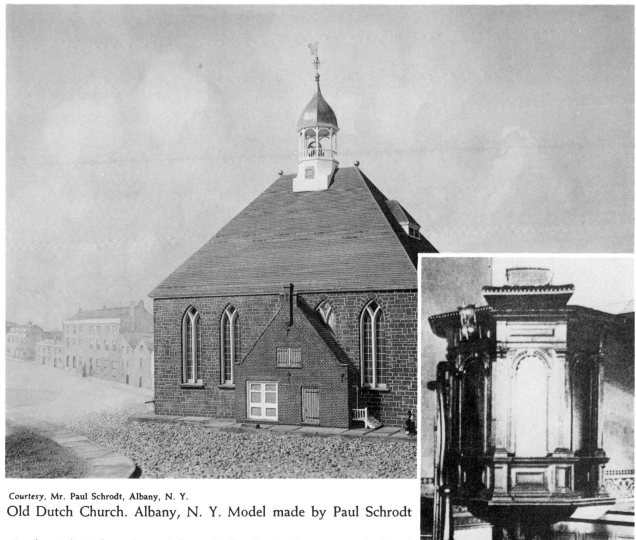

Courtesy, Mr. Paul Schrodt, Albany, N. Y.

Old Dutch Church. Albany, N. Y. Model made by Paul Schrodt

To the right Pulpit shipped from Holland, April, 1657, and placed in the Dutch Church at Fort Orange

Courtesy, Williams Press, Inc., Albany, N. Y.

Patroon

At Fort Orange lived the wealthy patroon Kiliaen Van Rensselaer. The Dutch West India Company granted large tracts of land and feudal privileges to patroons.

Left Portrait of Kiliaen Van Rensselaer
Courtesy, The New-York Historical Society, New York.

Below Manor of Rensselaerswyck. 1660
Courtesy, Holland Society, New York City.

Above Cannon of Rensselaerswyck. It was made in 1630
Courtesy, Williams Press, Inc., Albany, N. Y.

Left Title-page of the Dutch West India Company's publication setting forth the rights and privileges of patroons

Esopus

Esopus, later Kingston, N. Y., was an important settlement between Fort Orange and New Amsterdam.

Drawing by B. Eastman. Schoolcraft *Indian Tribes*. Pt. III. 1853.

Esopus Landing. Hudson River

Left Plan of Kingston

John Miller *New York Considered and Improved*. 1695.

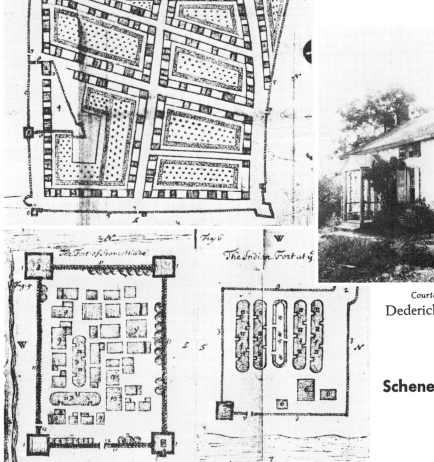

Courtesy, Holland Society, New York.

Dederick House, Kingston, N. Y.

Schenectady

Left Plan of Schenectady, N. Y.

John Miller *New York Considered and Improved*. 1695.

Villages

Courtesy, New-York Historical Society, New York City.

Courtesy, New-York Historical Society, New York City.

Above, at left is the Old Dutch Church at Shawan-gunk, N. Y., and to the *right* is the Billopp House, Staten Island, N. Y. At *right* and *below* are two views of Sleepy Hollow Church, Tarrytown, N. Y., built ca. 1699. At the *bottom* of the page we see Old Stone Church, Jamaica, L. I., built 1699.

Barber and Howe *Historical Collections in the State of New York.* 1842.

Courtesy, Branson Studio, Tarrytown, New York.

Onderdonk *History of the First Reformed Dutch Church, Jamaica, L. I.* 1884.

Dutch into English

In 1664 New Netherland was surrendered to the English. New Amsterdam and Fort Orange, henceforth known as New York and Albany, retained their Dutch character for many years. But the political power of the Dutch was broken, a power that had opened up the Hudson River Valley and challenged the English in Connecticut and Long Island, and which had, under domineering Peter Stuyvesant, successfully supplanted the Swedes on the Delaware. *Below* is a map of Virginia showing the Hudson and Delaware settlements. Designed in 1651, it is based on notes by John Farrer.

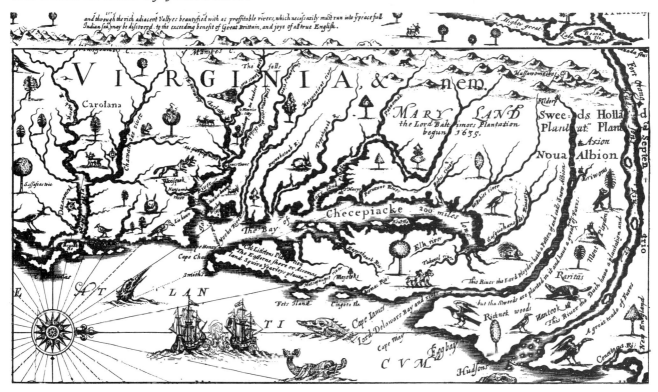

On the Delaware, New Amstel became known as Newcastle.

Old Dutch House, New Amstel (restored)

Tile House, New Amstel

Cosmopolis

Always of a mixed population New Amsterdam, after it became New York, took on a cosmopolitan aspect with the influx of the English, Jews, Negroes from Africa, friendly Indians, swashbuckling pirates from Madagascar, and exiled Huguenots from France, and many others. Eighteen languages could be heard in the streets. Religious tolerance and commercial activity was making New York a thriving port.

Pirates

and

Pirate

Gold

Left John Morgan, pirate

Right Francois Lolonois, pirate

Exquemeling *Bucaniers of America.* 1684.

Pirate coins. *Left* Algiers. Muhammad IV. 1648-1687 A. D. *Right* Morroco Filali Sherifs Ismail. 1672-1727 A. D. Coin struck at Fez and dated 1092 A. H.; i. e., 1681 A. D.

Courtesy, The American Numismatic Society, New York.

Into New York came trade goods from regions as widely separated as Africa and Spanish America.

Slave Trader

Thomas Gage *Nouvelle Relation.* 1720.

The fair of Porto Bello

Dapper *Umstandliche und eigentliche beschreibung von Africa.* 1670.

Quakers

There were a number of Quakers in New York and Long Island. Some of them settled at Flushing, Long Island. At the *top* is a view of Flushing showing the Bowne House, built in 1661. George Fox, the Quaker leader, visited the Quakers of Flushing shortly after William Penn founded Pennsylvania. He is shown, at the *bottom*, preaching to a group of them.

Illustrations from J. Milbert *A Series of Picturesque Views in North America.* 1825. *Courtesy,* Stokes Collection, The New York Public Library.

The Swedes on the Delaware

Mention has already been made of the Swedes. Their dream of empire was short-lived, but they added a memorable chapter to American history. Gustavus Adolphus, King of Sweden, died before his plans for American colonization were carried out, but his chancellor, Axel Oxenstierna, continued them.

Courtesy, Nordiska museet, Stockholm.

Globe engraved by William Jansson, Amsterdam, and dedicated to Gustavus Adolphus, 1617

Engraving from Thomas Campanius, *Description of New Sweden.*

Indians and settlers in New Sweden

Peter Minuit, the Dutch navigator, was employed by the Swedes to take the first contingent of Swedish and Finnish settlers to America in the ships *Kalmar Nyckel* and *Vogel Grip.* He sailed in 1637 and arrived at the present site of Wilmington, Del., in 1638. At this spot (*below, right,* in an etching by Robert Shaw) the Swedes built Fort Christina. *Below, left,* an old Swedish house, Wilmington, Del.

Courtesy, Historical Society of Delaware, Wilmington.

Colonial Society of America. *Courtesy,* Prints Division. New York Public Library.

Johan Printz

The Colony took root, and the arrival of Governor Johan Printz in 1643 was the beginning of expansion, for Printz meant to challenge Dutch supremacy in the region of the Delaware.

Left Portrait of Johan Printz

Courtesy, American Swedish Historical Museum, Philadelphia.

Below Silver mug used by Johan Printz in America

Courtesy, American Swedish Historical Museum, Philadelphia.

Printz brought along a fully equipped bodyguard and many servants and built a palace called Printzhof on Tinicum Island, some miles above Fort Christina.

Courtesy, The American-Swedish News Exchange, Inc., New York.

Swedish helmet. 17th Century. Kungl. Livrust-kammaren, Stockholm

Left Swedish block house. Naaman's, Del. ca. 1654

Courtesy, The Wilmington Institute Free Library, Wilmington, Del.

Below Swedish muskets. 17th Century. Kungl. Livrustkammaren, Stockholm

Courtesy, The American-Swedish News Exchange, Inc., New York.

The Swedes, among whom were a number of Finns, brought their costume, their furniture, and their style of architecture to America. The Finnish log cabin was soon adapted in the region of the Delaware. There is evidence to support the claim that Brandywine Creek in Delaware and Pennsylvania was named for Andrew Brandwyn, a Finn who lived on its banks.

A Collection of the Dresses of Different Nations. 1757-1772.

Swedish woman. 17th Century

Acerbi Travels Through Sweden. 1802.

Finns singing. The Finns held hands while singing. They achieved a closer harmony as a result

Finnish Bath

The Finns poured water over heated stones, thus producing a great quantity of steam. They beat their bodies with twigs to stimulate circulation. Afterwards they rolled in the snow to close their pores. Some American Indians followed a similar practice.

Right Finnish bath
Acerbi Travels Through Sweden. 1802.

Left Three-legged stool. Blekinge, Sweden

Courtesy, The American-Swedish News Exchange, Inc., New York.

In Wooden Things

The Swedes brought their clothing and table linens in chests like these. Wood was their favorite art medium, and they were born carpenters and wood workers.

Swedish chests. 17th Century
Courtesy, Nordiska Museet, Stockholm.

They Found Delight

Photo by Philip B. Wallace.
Courtesy, American Swedish Historical Museum, Philadelphia.
Wooden milk pail

Courtesy, American Swedish Historical Museum, Philadelphia, Pa.
Swedish chest. Brought to Delaware by the Sinnickson family. 17th Century

Courtesy, Nordiska Museet, Stockholm.
Swedish clothes chest. 1670

They Drank

Courtesy, Swedish Information Service, New York
Hooped drinking vessel. Dalecarlia, Sweden

Swedish drinking vessels

They Sat . . .

And Rocked the Cradle

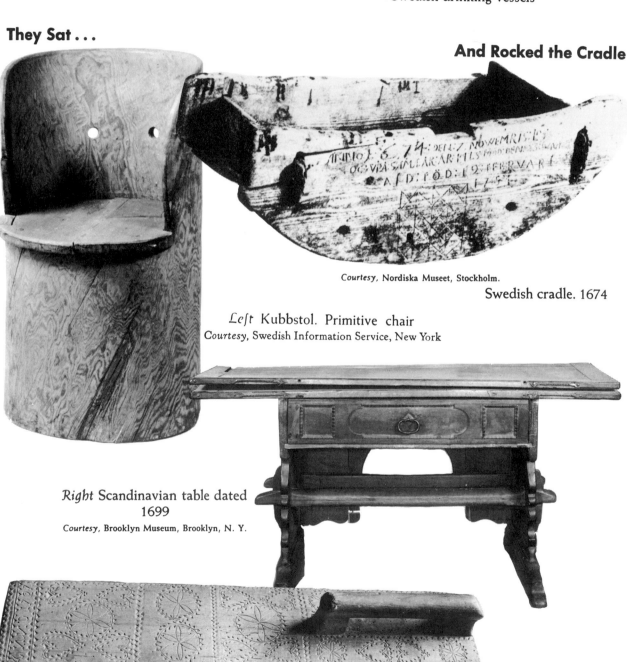

Courtesy, Nordiska Museet, Stockholm.

Swedish cradle. 1674

Left Kubbstol. Primitive chair
Courtesy, Swedish Information Service, New York

Right Scandinavian table dated
1699
Courtesy, Brooklyn Museum, Brooklyn, N. Y.

Courtesy, American Swedish Historical Society Museum, Philadelphia.   Photo by Philip A. Wallace.
Swedish mangle. A device for smoothing cloth

They Lived in Rooms Like These

Room from Dalarna, Sweden

Courtesy, Nordiska Museet, Stockholm.

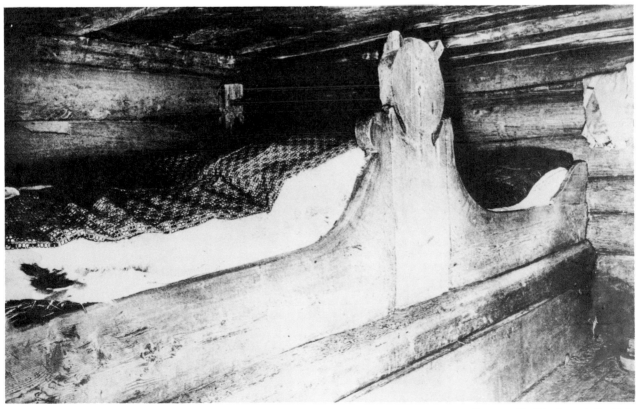

Built-in bed

Courtesy, Nordiska Museet, Stockholm.

Clocks

Courtesy, Swedish Information Service, New York

Swedish room showing a typical tall clock

Swedish clock

Courtesy, American-Swedish Historical Society Museum, Philadelphia.

Log Cabins

The cabin made of horizontal logs, so familiar on the American frontier, was brought to America by the Swedes and Finns.

Courtesy, Swedish Information Service, New York

Below Darby Creek Log House. Pennsylvania

Courtesy, Old Time New England, 1927.

This log storehouse in Sweden shows a roof-spanned opening between two log units. A log building was an indivisible structure, and to enlarge it another complete unit had to be built. This open space is called a "dog-trot" or "breeze-way" in our southern states.

Farm Life

Columbian Magazine. 1787.

Landscape near Wilmington, Del., country of the Swedes

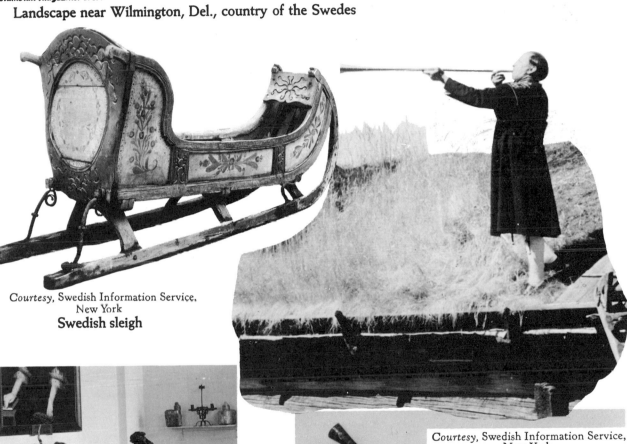

Courtesy, Swedish Information Service,
New York
Swedish sleigh

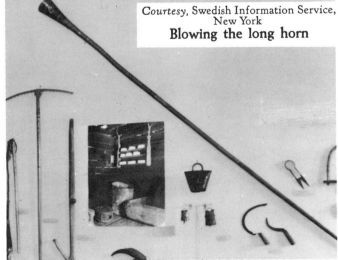

Courtesy, Swedish Information Service,
New York
Blowing the long horn

Exhibit in the American Swedish Historical Museum, Philadelphia, showing a model of a
Finnish farm

Exhibit in the American Swedish Historical Museum, Philadelphia, showing the long horn

Swedish Artist

One of America's foremost portrait painters was Gustavus Hesselius (1682-1755), a Swede. John Hesselius, a son, was also a prolific portrait painter.

Courtesy, Baltimore Museum of Art, Baltimore.

Portrait of Charles Calvert as a child. By Gustavus Hesselius

Tishcohan. Delaware chief. Painted from life by Gustavus Hesselius in 1735, at the request of John Penn. The original painting from which this print was made is owned by the Historical Society of Pennsylvania, at Philadelphia

McKenney and Hall *History of the Indian Tribes*. 1836.

They Built Churches

The Swedes in America have been immortalized in two famous churches, "Gloria Dei" in Philadelphia, and "Old Swedes" in Wilmington. The models for both existed in Stockholm, as the Braun view below will prove.

John C. Clay *Annals of the Swedes on the Delaware.* 1835.

"Gloria Dei". Swedish Lutheran Church. Philadelphia, Pa. Dedicated 1700

Below "Old Swedes" Swedish Lutheran Church. Wilmington, Del. Dedicated 1699. Engraved by John Sartain

Elizabeth Montgomery *Reminiscences of Wilmington.* 1851.

Braun *Civitates Orbis Terrarum.* 1618. Courtesy, The New York Public Library.

View of Stockholm

"Old Swedes" has a cupola similar to the one on the castle, and "Gloria Dei" has a steeple similar to the one on the church to the right. Note also the log cabins in the foreground.

They Planted Lutheranism in America

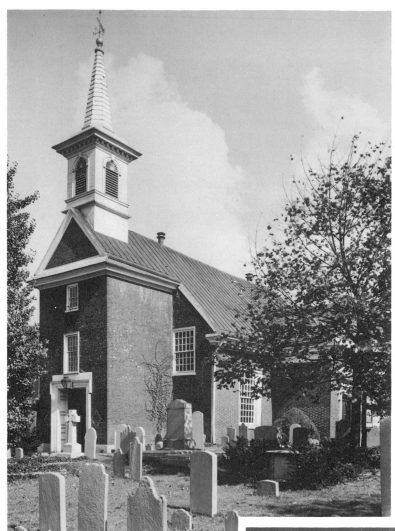

Photo by Philip B. Wallace.
Courtesy, Philip B. Wallace, Philadelphia.
A modern view of "Gloria Dei."
Philadelphia

John C. Clay *Annals of the Swedes on the Delaware*. 1835.
The Rev. Nicholas Collin. One of
the early ministers of "Gloria Dei"

Interior of "Gloria Dei"
Photo by Philip B. Wallace.

Cantankerous old Peter Stuyvesant finally broke the power of Johan Printz in 1655, and the
Swedish colony in America was taken over by the Dutch. When William Penn founded
Pennsylvania in 1683 he allowed the Swedes and the Finns on the Delaware to become English
citizens, and they lived in peace and harmony, contributing their peculiar gifts to the epic of
America.

Delaware Architecture

Other groups besides the Swedes settled along the Delaware.

Photo by Sanborn Studio.
Courtesy, Historical Society of Delaware, Wilmington.

Ferris *A History of the Original Settlements on the Delaware.* 1846.

Above, left, the Episcopal Church, New Castle, Del. 1704; *right,* Blackwater Presbyterian Church, between Frankford and Ocean View, Del.

Courtesy, Historical Society of Delaware.

Courtesy, Delaware State Museum, Dover, Del.

Above, left, Jacquett House, Long Hook Farm, Del., ca. 1660; *above, right,* Dickinson House, Kent County, Del. (restored). At *right* Stidham House, Wilmington, Del., 17th Century.

Courtesy, Historical Society of Delaware.

New Jersey

After the surrender of New Netherlands to the English, the region now known as New Jersey was divided between Sir George Carteret and John Lord Berkeley, favorites of the Duke of York. East Jersey was soon settled by Puritans from Connecticut and Long Island, and West Jersey by the Quakers under William Penn. Newark, in East Jersey, became a Puritan stronghold under the leadership of the Rev. Abraham Pierson. Burlington and Salem in West Jersey felt the Quaker influence.

Section of a view of Newark, New Jersey. The New England influence is at once visible in the layout of the town

Courtesy, Friends Historical Association, *Bulletin.*

Octagonal church Burlington, N. J., erected by the Quakers. It was based on the fifteenth century structure shown *Right,* the Abbot's kitchen of Glastonbury Abbey, Somersetshire, England

Courtesy, Historic American Buildings Survey.

Alexander Grant House, Salem, N. J.

Art in Colonial New Jersey

Governor Lewis Morris.
Portrait by John Watson in 1715
Courtesy, The Brooklyn Museum, Brooklyn, N. Y.

Architecture

Courtesy, Historic American Buildings Survey, Washington, D. C.

Hancock House. Hancock's Bridge, N. J.   Cedar Plank House, Hancock's Bridge, N. J.

Courtesy, Historic American Buildings Survey.
Revell House, Burlington, N. J. 1685

Courtesy, Historic American Buildings Survey.
Terheun House, Hackensack, N. J. ca. 1670

5

MARYLAND

"With a Gentle East Wind Blowing . . ."

Tanner *Societas Jesu Apostolorum Imitatrix.* 1694. *Courtesy,* The New York Public Library.

A Jesuit at prayer

Father White, a Jesuit priest, sailing for America wrote these words: "On the Twenty Second of the Month of November, in the year 1633, being St. Cecilia's day, we set sail from Cowes, in the Isle of Wight, with a gentle East wind blowing."

This gentle wind was carrying the *Ark* and the *Dove* to America to found Lord Baltimore's province of Maryland, chartered in 1632.

George Calvert, the first Lord Baltimore, died before the charter passed the Great Seal, but his son, Cecilius Calvert, the second Lord Baltimore, carried out his father's plans to found a Catholic settlement on Chesapeake Bay, sending his younger brother, Leonard, to act as governor.

The Calverts Founded a Dynasty

Courtesy, Maryland Historical Society, Baltimore, Md.

George Calvert, first Lord Baltimore

Cecilius Calvert, second Lord Baltimore

Leonard Calvert

Hand-Picked

Maryland's first settlers were carefully chosen by Cecilius Calvert, and as far as possible he personally interviewed the men and women who were to take passage on the *Ark* and the *Dove*. In 1633 he issued a pamphlet advertising the advantages of Maryland.

Mexico, there haue beene and are yet dayly yeare by yeare, brought thence to *Seuill*, 5. or 600. thousand Hides at a time: Goates likewise may be had from the Ilands nigh at hand; as many, as shall be desired. Besides these, there are Muske-rats, Squirrels, Beauers, Badgers, Foxes, Martins, Pole-cats, Weisels and Minkses; which yet hurt not the Poultry, nor their Egges. Among their Birds, the Eagle is the greatest deuourer. Hawkes there are of sundry sorts; which all prey commonly vpon fish: Sparrow-hawkes, Lanerets, Gosse-hawkes, Falcons, and Osperaics. Partridges not much bigger then our Quailes: but haue beene seene a hundred in a Couie. Infinite store of wild Turkeyes, nigh as big againe as our time. There are Owsels and Black-birds with red shoulders, Thrushes, and diuers sorts of smaller Birds, some redde, some blew, scarce so bigge as Wrens. In winter, is great plenty of Swannes, Cranes, and Pigeons, Herons, Geese, Brants, Ducks, Wigeon, Dottrell, Oxeis, Parrats, and much other fowle vnknowne in our parts. Limonds thriue wonderfully there, Apricockes and Meli-Cottons, come in such abundance, as a Gentleman in Towne protested hee cast a hundred bushels to the Hogs this last yeare, he had so many more then hee could spend. It hath Chochas and Garvanzas, and is excellent for Beanes, Pease, and all manner of Pults and Rootes: whereof Pease in ten dayes rise 14. inches high. The Corne is very plentifull in each of three Harvests in the same yeare, yeelding in greatest penurie two hundred for one, in ordinary yeares fiue or sixe hundred; and in the better, fifteene or sixteene hundred for one: which increase of Corne beeing so great, it is very easie to keepe all manner of Poultrie and Fowle for the Table all the yeare long. This Corne maketh good bread and beere. It is likely all the fruites of *Italy* will agree with that Soyle, as Figs, Melons, Pomegranates, Oranges, Oliues, Berenjenas, and

and the like: which in time, will be had there; as our Apples already are, where they grow to a much better taste and season then they doe heere. Of rich dyes, and drugs, there is no want; as of Tobacco, Saxaphrase, Bole-armoniacke and the like, though not to be esteemed with the former. As for Minerals little hath beene discouered, but seeing the lower grounds, giue many faire shewes, the Mountaines may not be doubted. As for Copper, the North-west Hils haue that store, as the Natiues themselues part the sollid meetall from the same without fire; and beate it into Plates from the raw oare, for Gold, this onely can be sayd, that the neighbouring nation, commonly weareth bracelets of rude gobbets of gold about their armes; and therefore, it is like there are mines of Gold not farre of. As for Pearle, they were large chaines thereof, though deformed by burning the Oisters and boaring them ill. I omit their Iron which they have already, their Glasse, Hempe, and Flaxe; which is very excellent in this land: with many other Commodities, which time, industry and Art will discover; The fruites whereof may be easier tasted, then beleeved.

February, 10. *anno* 1633.

Any man that desireth to aduenture in this Plantation, may bee informed of euery particular more at large concerning the Transportation and Provisions for their men, and also for the speedy raising of them, if hee repayre to the Lord BALTEMORE, who hath good aduantage to assist him in those things, by reason of the many Provisions hee maketh both for himselfe and others in that kinde: Prouided alwayes, that they assigne one to ouersee theyr Accompts for theyr better satisfaction, and his Lordships discharge. And this the sayd Lord BALTEMORE will bee able to doe for them, if

27

Courtesy, The New York Public Library.

Two pages from *A Declaration of the Lord Baltimore's Plantation in Maryland.* 1633

After a long voyage the colonists landed at an island called St. Clement's, and recorded that "On the day of the Annunciation of the Most Holy Virgin Mary in the year 1634, we celebrated the Mass for the first time, on this island."

This, and succeeding steps in the observance of the Mass, is from *Ceremonies and Religious Customs of the Various Nations of the Known World.* 1733-34.

the PRIEST begins MASS.

Left
Father White blessing the Indians

Tanner *Societas Jesu Apostolorum Imitatrix.* 1694.

Beautiful Robes

Father Marquette's
chasuble. 1618

Courtesy, The Archives of the University of Notre Dame, South Bend, Ind.

Throughout North America, from the time of Columbus, Spanish and French priests intoned the solemn words of the Mass. It was heard on Florida beaches, along the Mississippi, in Canada, in California, and in New Mexico. It was the one changeless ceremony in a world of change. In Maryland, between Anglican Virginia and Puritan New England, the Catholic Church was to gain a permanent foothold in the English colonies. Maryland Jesuits conducted Indian missions and made with their own hands the things they needed.

Tanner *Societas Jesu Apostolorum Imitatrix.* 1694.

Tanner *Societas Jesu Apostolorum Imitatrix.* 1694.

An Historic Document

In 1649 the Maryland Assembly passed a law often cited as a milestone of religious freedom; both partisans and critics can find support for their views by a careful analysis of this document shown *below*. In the fifth paragraph are sentiments that foreshadow the *Bill of Rights*.

A LAW
OF
MARYLAND
Concerning
RELIGION.

Oraſmuch as in a well-governed and Chriſtian Commonwealth, Matters concerning Religion and the Honour of God ought to be in the firſt place to be taken into ſerious conſideration, and endeavoured to be ſettled. Be it therefore Ordained and Enacted by the Right Honourable *CÆCILIUS* Lord Baron of *Baltemore*, abſolute Lord and Proprietary of this Province, with the Advice and Conſent of the Upper and Lower Houſe of this General Aſſembly, That whatſoever perſon or perſons within this Province and the Iſlands thereunto belonging, ſhall from henceforth blaſpheme GOD, that is curſe him; or ſhall deny our Saviour JESUS CHRIST to be the Son of God; or ſhall deny the Holy Trinity, the Father, Son, & Holy Ghoſt; or the Godhead of any of the ſaid Three Perſons of the Trinity, or the Unity of the Godhead, or ſhall uſe or utter any reproachful ſpeeches, words, or language, concerning the Holy Trinity, or any of the ſaid three Perſons thereof, ſhall be puniſhed with death, and confiſcation or forfeiture of all his or her Lands and Goods to the Lord Proprietary and his Heirs.

And be it alſo enacted by the Authority, and with the advice and aſſent aforeſaid, That whatſoever perſon or perſons ſhall from henceforth uſe or utter any reproachful words or ſpeeches concerning the bleſſed Virgin MARY, the Mother of our Saviour, or the holy Apoſtles or Evangeliſts, or any of them, ſhall in ſuch caſe for the firſt Offence forfeit to the ſaid Lord Proprietary and his Heirs, Lords and Proprietaries of this Province, the ſum of Five pounds Sterling, or the value thereof to be levied on the goods and chattels of every ſuch perſon ſo offending; but in caſe ſuch offender or offenders ſhall not then have goods and chattels ſufficient for the ſatisfying of ſuch forfeiture, or that the ſame be not otherwiſe ſpeedily ſatisfied, that then ſuch offender or offenders ſhall be publickly whipt, and be impriſoned during the pleaſure of the Lord Proprietary, or the Lieutenant or Chief Governor of this Province for the time being: And that every ſuch offender and offenders for every ſecond offence ſhall forfeit Ten Pounds Sterling, or the value thereof to be levied as aforeſaid; or in caſe ſuch offender or offenders ſhall not then have goods and chattels within this Province ſufficient for that purpoſe, then to be publickly and ſeverely whipt and impriſoned as before is expreſſed: and that every perſon or perſons before mentioned, offending herein the third time, ſhall for ſuch third offence, forfeit all his lands and goods, and be for ever baniſht and expelled out of this Province.

And be it alſo further Enacted by the ſame Authority, advice, and aſſent, That whatſoever perſon or perſons ſhall from henceforth upon any occaſion of offence, or otherwiſe in a reproachful manner or way, declare, call, or denominate, any perſon or perſons whatſoever, inhabiting, reſiding, trafficking, trading, or commercing within this Province, or within any the Ports, Harbours, Creeks or Havens to the ſame belonging, an Heretick, Schiſmatick, Idolater, Puritan, Presbyterian, Independant, Popiſh Prieſt, Jeſuit, Jeſuited Papiſt, Lutheran, Calviniſt, Anabaptiſt, Browniſt, Antinomian, Roundhead, Separatiſt, or other name or term in a reproachfull manner relating to matter of Religion, ſhall for every ſuch offence forfeit and loſe the ſum of Ten ſhillings Sterling, or the value thereof, to be levied of the goods and chattels of every ſuch offender and offenders, the one half thereof to be forfeited and paid unto the perſon & perſons of whom ſuch reproachful words are, or ſhall be ſpoken or uttered, and the other half thereof to the Lord Proprietary and his Heirs, Lords and Proprietaries of this Province: But if ſuch perſon or perſons who ſhall at any time utter or ſpeak any ſuch reproachful words or language, ſhall not have goods or chattels ſufficient and overt within this Province to ſatisfy the penalty aforeſaid, or that the ſame be not otherwiſe ſpeedily ſatisfied, that then the perſon and perſons ſo offending ſhall be publickly whipt, and ſhall ſuffer impriſonment without Bail or Mainpriſe untill he, ſhe, or they, reſpectively, ſhall ſatisfie the party offended or grieved by ſuch reproachfull Language, by asking him or her reſpectively forgiveneſs publickly, for ſuch his offence, before the Magiſtrate or chief Officer or Officers of the Town or place where ſuch offence ſhall be given.

And be further likewiſe enacted by the authority and conſent aforeſaid, that every perſon and perſons within this Province, that ſhall at any time hereafter prophane the Sabbath, or Lords day, called Sunday, by frequent ſwearing, drunkenneſs, or by any uncivil or diſorderly Recreation, or by working on that day when abſolute neceſſity doth not require, ſhall for every ſuch firſt offence forfeit two ſhillings ſix pence Sterling, or the value thereof; and for the ſecond offence five ſhillings Sterling. or the value thereof; and for the third offence, and for every time he ſhall offend in like manner afterwards, Ten ſhillings Sterling, or the value thereof; and in caſe ſuch offender or offenders ſhall not have ſufficient goods or chattels within this Province to ſatisfy any of the aforeſaid penalties hereby impoſed for prophaning the Sabbath or Lords day called Sunday as aforeſaid, then in every ſuch caſe the party ſo offending ſhall for the firſt and ſecond offence in that kind be impriſoned till he or ſhe ſhall publickly in open Court before the chief Commander, Judge or Magiſtrate of that County, Town, or Precinct wherein ſuch offence ſhall be committed, acknowledge the ſcandal and offence he hath in that reſpect given, againſt God, and the good and civil Government of this Province: and for the third offence and for every time after ſhall alſo be publickly whipt.

And whereas the inforcing of the Conſcience in matter of Religion hath frequently fallen out to be of dangerous conſequence in thoſe Commonwealths where it hath been practiſed, and for the more quiet and peaceable Government of this Province, and the better to preſerve mutual love & unity amongſt the Inhabitants here, Be it therefore alſo by the Lord Proprietary with the advice and aſſent of this Aſſembly, ordained and enacted, except as in this preſent Act is before declared and ſet forth, that no perſon or perſons whatſoever within this Province, or the Iſlands, Ports, Harbors, Creeks, or Havens thereunto belonging, profeſſing to believe in Jeſus Chriſt, ſhall from henceforth be any ways troubled, moleſted, or diſcountenanced, for, or in reſpect of his or her Religion nor in the free exerciſe thereof within this Province or the Iſlands thereunto belonging, nor any way compell'd to the belief or exerciſe of any other Religion, againſt his or her conſent, ſo as they be not unfaithfull to the Lord Proprietary, or moleſt or conſpire againſt the civil Government, eſtabliſhed or to be eſtabliſhed in this Province under him and his Heirs. And that all and every perſon and perſons that ſhall preſume contrary to this Act and the true intent & meaning thereof, directly or indirectly, either in perſon or eſtate, wilfully to wrong, diſturb, or trouble, or moleſt any perſon or perſons whatſoever within this Province, profeſſing to believe in Jeſus Chriſt, for or in reſpect of his or her Religion, or the free exerciſe thereof within this Province, otherwiſe then is provided for in this Act, that ſuch perſon or perſons ſo offending ſhall be compelled to pay treble damages to the party ſo wronged or moleſted, and for every ſuch offence ſhall alſo forfeit Twenty ſhillings Sterling in Money, or the value thereof, half thereof for the uſe of the Lord Proprietary and his Heirs, Lords and Proprietaries of this Province, and the other half thereof for the uſe of the Party ſo wronged or moleſted as aforeſaid; or if the party ſo offending as aforeſaid, ſhall refuſe or be unable to recompence the party ſo wronged, or to ſatisfy ſuch fine or forfeiture, then ſuch offender ſhall be ſeverely puniſhed by publick whipping and impriſonment during the pleaſure of the Lord Proprietary or his Lieutenant or chief Governor of this Province for the time being, without Bail or Mainpriſe.

And be it further alſo enacted by the authority and conſent aforeſaid, that the Sheriff or other Officer or Officers from time to time to be appointed and authorized for that purpoſe, of the County, Town, or Precinct where any particular offence in this preſent Act contained, ſhall happen at any time to be committed, and whereupon there is hereby a forfeiture, fine, or penalty impoſed, ſhall from time to time diſtrain, and ſeize the goods and eſtate of every ſuch perſon ſo offending as aforeſaid againſt this preſent Act or any part thereof, and ſell the ſame or any part thereof for the full ſatisfaction of ſuch forfeiture, fine, or penalty as aforeſaid, reſtoring to the party ſo offending, the remainder or overplus of the ſaid goods or eſtate, after ſuch ſatisfaction ſo made as aforeſaid.

St. Mary's City

The first permanent settlement was at St. Mary's City. The original temporary dwellings were flimsy, but it was not long before better homes were built. *Left,* Leigh House on St. Mary's Hill Freehold, St. Mary's City. *Below,* Manor of Cornwaleys' Crosse, St. Mary's County, Md., built ca. 1690. This is not the original house of 1642.

Photographs, *Courtesy,* H. Chandlee Forman, A.I.A., Easton, Md.

Early Maryland houses were modelled on those of the homeland such as the English houses of the period shown *below*.

P. Thompson *History and Antiquities of Boston*. 1856.

P. Thompson *History and Antiquities of Boston*. 1856.

Courtesy, Forbes Collection, Maryland Hall of Records. Photo by M. E. Warren.

Jonas Green House, Annapolis, Md. ca. 1680.

At *left*, old Treasury Building or Provincial Council House, Annapolis, Md., built 1735–37, as restored; *below*, Sands House, Annapolis, ca. 1680.

Photo by M. E. Warren, Annapolis, Md.

Courtesy, Historic Annapolis, Inc. Photo by M. E. Warren.

At *right*, fireplace, Tudor Hall, St. Mary's County, Md.

Below, artifacts found near the site of the Leonard Calvert House, St. Mary's City.

Courtesy, H. Chandlee Forman, A.I.A., Easton, Md.

Courtesy, H. Chandlee Forman, A.I.A., Easton, Md.

Below, Mount Airy, Prince George's County, Md., the old Calvert mansion, the earliest part of which was built ca. 1680 for a hunting lodge. Benedict Calvert, son of Charles, fifth Lord Baltimore, resided here. Originally called "His Lordship's Kindness."

Courtesy, Maryland Historical Society, Baltimore, Md.

Domestic Architecture of Maryland

The "Folly," St. Mary's County, Md.

Below, "Long Lane Farm," St. Mary's County.

All photographs *courtesy*, H. Chandlee Forman, A.I.A., Easton, Md.

Cedar Park, Anne Arundel County. Built *ca*. 1700 by Richard Galloway.

Photograph *courtesy*, H. Chandlee Forman, A.I.A., Easton, Md.

The Governor Lived In Style

The Governor's Castle at St. Mary's City, built in 1639, was excavated in 1940. Its foundations showed that it covered an area of 2,934 square feet, making it the largest structure ever erected in the English colonies, up to that time. It was blown up in 1694 when seventeen kegs of gunpowder exploded in its basement.

The Governor's "Castle" at St. Mary's City, 1639. It was the forerunner of the Governor's "Palace" at Williamsburg, Va. Reconstruction by Dr. Henry C. Forman, Wesleyan College, Macon, Ga.

Worldly Goods

What the colonists in Maryland wore, what tools and utensils they used, what furniture they had, etc., is strikingly revealed in the inventory of Justinian Snowe, dated 1639. The goods are valued in pounds of tobacco.

Gentleman Planter

Plantation life formed the basic pattern of colonial civilization in Maryland and Virginia. The hundreds of bays, inlets and rivers made construction of roads unnecessary. Transportation was chiefly by water. The tobacco growers had their private wharves in both Virginia and Maryland, and ships from England stopped at these wharves to unload manufactured articles in exchange for cargoes of tobacco, staves, American dye or drug-producing plants such as sumac, woad, sassafras and ginseng.

In this picture we see scantily dressed slaves, a cooper tightening the end of a tobacco hogshead, and a bookkeeper checking off the cargo. The loading crane and the ship appear in the background. Other hogsheads are seen in the warehouse.

Courtesy, Duke University Library, Durham, N. C.

Cartouche from the Fry and Jefferson map of Virginia and Maryland. 1775

At Right is a similar scene, even to the details of the coopers hammering hogsheads, and a gentleman with a pipe, who seems to be dickering over the price of the cargo.

Detail from a map by Henry Popple. 1733

Courtesy, Historic American Buildings Survey, Washington, D. C.

Tobacco barns, Calvert County, Md.

"Maryland, My Maryland"

Section of a map of Virginia and Maryland made by
Augustine Herrman in 1670. Engraved by William
Faithorne in 1673

Portrait of Augustine Herrman,
which was engraved on this map

Lord Baltimore called this "the best mapp that was ever Drawn of any Country Whatsoever,"
and was so pleased that he gave Herrman 13,000 acres of land in what is now Cecil County,
Maryland, upon which Herrman built Bohemia Manor, indicated in the upper right-hand
corner of the map.

Note the plantation houses that dot the irregular shores of Chesapeake Bay and the Patuxent River. Note St. Mary's at the bottom of the map. In 1694 the seat of government was
moved to Anne Arundel Towne (Arundelton on the map) which later became Annapolis.
Baltemore Towne, at the top of the map was not the present city of Baltimore, which was not
founded until 1729, on the Patapsco River, farther to the South.

He Stood His Ground

William Claiborne, of Virginia, had a profitable trading post on Kent Island in the Chesapeake, and resisted the encroachments of the Calverts. His name appears frequently in the early annals of Maryland.

She Gave A "Towne" Her Name

Portrait of William Claiborne. Owned by W. C. Claiborne, New Orleans, La.

At Right Anne Arundel, wife of Cecilius Calvert, second Lord Baltimore. Annapolis (Anne Arundel Towne), and Anne Arundel County, Md., perpetuate her name and memory

This Tree Still Stands

When Herrman made his map he may have rested under this very oak. If it could talk it would relate the history of Maryland from the beginning.

Courtesy, Maryland Geological Survey.

Wye Oak, Wye Mills, Talbot County, Md.

This Barn Stood Until 1937

This venerable structure, considered to be the original barn of Mrs. Mary Troughton, friend of Lord Baltimore, stood at St. Mary's until it was destroyed in 1937.

Courtesy, Dr. Henry C. Forman, Wesleyan College, Macon, Ga.

Old barn. St. Mary's City, Md. 17th Cent. Forman *Jamestown and St. Mary's.* 1938

Plantation Life

The Maryland planters remained near the water and there built their mansions. They had little intercourse with each other or the outside world, each plantation being an independent social and economic unit made up of the planter and his family, white indented servants and Negro slaves. This accounts for the scarcity and slow growth of towns and cities in Maryland and Virginia, as compared to New England. Even today Marylanders speak of counties more often than they do of towns. A stranger always received a hospitable welcome in Maryland, for he brought news of the outside world.

[4]

Should talk to you Unmannerly;
But if you please to go with me
To yonder House, you'll welcome be.
Encountring soon the smoaky Seat,
The Planter old did thus me greet:
" Whether you come from Goal or Colledge,
" You're welcome to my certain Knowledge;
" And if you please all Night to stay,
" My Son shall put you in the way.
Which offer I most kindly took,
And for a Seat did round me look:
VVhen presently amongst the rest,
He plac'd his unknown English Guest,
Who found them drinking for a whet,
A Cask of (b) Syder on the Fret,
Till Supper came upon the Table,
On which I fed whilst I was able.
So after hearty Entertainment,
Of Drink and Victuals without Payment;
For Planters Tables, you must know,
Are free for all that come and go.
While (i) Pon and Milk, with (k) Mush well sour'd,
In wooden Dishes grac'd the Board;
With (l) Homine and Syder-pap,
(Which scarce a hungry Dog wou'd lap)
VVell stuff'd with Fat, from Bacon fry'd,
Or with Molossus dulcify'd.
Then out our Landlord pulls a Pouch,
As greasy as the Leather Couch
On which he sat, and straight begun,
To load with VVeed his Indian Gun;
In length, scarce longer than ones Finger,
Or that for which the Ladies linger:
His Pipe smoak'd out with aweful Grace,
With aspect grave and solemn pace;
The reverend Sire walks to a Chest,
Of all his Furniture the best,
Closely confin'd within a Room,
VVhich seldom felt the weight of Broom;

(b) Syder-pap is a sort of Food made of Syder and small Homine, like our Oat-meal. (i) Pon is Bread made of Indian-Corn. (k) Mush is a sort of Hasty-pudding made with Water and Indian Flower. (l) Homine is a Dish that is made of boiled Indian Wheat...

[5]

From thence he lugs a Cag of Rum,
And nodding to me, thus begun:
I find, says he, you don't much care,
For this our Indian Country Fare;
But let me tell you, Friend of mine,
You may be glad of it in time,
Tho' now your Stomach is so fine;
And if within this Land you stay,
You'll find it true what I do say.
This said, the Rundlet up he threw,
And bending backwards strongly drew:
I pluck'd as stoutly for my part,
Altho' it made me sick at Heart,
And got so soon into my Head
I scarce cou'd find my way to Bed;
Where I was instantly convey'd
By one who pass'd for Chamber-Maid,
Tho' by her loose and sluttish Dress,
She rather seem'd a Bedlam-Bess:
Curious to know from whence she came,
I prest her to declare her Name.
She Blushing, seem'd to hide her Eyes,
And thus in Civil Terms replies;
In better Times, e'er to this Land,
I was unhappily Trapann'd;
Perchance as well I did appear,
As any Lord or Lady here,
Not then a Slave for twice two (a) Year.
My Cloaths were fashionably new,
Nor were my Shifts of Linnen Blue;
But things are changed now at the Hoe,
I daily work, and Bare-foot go,
In weeding Corn or feeding Swine,
I spend my melancholy Time.
Kidnap'd and Fool'd, I hither fled,
To shun a hated Nuptial (b) Bed,

(a) Tis the Custom for Servants to be obliged for four Years to very servile Work; after which time they have their Freedom.
(b) These are the general Excuses made by English Women, which are sold, or sell themselves to Mary-Land.

C   And

Two pages from Ebenezer Cook's *Sot-Weed Factor*. 1708, describing a visit to a Maryland plantation

One of the delicacies of Maryland often seen on the planter's table was the canvas-back duck.

The Cabinet of Natural History. 1830-34.

Three-Notch Roads and Ox Carts

When a land journey was undertaken it meant dangerous travel along trails through woods filled with Indians. Trees were notched to keep the wayfarer from getting lost. Some of the old three-notch roads still exist in Maryland.

Three-notch road, St. Mary's County, Md. The three notches are shown on the tree below

Courtesy, Maryland Geological Survey.

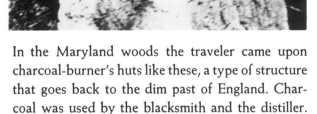

Now and then a traveler met a two-wheeled ox cart. Ox carts are still used in certain sections of Maryland

Below Two-wheeled ox carts, Port Tobacco, Charles County, Md.

Courtesy, Maryland Geological Survey.

In the Maryland woods the traveler came upon charcoal-burner's huts like these, a type of structure that goes back to the dim past of England. Charcoal was used by the blacksmith and the distiller.

Iron furnaces were built in Maryland at an early date. Here are the ruins of two of them.

Courtesy, Maryland Geological Survey.

Curtis Creek Furnace, Furnace Creek, Anne Arundel County, Md.

Nassawango Furnace, near Snow Hill, Worcester County, Md.

Courtesy, Maryland Geological Survey.

Charcoal-burner's hut. Cecil County, Md.

The Church of England

The Maryland planter ordered his Sunday clothes direct from London. If he was a member of the Church of England he went to a church like this.

Left Male costume. 1700

Pugh *London.* v. 4. 1807.

Below St. Luke's church. "Old Wye."
Wye Mills, Md. ca. 1700

Courtesy, Enoch Pratt Free Library, Baltimore, Md.

He could borrow books from the parish libraries founded by the Reverend Thomas Bray, that indefatigable promoter of useful knowledge.

Courtesy, The New York Public Library.
Bookplate used in Maryland

Note in Bray's essay the suggestion that there should be a bookplate in each book designating the parish library it belonged to, to avoid loss and theft. One of these bookplates is shown here.

Two pages from Thomas Bray's *An Essay Towards Promoting All Necessary and Useful Knowledge.* 1697

Bray had the quaint notion that the size of a book, regardless of the size of the type, should determine the number of days it could be kept by the reader, as this excerpt will show.

"In My Father's House Are Many Mansions"

Catholics and Protestants lived side by side in Maryland, and the latter often boasted a majority in the Maryland Assembly, despite the fact that the Proprietors, the Calverts, were staunch Catholics. When William and Mary came to the English throne a band of Maryland Protestants took up arms against the Catholics. They captured St. Mary's City in 1689, and printed there this *Declaration*.

Courtesy, H. Chandlee Forman, A.I.A., Easton, Md.

Above, an interior view of Old Gunpowder Friends' Meeting, Baltimore County, Md.

Courtesy, The Library of Congress.

Below, Old Trinity Church, Church Creek, Md., built ca. 1675. This photograph shows the church as recently restored.

Courtesy, Maryland Department of Economic Development, Annapolis, Md.

A Poet Advertises Maryland

The beauties of Maryland were sung by George Alsop, an indented servant, who upon working out his term of service, was so pleased with Maryland and the opportunities it afforded that he wrote its history in verse. The burden of his song was that his friends in England should settle without delay in this sylvan paradise. In Maryland one breathed freedom's air. How else could one explain the unprecedented request of Margaret Brent before the Maryland Assembly in 1639. She asked for the right to vote! She was almost three hundred years ahead of her time.

Vow here the Shadow whole Ingenuous Hand
Hath drawne exact the Province Mary Land.
Display her Glory in such Scenes of Witt
That those that read must fall in Love with it
For which his Labour hee deserves the praise
As well as Poets doe the wreath of Bay's.
Anno Dồ 1666. Aeta Sue 28.   H.W.

George Alsop

Frontispiece of his *A Character of the Province of Mary-Land.* 1666

Women's Rights

ffriday 21ᵗʰ Jan.

The ffreemen bownd to attend the Assembly appeared except mʳ ffenwick, mʳ Thorneborough, Mʳ Brookes & George Saphyer

Summons to George Saphyer to be att the Assembly forthwᵗʰ vppon sight &c

was read certaine orders to be obserued in the howse during the Assembly

Came Mʳˢ Margarett Brent and requested to have vote in the howse for her selfe and voyce allso for that att the last Court 3ᵈ Jan: it was ordered that the said Mʳˢ Brent was to be lookd uppon and received as his Lᵖˢ Attorney. The Gouᵗ denyed that the sᵈ Mʳˢ Brent should have any uote in the howse. And the sᵈ Mʳˢ Brent protested agst all proceedings in this pñt Assembly, unlesse shee may be pñt. and have vote as aforesᵈ

Orders &c.

Published eod. 1 That noe one of the howse shall use any reuyling speeches or name any one by name but by another signification Viz. the Gent. that spoke last or the like.

Maryland Archives.

Margaret Brent's request denied

"Of Thee I Sing"

Picturesque Views of American Scenery. Published by M. Carey & Son, Philadelphia. 1820.

Jones' Falls near Baltimore. Painted by J. Shaw. Engraved by J. Hill

6

THE CAROLINAS AND GEORGIA

Plato Refuted

Plato's ideal republic was one managed by philosophers. In planning the government of the Carolinas the philosophical mind of John Locke evolved an elaborate *Constitution*, but it was doomed to failure. It was not adapted to the realities of colonial life. Locke, as secretary to Anthony Ashley Cooper, later to become the Earl of Shaftesbury, was delegated to write this bizarre document, which provided for such offices as palatine, chamberlain, high steward, landgrave, cazique, and eight supreme courts, and such land divisions as signiories, baronies, and manors.

The Earl of Shaftesbury

John Locke

Fundamental Constitutions
OF
CAROLINA.

OUR Sovereign Lord the King having out of His Royal Grace and Bounty, granted unto us the Province of *Carolina*, with all the Royalties, Proprieties, Jurisdictions and Privileges of a *County Palatine*, as large and ample as the County Palatine of *Durham*, with other great Privileges; for the better Settlement of the Government of the said Place, and establishing the Interest of the Lords Proprietors with Equality, and without Confusion, and that the Government of this Province may be made most agreeable to the Monarchy under which we live, and of which this Province is a Part; and that we may avoid erecting a numerous *Democracy*, we the *Lords* and *Proprietors* of the Province aforesaid, have agreed to this following Form of *Government*, to be perpetually established amongst us, unto which we do oblige our selves, our Heirs and Successors, in the most binding Ways that can be devised.

§. 1. THE *Eldest* of the *Lords Proprietors* shall be *Palatine*, and upon the Decease of the *Palatine*, the *Eldest* of the Seven surviving *Proprietors* shall always succeed him.

§. 2. There shall be *Seven* other *Chief Offices* erected, *viz.* The *Admirals*, *Chamberlains*, *Chancellors*, *Constables*, *Chief-Justices*, *High-Stewards* and *Treasurers*; which Places shall be enjoy'd by none but the *Lords Proprietors*, to be assign'd at first by Lot, and upon the Vacancy of any one of the Seven Great Offices by Death, or otherwise, the Eldest *Proprietor* shall have his Choice of the said Place.

§. 3. The whole Province shall be *divided* into *Counties*; each County shall consist of Eight *Signiories*, Eight *Baronies*, and Four *Precincts*; each *Precinct* shall consist of Six *Colonies*.

Carolina. 37

...part thereof, either... or *One and Twenty*...

§. 28... ...ll be *divided* amongst Co-heirs... ...shall all entirely *descend* to the... ...If there be more *Mannors* than one, ...shall have her *Choice*, the Second next, and so on, beginning again at the Eldest, till all the *Mannors* be taken up; that so the *Privileges* which belong to *Mannors* being *indivisible*, the Lands of the *Mannors* to which they are annexed, may be *kept entire*, and the *Mannor* not lose those *Privileges*, which upon parcelling out to several Owners, must necessarily cease.

§. 21. Every Lord of a *Mannor*, within his *Mannor*, shall have all the Powers, Jurisdictions, and Privileges, which a *Landgrave* or *Cassique* hath in his *Baronies*.

§. 22. In every *Signiory*, *Barony*, and *Mannor*, all the *Leet-Men* shall be under the Jurisdiction of the respective Lords of the said *Signiory*, *Barony*, or *Mannor*, without Appeal from him. Nor shall any *Leet-Man* or *Leet-Woman* have Liberty to go off from the Land of their particular Lord, and live any where else, without License obtained from their said Lord, under Hand and Seal.

§. 23. All the Children of *Leet-Men* shall be *Leet-Men*, and so to all Generations.

§. 24. No Man shall be capable of having a *Court-Leet* or *Leet-Men*, but a *Proprietor*, *Landgrave*, *Cassique*, or *Lord of a Mannor*.

§. 25. Whoever shall voluntarily enter himself a *Leet-Man* in the Registry of the County Court, shall be a *Leet-Man*.

§. 26. Whoever is Lord of *Leet-Men*, shall upon the *Marriage* of a *Leet-Man* or *Leet-Woman* of his, give them Ten Acres of Land for their Lives, they paying to him therefore not more than one Eighth part of all the Yearly Produce and Growth of the said Ten Acres.

§. 27. No *Landgrave* or *Cassique* shall be try'd for any Criminal Cause, in any but the *Chief-Justice's* Court, and that by a Jury of his *Peers*.

§. 28. There shall be *Eight Supreme Courts*. The First called, *The Palatine's Court*, consisting of the *Palatine*, and the other Seven *Proprietors*. The other Seven Courts of the other Seven Great Officers, shall consist each of them of a *Proprietor*, and Six *Councellors* added to him. Under each of these latter Seven *Courts* shall be a *College* of Twelve *Assistants*. The Twelve *Assistants* of the several *Colleges* shall be chosen; Two out of the *Landgraves*, *Cassiques*, or eldest Sons of *Pro-*

The Lords Proprietors

John Colleton, a planter of Barbadoes, friend of King Charles II, had obtained for himself and seven other proprietors a charter for Carolina in 1664. The eight proprietors were Colleton, Lord Ashley, Sir William Berkeley, John Lord Berkeley, Lord Craven, the Duke of Albemarle, the Earl of Clarendon, and Sir George Carteret.

From Public Records Office, London

The Great Seal of the Lords Proprietors of the Province of Carolina, showing on the reverse the coats of arms of the eight signatories

Charles Towne

The first settlers in South Carolina, mostly from Barbadoes, founded Charles Towne on the Ashley River in 1670, naming it in honor of their sovereign. The plantation system, patterned on the prevailing system in the West Indies, was established from the very beginning. Negro labor was an important factor.

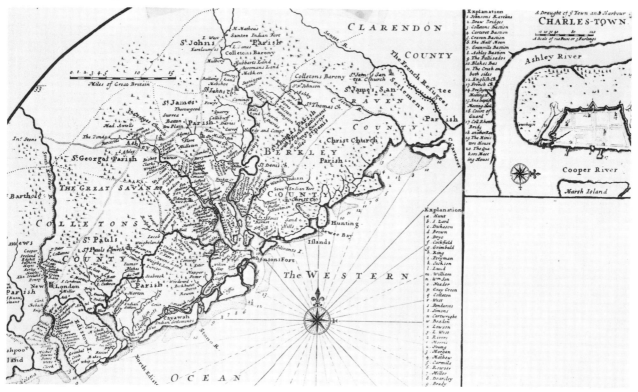

Herman Moll's map showing the names of the early settlers in South Carolina. 1715

The Roberts view of Charles Town. 1739
Courtesy, Stokes Collection, The New York Public Library.

At the Edge of the Unknown

Beyond the narrow limits of the town stretched the swampy wilderness. Early waterfront towns gave the effect of a stage setting, lacking depth. The urban fringe was a narrow wedge between the mystery and immensity of the sea and the mystery and wildness of the unexplored forests and streams. The spire of St. Philip's Church, marked (E) on the Roberts view, punctuated the wilderness like an exclamation point of God.

St. Philip's Church

Designs for church clock towers taken from *A Book of Architecture* by James Gibbs. 1726

Charles Town. (Second section)

Guns and Steeples

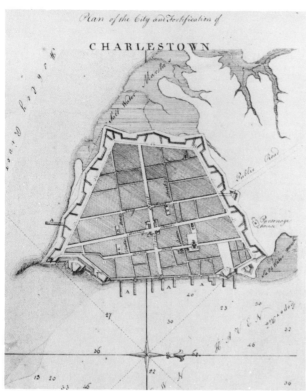

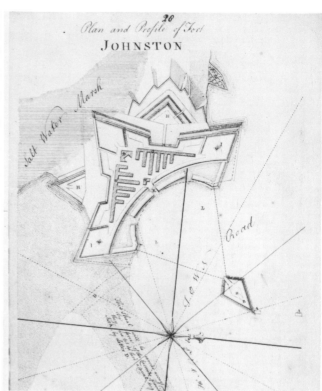

Plan by William Gerard De Brahm. ca. 1760. It shows how the town had expanded.

Plan by William Gerard De Brahm. ca. 1760. Fort Johnson was built to protect Charlestown from the Spanish threat from Florida

St. Michael's Church. 1752. It was copied from St. Martin's-in-the-Fields, London

Stoney *Plantations of the South Carolina Low Country.* 1939. Courtesy, Carolina Art Association, Charleston, S. C. Photo by Frances B. Johnston.

Interior of St. James' Church, Goose Creek, S. C. 1711

Huguenots and Acadians

Charleston, even today, has a certain French atmosphere. Huguenot names are sprinkled through the telephone book. The Huguenots were driven from France in 1685-86, and many found refuge in South Carolina. Another French stream poured from Nova Scotia in 1755, the ill-fated Acadians immortalized in Longfellow's *Evangeline*. The French exiles were industrious and thrifty. They built beautiful mansions among the oak and cypress trees laden with Spanish moss, and their rice and indigo plantations were sources of ever-increasing wealth.

Photo by U. S. Forest Service.

Courtesy, Carolina Art Association, Charleston, S. C.

Scene near Charleston. Water color by Charles Fraser. 1801

Right Hampton, near Charleston. Begun by Noe Serre in 1735. Home of the Horry family, prosperous Huguenots

Courtesy, Mr. Archibald Rutledge, the present owner.

Under the Magnolias

The English planters vied with the Huguenots in the extent of their rice fields and in the elegance of their mansions.

Below "Brabants", near Charleston. Water color by Charles Fraser

Courtesy, Carolina Art Association, Charleston, S. C.

Courtesy, University of North Carolina Press.

Rose Hill Plantation, home of Charles Heyward

Left Medway. Built by Jan Van Arrsens in 1686. It shows the Dutch influence

Stoney *Plantations of the Carolina Low Country.* 1939. *Courtesy,* Carolina Art Association, Charleston, S. C. Photo by Frances B. Johnston.

Right Fenwick Hall. Stono River, near Charleston. Built by John Fenwick in 1730

Courtesy Carolina Art Association, Charleston, S. C. Stoney *Plantations of the Carolina Low Country.* Photo by Ben Judah Lubschez.

Middleton Place

Courtesy, Carolina Art Association, Charleston, S. C. Photo by Ben Judah Lubschez.

Above, house at Middleton Place. Built by John Williams in 1738, enlarged 1755. Note the prominent Dutch gables. *Below,* view of the Ashley River from Middleton Place.

Courtesy, The Library of Congress. Photo by Frances B. Johnston.

Rice Seed from Madagascar

What tobacco was to Virginia and Maryland, rice was to South Carolina. Rice seed was brought to South Carolina from Madagascar around 1694. The rice was threshed with flails and forks, and the husks were removed by pounding them with a wooden pestle in a mortar made of a hollow stump. The Negroes of South Carolina still pound rice in this primitive fashion.

Catesby Natural History of Carolina. 1754.

Rice plant

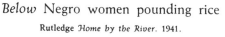

Below Negro women pounding rice

Rutledge Home by the River. 1941.

Below Hoes and rice hook

Courtesy, The Charleston Museum, Charleston, S. C.

Mules bogged down in the soggy rice fields, and special boots had to be strapped to their feet.

Mule boots

Courtesy, The Charleston Museum, Charleston, S. C.

Winnowing Rice

Courtesy, The Charleston Museum, Charleston, S. C.

Rice scales

Courtesy, The Charleston Museum, Charleston, S. C.

Winnowing house. Hopsewee Plantation, South Santee River, S. C.

Courtesy, The Charleston Museum, Charleston, S. C.

Piggins. Used on a rice plantation

Water color by Alice R. Huger Smith. Sass *A Carolina Rice Plantation of the Fifties*. 1936. Courtesy, William Morrow & Co., Inc., New York.

Winnowing Rice

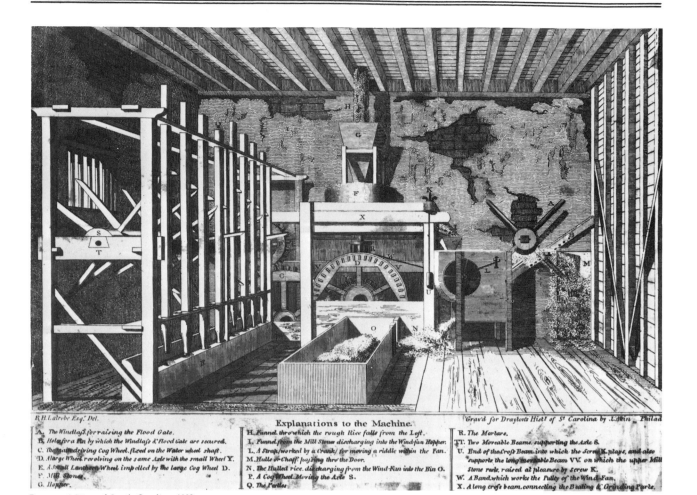

R.H.Latrobe Esqr. Del.

Explanations to the Machine.

'Grav'd for Drayton's Hist^y of St Carolina by J.Akin .. Philad

A. *The Windlass for raising the Flood Gate.*
B. *Holes for a Pin by which the Windlass & Flood Gate are secured.*
C. *The main driving Cog Wheel, fixed on the Water wheel shaft.*
D. *A large Wheel revolving on the same Axle with the small Wheel Y.*
E. *A Small Lanthern Wheel impelled by the large Cog Wheel D.*
F. *Mill Stone.*
G. *Hopper.*

H. *Funnel thro'which the rough Rice falls from the Loft.*
I. *Funnel from the Mill Stone discharging into the Wind-fan Hopper.*
L. *A Strap worked by a Crank for moving a riddle within the Fan.*
M. *Hulls or Chaff, flying thro' the Door.*
N. *The Hulled rice discharging from the Wind-fan into the Bin O.*
P. *A Cog Wheel Moving the Axle S.*
Q. *The Pestles.*

R. *The Mortars.*
TT. *Two Moveable Beams, supporting the Axle S.*
U. *End of the Cross Beam, into which the Screw K, plays, and also supports the long moveable Beam VV. on which the upper Mill Stone rests, raised at pleasure by screw K.*
W. *A Band which works the Pulley of the Wind-Fan.*
X. *A long cross beam, connecting the Beating & Grinding Parts.*

Drayton *A View of South-Carolina.* 1802.

Water rice machine

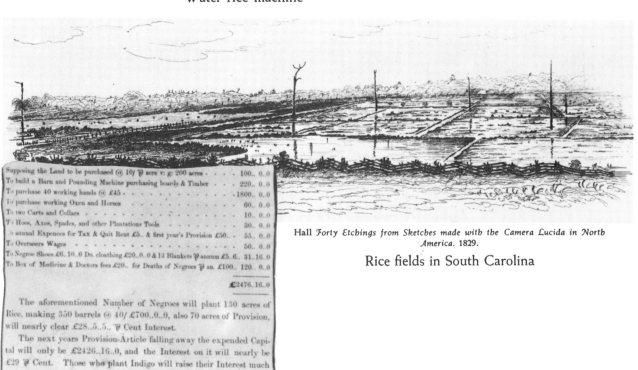

Supposing the Land to be purchased @ 10/ ℔ acre v: g: 200 acres . . . . 100.. 0..0
To build a Barn and Pounding Machine purchasing boards & Timber . . . 220.. 0..0
To purchase 40 working hands @ £45 . . . . .1800.. 0..0
To purchase working Oxen and Horses . . . . 60.. 0..0
To two Carts and Collars . . . . 10.. 0..0
To Hoes, Axes, Spades, and other Plantations Tools . . . . . . 30.. 0..0
To annual Expences for Tax & Quit Rent £5.. & first year's Provision £50.. . 55.. 0..0
To Overseers Wages . . . . 50.. 0..0
To Negroe Shoes £6..10..0 Do. cloathing £20..0..0 & 13 Blankets ℔ annum £5..6.. 31..16..0
To Box of Medicine & Doctors fees £20.. for Deaths of Negroes ℔ an. £100.. 120.. 0..0
                                                    £2476..16..0

The aforementioned Number of Negroes will plant 130 acres of
Rice, making 350 barrels @ 40/ £700..0..0, also 70 acres of Provision,
will nearly clear £28..5..5.. ℔ Cent Interest.
    The next years Provision-Article falling away the expended Capi-
tal will only be £2426..16..0, and the Interest on it will nearly be
£29 ℔ Cent. Those who plant Indigo will raise their Interest much
higher. NB. the above Calculation is on Land, which is ready
cleared and fenced, for if this is to be done, so full a Crop cannot be
expected the first, and at times not the second year, especially if the
Undertaker is not a professed Planter, and has not a very faithfull
and industrious well experienced Overseer.

Hall *Forty Etchings from Sketches made with the Camera Lucida in North America.* 1829.

Rice fields in South Carolina

Around 1750 William Gerard De Brahm, a surveyor,
estimated the cost of operating a 200 acre rice plantation, at *left.*

Slavery

To make rice growing profitable the planters of South Carolina needed cheap labor. Lacking White laborers they imported Negro slaves from the West Indies. The West Indies were clearing houses for slaves brought from Africa. The Dutch, French, Portuguese, and English traders were all interested in this traffic.

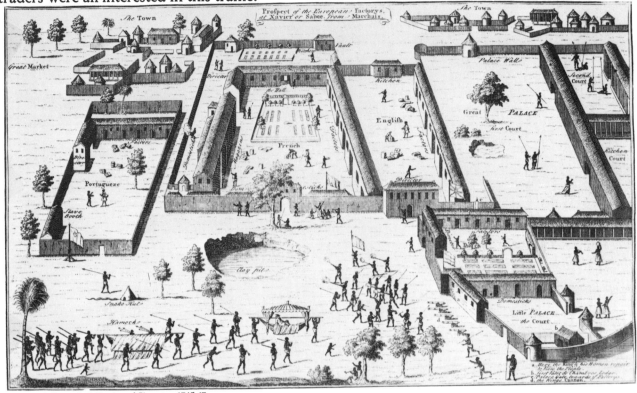

A New and General Collection of Voyages. 1745-47.

European trading center in Africa

Through the hot, still nights came the sound of the drums, and the voices of Negro songsters, voices that sang the strange music of Africa.

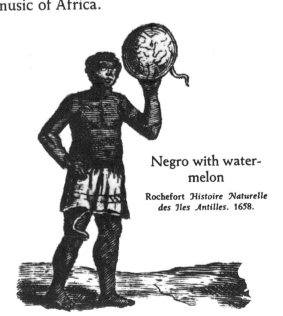

Negro with water-melon

Rochefort Histoire Naturelle des Iles Antilles. 1658.

A New and General Collection of Voyages. 1745-47.

Negro musical instruments

Negro fisherman

Duhamel du Monceau Traité générale des pesches. 1769-77.

Links With the Past

Left Water color paint-
ing discovered near
Orangeburg, S.C. Early
19th century

Courtesy, Abby Aldrich
Rockefeller Folk Art
Collection, Williamsburg, Va.

Hot and thirsty Negroes
trudged along behind crude
wooden plows, drank from
gourd dippers, and when the
day's work was done retired
to slave quarters near the
plantation house.

Guion G. Johnson *A Social History of the Sea Islands.* 1930. *Courtesy,* University of North Carolina Press.

Courtesy, North Carolina Historical Commission,
Raleigh, N. C.

Courtesy, Rutledge Home by the River. 1941.

Slave quarters, "Melrose", Wedgefield
Vicinity, S. C.

Courtesy, Historic American Buildings Survey,
Washington, D. C.

Indigo

Next to rice, indigo was the most important crop in South Carolina. Governor West instructed that the indigo plant be brought from Barbadoes as early as 1674. Eliza Lucas in 1744 was the first to make it profitable. She hired Andrew Deveaux to perfect a new process of producing indigo, from which a blue dye, much in demand in Europe, could be obtained, and she advocated the use of slave labor. The Huguenots, particularly the Legares, Ravenels, St. Juliens, Marions, Mottes, and Peronneaus, made their fortunes in indigo.

Indigo plant

Courtesy, Lesesne Family of Charleston, S. C.

Processing of indigo on a plantation near Charleston, S. C.

Pomet *A Compleat History of Druggs.* 1725.

Negroes processing indigo

Institut de France. Academie des Sciences. Descriptions des Arts et Metiers. 1770.

Negroes cultivating indigo

Salt

Salt was a Carolina product of great value. Salt marshes were converted into salt yards. By a process of evaporation the saline content of sea water became crystalized, and the piles of salt were conveyed to the plantations by boat.

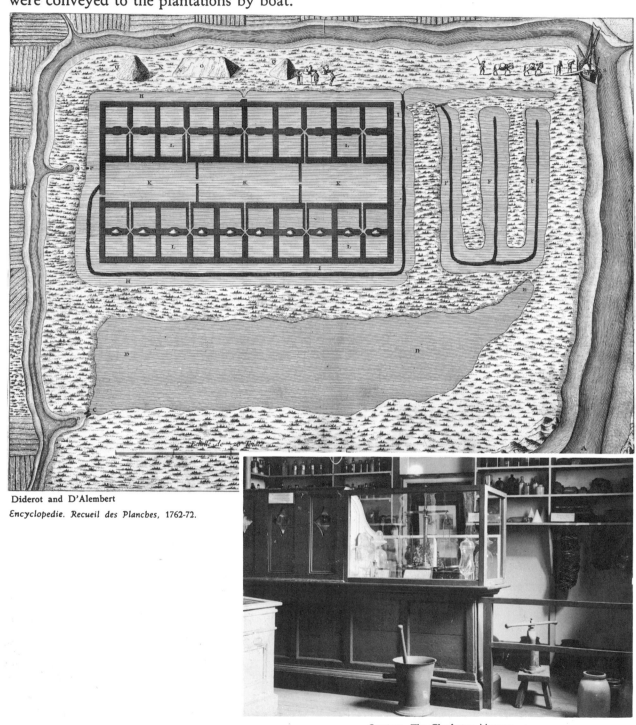

Diderot and D'Alembert
Encyclopedie. Recueil des Planches, 1762-72.

Courtesy, The Charleston Museum.
Apothecaries' Hall. Charleston

Yellow Fever

The climate of South Carolina before the development of modern medical science took a heavy toll of lives. Yellow fever, smallpox, and other diseases ran rampant. The apothecary shop was a popular place in old Charleston. The planter stopped there to lay in supplies, for he performed the duties of a doctor when his family or slaves needed medical attention.

North Carolina

North Carolina and South Carolina were under the same English governors until 1712. North Carolina became a Royal Colony in 1729 when the King bought out the proprietors. Bath was the first North Carolina settlement of any size, and was incorporated in 1705, followed shortly thereafter by New Bern, Edenton, Beaufort, and Brunswick.

St. Thomas Church. Bath. 1734

St. Paul's Church, Edenton. 1736

Courtesy, State Department of Archives and History, Raleigh, N. C.

North Carolina was a wild country filled with animals like these if we are to believe John Brickell.

Brickell *The Natural History of North Carolina*. 1737.

Pioneer Life

In the back country settlers might look out from their cabin doors and see a bear and cub lumbering across the clearing, and as they walked through the underbrush they might hear the spine-chilling warning of the deadly rattlesnake.

Catesby *Natural History of Carolina.* 1754.

Mason *The Lure of the Great Smokies.* 1927.
Courtesy, Houghton Mifflin. Boston.

Bowman *Land of High Horizons.* 1938.
Courtesy, Southern Publishers, Kingsport, Tenn.

Flying squirrel

Kalm *Reis door Noord Amerika.* 1772.

Raccoon

Indians

The Tuscarora War in 1711 almost wiped out the white settlers in North Carolina, and the Cherokee were to be feared as well as the Tuscarora. Remnants of the Cherokee still reside in the mountains of North Carolina.

Scalps

Maxwell *Valhalla in the Smokies*. 1938.
Courtesy, Mr. George A. Exline, Cleveland, O.

Cherokee

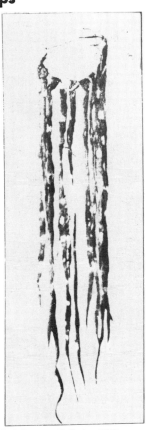

Courtesy, American Ethnological Bureau. *Bulletin*. 1918.

Engraving by F. O. C. Darley.

Sudden attack

Schoolcraft *Indian Tribes*. 1853.

Johnson *A General History of the Lives and Adventures of the Most Famous Highwaymen . . . (etc.). 1736.*

Captain Teach, better known as Black Beard

Pirates

Along the seacoast bold pirates captured the planters' ships. The boldest of all, the notorious Black Beard, had a hangout on the North Carolina coast.

Black Beard carried a small arsenal on his person, and stuck lighted tapers in his hair.

Here we see Governor Spotswood's *Proclamation* concerning Black Beard.

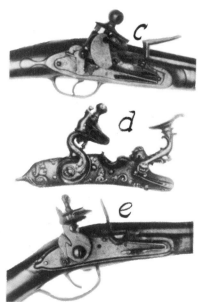

Courtesy, The Magazine *Antiques,* New York.

Details of colonial muskets (c) Miquelet (d) Snaphaunce (e) Flintlock

Right Proclamation of Governor Alexander Spotswood of Virginia. 1718. Spotswood's men brought Black Beard to bay, captured his ship, and brought his head back on a pole

Of BLACK-BEARD. 79

By his Majesty's Lieutenant Governor, and Commander in Chief, of the Colony and Dominion of *Virginia,*

A PROCLAMATION,

Publishing the Rewards given for apprehending, or killing, Pyrates.

Whereas, by an *Act of Assembly, made at a Session of Assembly, begun at the Capital in* Williamsburgh, *the eleventh Day of* November, *in the fifth Year of his Majesty's Reign, entitled,* An Act to encourage the apprehending and destroying of Pyrates: *It is, amongst other Things enacted, that all and every Person, or Persons, who, from and after the fourteenth Day of* November, *in the Year of our Lord one thousand seven hundred and eighteen, and before the fourteenth Day of* November, *which shall be in the Year of our Lord one thousand seven hundred and nineteen, shall take any Pyrate, or Pyrates, on the Sea or Land, or in Case of Resistance, shall kill any such Pyrate, or Pyrates, between the Degrees of thirty four, and thirty nine, of Northern Latitude, and within one hundred Leagues of the Continent of* Virginia, *or within the Provinces of* Virginia, *or* North-Carolina, *upon the Conviction, or making due Proof of the killing of all, and every such Pyrate, and Pyrates, before the Governor and Council, shall be entitled to have, and receive out of the publick Money, in the Hands of the Treasurer of this Colony, the several Rewards following; that is to say, for* Edward Teach, *commonly call'd Captain* Teach, *or* Black-Beard, *one hundred Pounds, for every other Commander of a Pyrate Ship, Sloop, or Vessel, forty Pounds; for every Lieutenant, Master, or Quarter-Master, Boatswain, or Carpenter, twenty Pounds; for every other inferior Officer, fifteen Pounds, and for every private Man taken on Board such Ship,*

Sloop,

Tidewater and Piedmont

The Anglican gentry developed their plantations in the Tidewater region, and tobacco became the chief crop. Ships from England docked at the private wharves of the planters, bringing books, clothing, furniture, tools, utensils, and drugs from London. There was a distinct social cleavage between Tidewater and Piedmont, between landed gentry and "buckskins."

At *right*, Orton Plantation, Cape Fear, N. C., 1725. *Below*, Indian dugout found in Great Dismal Swamp, North Carolina.

Courtesy, State Department of Archives and History, Raleigh, N. C.

Courtesy, The Mariners Museum, Newport News, Va.

Courtesy, Metropolitan Museum of Art, New York City. Gift of Mrs. J. Amory Haskell.

At *left*, a buckskin suit. *Above*, silver tea set by John Letelier and Thomas Shields, Baltimore, Md.

Courtesy, The Valentine Museum, Richmond, Va.

Brick

Here are three types of early North Carolina houses.

Left Newbold-White House. Early 18th Century. Harveys Neck, Perquimans County, N. C. Note the huge chimney, the small end windows and the dormers, called "dog houses" by the Negroes. This is a 17th Century Virginia type reminiscent of Jamestown

Illustrations from Johnston & Waterman *The Early Architecture of North Carolina* 1940. Courtesy, University of North Carolina Press.

Log

Courtesy, Library of Congress.
Above McIntyre Log Cabin. ca. 1726. Near Charlotte, Mecklenberg County, N. C. Note the saddle-notched corners

Stone

Left Michael Braun Rock House. 1766. Near Salisbury, Rowan County, N. C. This shows the Moravian influence. The Moravians built the same type in Pennsylvania

Illustrations from Johnston & Waterman, *The Early Architecture of North Carolina* 1940. Courtesy, University of North Carolina Press.

Moravians

A Moravian sect settled at Salem, now Winston-Salem, North Carolina, and influenced the domestic and ecclesiastical architecture of the surrounding region. Other Moravian groups settled in Georgia and Pennsylvania, as we shall see when we come to those colonies.

Log house. Winston-Salem, N. C. 1766

Right Adam Spach House, near Winston-Salem, N. C. 1774

Courtesy, North Carolina Historical Commission, **Raleigh, N. C.**

Kurze Zuverlassige Nachricht. 1757.
Moravians baptising the Indians

Kurze Zuverlassige Nachricht. 1757.
Moravians teaching Negroes the religious rites of Christianity

Mountain Country

The great mountain barriers in the western part of North Carolina beckoned to hardy settlers, for beyond them lay unclaimed wealth. Pioneers probed the gaps in these mountains looking for trails that would lead them to the "Promised Land". The Scotch-Irish, fiercely independent and disdaining the soft life of the Tidewater region, were among the first to flock to the mountain country.

Picturesque America. 1872-74.

The Great Smoky Mountains

Mason *The Lure of the Great Smokies.* 1927.
Courtesy, Houghton, Mifflin, Boston

Mountain grist mill

Courtesy, Columbia University Press, New York.
Dorothy Scarborough *A Song Catcher in the Southern Mountains.* 1937.

Ballads

Folk ballads of England and Scotland were heard in the mountains of North Carolina. A favorite was "Barbara Allen".

Georgia

Georgia was founded as the result of salesmanship. Months before the actual settlement, reformers, speculators, visionaries, adventurers, and persecuted religious sects printed and had circulated books, pamphlets, and magazine articles setting forth in glowing terms the advantages of Georgia. A Board of Trustees was to manage this Utopia, which was to be run along the lines of a huge philanthropic institution. Rum and slavery were prohibited, and debtors' prisons were emptied in order to find willing pioneers. One of the active promoters of the project was James Edward Oglethorpe. In 1732 he and nineteen other persons obtained a charter from King George II, in whose honor the new colony was named. With Oglethorpe at their head the first settlers landed in February, 1733.

Left The Trustees of Georgia Receiving the Indians in 1734. A painting by Verelst

Courtesy, Henry Francis du Pont Winterthur Museum

James Oglethorpe. Portrait by Ravenet

Left James Oglethorpe as an old man. The sketch was made while he was attending the sale of the library of Dr. Samuel Johnson in London

Savannah

The first permanent settlement in Georgia was at Savannah, laid out along formal lines at the edge of a mighty forest of pines.

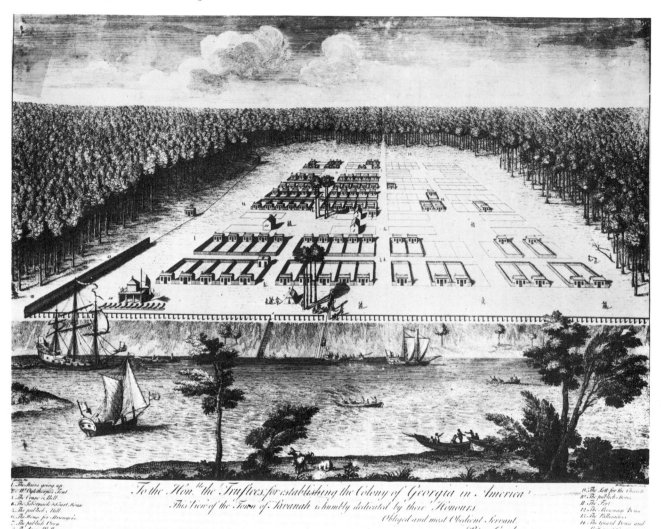

Peter Gordon's view of Savannah. 1734

Urlsperger Der Ausfubrlichen Nacbrichten. 1747.

Map of the County of Savannah, showing the Moravian town of Ebenezer

The Salzburgers

The first religious sect to immigrate to Georgia was the Salzburger Lutherans in 1734. We see *below*, in a contemporary print, a view of the welcome given them in Leipzig on their way to America. The great frontier trek did not begin at the Cumberland Gap and western New England. It began in Holland and Germany, in Scotland and Ireland, and was merely continued in America.

Courtesy, New York Public Library.

The leader of these Salzburger immigrants was John Martin Bolzius (*right*).

Below, Log cabin in Georgia.

Hall *Forty Etchings from Sketches Made with the Camera Lucida in North America.* 1829.

Urlsperger *Americanisches Ackerwerk Gottes.* 1754.

Ebenezer

Another German sect, the Moravians, came to Georgia in 1735, 1736, and 1738, under A. G. Spangenberg, David Nitzchmann, and Peter Boehler. They founded the town of Ebenezer in 1734. In 1736 they abandoned this settlement and founded New Ebenezer.

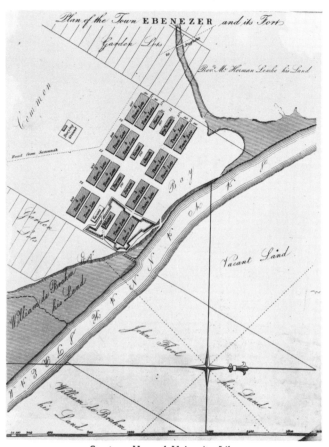

Urlsperger *Der Ausfuhrlichen Nachrichten.* 1735.
Tomo-Chi-Chi and his nephew

Courtesy, Harvard University Library.
Plan by William Gerard De Brahm. ca. 1770

Creek Indians

To the west were the Creek Indians and other tribes. They were friendly to Oglethorpe and he took some of them to London for an interview with the King. While on this trip Chief Tomo-Chi-Chi had his portrait painted.

Schoolcraft *Indian Tribes.*

Creek house

Right Creek Indian. Pencil sketch by John Trumbull.

Fur Trade

Pack trains loaded with furs, sold to the white traders by the Indians in exchange for bottles and beads and other trinkets, wended their way from the Alabama country to the fur marts of Savannah and Charleston. Augusta, Georgia, was destined to become the center of this lucrative trade which had been inaugurated as early as 1685 by Charleston merchants.

Courtesy, The Alabama Anthropological Society.

Trade bottles unearthed at Indian sites in Alabama. They date from 1685 to around 1810. The square bottles were called Dutch gins.

Silk Trade

The presence of mulberry trees in Georgia had encouraged the Trustees to believe that silk could be produced on a large scale, and the Moravians took instructions in its manufacture. Some silk was actually exported, but the industry never flourished.

Pomet A Compleat History of Druggs. 1725.

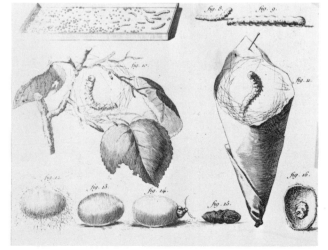

Diderot and D'Alembert Encyclopedie. Recueil des Planches, 1762-72.

Fear of Spain

It soon became apparent that the real motive behind the colonization of Georgia was the creation of a buffer state between South Carolina and Spanish-held Florida. Strong fortifications were constructed in Georgia to repel the Spanish attack, as these plans will reveal.

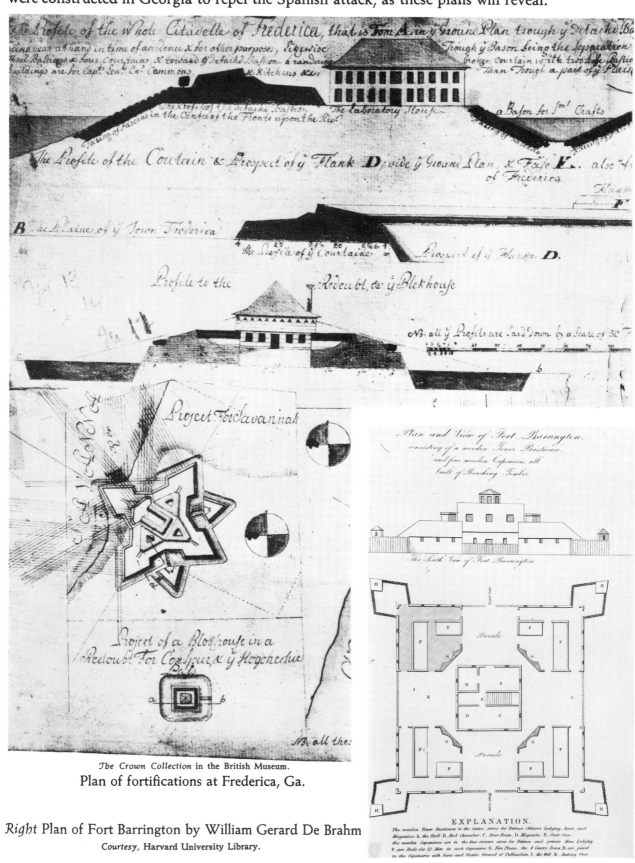

The Crown Collection in the British Museum.

Plan of fortifications at Frederica, Ga.

Right Plan of Fort Barrington by William Gerard De Brahm

Courtesy, Harvard University Library.

The War of Jenkins' Ear

In 1739-43 Great Britain and Spain fought the War of Jenkins' Ear. The Georgia settlements were threatened with extinction, but Oglethorpe thwarted Spanish plans by marching boldly into Florida. He failed in an attempt to capture St. Augustine.

The Crown Collection in the British Museum.

View of the Governor's House. St. Augustine, Fla.

The Crown Collection in the British Museum.

View from the Governor's House. St. Augustine.

Views of Fort San Marco, St. Augustine. Begun in the 17th Century and completed in 1756.

Courtesy, Historic American Buildings Survey, Washington, D. C.

Oglethorpe was able to isolate the Pensacola garrison on the Gulf of Mexico from the stronger force at St. Augustine. Driven back to Georgia he won the decisive battle of Bloody Marsh on St. Simon Island, thus ending the Spanish threat.

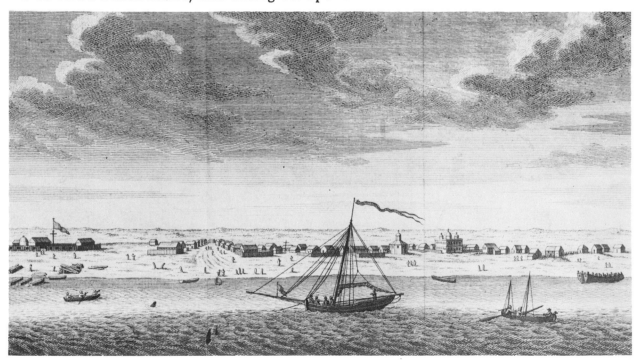

View of Pensacola, Fla. 1743   *Courtesy*, Stokes Collection, The New York Public Library.

Methodists

John Wesley, the founder of Methodism, accepted the charge of the Georgia mission in 1735, but did not stay long. His disciple, George Whitefield, came to Georgia in 1738 and founded an orphanage named Bethesda, near Savannah. He placed it under the management of James Habersham, who soon went to Charleston, S. C., to found the great mercantile establishment of Habersham and Harris. Whitefield visited the other English colonies in America, raised huge sums of money for charitable purposes, and set in motion a frenzy of evangelism.

John Wesley

George Whitefield

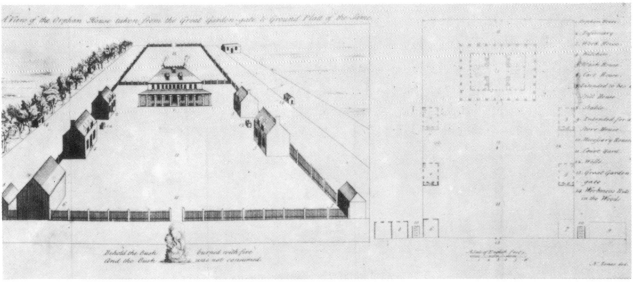

Whitefield *An Account of Money Received and Disbursed for the Orphan-House in Georgia.* 1741.

Orphanage at Bethesda

Georgia became a Royal Province in 1752, the Trustees being forced to sell out to their King. Their Utopia had collapsed. The Moravians moved to Pennsylvania. The Scotch settlers remained, prospered and survived. Rum and slavery were introduced. The stage was set for cotton.

7

PENNSYLVANIA

Courtesy, New York Public Library. Prints Division.
Engraving by John Sartain.

Courtesy, New York Public Library. Prints Division.
Engraving by John Sartain.

It was fortunate that William Penn's father was a wealthy and influential admiral in His Majesty's Navy—fortunate for Pennsylvania and the Quakers. Charles II, to discharge a debt of £16,000 owed to Admiral Penn, gave Pennsylvania to his son. At left, *above* is the younger Penn; at *right*, we see him in Quaker dress, after a painting by Inman.

The handsome and brilliant young Penn had been a disappointment to his father. He had embraced the religion of the Quakers, a persecuted sect founded by George Fox. William Penn publicly defended the Quakers and was imprisoned in the Tower of London (at extreme right in the 1657 view of London *below*) where he wrote some of the masterpieces of Quaker literature.

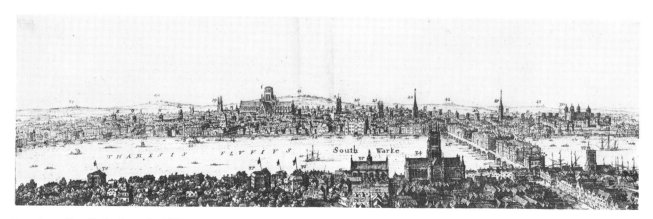

From James Howell, *Londonopolis*, 1657.

Towns on the Delaware

The Pennsylvania charter was granted in 1681, and William Penn made preparations to found a Quaker settlement. Thomas Holme surveyed the region between the Delaware and Schuylkill rivers, and located the site of Philadelphia.

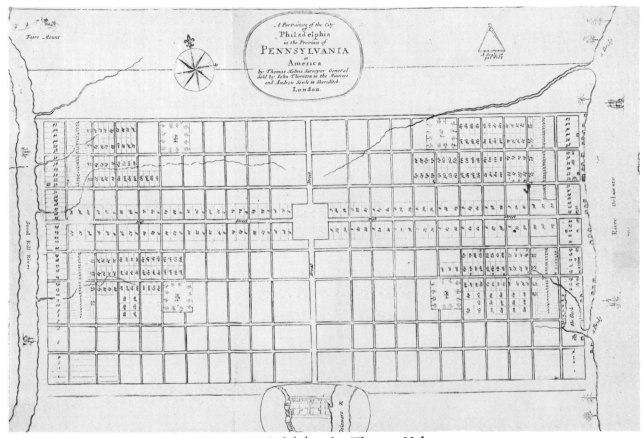

Plan of Philadelphia, by Thomas Holme

Contrast the broad, straight streets with the narrow, crooked streets and alleys of contemporary European cities. This is an early example of intelligent city planning. Note spaces provided for parks

Penn first took possession of New Castle on the Delaware, ceded to him by the Duke of York, and also of the Swedish town of Upland, which he renamed Chester. From these he proceeded up the Delaware to Philadelphia, where he arrived in October, 1682, on the ship *Welcome*.

Penn landing at Chester   John F. Watson *Annals of Philadelphia.* 1830.   Penn landing at Philadelphia

"Never Sworn to and Never Broken"

One of the first things that Penn accomplished was a lasting treaty with the Indians. His policy, like that of the Swedes on the Delaware, was to live in peace and harmony with the Indians and to pay them for their land. Voltaire remarked that this was "the only treaty never sworn to and never broken."

Advertising Pennsylvania
on playing cards

From Worcester College, Oxford University.

Penn's treaty with the Indians, at Shackamaxon (now Kensington), in 1682. Painting by Benjamin West

Benjamin West (1728-1820), who painted the famous treaty scene, was born not far from the site depicted. This American painter was to achieve the honor of becoming the President of the Royal Academy in London in 1792, succeeding Sir Joshua Reynolds.

Excerpt from *The Life of William Penn*,
by Mason Locke Weems. 1822

Mason Locke Weems, later known as "Parson" Weems who created the legend of George Washington and the cherry tree, wrote a life of Penn, and in it is a list of goods given to the Indians in exchange for land.

The Walking Purchase

In 1686 the Delaware Indians deeded to William Penn a tract in the fork of the Delaware and Lehigh rivers embracing an area in depth as far as a man could walk in a day and a half, or about forty miles. In 1737 Thomas Penn, by the ruse of hiring expert walkers increased the distance to 66½ miles, thereby arousing the ire of the Delaware Indians.

McKenney and Hall *History of the Indian Tribes*. 1836.

Lappawinsoe, Delaware Chief, one of the signers of the Walking Purchase. From a painting by Gustavus Hesselius, 1735

Cabin in the clearing

Below Log cabin in Pennsylvania   Shurtleff *Log Cabin Myth*. 1939. *Courtesy,* Harvard University Press.

The Sawkill

The American Landscape. 1830.

Falls of the Sawkill

Day Historical Collections of the State of Pennsylvania. 1843.

Old Assembly House and Penn's Landing Place. Chester, Pa.

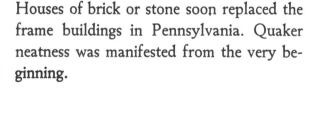

Right Town Hall. Chester, Pa.
Built 1724

George Smith *History of Delaware County Pennsylvania.* 1862.

About a mile and a half northwest from Chester, on the left Chester cr., and a short distance above the mill of Richard Flower still exists an humble cottage, built principally of brick, of which nexed is a correct sketch. This is the original dwelling erected ard Townsend, for the accommodation of his family while he was tend-

Richard Townsend's original dwelling.

ing the first mill erected in the province. The mill stood some forty rods above the cottage. The original mill is all gone, but the rocks around bear traces of its existence, and the log platform still remains under water at the place where the original ford was, on the road to Philadelphia. The partners in this mill were William Penn, Caleb Pusey, and Samuel Carpenter, and their initials are inserted in the curious antiquated iron vane which was once erected on the roof of the mill, and is still engaged in its 144th year of duty on the top of Mr. Flowers' house. In this cottage, no doubt, Penn, Pusey, and Carpenter have often met to count their gains, and to devise plans for the future good of the province. The hipped roof of the cottage was added by Samuel Shaw, who, before the revolution, erected the second mill near this place.

Houses of brick or stone soon replaced the frame buildings in Pennsylvania. Quaker neatness was manifested from the very beginning.

Left Caleb Pusey House, near Chester, Pa.
Day Historical Collections of the State of Pennsylvania. 1843.

Letitia Street House

William Penn lived at the Letitia Street House in Philadelphia, built for him, 1682-83.

Watson *Annals of Philadelphia.* 1830.

Letitia House. Named for Penn's daughter

Right Letitia Street House as it appears today

Courtesy, Philadelphia Museum of Art, Philadelphia.

Penn Lived Here

Left Letitia Street House. First
floor front

Courtesy, Philadelphia Museum of Art, Philadelphia.

Right Letitia Street House. First
floor rear

Courtesy, Pennsylvania Museum of Art, Philadelphia

The Penn Doll

Courtesy, Mrs. Imogene Anderson, New York, the owner.

"Letitia Penn", a doll brought to Pennsylvania by William Penn in 1699

Slate Roof House. Philadelphia. Occupied by William Penn, 1699-1700

Quaker Meeting Houses

Left Quaker meeting

Ernst von Hesse-Wartegg, *Nord Amerika*, 1880.

Below William Penn's Meeting House. Chester, Pa.

"Many Mansions"

George Smith *History of Delaware County Pennsylvania.* 1862.

Friends Meeting House. Haverford, Pa. Built 1700.
Note the wagon shed

Views of Philadelphia. 1827-30.

Friends Meeting House. Merion, Pa. Built ca. 1700

Smith *History of Delaware County Pennsylvania.*

St. David's Church, Radnor, Pa.

Below Modern view of Friends
Meeting House. Merion, Pa.
Photo by Philip B. Wallace.

Photo by Philip B. Wallace.

Modern view of St. David's Church.
Radnor, Pa.

Right St. Paul's Church. Chester, Pa. 1703
Smith *History of Delaware County, Pennsylvania.*

Quaker Women

The Society of Friends permitted women to preach, and Rebecca Jones of Philadelphia was one of the best known. Here we see some of her relics.

Photo by Philip B. Wallace.

Miniature facsimile of the dress worn by Rebecca Jones

Photo by Philip B. Wallace.

Linen mittens and silk reticule belonging to Rebecca Jones

Photo by Philip B. Wallace.

Tea pot, pot, and skillet belonging to Rebecca Jones

Quaker bonnet of silk

Photo by Philip B. Wallace.

Photo by Philip B. Wallace.

Utensil holder made by a Quakeress

All objects on this page are furnished through the courtesy of the Atwater Kent Museum, Philadelphia

Quakeress Costumes

Courtesy, Philadelphia Museum of Art.

Quaker Farm

Primitive painting by Edward Hicks of the residence of David Twining, Bucks County, Pa., 1787.

Courtesy, Abby Aldrich Rockefeller Folk Art Collection, Williamsburg, Va.

The Moravians Arrive

The Moravians in Georgia, refusing to bear arms under Oglethorpe, moved to Pennsylvania. They founded the towns of Bethlehem and Nazareth. Swarms of persecuted Moravians in Saxony fled to Pennsylvania to join their brethren.

Moravian colonists being married in a group ceremony before departing for America

Kurze Zuverlassige Nachricht. 1757.

Left Pottery. Sgraffito decoration. Pennsylvania

Courtesy, The New York Historical Society, New York.

Bethlehem, Pa. Sketch by Governor Thomas Pownall, engraved by Paul Sandby. 1761.

Henry *History of the Lehigh Valley.* 1860.

Bethlehem Islands in the Lehigh River

Kurze Zuverlassige Nachricht. 1757.

Moravian christening

Kurze Zuverlassige Nachricht. 1757.

Children's love-feast

Music and Mysticism

The Moravians brought to America a lively appreciation of church music. Bethlehem, Pa., even today, is noted for its music festivals.

Kurze Zuverlassige Nachricht. 1757.

Left, The Moravians brought their beautiful custom of the Easter liturgy to Pennsylvania.

Below, left, the first pipe organ built in America. Made by Gustavus Hesselius and John G. Klemm in Philadelphia. It was installed in the "Gemein-House," Bethlehem, 1746.

The Germans were also inclined to mysticism. Johannes Kelpius (*below, right*), founded the Pietist sect called The Woman of the Wilderness. He lived in a cave near Germantown, Pa.

courtesy of the Prints Division, New York Public Library

Courtesy, Moravian Historical Society, Nazareth, Pa.

Lutherans

The German followers of Martin Luther found in hospitable Pennsylvania a seed-plot for their faith. Their church at Trappe (*right*) is a Lutheran shrine.

Day *Historical Collections of the State of Pennsylvania.* 1843.

Inside of the Lutheran Church, York, Pa., 1800.

Drawing by Lewis Miller. *Courtesy,* The Historical Society of York County, York, Pa.

Good Earth

At *left*, "Metamorphosis of an American Farm." Sketch by Governor Thomas Pownall, engraved by James Peake. 1761.

Below, traditional decorations characteristic of Pennsylvania German folk art.

At the *bottom*, view of Pennsylvania Dutch barn, with designs, Lancaster County, Pa.

Courtesy, New York Public Library, Prints Division.

Photo by Pennsylvania Historical and Museum Commission, Harrisburg, Pa.

Photo by Pennsylvania Historical and Museum Commission, Harrisburg, Pa.

Logs

Following the example of the Swedes and Finns the early settlers in Pennsylvania erected log cabins and barns.

Courtesy, Pennsylvania Farm Museum of Landis Valley, Lancaster Co., Pa.

Log barn

Locks

Courtesy, Pennsylvania German Society.

Landis' Store

Barn locks   Courtesy, Pennsylvania Farm Museum of Landis Valley, Lancaster Co., Pa.

Meat and Lard

Meat barrel

Courtesy, Pennsylvania Farm Museum of Landis Valley, Lancaster Co., Pa.

Outdoor furnace with iron kettles. In these kettles were made soap, lard, and apple butter, and on wash day they were used for boiling clothes

Butcher . . .

Courtesy, Pennsylvania Farm Museum of Landis Valley, Lancaster Co., Pa.

Pennsylvania butchering tools and utensils

Baker . . .

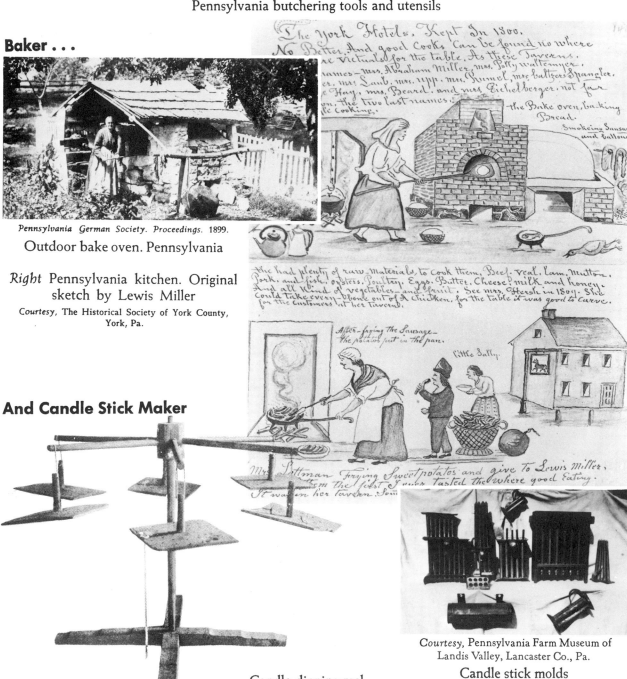

Pennsylvania German Society. Proceedings. 1899.

Outdoor bake oven. Pennsylvania

Right Pennsylvania kitchen. Original sketch by Lewis Miller

Courtesy, The Historical Society of York County, York, Pa.

And Candle Stick Maker

Candle-dipping reel

Courtesy, Bucks County Historical Society, Doylestown, Pa.

Courtesy, Pennsylvania Farm Museum of Landis Valley, Lancaster Co., Pa.

Candle stick molds

Home Made Bread!

Courtesy, The Metropolitan Museum of Art, New York.

Pennsylvania dough trough

Right Bread basket

Courtesy, Pennsylvania Farm Museum of Landis Valley, Lancaster Co., Pa.

Below Rolling pins, towel rollers, etc.
Courtesy, Pennsylvania Farm Museum of Landis Valley, Lancaster Co., Pa.

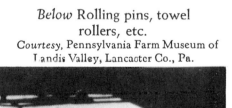

Courtesy, Pennsylvania Farm Museum of Landis Valley, Lancaster Co., Pa.

Dough troughs and other kitchen equipment

Cheese

Cheese making

Diderot and D'Alembert *Encyclopedie. Recueil des planches.* 1762-72.

Marzipan

The Pennsylvania Germans loved cakes and cookies. Artistic moulds were made for the special festival cookies called "Marzipan."

Designs in marzipan moulds

The same folk-art was carried over into butter mould designs.

Butter Moulds

Wooden butter moulds. Pennsylvania

All items shown are *courtesy* of the Pennsylvania Farm Museum of Landis Valley, Lancaster Co., Pa.

Tulips

The favorite decorative motif of the Pennsylvania Germans was the tulip. It appeared time and again in various forms.

Butter mould. Tulip design

Courtesy, Philadelphia Museum of
Art, Philadelphia.

Pennsylvania German
pottery dish. Slip decoration (Sgraffito). 1769

Left Pine wall corner cupboard. Pennsylvania Ger-
man. Note the tulip design
in the piece of pottery

Courtesy, Philadelphia Museum of
Art, Philadelphia.

Below Dower chest made
by Christian Setzer. 1785

Courtesy, The Magazine Antiques,
New York.

They Never Dreamed of Electricity, Aluminum, or Stainless Steel

Wooden sink and drain board

Right Settle used in front of the kitchen fireplace

In every Pennsylvania kitchen were ingenious hand-made utensils and gadgets.

Knife and fork cleaner

Miscellaneous kitchen utensils

Dutch oven

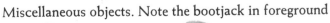

Miscellaneous objects. Note the bootjack in foreground

Left Muffin irons

All items on this page are by *courtesy* of the Pennsylvania Farm Museum of Landis Valley, Lancaster Co., Pa.

They Could Make Anything

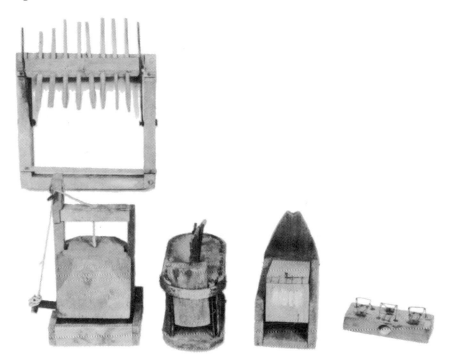

Mouse traps

Courtesy, Bucks County Historical Society, Doylestown, Pa.

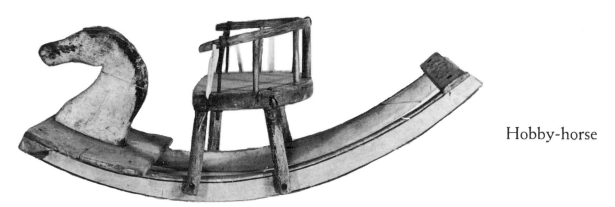

Hobby-horse

Courtesy, Pennsylvania Farm Museum of Landis Valley, Lancaster County, Pa.

Foot stool

Courtesy, Pennsylvania Farm Museum of Landis Valley, Lancaster County, Pa.

Mills

Along the rivers of Pennsylvania were mills and furnaces

Ruins of an old mill on
Cresheim Creek, Pennsylvania

Courtesy, Pennsylvania German Society.

Birthplace of David Rittenhouse, Germantown, Pa.
The Rittenhouse family had a paper mill here
as early as 1690.

Mill stone.
Used to crush oak bark for tannery

Courtesy, Pennsylvania Farm Museum of Landis Valley, Lancaster Co., Pa.

At right Mill at Ephrata Cloister, Ephrata, Pa.

Courtesy, Pennsylvania Farm Museum of Landis Valley, Lancaster Co., Pa.

The Wall of the Alleghenies

The Pennsylvania settlers occupied the farm lands east of the Alleghenies. They crouched at the slopes of these mountains, for beyond them lay danger—the French and Indians. They sent a few traders, missionaries, and explorers into the mountains and built outposts on the Susquehanna River, but the great westward push awaited its appointed hour.

Below The Susquehanna
Picturesque America. 1872-74.

Courtesy, Mrs. Evan Randolph and J. B. Lippincott Co., Philadelphia.

Shoomac Park. Ridge Road. Falls of the Schuylkill

Water color by Köllner

Lancaster, Pa.

Carlisle, Pa.

Edouard C. V. Colbert, Comte de Maulevrier *Voyage.* ca. 1796-98.

Courtesy, Institut Francais de Washington, and the Johns Hopkins Press, Baltimore.

8

THE FIRST HALF
OF THE EIGHTEENTH CENTURY

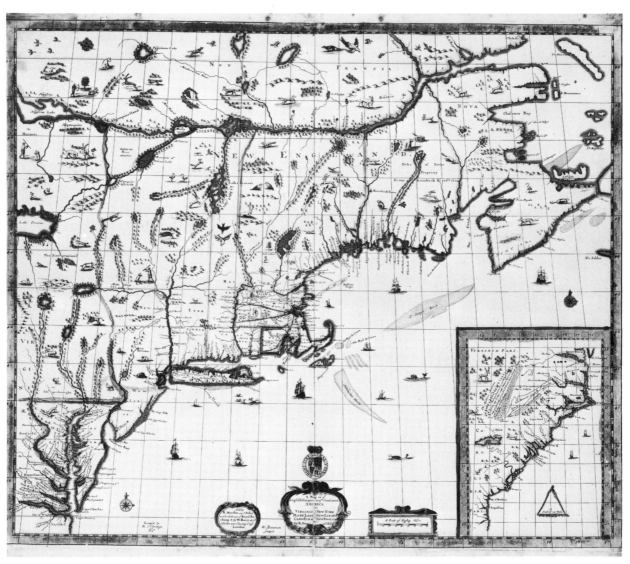

Courtesy, The New York Public Library.

Map of the English colonies in North America. ca. 1700

At the beginning of the Eighteenth Century the American colonies were firmly established, with the exception of Georgia (chartered 1732), but in spite of the common dangers and hardships of the wilderness there was as yet no general realization of a common destiny. Each colony clung tenaciously to its own form of political and economic organization—to its trade with the hinterland or its trade from the sea. Schemes for colonial union found no soil in which to take root. Each of the colonies looked first to itself, next to the Mother Country, and scarcely at all to its sister colonies up and down the Atlantic seaboard.

It is interesting to note that Jamestown, St. Mary's City, and Plymouth were declining, while Williamsburg, Charleston, Boston, New York, and Philadelphia were growing in size and importance. Commerce and population increased wherever the Royal governors held court, and where good natural harbors existed.

Where Virginia's Royal Governor Presided

Photo by Richard Garrison. *Courtesy*, Colonial Williamsburg, Inc.
The Capitol at Williamsburg, Va. Restored

Williamsburg's "Rosetta Stone"

The "Frenchman's map" of Williamsburg, Va. 1782

The previous discovery of this map, which gave the exact location of every building, greatly facilitated the recent restoration of this colonial capital.

Courtesy, Colonial Williamsburg, Inc.

New York

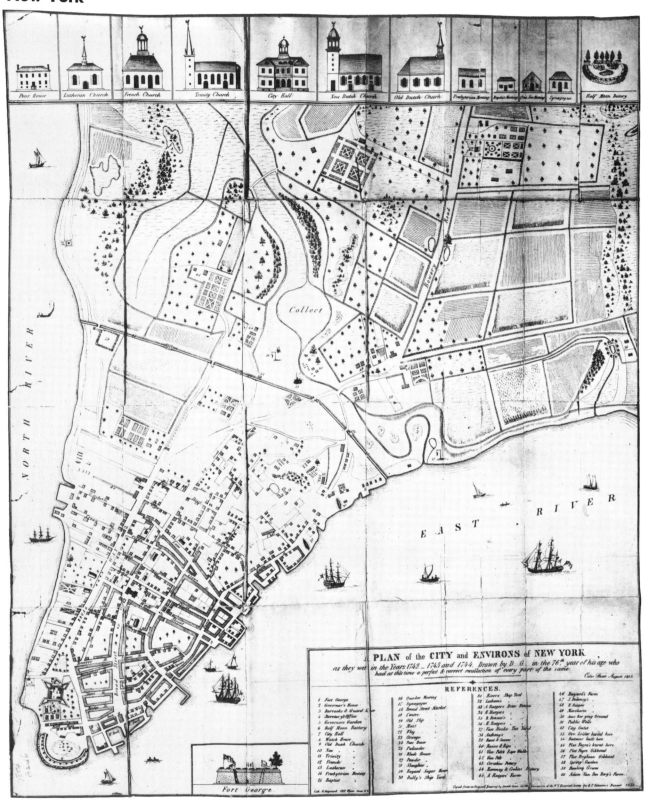

Valentine's Manual. 1854.

New York and environs. 1742-44

Dutch New Amsterdam ended at Wall Street. Note how the town has spread northward. The number of churches, including a synagogue and a Quaker meeting house, indicate that religious tolerance was at work. Almost every church had a crowing cock for a weathervane. Even at this early period New York was developing its cosmopolitan aspect, a characteristic which it has never lost.

Sky Line

London Magazine. Aug. 1761. Date depicted 1746. *Courtesy,* The New York Public Library.

Note the busy New York harbor scene *above*. In the lower right-hand corner is an old Dutch house and the Brooklyn ferry. The buildings across the water still bear the mark of Dutch architecture. By looking at the foregoing map of New York many of the churches and other buildings in this view can be identified.

At *right*, the New Dutch Church, New York City, completed 1731, from a print by William Burgis. *Below*, the first St. Peter's Church, Albany, N. Y., from a water color drawn ca. 1800.

I. N. Phelps Stokes *Iconography of Manhattan Island.* 1915-28.

Hooper *A History of St. Peter's Church.* 1900.

Boston

Carwitham view of Boston. Date depicted ca. 1731-36. Based on the Burgis view of 1722

Note the many churches, the long wharf, and the rural aspects of the environs. American seaport towns clustered around the waterfront. Rivers and harbors were the main highways of commerce.

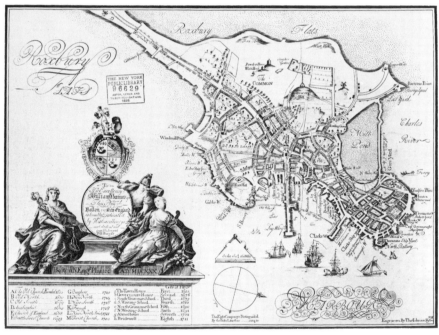

Plan of Boston, *ca.* 1728—the Burgis-Johnston Map.

Philadelphia

Peter Cooper's painting of Philadelphia. 1718-20

Back of These Towns—Wilderness

Henry *History of the Lehigh Valley.* 1860.

Slatington, Lehigh County, Pennsylvania

Hanson *Old Towns of Norridgewock and Canaan.* 1849.

Skowhegan and Bloomfield, Maine

Left Red fox

The Cabinet of Natural History. 1830-34.

Collot *Voyage dans L'Amerique Septentrionale.* 1826.

Cabin in the clearing

Left Vignette by F. O. C. Darley

Civilization

In spite of the primitive life on the frontier fringes a high state of civilization prevailed among the wealthier inhabitants of American cities and plantations. Their houses were elegantly furnished. Their costume followed the latest London and Paris styles. The houses of the poor have not been preserved, but many of the mansions of the wealthy merchants and planters have survived intact. Let us open the doors and enter some of them.

Doorway. Stenton, Logan Park, Philadelphia. ca. 1721

Courtesy, The Essex Institute, Salem, Mass. Photo by Frank Cousins.

Courtesy, Pocumtuck Valley Memorial Association of Deerfield, Mass.

Doorway, Sheldon House, Deerfield, Mass.

Courtesy, The Essex Institute, Salem, Mass. Photo by Frank Cousins.

Doorway. Warner House, Portsmouth, N. H.

New England

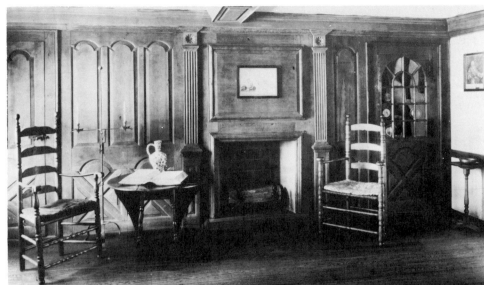

Room from Newington, Conn. 2nd quarter of 18th Century

Low ceilings prevailed in New England. The Holy Bible rests on the butterfly table. Note the built-in cupboard and the slat-back chairs. Pictures began to adorn the carefully plastered walls.

Courtesy, American Wing, The Metropolitan Museum of Art, New York.

Whitefield *The Homes of Our Forefathers*. 3 v. 1880-86.

Silliman House. Bridgeport, Conn.

King House. Newport, R. I. ca. 1710

Shumway House, Fiskdale, Mass. ca. 1740

Note the cupboard, the long hinges of the doors, the unique chest of drawers above the fireplace, and the warming pan and fireback. The chair at the gate-legged table is the Dutch style, with its cyma curves.

Courtesy, Museum of Fine Arts, Boston, Mass.

Courtesy, Museum of Fine Arts, Boston.

Room from West Boxford, Mass. ca. 1725

Whitefield *The Homes of Our Forefathers*. 1880-86.

Moll Pitcher House, Marblehead, Mass. ca. 1720.
(Not to be confused with the Moll Pitcher who was
a heroine of the American Revolution)

Details of stairways, "The Lindens"
Danvers, Mass. 1745

Courtesy, Essex Institute, Salem, Mass.

Orne House. Marblehead,
Mass. ca. 1730

Courtesy, Museum of Fine Arts,
Boston.

Pennsylvania

Rooms from Millbach,
Lebanon County,
Pa. 1752

The Pennsylvania
Germans loved deco-
rative design and color

Courtesy, Philadelphia Museum
of Art, Philadelphia.

Maryland

Living room. Henry Sewall House. Secretary, Md. 1720. Note the high ceiling, the cane chairs, and the wide door, designed for a warm climate

Courtesy, The Brooklyn Museum, Brooklyn, N. Y.

Room from Eltonhead Manor, Calvert County, Md. ca. 1720

Courtesy, Baltimore Museum of Art.

Entrance hall of Drayton Hall, Ashley River, S. C. 1740

Courtesy, Carolina Art Association, Charleston, S. C.

Old Virginia

Bed chamber of Governor's Palace, Williamsburg, Va.

In Virginia expensive carved beds were imported from England. Most New England beds were home made, and much simpler.

Courtesy, Colonial Williamsburg

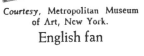

Courtesy, Metropolitan Museum of Art, New York.

English fan

Portrait of Evelyn Byrd, a Virginia belle
Courtesy,
Colonial Williamsburg

Kitchen. Governor's Palace, Williamsburg, Va.

The Governor's Palace in Williamsburg was built 1706-20, and was the center of fashion and social life in Virginia.

Courtesy, Colonial Williamsburg

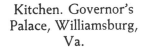

Exteriors

The exterior of American houses during this period show even more striking regional differences.

Joseph Cabot House, Salem, Mass. 1748

Whitefield *The Homes of Our Forefathers,* 1880-86.
Tillinghast Mansion, Providence, R. I. ca. 1710

Frary House, Deer-
field, Mass.

Van Courtlandt Mansion,
New York. 1748

Brick and Stone

Gov. Keith House, Graeme Park, Pennsylvania. 1721

Left Abel Nickolson House, Salem County, N. J. 1722

Maryland Mansion

Doughoregan Manor, Howard County, Md. The home of the Carroll family. 1727

South Carolina

Drayton Hall, Ashley River, S. C. 1740

Mansions of the Old Dominion

"Westover." North front, Charles City County, Va.

Built by William Byrd II. 1726. One of the finest examples of Georgian architecture in America

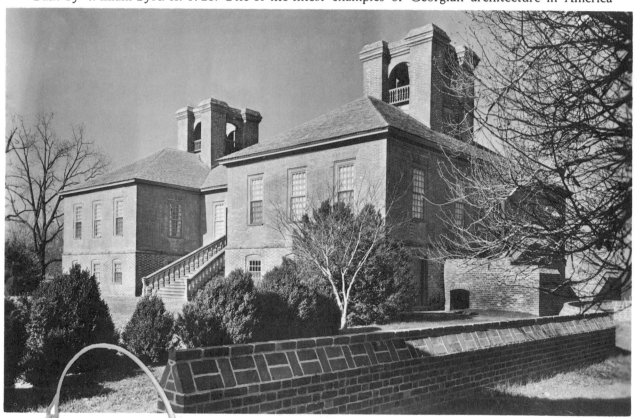

"Stratford," Westmoreland County, Va.

Built by Thomas Lee between 1725 and 1730. Birthplace of Robert E. Lee. The huge chimneys are a feature. The kitchen and servants' quarters were separate dependencies a few yards away from the main house. These dependencies were typical of the South. The planter did not want the odors of the kitchen to permeate the dining room. Food was carried to the house in covered dishes.

Left Brass kettle used at "Eagle Point", Gloucester County, Va., and later at "Brampton", Madison County, Va.

Courtesy, Valentine Museum, Richmond, Va.

Costume

Let us look at the costume worn by the occupants of beautiful homes such as those just shown.

Wedding slipper worn by Elizabeth Wilson of Kingston, R. I. Oct. 15, 1730

Courtesy, United Shoe Machinery Corporation, Boston, Mass.

Dress worn at wedding of Mary, granddaughter of Gov. Leverett of Massachusetts. 1719

Courtesy, Essex Institute, Salem, Mass.

Costume dolls were the fashion. Here we see "Mehetable Hodges" or the Salem Doll

Courtesy, Museum of the City of New York.

Button samples. 18th Century. Colonial costume required many buttons, and button salesmen called on fashionable ladies and gentlemen and allowed them to choose their buttons from sample cards.

Courtesy, Cooper Museum for the Arts of Decoration, New York.

Puritan Face

Abigail Gerrish and her grandmother, Abigail (Flint) Holloway Gerrish. Painted by John Greenwood, ca. 1750

A Gentleman from Maine

William Bowdoin
Portrait by Robert Feke. 1748

Mayor of New York

Caleb Heathcote. Portrait made ca. 1710, by an unknown artist. Heathcote lived at the Manor of Scarsdale in Westchester County, N. Y., and was mayor of New York City, 1711-13

Patron of Yale College

Elihu Yale. Portrait by Zeeman. Yale gave funds to the Collegiate School at Saybrook, Conn., which honored him by renaming the institution Yale College in 1745, after its removal to New Haven

The Deerfield Massacre

To regard these elegant homes and this expensive costume as a true index of American life during the first half of the Eighteenth Century would be misleading. The bulk of the population were not rich or clad in fine clothes. They faced daily hardships, and on the frontier fringe were subjected to dangers of all kinds. We may cite as one example that on the early morning of February 29, 1704, a body of French soldiers and Indian allies surprised the sleeping inhabitants of Deerfield, a western outpost in Massachusetts, massacred about fifty men, women, and children, and carried over a hundred into captivity. The town was burned to the ground with the exception of a few houses.

Left Indian House, Deerfield, Mass. Restored

In this house a small group of defenders successfully resisted the Indian raid of 1704.

Courtesy, Pocumtuck Valley Memorial Association of Deerfield, Mass.

The attack on Indian House
Woodcut by Alexander Anderson

Captives
A drawing by F. O. C. Darley

Blockhouse and Garrison

The Deerfield tragedy shocked the American colonies. Frontier defenses were strengthened. The French and Indians lurked in the woods from Maine to western Pennsylvania, and along the whole length of the Appalachian chain of mountains. No one knew where the enemy would strike next. The English blamed the French for stirring up Indian hatred. Father Rasle, a French missionary at Norridgewock, Me., was killed by the English in 1724, accused of fomenting trouble among the Abenaki Indians.

Blockhouse and sawmill
Anburey *Travels Through America.* 1789.

Courtesy, Maine Historical Society.
Strong box belonging to
Father Rasle

Courtesy, Maine Historical Society.
Bell belonging to Father
Rasle

July 14th. 1703.
Prices of Goods

Supplyed to the

Eastern Indians,

...eral Truckmasters ; and of the Peltry received
by the Truckmasters of the said *Indians.*

ONe yard Broad Cloth, *three* Beaver skins, *in season.*
One yard & half Gingerline, *one* Beaver skin, *in season*
One yard Red or Blew Kersey, *two* Beaver skins, *in season.*
One yard good Duffels, *one* Beaver skin, *in season.*
One yard & half broad fine Cotton, *one* Beaver skin, *in season*
Two yards of Cotton, *one* Beaver skin, *in season.*
One yard & half of half thicks, *one* Beaver skin, *in season.*
Five Pecks Indian Corn, *one* Beaver skin, *in season*

What shall be accounted in *Value* equal
One Beaver in season : *Viz.*

ONe Otter skin in season, is one Beaver
One Bear skin in season, is one Beaver,
One Half skin in season, is one Beaver

Courtesy, The New York Public Library.

Travel

Between the cities and the frontier blockhouses, were isolated farms and plantations connected by water or narrow, foot-worn Indian trails. Roads, if they existed, were full of snow drifts in the winter, and mud holes in the spring. A few hardy souls traveled by horseback, and around New York and Philadelphia short stage coach routes were laid out. The large rivers were not bridged and the ferryman did a brisk business, particularly if he ran a tavern at the water's edge.

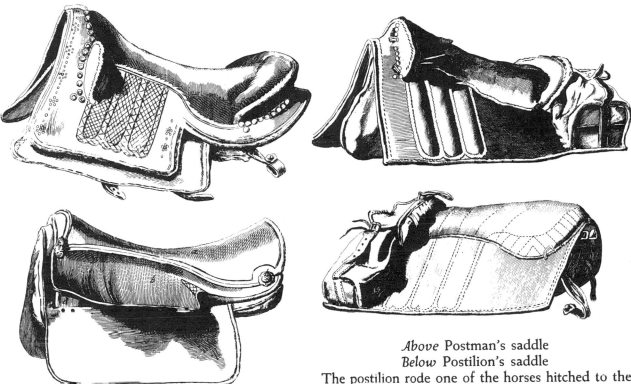

Above Postman's saddle
Below Postilion's saddle
The postilion rode one of the horses hitched to the stage coach.

Diderot and D'Alembert *Encyclopedie. Recueil des planches.* 1762-72.

English saddles. 18th Century

Valentine's Manual. 1853.
Cato's Tavern on the Boston Post Road. ca. 1712

Below Old Spread Eagle Inn near Lancaster, Pa.

Note the worm fence made of hand-hewn rails, and the stumps in the clearing.

Courtesy, Pennsylvania German Society.

Ferry and Tavern

This Act was passed in the 6th Year of the Reign of his present Majesty King George II.

An ACT to regulate the Ferry between the City of New-York and the Island of Nassau, and to establish the Ferriage thereof.

BE it Enacted by his Excellency the Governor, the Council, and the General Assembly, and it is hereby Enacted by the Authority of the same, That from the Twelfth Day of June next ensuing, and at all Times hereafter, the Ferriage for transporting Men, Women, Horses, Cattle, Grain, and all Manner of Goods, Wares and Merchandizes, over the said Ferry, either forward or backward, shall be, and hereby are established, to be and remain after the Rates and Prices following, That is to say,

Rates to be taken for Ferriage.

For transporting every Person from the City of New-York to the Island of Nassau, or from the Island of Nassau to the City of New-York, Ten Grains of Sevil, Pillar or Mexico Plate, or Two Pence in Bills of Credit, made current in this Colony; and if after Sun-set, double that Rate; unless a Neglect or Refusal in the Ferry-Man, to transport Passengers over sooner: Always Provided, That a Sucking-Child, or some Remnants of Goods, or other small Goods (not herein-after-rated) which a Woman carries in her Apron, or a Man or a Boy under his Arm, shall be free from Ferriage.

For every Horse or Beast, One Shilling in like Money.
For every live Calf or Hog, Four Pence in like Money.
For every live Sheep or Lamb, Three Pence in like Money.
For every dead Hog, Three Pence in like Money.
For every dead Sheep, Lamb or Calf, Two Pence in like Money.
For every Barrel of Rum, Sugar, Molasses, or other full Barrel, Eight Pence in like Money.
For every empty Barrel, Three Pence in like Money.
For every empty Pipe or Hogshead, Nine Pence in like Money.
For every Beast's Hide, Three Pence in like Money.
For every undressed Calf, Sheep or Deer Skin, One Penny in like Money.
For every Pail of Butter, One Penny in like Money.
For every Firkin or Tub of Butter, Two Pence in like Money.
For every Bushel of Salt, Wheat, Grain, Seeds, or any other Thing usually measured, and sold by the Bushel, One Half-penny in like Money.
For every full Pipe or full Hogshead, Four Shillings in like Money.
For every Inch Board, One Penny in like Money.
For every Board of one Inch and a Half, One Penny Ha[lf]
For every Waggon, Five Shillings in like Money.
For every Pair of Cart-Wheels, Eighteen Pence in like
For every Cupboard, Press for Cloaths, or Writing-D[esk] like Money.
For every full Trunk or Chest, One Shilling in like M[oney]
For every empty Trunk or Chest, Nine Pence in like
For every Half Barrel of Flour, or any other Half Ba[rrel] Money.
For every Barrel of Bread, Six Pence in like Money.
For every Bag of Bread, One Penny Half-penny in like
For every Gammon of Bacon, Turkey or Goose, One H[alf]
For every Hundred of Eggs, Three Eggs, and so in P[roportion] or lesser Number.
For every Dunghill Fowl, Brant, Duck, Heath-Hen o[r] in like Money.

For every Dozen of Pigeons, Quails or Snipes, One Penny in
For every Dozen of smaller Birds, One Half-penny in like Mon[ey]
For every Hundred Weight of Iron, Steel, Shot, Pewter or Iron, Copper or Brass Kettles or Pots, Six Pence in like [Money] in that Proportion for a greater or lesser Quantity.
For every Hundred Weight of Gun-Powder, One Shilling in l[ike]
For every Sythe or Sith, One Half-penny in like Money.
For every Firkin of Soap, Two Pence in like Money.
For every Cheese, One Half-penny in like Money.
For every Corn Fan, Three Pence in like Money.
For every Hundred of Shingles, Six Pence in like Money.
For every Cedar Bolt, One Penny in like Money.
For every common Bag of Cotton-Wool, One Penny in like Money.
For every Bale of Cotton-Wool or Hops, Eighteen Pence in like Money.
For every Coach, Six Shillings in like Money.
For every Chaise, Three Shillings in like Money.
For every single Sleigh, Eighteen Pence in like Money.
For every double Sleigh, Two Shillings in like Money.
For every Piece of Ozenbrigs, Two Pence in like Money.
For every Piece of Blankets or Duffils, Eighteen Pence in like Money.
For every Piece of Cotton, Pennistone, Flannel or Frize, Four Pence in like Money.
For every Piece of Broad-Cloth, Kersey, Strouds, Halfthicks and Druggets, Three Pence in like Money.
For every Piece of Wadding, Two Pence in like Money.
For every Piece of Duroys, Calamincos, Shalloons, or other Stuff, and for every Piece of Garlix, Holland, or other Linnen, One Penny in like Money.
For every empty Firkin or Pail, One Half-penny in like Money.
For every Side of Sole-Leather, Two Pence in like Money.
For every Side of Upper-Leather, One Penny in like Money.
For every Hundred Weight of Bever, Raccoon-Skins, or Cat's, Nine Pence in like Money, and so in Proportion for a greater or lesser Quantity.
For every half Dozen of Hats, One Penny Half-penny in like Money.
For every Dozen of Fish, called Sheepshead, Two Pence in like Money.
For every Hundred Weight of Dying-Wood, Eight Pence in like Money, and so in Proportion for a greater or lesser Quantity.
For every Hundred Weight of Copperas, Allom or Brimstone, Six Pence in like Money, and so in Proportion for a greater or lesser Quantity.
For every Chair, One Penny in like Money.
For every half Dozen Pair of Wool-Cards, One Penny in like Money.
For every Saddle without a Horse, Two Pence in like Money.
For every Rug, One Penny in like Money.
For every Gun, One Penny in like Money.
For every Spade, One Half-penny in like Money.
For every Case with Bottles, Three Pence in like Money.
For every Looking-Glass of Two Foot high and upwards, Four Pence in like Money.
For every Looking-Glass of One Foot high, Two Pence in like Money.
For every Hundred Weight of Rice, Two Pence in like Money, and so in

Ferry rates. ca. 1733

The Red Lion Inn near Holmesburg, Pa. Built 1730

Philadelphia Ferry

From George Heap's View of Philadelphia.

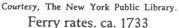

Tavern sign of the Red Lion Tavern, shown above

The Great Awakening

Around the year 1740 a wave of religious frenzy swept the American colonies. It has been called The Great Awakening. Eloquent preachers like George Whitefield and Jonathan Edwards attracted huge crowds wherever they went. This common religious excitement helped to break down the inter-colonial isolation. The evangelists and their followers carried news from one town to another, rich and poor alike were linked by a new bond of fellowship, and the spirit of democracy was emerging.

Rev. George Whitefield

After bringing Methodism to Georgia, Whitefield visited other colonies. He enjoyed a sensational success as an evangelist and raised large sums of money for charitable institutions.

Rev. Jonathan Edwards

An engraving after a painting now thought to have been the work of Joseph Badger.

George Ninde *George Whitefield.* 1924.
Courtesy, Abingdon Press, Nashville, Tenn.

Field pulpit used by George Whitefield
George Ninde *George Whitefield.* 1924

Courtesy, The Forbes Library, Northampton, Mass.
Home of Jonathan Edwards, Northampton, Mass.

Sinners In the Hands of an Angry God

Jonathan Edwards preached a sermon at Enfield, Mass., in 1741 entitled *Sinners in the Hands of An Angry God* which pictured the torments of Hell. Mass hysteria often followed the fiery sermons preached by Edwards.

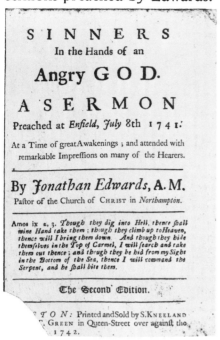

Mrs. Jonathan Edwards. Portrait by Joseph Badger. Sarah Pierpont of New Haven married Jonathan Edwards in 1727, and was described by her husband as being "always full of joy and pleasure". *Courtesy,* Museum of Fine Arts, Boston.

Camp meeting in the woods. Drawing by F. O. C. Darley

Log College and the Presbyterians

Many sectarian schools and colleges were founded as a result of this religious stirring. Log College, established in 1726 at Neshaminy, Pennsylvania, by William Tennent, was the nucleus from which Princeton University, as well as many other Presbyterian schools and churches, sprang. Samuel Finley conducted a school for ministers at Nottingham, Pa., 1744-1761, and became president of the College of New Jersey (Princeton).

Samuel Finley. Portrait engraved by
John Sartain

Ferris *History of the Original Settlements on the Delaware.* 1846.

First Presbyterian Meeting House, Wilmington, Del. 1740

Lutherans

In 1742, Heinrich Melchior Muhlenberg came to Pennsylvania to serve as a German Lutheran missionary. He founded churches and schools, and his sons, Frederick Augustus Conrad and John Peter Gabriel, became distinguished clergymen.

Courtesy, Pennsylvania German Society. Proceedings

Heinrich Melchior Muhlenberg

Courtesy, The Historical Society of York County, York, Pa.

Lutheran christening. Sketch by Lewis Miller

In 1745 Heinrich Melchior Muhlenberg married Anna Maria, daughter of Conrad Weiser of Tulpehocken.

Conrad Weiser House, near Womelsdorf, Pa. Weiser was a famous interpreter of Indian languages at treaty conferences

Right Conrad Weiser

Courtesy, Pennsylvania German Society. Proceedings. 1898.

Mennonites

The sect of Amish Mennonites around Lancaster, Pennsylvania always dressed in austere black. They were industrious farmers and lived to themselves.

Courtesy, Landis Valley Museum.

Mennonite buggy

Courtesy, Pennsylvania German Society. Proceedings. 1911.

Amish couple

Kurze Zuverlassige Nachricht. 1757.

Foot washing, a ritual practiced by the Amish and Moravian sects

Ephrata Cloister

None of the German sects in Pennsylvania were more interesting or culturally significant than that established at Ephrata near Lancaster under the leadership of Conrad Beissel in 1735. The Brethren and Sisters lived in humble simplicity in the manner of medieval monks and nuns. Ephrata had its own grist mill, paper mill, printing press, book bindery, bakery, tannery and other self-supporting adjuncts. The Brethren made furniture and other necessaries, and the Sisters illuminated manuscripts, copied musical scores, and did exquisite needlework.

Photo by Philip B. Wallace.

Saal and Sister House. Ephrata Cloister

Kimball *Domestic Architecture of the American Colonies.*
1922.

Porch of the Sister House. Ephrata
Cloister

Ephrata Sister. Illuminated manuscript

Jews

Synagogues in New York, Newport, Charleston, and other American cities provided places
of worship for the growing Jewish population.

Ceremonies and Religious Customs of the Various Nations of the Known World. 1733-34.

Blowing the shophar on the Jewish New Year, an ancient custom. The interior of Trouro Synagogue in Newport, R. I., is strikingly similar to the one shown here.

Courtesy, Redwood Library, Newport, R. I.

Jacob Rodriguez Rivera of Newport, R. I. Portrait by
Gilbert Stuart. The Rivera family improved lighting
facilities in the 1740's by the introduction of spermaceti candles

Courtesy, Museum of the City of New York.

Silver tankard made for the Livingston family by the
Jewish silversmith, Myer Myers

Puritans and Anglicans

The Puritans and Anglicans were the leading religious groups in America and dominated the ecclesiastical and political life of the colonies. The provincial governors, being Church of England men, were in a position to exert considerable authority, particularly in the southern colonies, whereas the Puritans of New England, by sheer force of numbers, constituted a serious threat to Anglican leadership.

Courtesy, Essex Institute, Salem, Mass.
St. Peter's Church. Salem, Mass. Water color by George Perkins 1733

Right Bruton Parish Church, Williamsburg, Va. 1710-15
Courtesy, Colonial Williamsburg, Inc.

Whitefield *The Homes of Our Forefathers.* 3 v. 1880-86.
St. Michael's Church. Marblehead, Mass. 1714

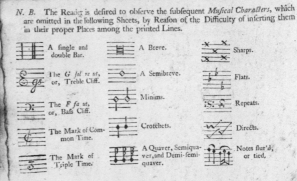

Specimen of New England church music

Walter Grounds and Rules of Musick Explained. 1721.

Louisburg

If the Great Awakening brought the American colonies together spiritually, the successful military and naval engagements against the French at Louisburg on Cape Breton Island in 1744-45, gave them visions of future independence. The much-publicized Louisburg campaign proved to the raw provincial troops that they could fight and win battles as well as the better-trained British regulars. The Americans began to feel cocky.

London Magazine. 1746.

British Foot Guards. Exercises from the British Manual of Arms

Sir William Pepperell of Kittery, Me., was chosen to lead the American troops at the siege of Louisburg. He knew little about the art of siege, and his troops knew even less, but in spite of recklessness, lack of discipline, and inexperience they carried the day.

Sir William Pepperell. From a painting
by John Smibert

Courtesy, The New-York Historical Society, New York.

Flag carried at the siege of Louisburg

Fear Was Routed

Fear of the French, a New England complex, was partially overcome by the victory at Louisburg. New England breathed easier. Bonfires of victory were lighted, Louisburg was celebrated in poem and sermon.

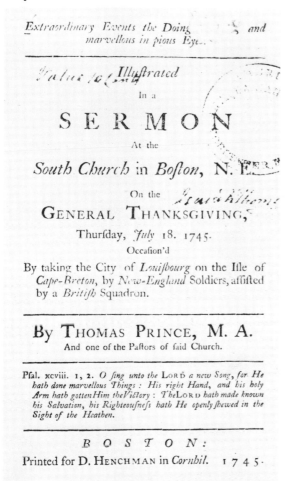

Bookplate of Thomas Prince

Handwriting of Thomas Prince

Courtesy, American Antiquarian Society, Worcester, Mass.

View of Louisburg

Courtesy, The Stokes Collection, The New York Public Library.

Currency Was Stabilized—Business Boomed

The expenses of the Louisburg adventure all but bankrupted the New England colonies, particularly Massachusetts. Great Britain, to keep Massachusetts solvent, shipped £183,649 to Boston. This precious cargo included 217 chests of Spanish dollars and 100 barrels of copper coin. This enabled Massachusetts to stabilize her currency and pay off her debts. Business boomed immediately. The previous currency had been called old tenor, and it had depreciated in value so much that a pound sterling was equivalent to eleven pounds old tenor. Each colony had a different rate of exchange, further complicating business transactions.

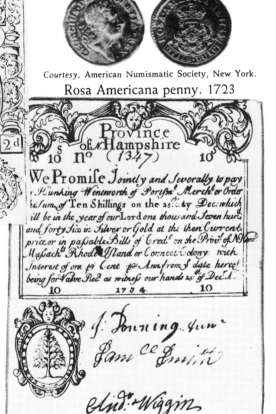

Courtesy, American Numismatic Society, New York.

Rosa Americana penny. 1723

Courtesy, Old-Time New England.

Massachusetts paper money. 1744

Promissory note. New Hampshire. 1734

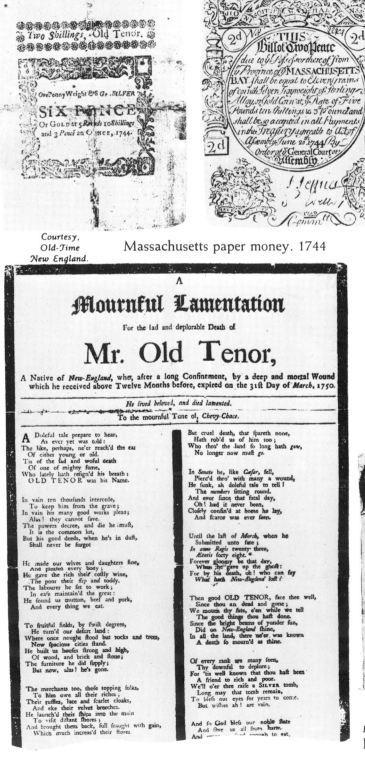

Reverse of same *above*

Courtesy, Colonial Society of Massachusetts.

Broadside lamenting the death of old tenor

Courtesy, The Massachusetts Historical Society, Boston.

"Old Fan'l"

Men like Peter Faneuil, Huguenot merchant prince of Boston, foresaw the glorious future of the American colonies. He built Faneuil Hall and offered it as a gift to the citizens of Boston, but the gift was accepted by the close vote of 367 to 360.

Willis *American Scenery*. 1840.

Faneuil Hall. Designed by John Smibert. In 1805 Charles Bulfinch added a third story to Smibert's original design of 1740-42

BOSTON.

POMPEY for Plays, a Theatre gave *Rome*,
    GRESHAM to *London*, an Exchange for Wealth,
FANEUIL to *Boston*, gives a worthier Dome,
    A Hall for LIBERTY, a Change below for *Health*.

Monday laſt being the Annual Meeting of the Town, to chuſe meet Perſons to ſerve in the ſeveral Offices the Year enſuing, the ſame was opened with Prayer, by the Rev. Dr. CHAUNCY: After which Mr. JOHN LOVELL, Maſter of the firſt Grammar-School in the Town, pronounced an Oration to the Acceptance of a great Aſſembly on the Death of PETER FANEUIL Eſq; the generous Benefactor to the Town, of the ſtately Edifice wherein they were convened. And then the Town proceeded to the Choice of Officers, & the following were choſen, Viz.

The Hon. *Thomas Cuſhing*, Eſq; Moderator.

Mr. *Ezekiel Goldthwait* Town-Clerk.

For Select-Men, the Hon. *John Jeffries* Eſq; Capt. *Alexander Forſyth*, *Jonas Clark* Eſq; *Thomas Hutchinſon* Eſq; Mr. *Thomas Hancock*, Mr. *Middlecott Cooke*, and Capt. *John Steel*.

For Town-Treaſurer, the Hon. *Joseph Wadſworth* Eſq;

For Overſeers of the Poor, the Hon. *Jacob Wendell* Eſq; *William Tyler*, Eſq; Col. *John Hill*, *Thomas Hubbard* Eſq; *Daniel Henchman* Eſq; Mr. *Edward Bromfield*, Col. *William Downe*, *Andrew Oliver*

For Aſſeſſors, Meſſi. *Richard Buckley*, *Joſhua Blanchard*, *Jacob Parker*, *Daniel Pecker*, *Nathaniel Barber*, *William Fairfield*, *Nathaniel Gardner*.

Clerk of *Faneuil-Hall* Market, Mr. *John Staniford*.

The Town have voted that *Faneuil-Hall* Market ſhall be opened three Days in the Week only, viz. *Tueſdays*, *Thurſdays* and *Saturdays*, and be ſhut up on thoſe Days at 12 o'Clock, till the Meeting in *May* next; and the Select-Men are deſired to conſult what is farther neceſſary to be done for the better regulating ſaid Market, and report to ſaid Meeting.

A Number of the Inhabitants having petitioned for Part of Fort-Hill to be improved for a Bowling-green, the Select Men were impowered to leaſe out to ſuch of the Petitioners as appeared for the ſame, ſo much of ſaid Hill as they tho't proper for that Purpoſe, with this Reſtriction, That the ſame ſhall be quitted by the Leſſees whenever the Town require it.

Custom-Houſe, BOSTON.

Entred In, Kilder from Bonavyar, Blackador from Honduras, Gorham from N. Carolina, Elwell from Maryland.

Outward Bound, Everden for

Boston Weekly Magazine, May 16, 1743.

Note the references to Faneuil

More Ships

Shipbuilding boomed after Louisburg. The Royal Navy increased its orders for American-built vessels, and colonial merchants began to expand their private shipping business.

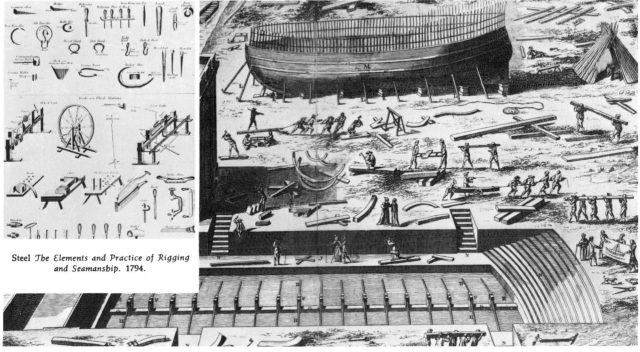

Steel *The Elements and Practice of Rigging and Seamanship*. 1794.

Diderot and D'Alembert *Encyclopedie. Recueil des Planches*, 1762-72.

Shipbuilding yard. 18th Century

Rope

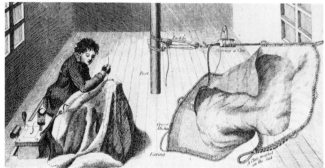

Diderot and D'Alembert *Encyclopedie. Recueil des Planches,* 1762-72.

Twisting hemp into ropes for ships

Sail

Steel *The Elements and Practice of Rigging and Seamanship.* 1794.

A sail loft

Right Commodore Edward Tyng. ca. 1744

Courtesy, Yale University Art Gallery.

Barrels

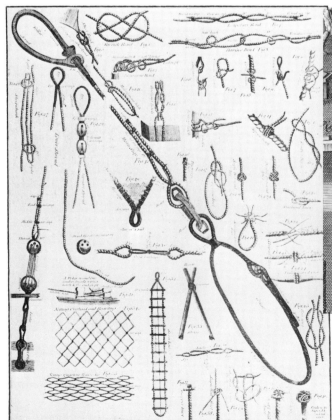

Institut de France. Academie des Sciences. Descriptions des Arts et Metiers.

Coopers at work

Steel *The Elements and Practice of Rigging and Seamanship.*

"Rule of Three"

Young apprentices were needed for all the trades. Boys entering trade were expected to know the mathematical "Rule of Three", a short-cut to calculation.

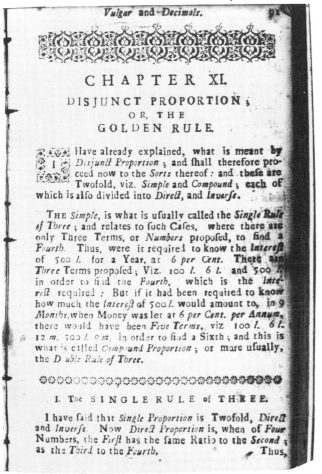

Vulgar and Decimals. 91

CHAPTER XL
DISJUNCT PROPORTION;
OR, THE
GOLDEN RULE.

I Have already explained, what is meant by *Disjunct Proportion*; and shall therefore proceed now to the *Sorts* thereof: and these are Twofold, viz. *Simple* and *Compound*; each of which is also divided into *Direct*, and *Inverse*.

THE *Simple*, is what is usually called the *Single Rule of Three*; and relates to such Cases, where there are only Three Terms, or *Numbers* proposed, to find a *Fourth*. Thus, were it required to know the *Interest* of 500 *l.* for a Year, at 6 *per Cent*. There are *Three* Terms proposed; Viz. 100 *l.* 6 *l.* and 500 *l.* in order to find the *Fourth*, which is the *Interest* required: But if it had been required to know how much the *Interest* of 500 *l.* would amount to, in 9 *Months*, when Money was let at 6 *per Cent. per Annum*, there would have been *Five* Terms, viz. 100 *l.* 6 *l.* 12 *m.* 500 *l.* 9 *m.* in order to find a Sixth; and this is what is called *Compound Proportion*; or more usually, the *Double Rule of Three*.

I. The SINGLE RULE of THREE.

I have said that *Single Proportion* is Twofold, *Direct* and *Inverse*. Now *Direct Proportion* is, when of *Four* Numbers, the *First* has the same Ratio to the *Second*; as the *Third* to the *Fourth*. Thus,

Courtesy, Plimpton Collection, Columbia University Library, New York.

Page from Isaac Greenwood's *Arithmetick*. 1729. The beginning of a lengthy explanation of the "Rule of Three"

An Indenture for placing forth an Apprentice.

THIS Indenture made, &c. Witnesseth, That *A. B.* Son of, &c. hath of his own free and voluntary Will (or by and with the Consent of his Father) placed and bound himself Apprentice unto *D. E.* of, &c. Pewterer, to be taught in the said Trade, Science or Occupation of a Pewterer, which he the said *D. E.* now useth, and with him as an Apprentice to dwell, continue and serve from the Day of the Date hereof unto the full End and Term of Seven Years from thence next ensuing, and fully to be compleat and ended; During all which Term, the said Apprentice his said Master well and faithfully shall serve, his Secrets keep, his lawful Commands gladly do, Hurt to his said Master he shall not do, nor wilfully suffer to be done by others, but of the same to his Power shall forthwith give Notice to his said Master. The Goods of his said Master he shall not imbezle or waste, nor them lend without his Consent to any; at Cards, Dice, or any other unlawful Games he shall not play; Taverns or Alehouses he shall not frequent; Fornication he shall not commit, Matrimony he shall not contract; from the Service of his said Master he shall not at any Time depart or absent himself without his said Master's Leave; But in all Things, as a good and faithful Apprentice, shall and will Demean and Behave himself towards his said Master and all his, during the said Term. And the said Master his said Apprentice the said Trade, Science, or Occupation of a Pewterer, with all Things thereunto belonging, shall and will teach and instruct, or cause to be well and sufficiently taught and instructed, after the best Way and Manner that he can; And shall and will also find and allow unto his said Apprentice, Meat, Drink, Washing, Lodging, and Apparel, both Linnen and Woollen, and all other Necessaries fit and convenient for such an Apprentice during the Term aforesaid. And at the End of the said Term shall and will give to his said Apprentice one new Suit of Apparel, &c. In Witness, &c.

Bb 2   Licence.

Form of indenture, from *The American Instructor*. 1748.

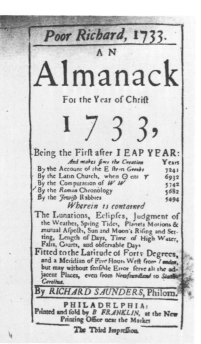

Poor Richard, 1733.
AN
Almanack

For the Year of Christ

1733,

Being the First after LEAP YEAR:

And makes since the Creation   Years
By the Account of the Eastern *Greeks*   7241
By the Latin Church, when ☉ ent ♈   6932
By the Computation of W.W.   5742
By the *Roman* Chronology   5682
By the *Jewish* Rabbies   5494

Wherein is contained

The Lunations, Eclipses, Judgment of the Weather, Spring Tides, Planets Motions & mutual Aspects, Sun and Moon's Rising and Setting, Length of Days, Time of High Water, Fairs, Courts, and observable Days.

Fitted to the Latitude of Forty Degrees, and a Meridian of Five Hours West from *London*, but may without sensible Error serve all the adjacent Places, even from *Newfoundland* to *South-Carolina*.

By RICHARD SAUNDERS, Philom.

PHILADELPHIA:
Printed and sold by B. FRANKLIN, at the New Printing Office near the Market.

The Third Impression.

Benjamin Franklin began his career as a "printer's devil", and the moral precepts of his *Poor Richard's Almanack* did much to form the character of the young tradesmen.

Whitefield *The Homes of Our Forefathers*.
Old schoolhouse, Connecticut

Printing press used by Benjamin Franklin

Courtesy, National Museum, Washington, D. C.

Some Went to College

Yale College. 1749
Engraved by Thomas Johnston after a drawing
by John Greenwood

Courtesy, Connecticut Magazine.
First building at Yale College

Home of George Berkeley, Middletown, R. I. Bishop Berkeley of Ireland was one of the benefactors of
Yale College and gave it many books

For Tender Minds

Courtesy, Plimpton Collection,
Columbia University Library,
New York.

Above Pages from the
Massachusetts Primer

Left Pages from the
New England Primer
Enlarged. 1736

Courtesy, Plimpton Collection,
Columbia University Library,
New York.

Books

Benjamin Franklin founded the Library Company of Philadelphia in 1731. Abraham Redwood founded the Redwood Library in Newport, R. I., in 1748. James Logan in Philadelphia, Thomas Prince and the Mathers in Boston, William Byrd in Virginia, and a few other patrons of letters had fairly large private libraries.

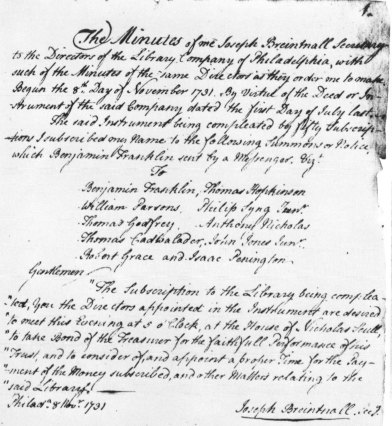

Excerpt from the *Minutes* of the Library Company, Philadelphia, 1731

The Redwood Library

Bookplate of James Logan

Trade card of Andrew Barclay, bookbinder

Freedom of the Press

In 1733, Peter Zenger criticized the high-handed policies of Governor William Cosby in the pages of *The New-York Weekly Journal.* Cosby issued a proclamation offering a reward for the apprehension of the author of the offending articles. Zenger was arrested and brought to trial, and through the eloquent defense made by his lawyer, Andrew Hamilton of Philadelphia, was acquitted. This famous trial helped to establish the idea of the freedom of the press in America.

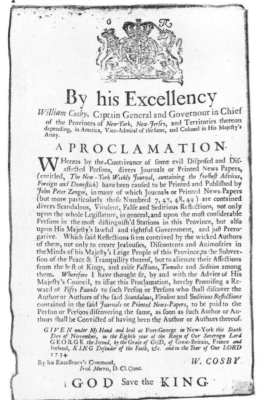

Courtesy, The New York Public Library.

Left Typical front page of an American newspaper

Courtesy, Maryland Historical Society, Baltimore, Md.

Crime and Punishment

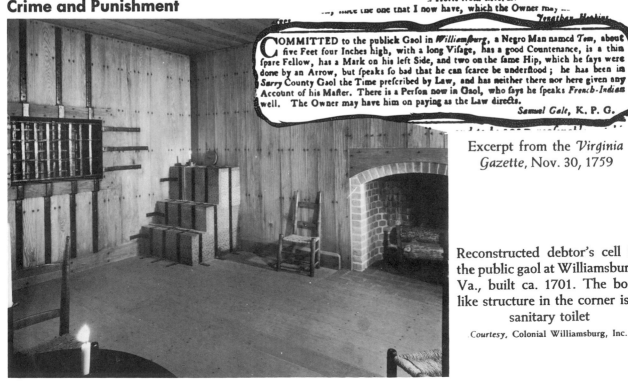

Excerpt from the *Virginia Gazette*, Nov. 30, 1759

Reconstructed debtor's cell in the public gaol at Williamsburg, Va., built ca. 1701. The box-like structure in the corner is a sanitary toilet

Courtesy, Colonial Williamsburg, Inc.

Laws Were Passed

House of Burgesses. The Capitol. Williamsburg, Va.

The General Assembly of Virginia met here from the early years of the eighteenth century until 1779, when it was moved from Williamsburg to Richmond.

Williamsburg, Va.
ca. 1740

A copper plate found in the Bodleian Library, Oxford, which may have been the work of John Bartram, the colonial botanist. The upper panel shows William and Mary College, (1) Brafferton Hall. (2) The Wren Building, and (3) the President's House. The middle panel shows (4) the Capitol. (5) West elevation of the Wren building. (6) the Governor's Palace.

The Art of the Silversmith

The arts developed slowly in America, due to lack of schools and the absence of patrons, and to Puritan prejudice, but as merchants and planters accumulated wealth they built finer houses and furnished them with more expensive objects. Almost from the beginning the silversmiths were active, and their art developed much more rapidly than the fine arts of music and painting.

Left Silver porringer by John Burt, Boston
Courtesy, Museum of Fine Arts, Boston.

Silver cup by John Coney, Boston
Courtesy, Museum of Fine Arts, Boston.

Silver porringer by Benjamin Burt, Boston
Courtesy, Metropolitan Museum of Art, New York.

Below Left Silver tankard by Edward Winslow, Boston
Courtesy, Philadelphia Museum of Art, Philadelphia.

Below Silver brazier by Johann de Nys, Philadelphia
Courtesy, Philadelphia Museum of Art, Philadelphia.

Courtesy, Mabel Brady Garvan Collection, Yale University Art Gallery.

Silver tankard by Peter Van Dyck, New York. It has
the Wendell coat of arms

Courtesy, Yale University Art Gallery.

Silver tray by Jacob Hurd

Left Silver teapot by Jacob Hurd
Courtesy, Yale University Art Gallery.

Right Silver casters by Adrian Bancker, New York

*Courtesy, Collection of Herbert L. Pratt and the Museum of
the City of New York.*

Courtesy, Pleasants and Sill Maryland Silversmiths.
1930.

Design for a teapot by William Faris,
Baltimore

Courtesy, Mabel Brady Garvan Collection, Yale University Art Gallery.

Sugar box by Edward Winslow, Boston

Left Monteith bowl by John Coney, the earliest form of the "Monteith" in America

Below Silver dish ring by Myer Myers. Unique sample of an American dish ring

Courtesy, Mabel Brady Garvan Collection, Yale University Art Gallery.

Silver nutmeg grater by William Cross, Boston

Courtesy, Metropolitan Museum of Art, New York.

The Hunger For Beauty

Puritan austerity could not kill the human instinct for artistic expression. In spite of rigid taboos the busy fingers of many a young woman recorded the dreams of the heart in lively flights of the imagination.

American embroidered pieces. ca. 1740

Courtesy, Museum of Fine Arts, Boston.

9
THE SELF-CONSCIOUS ERA

After 1750 the American colonies grew more self-conscious; more critical of Great Britain's colonial attitude; more articulate in the cause of liberty. American harbors were filled with shipping; tremendous natural resources were being tapped; the arts and sciences were beginning to take root; newspapers were multiplying. The panoramic view of Philadelphia *below* was executed by George Heap at some time prior to 1754 when the engraving was issued.

Courtesy, The Historical Society of Pennsylvania, Philadelphia.

Newspapers

THE
NEWPORT MERCURY,
OR,
Weekly
THE
Advertiser;

NUMB: 27.

With the freſheſt ADVICES,

FOREIGN and DOMESTIC.

TUESDAY, DECEMBER 19, 1758.

LONDON.

Shall, for the ſake of variety, this week entertain my readers with a few obſervations, that have little or no relation to party, and yet, ſuch as concerns every Engliſhman to know.

There is not a reader of common underſtanding, who does not perceive that affairs are now in ſuch a ſituation upon the continent, that no power in Europe has any thing to hope or to fear, but from England. This vaſt, but late growth of importance, calls for all her caution, as her ſmalleſt failure of conduct, may be fatal to her allies. Even hiſtory and experience are but of little uſe upon this emergency, becauſe the ballance of power which our anceſtors were ſo careful to maintain, no longer exiſts in the ſame manner as heretofore, and a new ſyſtem has taken place all over Europe, and how much it is in favour of Eng-

Almoſt the ſame obſervation holds good with regard to the Swedes, who likewiſe have put in for their ſhare of the ſpoils of the houſe of Brandenbourg. They lie indeed more convenient for annoying his Pruſſian Majeſty, and they have hitherto proceeded with more ſpirit, or rather with leſs caution, than the Ruſſians have done, but with all the poverty of the Ruſſians, they have the misfortune of being governed by a faction that has wreſted all power from their King, and ſeem to follow no dictates, but thoſe of blind revenge and deſpair. In what a condition then muſt ſuch a government be, ſhould the greateſt maritime power in the world take advantage of the diviſions that now rend their country, and have forced their King to act a part, that is directly the reverſe of his intereſt, inclination, and honour?

Upon the whole therefore, it appears, that as ſoon as his Majeſty ſhall be of opinion, that the intereſt of his dominions or allies call upon him to declare as a principle in the war upon the continent; the weight both

April 3, 1752.

THE
VIRGINIA GAZETTE.

Numb. 66.

With the freſheſt Advices,

Foreign and Domeſtic.

The SPEECH of TOM TELLTRUTHIA, againſt Virginia, and Bombaſtia.

THE
GEORGIA GAZETTE.

NUMBER 27.   THURSDAY, OCTOBER 6, 1763.

Specimens of newspaper printing in the American colonies

The Mason and Dixon Line

Boundary disputes which had retarded progress were slowly being settled. Maryland had long been the chief sufferer in this respect. To reach Philadelphia by sea one had to enter Maryland territory. William Penn and his descendants carried on a fight for this vital strip. In 1763 two English surveyors, Charles Mason and Jeremiah Dixon, began their survey of the boundary between Pennsylvania and Maryland now known as the Mason and Dixon Line, completed in 1767. One of the original markers, bearing the Calvert coat of arms on one side, and the Penn coat of arms on the other, is shown here. Had the full claims of either Penn or Calvert been honored, Baltimore would now be in Pennsylvania or Philadelphia in Maryland.

Photo by Philip B. Wallace.

Baltimore was still a village. Here we see a portrait of Mrs. John Moale (Ellin North), said to have been the first white child born in Baltimore. Her father, Robert North, helped lay out Baltimore Town in 1729.

Mrs. John Moale (1740-1825) and her granddaughter. Painting by Joshua Johnson, Negro artist. ca. 1800

Courtesy, Mr. Roswell P. Russell, Baltimore, the owner of the portrait, and Dr. J. Hall Pleasants, Baltimore.

Baltimore

View of Baltimore, Md. Aquatint based on a sketch made by John Moale in 1752. It was then a town of less than fifty houses and two hundred inhabitants. Note the sloop (26), the brig (27) and the architectural style of the buildings. The untamed wilderness lay at the backdoor of every Maryland house, even as late as 1752

Colleges Were Springing Up

View of the College of New Jersey, later to become Princeton University, Princeton, N. J. 1764. The architect was Robert Smith of Philadelphia. This view was engraved by H. Dawkins after a drawing by W. Tennent

View of Rhode Island College, Providence, R. I., later to become Brown University. Founded 1764. This view was made in 1793

Courtesy, John Carter Brown Library.

View of Kings College, New York. Founded 1754. It was then located on lower Manhattan, not far from Trinity Church. It became Columbia College in 1784

Merchant Princes Were Arising

John Amory of Boston. Portrait by John Singleton Copley. 1768

For LONDON,

THE Ship FRIENDSHIP, Benfon Fearon Mafter, lying at Bermuda Hundred, on James River, will take in Tobacco at 12 Pounds per Ton, with Liberty of Confignment.

All Perfons inclinable to fhip, are defired to apply to Meff. Atkinfon and Newfum, Merchants in Peterfburg; to Colonel Thomas Tabb in Amelia, or to the Captain on board.

For MADEIRA,

THE Brigantine BETSEY, Captain Stagg, a Letter of Marque, well provided.

Gentlemen defirous of Wine from Madeira, by the Return of the Veffel, are defired to fend their Orders, immediately, to Colonel Lewis Burwell, as fhe will fail in a few Days.

To be SOLD to the highest Bidders, on Monday the 17th of December next, if fair (if not, the next fair Day) at the late Dwelling-House of Mr. Thomas Thorpe, deceafed, in King and Queen, ALL the Houfhold-Goods, Plate and Books, with a new Chair and Harnefs, the Stocks of Cattle, Horfes and Hogs; alfo 20 Negroes. Six Months Credit will be allowed, the Purchafers giving Bond and Security to

Graham Frank, Executor.

JUST imported in the Good-Intent, Capt. Reddick, and to be fold cheap, for ready Money, by the Subfcriber, living at the Palace, in Williamfburg; where Gentlemen may depend on being well ferved, with the following Garden-Seeds, by

Their humble Servant, Chriftopher Ayfcough.

Six-Week Peas, Charlton Hotfpur Peas, Marrowfat Peas, Nonpareil Peas, Spanifh Morrotto Peas, Sugar Dwarf Peas, Windfor Beans, Long-poded Beans, White Bloffom Beans, Green Beans, Nonpareil Beans, large Englifh Turnip, early Dutch Turnip, early Dutch Cabbage, Sugar-Loaf Cabbage, Batterfea Cabbage, large Winter Cabbage, Red Cabbage, Yellow Savoy Cabbage, Green Savoy Cabbage, early Colliflower, late Colliflower, Colliflower Brocoli, Purple Brocoli, curled Colewort, Scarlet Raddifh, fhort-topped Raddifh, white Turnip Raddifh, black Turnip Raddifh, white Gafs Lettuce, black Gafs Lettuce, brown Dutch Lettuce, Nonpareil Lettuce, Silefia Lettuce, white curled Endive, white Spanifh Onion, Englifh Onion, Leek, Chardoon, Italian Cellery, white Muftard, Garden

Shipping notices from the *Virginia Gazette*

Stephen Cleveland

Left Bookplate of Stephen Cleveland, showing nautical influence

Moses Brown, merchant of Providence

Salem Magnate

Elias Hasket Derby of Salem, Massachusetts, operated a large fleet of ships. He and other merchant princes could afford fine mansions, rare china, elegant costumes, and all the luxuries of Europe. They had their private wharfs and warehouses.

Elias Hasket Derby (1734-99)
Portrait by James Frothingham

Courtesy, Peabody Museum, Salem, Mass.

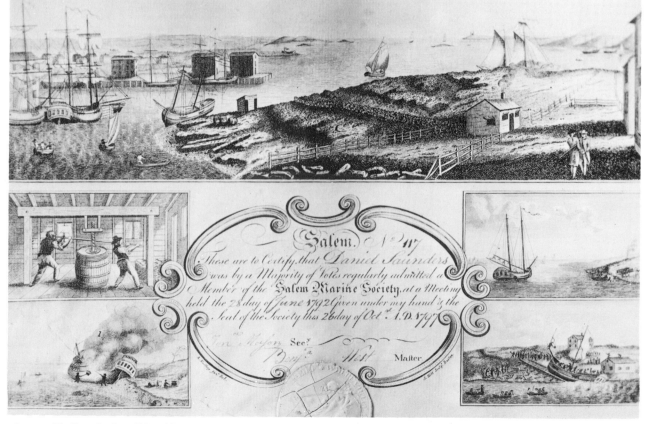

Courtesy, The Essex Institute, Salem, Mass.

View of Salem showing Derby's wharf. The view depicted is earlier than the date on the certificate.

His Plate

Chinese export porcelain plate
made especially for
Elias Hasket Derby

Courtesy, Museum of Fine Arts, Boston.

His Tea House

Courtesy, The Essex Institute, Salem, Mass.

His Ship

Ship *Grand Turk*. 1781. Built for Elias Hasket
Derby, and used in the China trade

Courtesy, The Essex Institute, Salem, Mass.

Ship Figureheads

Courtesy, The Essex Institute, Salem, Mass.
Figurehead by Samuel McIntire of Salem

Courtesy, The Essex Institute, Salem, Mass.
Bill for carving figureheads and other
ship decorations sent to Elias Hasket
Derby by the noted wood carvers,
the brothers Skillin of Boston

Left Ship's figurehead found near Nantucket, Mass.
18th Century
Courtesy, The New-York Historical Society, New York.

Below Making rope for ships
Steel *The Elements and Practice of Rigging and Seamanship.* 1794.

Rope

Counting House

Merchant's Counting House. Published by T. Dolson, Philadelphia. 18th Century

18th Century ships

Shipping

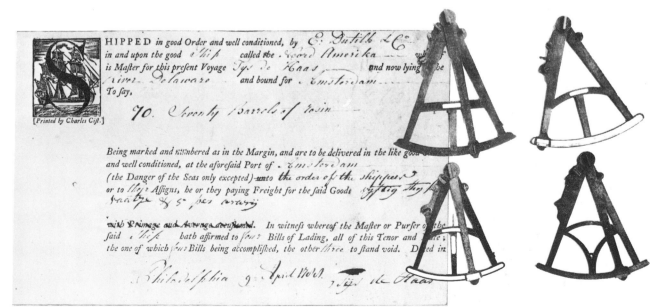

Shipping bill. 1755

Navigator's quadrants

Master and Seamen

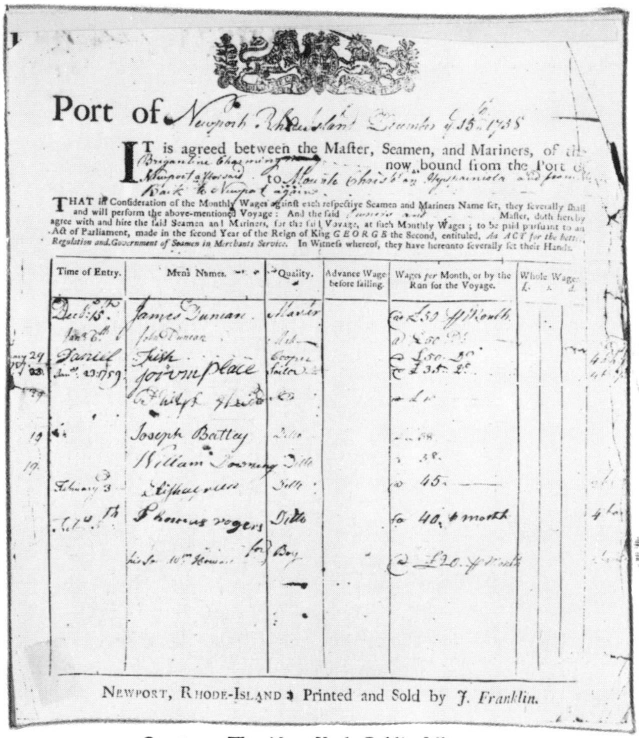

Courtesy, The New York Public Library.

Agreement between master and seamen. 1758

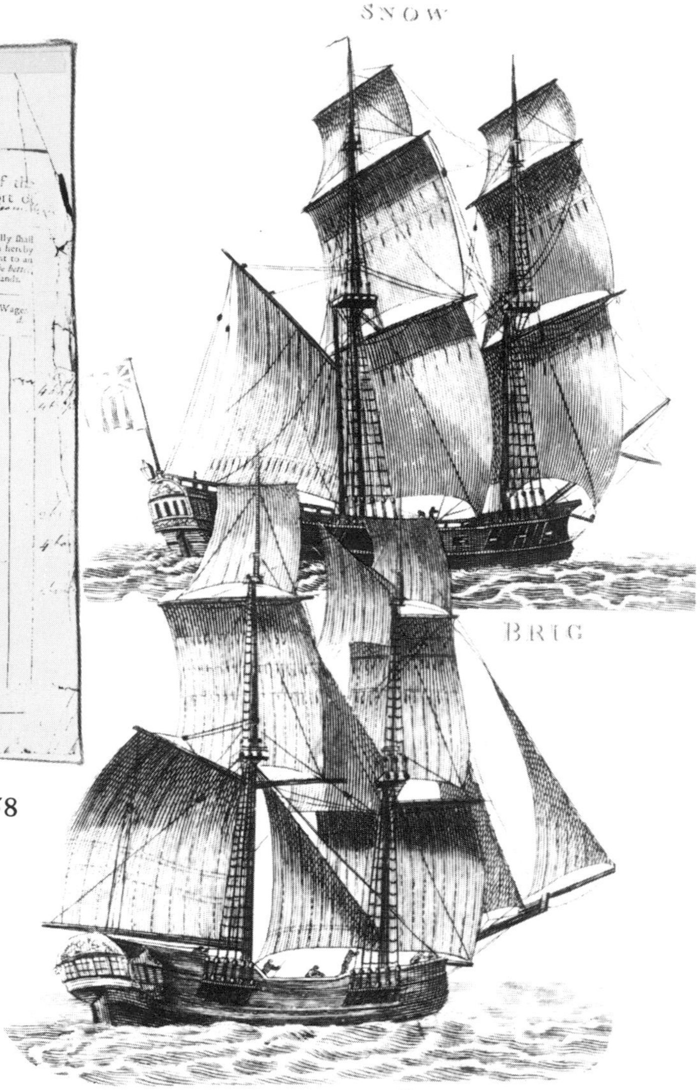

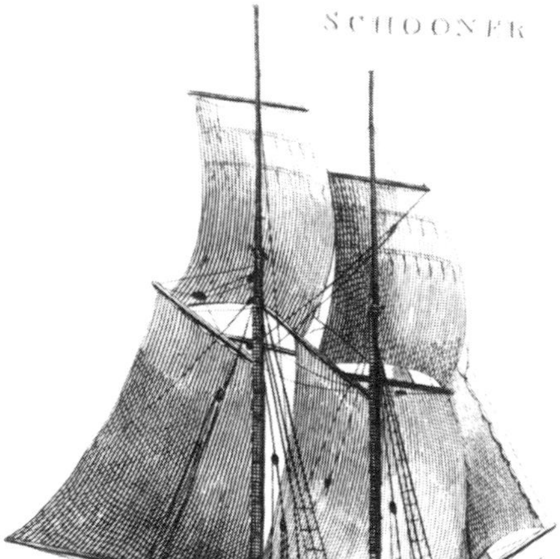

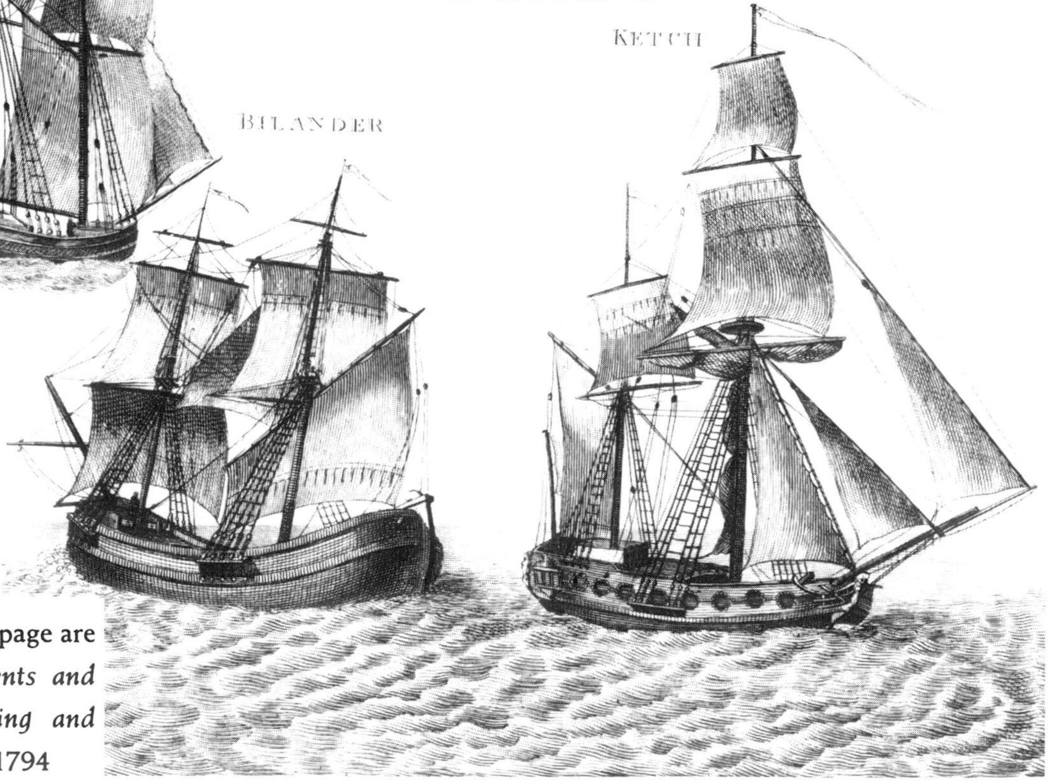

The ships on this page are
from Steel *Elements and
Practice of Rigging and
Seamanship*. 1794

Chamber of Commerce

The first Chamber of Commerce in America was founded in New York City in 1768, and is still in existence. It was the Chamber of Commerce of the State of New York. It met first in Fraunces Tavern, and the next year moved to the Royal Exchange.

Courtesy, The Emmet Collection, The New York Public Library.
Royal Exchange. New York. 1754

Great Seal of the Chamber of Commerce of the State of New York. 1770

Courtesy, The Bella C. Landauer Collection. The New-York Historical Society, New York.
Trade card of Francis Hopkinson

"Pieces of Eight"

Among the coins that circulated in New York were the Spanish Eight Reales, called "Pieces of Eight".

Courtesy, American Numismatic Society, New York.
Eight Reales. 1767. The silver mines of Potosi (Bolivia) supplied the metal for these coins

Courtesy, American Numismatic Society, New York.
Shilling. George II. 1758

A La Mode

Fine cloth was imported from England, Holland, and France, and the ladies and gentlemen of the American colonies kept abreast of the London and Paris styles.

Courtesy, Litchfield Historical Society and The Metropolitan Museum of Art.

Benjamin Tallmadge and son, of Litchfield, Conn.   Mrs. Benjamin Tallmadge and children, of Litchfield, Conn.

Portraits by Ralph Earl

Courtesy, Carolina Art Association, Charleston, S. C.

Bernard Eliot of Charleston   Mrs. Bernard Eliot of Charleston

Portraits by Jeremiah Theus

Presenting . . .

Mr. and Mrs. Isaac Winslow. Portraits by John Singleton Copley

Gov. Jonathan Trumbull, Jr., of Conn., with his wife and eldest daughter. Portraits by John Trumbull

Whitefield *The Homes of Our Forefathers.* 1880-86.

They Sat For Copley Gov. Trumbull's house and war office, Lebanon, Conn.

It was fashionable to have a portrait painted by John Singleton Copley, the Boston artist.

Thomas Boylston   Mrs. Thomas Boylston

Portraits by John Singleton Copley

The Hairdresser's Art

Courtesy, Museum of Fine Arts, Boston.

Portrait of Miss Skinner by John Singleton Copley

Courtesy, Essex Institute, Salem, Mass.

Portrait of Esther (Gerrish) Carpenter by an unknown artist

RICHARD THOMPSON,
PERUKE-MAKER and HAIR-CUTTER from LONDON,
GIVES this publick notice, that he intends following
his busineſs, at the houſe of Mr. Chriſtopher Ring in
Broughton-ſtreet. Whoever pleaſe to favour him with their
cuſtom ſhall be duly attended at a reaſonable price.

ALEXANDER BELL, from VIRGINIA,
GIVES notice to the publick, that he will erect machines
for preventing houſes from being ſtruck by lightening, after the neweſt and beſt manner, at a reaſonable rate.
Thoſe who chuſe to employ him, may call on him at Mr.
John Lyons's ſhop, where they may ſee the machines. His
ſtay will be but about three weeks in this place.

A Gentleman's Watch . . .

Courtesy, The New-York Historical Society, New York.

Watch made by Green of London, 1763-64, and owned by Major-General Philip Schuyler of New York

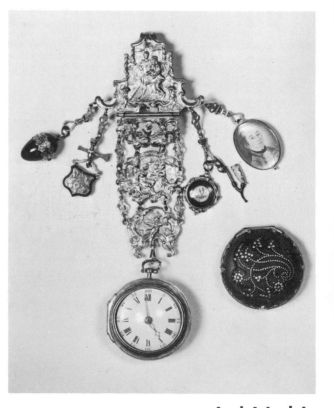

. . . And A Lady's

Gold chatelaine and watch

Courtesy, Collection of
Miss Julia Lawrence
Wells, and the Museum
of the City of New York.

Philipse Manor

The portraits *above* represent Mr. and Mrs. Philip Philipse and were painted by John Wollaston. The 19th Century engraving of their home, Philipse Manor, Yonkers, N. Y., seen at the *left, below*, was the work of James Smillie.

At *right*, portrait of Margaret Sylvester Chesebrough by Joseph Blackburn.

Flowered Silk

Dress of cream-colored silk worn by Jane Galloway, who married Col. Joseph Shippen of Philadelphia in 1768. The blue quilted petticoat was made ca. 1775

Courtesy, Philadelphia Museum of Art, Philadelphia.

Embroidery

Courtesy, Old Quinabaug Village, Sturbridge, Mass.

Embroidered crewelwork lady's pocketbook. 1762

Courtesy, Essex Institute, Salem, Mass.

Pocketbook made by Eliza Willard in 1760

Left Embroidery frame. ca. 1755
Courtesy, Metropolitan Museum of Art, New York.

Below Needlepoint picture worked by Sarah Warren,
Massachusetts. 1748
Courtesy, Estate of Francis Sever, and The Museum of Fine Arts, Boston.

Textiles

Early American quilt

Early American textiles, two-toned blue resist
Courtesy, Cooper Union Museum for the Arts of Decoration, New York.

The Tailor

Diderot and D'Alembert *Encyclopedie. Recueil des planches.* 1762-72.

Tailor

Courtesy, Valentine Museum, Richmond, Va.

Velvet suit worn by Dr. John Peter Le Mayeur, George Washington's dentist

PATRICK AUDLEY, Taylor,
who for many years paft, hath work'd in the beft fhops in *Great-Britain* and *Ireland*; has, on the encouragement of fome gentlemen, fettled in this city, where he will carry on his trade, and engage to finifh any kind of work, in the neweft and neateft manner, now ufed either in *London* or *Paris*. He makes gentlemen's laced and plain cloaths, hunting dreffes, uniforms for horfe and foot, pantine fleeve, racolues for clergymen and others, ladies jofephs, riding, habits: Thefe, and all other kinds of dreffes, that are wore in *London, Paris* or *Dublin*, fhall be done in the moft agreeable fafhions, at reafonable prices, and finifh'd without lofs of time. *N. B.* As he is a ftranger in this part of the world, he humbly hopes that gentlemen and ladies will be pleafed to favour him with their commands, which fhall be carefully executed, by their moft humble, and obedient fervant, PATRICK AUDLEY.

Tailor's advertisement

New York Mercury. 1753.

The Shoemaker

Diderot and D'Alembert *Encyclopedie. Recueil des planches.* 1762-72.

Courtesy, Rhode Island School of Design, Providence, R. I.

Portrait of Theodore Atkinson, Jr., by Joseph Blackburn

The Hatter

Institut de France. Academie des sciences. Descriptions des arts et metiers. 1765.

Preparing wool for felt   Hatters at work

Institut de France. Academie des sciences. Descriptions des arts et metiers. 1765.

Hat shop

A PRICE CURRENT of SKINS, &c. usually imported at London, from NORTH - AMERICA.

		Season'd	Damag'd Stage.
		s. d. s. d.	s. d. s. d.
First Sort,	Beaver Parchment, per lb.	7 7—7 9	3 2—3 7
Second Do.	Ditto	4 0—5 3	2 0—3 6
First Sort.	Beaver Cub	5 2—0 0	2 3—2 5
Second Do.	Ditto	3 9—4 9	2 0—2 2
	Beaver Coat	5 0—5 5	1 7—4 0
	Bear per Skin	15 6—22 6	6 0—10 0
	Ditto Cub	10 6—16 0	Mix'd.
	Otter	14 0—19 0	7 6—12 0
	Fisher	4 7—6 0	Mix'd.
	Martin	4 6—7 0	3 0—4 1
	Ditto fine	8 0—13 0	4 6—5 6
	Wolf	9 6—18 6	5 6—6 6
	Wolverin	10 0—12 0	Mix'd.
	Cat cased	4 6—5 0	
	Ditto fine	12 0—15 6	6 0—7 0
	Cat open	3 6—4 6	1 6—2 0
	Mink	3 9—5 6	0 11—2 0
	Fox Silver	15 0—60 0	
	Fox Cross	10 0—12 0	
	Fox Red	4 6—7 0	2 0—2 6
	Fox Grey	2 4—3 6	1 0—1 6
	Raccoon	1 6—2 11	0 4—0 11
	Musquash	0 4—0 8	Mix'd.
	Elk	25 6—27 0	
	Deer in the Hair	3 6—7 6	2 4—3 11
	Deer half drest per lb.	3 0—3 1	1 5—1 10
	Castorum	5 8—8 2	

. To Sale, February 25 and 26, 1767.   *Your most humble Servant,* SAMUEL ROBINSON.

Price list of skins. 1767

The best hats were made from beaver skins.

Hatters

Universal Magazine. London. Apr. 1750.

Colonial Life At Its Best

Door of Mt. Pleasant, Philadelphia

Let us step in the door of a fine house in Philadelphia and see the hall.

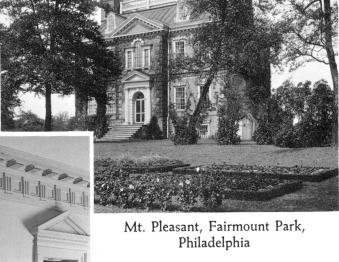

Mt. Pleasant, Fairmount Park, Philadelphia

Entrance hall, Mt. Pleasant

Front bedroom, Mt. Pleasant

All photographs on this page *Courtesy*, Philadelphia Museum of Art, Philadelphia.

New York Elegance

Let us step into the Beekman mansion in New York, seen at *right* in a mid-19th Century print.

The Blue Room *above* and the Green Room at *right* have been restored and are to be seen in the museum of The New-York Historical Society.

Two above photographs *Courtesy*, The New-York Historical Society, New York City.

Portsmouth, New Hampshire

Room from the Samuel
Wentworth House,
Portsmouth, N. H.
1761

Courtesy, The Metropolitan Museum of Art, New York.

Room from the Metcalf
Bowler House, Portsmouth, N. H. Before
1765

Courtesy, The Metropolitan Museum of Art, New York.

Gov. Benning Wentworth House, Little
Harbor, N. H. 1755

Whitefield *The Homes of Our
Forefathers*. 1880-86.

Wall Decorations

Courtesy, The Metropolitan Museum of Art, New York City.

Section of the great hall of the Van Rensselaer Manor House, Albany, N. Y. The wall paper was painted in London especially for this room, now restored in its 18th Century elegance in the American Wing of The Metropolitan Museum of Art, in New York.

Below is a view of the stairway of the Jeremiah Lee Mansion, Marblehead, Mass., (built 1768), also decorated with wall paper from London.

Courtesy, The Essex Institute, Salem, Mass.

Down South

Left Daphne Room, Raleigh Tavern, Williamsburg, Va.

Courtesy, Colonial Williamsburg, Inc.
Photo by Richard Garrison.

Right Room from Almodington, Maryland. ca. 1750

Courtesy, Metropolitan Museum of Art, New York.

Left Room from "The Abbey", Chestertown, Md.

Courtesy, Baltimore Museum of Art, Baltimore.

Right Room from "Habre de Venture", Port Tobacco, Charles County, Md.

Courtesy, Baltimore Museum of Art, Baltimore.

Annapolis

Left Brice House, Annapolis, Md. 1740

Below Paca House, Annapolis, Md. 1763

Both pictures *courtesy*, Hayman Collection, Hall of Records, Annapolis, Md.

Baltimore

Below Mount Clare, Baltimore, Md. 1754

Courtesy, Mr. Laurence Hall Fowler, Baltimore.

Charleston

Above Gibbes House, Charleston, S. C.

Left Pringle House, Charleston, S. C.

Humble Architecture

Despite the sumptuousness of many colonial mansions there was nothing approaching modern plumbing or even that of ancient Rome. The "temple" was a necessary adjunct to every home, but in spite of its architectural adornments it was still a privy.

Courtesy, Historic American Buildings Survey,
Washington, D. C.

Nathan Dean's privy. East Taunton,
Mass.

Stoney *Plantations of the Carolina Low Country.* 1939.
Courtesy, Carolina Art Association, Charleston, S. C. Photo by Ben Judah Lubschez.

Kitchen. "Oakland", in South Carolina

Courtesy, Historic American Buildings Survey,
Washington, D. C.

Judge Samuel Horton's privy.
Danvers, Mass.

Courtesy, Historic American Buildings Survey, Washington, D. C.

Meat house. "Old House of the Hinges",
East New Market, Md.

Right Smokehouse. "Mordington"
Frederica vicinity, Delaware

Courtesy, Historic American Buildings Survey,
Washington, D. C.

Poems In Silver

The silverware of the period was in keeping with the fine houses. It has never been surpassed.

Silver chafing dish by John Burt, Boston
Courtesy, Metropolitan Museum of Art, New York.

Silver salt cellars by Charles Le Roux, New York
Courtesy, Metropolitan Museum of Art, New York.

Courtesy, Collection of Mrs. de Lancey Walton Ward and the Museum of the City of New York. Silver marrow spoon by Thomas Hammersley

Top of silver caster by Jonathan Otis, Newport, R. I
Courtesy, Metropolitan Museum of Art, New York.

Silver cream pitcher and sugar bowl by Paul Revere, Boston
Courtesy, Metropolitan Museum of Art, New York.

Silver tongs by William Grigg, New York
Courtesy, Metropolitan Museum of Art, New York.

Silver tankard by John Le Roux,
New York

Moulds for "rat tail" spoons

Proud . . .

And Humble

Gourd dipper

Silver soup tureen and pair of vegetable dishes belonging to the
Livingston family. By J. B. Fouache. These reflect contemporary
European taste

Fine China

Monteith Lowestoft
China objects from the table service of Samuel Chase, Annapolis, Md., with Chase
coat of arms

Stiegel Glass

The most beautiful glassware and ironware of America was made by William Henry Stiegel in Lancaster County, Pennsylvania. The self-styled "Baron" Stiegel operated Elizabeth Furnace and Charming Forge, the very names of which reflect the romantic spirit of this master craftsman.

Glassware by Stiegel

Courtesy,
Metropolitan Museum of Art, New York.

Courtesy, The Philadelphia Museum of Art, Philadelphia.

Courtesy, Metropolitan Museum of Art,
New York.

Courtesy, Metropolitan Museum of Art, New York.

Glassmakers at work

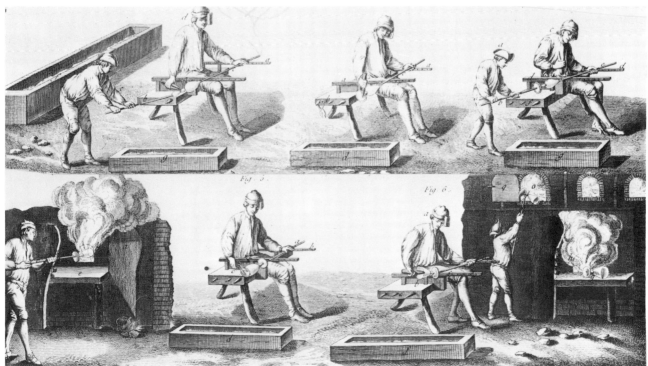

Diderot and D'Alembert *Encyclopedie. Recueil des planches.* 1762-72.

Fine Furniture

Courtesy, The Magazine Antiques.
Lowboy in style of William Savery, Philadelphia.
ca. 1750

Courtesy, The Magazine Antiques and Philip J. Birckhead.
Lowboy by John Goddard, Newport, R. I.
ca. 1760

Courtesy, Yale University Art Gallery.
Secretary by John Goddard, Newport, R. I. ca. 1770

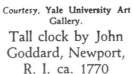

Courtesy, Yale University Art Gallery.
Tall clock by John Goddard, Newport, R. I. ca. 1770

Courtesy, Estate of George Drew Egbert, and the Museum of the City of New York.
Highboy. ca. 1760

Block-front escrutoire. 1760-70

Tall clock by William Claggett

Courtesy, The Magazine Antiques, New York.

Furniture label of William
Savery, Philadelphia

**Tick! Tock!
Tick! Tock!**

Courtesy, Mr. Charles W. Lyon, New York, and The Magazine Antiques.

Clock label of Aaron Willard, Boston

*Courtesy, Dr. J. Hall Pleasants,
Baltimore, Md.*

Clock face design by
Hyram Faris of An-
napolis

*Courtesy, Old Quinabaug Village,
Sturbridge, Mass.*

Tall clock by Benjamin
Cheney of Hartford,
Conn.

The Franklin Stove

Heating was a problem in the colonial house. One either baked in front of the fireplace or froze in the far corners of the room. Benjamin Franklin, the universal genius of the period, came forward with a stove which proved a blessing to mankind.

Courtesy, Landis Valley Museum, Landis Valley, Pa.

Cannon stove of the type designed by "Baron" Stiegel

Courtesy, The Metropolitan Museum of Art, New York.

The Franklin stove

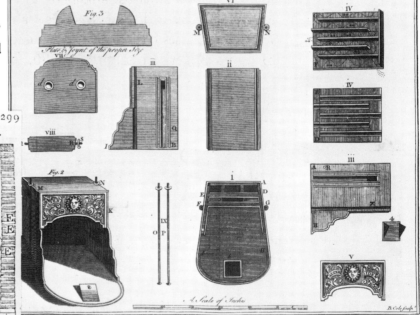

PROFILE of the CHIMNEY and FIRE-PLACE.

M The mantle-piece, or breast of the chimney.

C The funnel.

B The false back and closing.

E True back of the chimney.

T Top of the fire-place.

F The front of it.

A The place where the fire is made.

D The air-box.

K The hole in the side-plate, through which the warmed air is discharged out of the air-box into the room.

H The hollow filled with fresh air, entering at the passage I, and ascending into the air-box through the air-hole in the bottom plate near

G The partition in the hollow to keep the air and smoke apart.

P The passage under the false back and part of the hearth for the smoke.

The arrows show the course of the smoke.

The fire being made at A, the flame and smoke will ascend and strike the top T, which will thereby receive a considerable heat. The smoke, finding no passage upwards, turns over the top of the air-box, and descends between it and the back plate to the holes at B, in the bottom plate, heating, as it passes, both plates of the air-box,

Benjamin Franklin *Experiments and Observations on Electricity.* 4th edition. 1769.

Illustration showing the construction of the Franklin stove

Stove Plates

Pennsylvania craftsmen designed beautiful stove plates and fire backs.

Courtesy, Bucks County Historical Society, Doylestown, Pa.

Amusements

Courtesy, National Gallery of Art, Washington, D. C.

The men and women of the American colonies enjoyed life. Those who could afford it went to the theatre, rode to hounds, played billiards, attended balls and assemblies. The poor played cards, went fishing and hunting, attended horse races, fairs, markets, husking bees, or got drunk in the local taverns. All classes consumed enormous quantities of cider, beer, and rum. *Above*, "End of the fox hunt," American school, ca. 1780.

TO BE RUN FOR,
At SUNBURY, on THURSDAY the firſt of DECEMBER next,
A GIVE-AND-TAKE-PURSE OF
TWENTY POUNDS STERLING,
The beſt in three heats, each heat two miles, on the follow-
ing conditions, viz.

HORSES 14 hands high to carry 10 ſtone, all above that to carry weight for inches, and all under to be allowed the odds.

No horſe to ſtart, unleſs proof is made that the horſe has been ten weeks in the province before the day of running.

Each perſon entering a horſe, if a ſubſcriber, to pay half a guinea for each horſe, and every other perſon to pay a gui-nea and a half; provided the horſes be entered ten days be-fore the day of running; any horſe entered after that day to pay three guineas.

No ſubſcriber allowed to enter another man's horſe to ſave the entrance money.

Likewiſe to be run the day following, a PURSE, value FIFTEEN POUNDS STERLING. The conditions as a-bove.—No horſe who run the firſt day to ſtart for this purſe. The third day's ſport is the INNKEEPER's PURSE, va-lue at leaſt SIX POUNDS STERLING, for Galloways not above 13 hands high, to carry 8 ſtone, all under to be allow-ed weight for inches.

An ASSEMBLY each night at Mr. WILLIAMS's long-room.

There will be encouragement for cudgel-playing every forenoon, &c. &c. &c.

Georgia Gazette, Oct. 20, 1763.
Courtesy, Massachusetts Historical Society, Boston.

To be SOLD, by
LEAKE & BANCKER,
Near the *Fly-Market*,
A parcel of choice Weſt-India &
New-York *diſtill'd* RUM, *molaſſes, coarſe and fine ſalt, cordage, and a parcel of ſoal and upper leather, alſo a few caſes of drinking-glaſſes, and decanters,* &c.

To be SOLD, by
Benjamin Payne,
At his Houſe oppoſite the *Old-Slip-Market*, at the Sign of Admiral WARREN;
*Choice*Madeira *wine, rum, brandy, geneva and arrack ; bohea tea and* Muſcovado *ſugar, with ſundry other liquors by wholeſale or retale.*

From *New York Mercury*, Oct. and Dec., 1753.
Courtesy, New-York Historical Society.

The Cup That Cheers

Courtesy, Metropolitan Museum of Art, New York.

Doorway. Captain Clapp's Tavern, Westfield, Mass. ca. 1750

Raleigh Tavern   *Courtesy, Colonial Williamsburg*

Virginia gentlemen talked politics, horses, and intrigues
in the barroom of the Raleigh Tavern in Williamsburg.

Billiards

Diderot and D'Alembert *Encyclopedie. Recueil des planches.* 1762-72.

The Early Theatre

Some of the gentlemen in the Raleigh Tavern bar may have just come from a performance of Shakespeare's *The Merchant of Venice*.

They also bought lottery tickets. Lotteries were the rage. Americans have always liked to bet or take chances. Lottery tickets helped build some of the early American colleges and hospitals.

By Permission of the Honble ROBERT DINWIDDIE, Esq; His Majesty's Lieutenant-Governor, and Commander in Chief of the Colony and Dominion of *Virginia*.

By a Company of COMEDIANS, from LONDON, At the THEATRE in WILLIAMSBURG, On *Friday* next, being the 15th of *September*, will be presented, A PLAY, Call'd,

THE MERCHANT of VENICE.

(Written by *Shakespear*.)
The Part of ANTONIO (the MERCHANT) to be perform'd by **Mr. CLARKSON.**

GRATIANO, by Mr. SINGLETON, *Lorenzo*, (with Songs in Character) by Mr. ADCOCK. The Part of BASSANIO to be perform'd by **Mr. RIGBY.**

Duke, by Mr. Wynell.
Salanio, by Mr. Herbert.
The Part of LAUNCELOT, by Mr. HALLAM. And the Part of SHYLOCK, (the Jew) to be perform'd by **Mr. MALONE.**

The Part of NERISSA, by Mrs. ADCOCK, *Jessica*, by Mrs. Rigby. And the Part of PORTIA, to be perform'd by **Mrs. HALLAM.**

With a new occasional PROLOGUE. To which will be added, a FARCE, call'd,

The ANATOMIST: OR, SHAM DOCTOR.

The Part of *Monsieur le Medecin*, by **Mr. RIGBY.**

And the Part of BEATRICE, by Mrs. ADCOCK.
No Person, whatsoever, to be admitted behind the Scenes.
BOXES, 7s. 6d. PIT and BALCONIES, 5s. 9d. GALLERY, 3s. 9d.
To begin at Six o'Clock.

Vivat Rex.

THE Snow *Frances*, Paul *Loyall*, Master, who will be at his Moorings, at Capt. Danfie's, in Pamunky, will take in Tobacco for London, either from York or Rappahanock River, at 7 l. per Ton, with Liberty of Consignment. Gentlemen inclined are defired to send their Orders to Mr. *John Norton*, Mr. Hugh Mills the Printer hereof, or to

Theatre advertisement in the *Virginia Gazette*, Williamsburg, Va. Aug. 28, 1752

Courtesy, Bella C. Landauer Collection, The New-York Historical Society, New York.

Lottery ticket of George Washington, 1768

Courtesy, Bella C. Landauer Collection, The New-York Historical Society, New York.

Lottery ticket of William Byrd, 1767

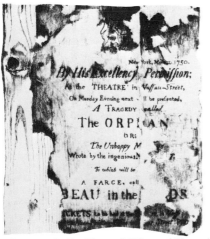

Courtesy, the President and Fellows of Harvard College.

Earliest American playbill extant, 1750. Nassau-Street Theatre, New York. The play was Otway's *The Orphan*, followed by a farce called *Beau in the Sudds*

By Permission.
THIS is to inform the PUBLICK, That this EVENING, being Monday the 3d Instant, Will be exhibited (*for the last Night but five*) at a new House built for that Purpose, in *Adam Van Denberg's* Garden, The usual Performances of the celebrated *Anthony Joseph Dugee*, On a Slack Wire scarcely perceptible, with and without a Balance. I. He raises the Wire to a Swing, then rises on his Feet, walking forwards and backwards in full Swing; and turns himself, and swings to Admiration on one Foot. II. He will balance a Hat on his Nose. III. He balances a Straw on the Edge of the Rim of his Hat. IV. He plays with four Balls at once, in a surprizing Manner. V. He balances a Pyramid of Glasses full of Wine, on the Edge of a drinking Glass. VI. He will stand on his Head on the Wire, in full Swing. VII. He wheels a Whell-barrow, with his Negro Boy in it on the Wire. Also, Several new Exercises on the Stiff-Rope, by Mr. DUGEE, the Indian, and young Negro Boy. In particular, the Indian intends to entertain the Company, by eating his Supper standing on his Head at the same Time, on the Nob of a Chair. With several curious Equilibres, on a Table, three Pins and a Chair, by the young Negro Boy. The whole to conclude with a Dance, called, the Drunken Peasant. Doors open'd at six o'Clock, and to begin precisely at Seven. TICKETS to be Sold at the House of Mr. *James Ackland*, at the Royal-Exchange; and at the Printing-Office opposite the Old-Slip-Market, PITT, four Shillings, GALLERY, two Shillings.
N. B. Mr. Dugee intends to perform every Monday, Wednesday and Friday, in every Week during his Residence here, but there will be different Performances every Night.

Advertisement in the *New York Mercury*. 1753

Harvard Boys Played Cricket . . .

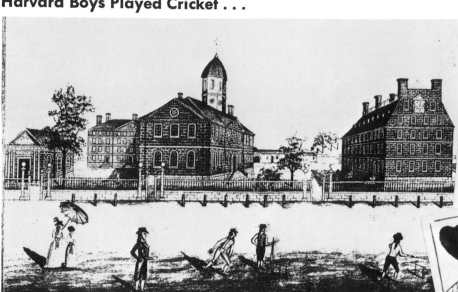

Courtesy, The Colonial Society of Massachusetts, Boston.

View of Harvard College. 1795

Or Rode Over to Charlestown
To See a Spectacle . . .

or Played At Cards

A few LINES on
Magnus Mode, Richard Hodges & J. Newington Clark.
Who are Sentenc'd to stand one Hour in the

Pillory at Charlestown;

To have one of their EARS cut off, and to be Whipped 20 Stripes at the public Whipping-Post, for making and passing Counterfeit DOLLARS, &c.

BEHOLD the villains rais'd on high !
(The Post they've got attracts the eye :)
Both Jews and Gentiles all appear
To see them stand exalted here ;
Both rich and poor, both young and old,
The dirty slut, the common scold :
What multitudes do them surround,
Many as bad as can be found.
And to encrease their sad disgrace,
Throw rotten eggs into their face,
And pelt them sore with dirt and stones,
Nay, if they could wou'd break their bones.
Their malice to such height arise,
Who knows but they'll put out their eyes :
But pray consider what you do
While thus expos'd to public view.
Justice has often done its part,
And made the guilty rebels smart ;
But they went on did still rebel,
And seem'd to storm the gates of hell.
To no good counsel would they hear,
But now each one must loose an EAR,

And they although against their will
Are forc'd to chew this bitter pil :
And this day brings the villains hence
To suffer for their late offence ;
They on th' Pillory stand in view :
A warning firs to me and you !
The drunkards sung, the harlots scorn,
Reproach of some as yet unborn.
But now the Post they're forc'd to hug,
But loath to take that naufeous drug
Which brings the blood from out their veins,
And marks their back with purple stains.
From their disgrace, now warning take,
And never do your ruin make
By stealing, or unlawful ways ;
(If you would live out all your days)
But keep secure from Theft and Pride ;
Strive to have virtue on your side.
Despise the harlot's flattering airs,
And hate her ways, avoid her snares ;
Keep clear from Sin of every kind,
And then you'll have true peace of Mind.

Courtesy, The New York Public Library.

Broadside. 1767

Courtesy, Cincinnati Art Museum, Cincinnati.

18th Century playing cards exported to America by Henry Hart of London

Extra! Extra!

Morbid broadsides took the place of sensational newspaper stories in the colonial era. Here is a typical one from Salem, Massachusetts, with all its gruesome details.

S B M D N D E M M W W W D H L K P K R G

THE

PARTICULARS

Of the late melancholly and shocking

TRAGEDY,

Which happened at *Salem*, near *Boston*, on Thursday, the 17th Day of *June*, 1773.

Which Particulars, together with the Verses that are annexed, are printed in this Form at the Request of the Friends and Acquaintance of the Ten deceased Persons, and are recommended as very proper to be posted up in every House in NEW-ENGLAND, to keep in Remembrance the most sorrowful Event, of the Kind, that has happen'd in AMERICA since its first Discovery. But to depicture this unhappy Catastrophe in its true Colours, must shock the tenderest Feelings of Humanity, and would serve to extenuate this Detail to the Size of a Volume, instead of a Sheet.— Shocking indeed must one imagine it for their Friends on Shore at MARBLEHEAD, and at the small Distance of an Hundred Yards, to behold these distressed People just launching into Eternity, and not able to afford them the least of their wonted Assistance! Surely the Shrieks and Cries of the poor drowning Souls, which seemed to reach the Heavens (more especially the Lamentations of the Women, as the pregnant Situation of Five of them made the Scene more dreadful) must pierce the Soul of the Spectator, and melt his Heart, ever were it adamant!

SALEM, June, 1773.

THURSDAY, the Seventeenth, towards the Evening, (the preceeding Part of the Day having been very warm) the Horizon, Westward and Northward, was rendered very dark and gloomy by the extensive Appearance of many black Clouds, presaging a Thunder Storm ; it however consisted chiefly of heavy Gusts of Wind. At this Time four or five Boats from the Harbour, were employed in bringing paving Stones from the Islands below ; after much Concern with Regard to their Safety they all happily returned the next Day. Two or three Boats were also out, at the same Time, from this Place, on Parties of Pleasure ; but all returned safe excepting one, the Fate of which was, perhaps, one of the most distressing Events that ever happen'd in or near this Place, an Account of which is as follows :

A large two-mast Boat, belonging to the Custom-House, of twenty-nine Feet Keel, with a Deck extending about half-way from Head to Stern, forming a considerable Cabbin, with about seven Tons of Ballast, sailed from Capt. Derby's Wharf between 10 and 11 o'Clock in the Forenoon, proceeded to Baker's Island, where they went ashore, staid and dined. In the Afternoon they went on board the Boat, and stood to the Eastward of the Island, for the Purpose of Fishing ; then, about the Middle of the Afternoon, returned and anchored between Baker's-Island and the Misery (Island,) where they drank Tea. After they came to Sail again the Clouds were seen rising ; and as the Weather appeared dark and threatening, they determined to try for Marblehead Harbour. As the Wind arose, they furl'd the Jibb, and took a double Reef in their Mainsail.— Mr. William Ward was the Commander of the Boat ; and as the Wind increased, he was desired by the other Men, who apprehended Danger, to lower the Sails ; but he declined, saying the Boat would stand it ; and the others, trusting his Judgment, thought proper to submit. The 7 Women were all confined in the Cabbin. About 7 o'Clock, Ward being at Helm, a sudden, smart

Gust of Wind canted the Boat over on one Side ; Mr. John Becket, who stood near the Cabbin, opened the Door, but had only Time to tell the Women they were all going to the Bottom ; he heard their Shrieks, immediately jumped upon the Deck, and the Boat instantly sunk. Out of 12 Persons on board, 10 were drowned.

The Names of the Deceased are as follow, viz.

Mrs. *Sarah Becket*, Wife of Mr. John Becket, and Daughter of Mr. William Brown, deceased.
Mr. *Nathaniel Diggadon*, Tidewaiter ; and Mrs. *Diggadon*, his Wife.
Mr. *William Ward*, Boatman ; and Mrs. *Mary Ward*, his Wife, Daughter of Mr. John Masury.
Miss *Esther Masury*, Sister to the above Mrs. Ward.
Mrs. *Desire Holman*, Wife of Mr. John Holman, Mariner, now at Sea.
Mr. *Paul Kimball*, Cooper, and Mrs. *Lydia Kimball*, his Wife, Daughter of Dr. Fairfield.
Mrs. *Rebecca Giles*, Widow of the late Mr. Eleazer Giles, and Daughter of Capt. John White.

Mr. *John Becket*, Husband to the above Mrs. *Becket*, and his Apprentice, named *Philip Becket*, were the only two who were saved.

Mr. Becket found that they, Kimball, Ward, and Diggadon, had got into a small Skiff, (which floated off the Boat as she sunk) and the Lad had hold of a Piece of Plank, about three Feet long. Mr. Becket swam for the Skiff, which before he could reach, overset, when Kimball and Diggadon sunk ; Ward got hold of Mr. Becket, but in a Minute or two was disengaged and sunk also. There were now none left but Mr. Becket and the Lad, the former held to the Skiff, and the latter to the Piece of Plank.—As this Disaster happened within about one Mile of Marblehead, it was

seen by some People there, who, by their timely and vigorous Efforts, got off a small Schooner, which the Tide had left a-Ground near a Fort, and happily took up Mr. Becket and the Lad, after they had been in the Water about half an Hour.

The next Day, Friday, a great Number of People, from this Town and Marblehead, in two Sloops and a Number of Boats, went off to endeavour to weigh the sunken Boat, (one of the Masts of which could just be seen at low Water) and also to recover the Bodies.— They succeeded in getting up the Boat, and after towing her up to a Wharf, which they reached between 8 and 9 o'Clock in the Evening, searched the Cabbin for the Bodies of the unfortunate Women, when those of Mrs. Giles, Mrs. Becket, Mrs. Kimball, Mrs. Ward, Mrs. Holman, and Miss Masury, were found, all of which were landed on the same Wharf from which so much Cheerfulness and Gaiety they departed the Day before.

The Bodies of the three Men are not found : And that of Mrs. Diggadon, which was thought to be in the Cabbin, is missing. The six that were found were all buried on Saturday, Mrs. Ward and her Sister (Miss Esther Masury) in one Grave, and the others separate. The Solemnity of the several Processions drew together a vast Number of People, and the Funerals were attended by People of all Ranks.

This Event is rendered still more affecting by the Situation of the five married Women, who, it is said, were all pregnant, and 2 or 3 of them far advanced.

We are desired to mention, that it was owing to the Assistance received from Marblehead, that the Attempt to weigh the Boat so well succeeded as to get her up on Friday : Some of the most respectable Inhabitants of that Town, Captains of Vessels, and a great Number of others, exerted themselves in an extraordinary Manner for that Purpose ; for which they have the sincere Thanks of the Friends of the deceased in particular, as well as the most grateful Acknowledgment of the Town in general.

The *Salem* TRAGEDY.

Being a Relation of the drowning of Ten Persons, who were taking their Pleasure on the Water, June 17th, 1773.

YOU who at Morning call your Friends
To mingle in Delight,
Think seriously what sad Events
Happen before Night.

2. This smiling Company were met,
And left the Wharf all gay,
Which of them when he trod the Boat
Thought it was their dying Day.

3. The Pastimes of the Day were o'er,
They sat at chearful Tea :
The Winds and Waves begin to roar,
And Death demands his Prey.

4. How couldst thou, Pilot, hear the Cry,
O low'r, O low'r the Sail !"
Fool-hardy thou thy Skill must try,
Nor female Shrieks prevail.

5. See how the Picture shews all this,
So dismally adorn'd !
Frolicks are finish'd, Sports are past,
And Boats to Coffins turn'd.

Salem tragedy. Broadside dated 1773

Fire! Fire!

Fires were always exciting events for young and old. Everyone came running post haste to the scene of the blaze.

Courtesy, North Carolina Historical Commission, Raleigh, N. C.

Fire engine. Salem, N. C. It was ordered from Europe in 1784

Courtesy, Old Quinabaug Village, Sturbridge, Mass.

Leather fire buckets from Portsmouth, N. H. 1789

Courtesy, New Hampshire Antiquarian Society, Hopkinton, N. H. Kimball Studio.

Fire engine, New Hampshire

Fireman's certificate. New York. 1787

Valentine s Manual. 1851.

Public Health

Poor sanitation, the lack of doctors, cold houses, and the rigors of colonial life resulted in a high mortality rate. Quack doctors flourished, surgery was brutal, and epidemics raged uncontrolled. The apothecary's shop dispensed pills and powders.

Drugs

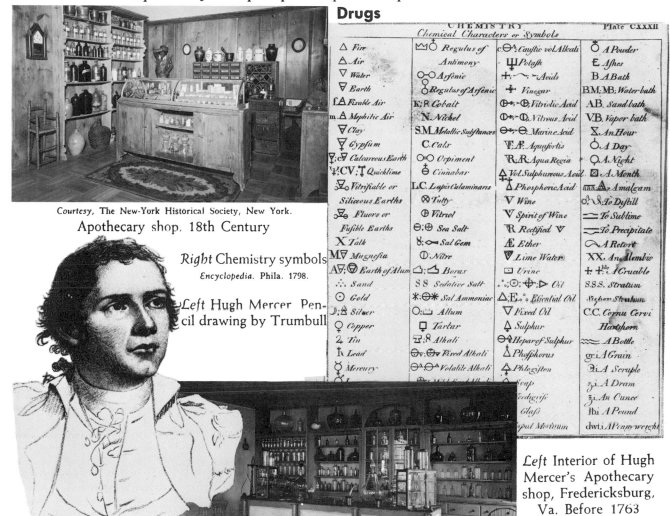

Courtesy, The New-York Historical Society, New York.
Apothecary shop. 18th Century

Right Chemistry symbols
Encyclopedia. Phila. 1798.

Left Hugh Mercer Pencil drawing by Trumbull

Left Interior of Hugh Mercer's Apothecary shop, Fredericksburg, Va. Before 1763
Courtesy, Mrs. Louise W. Carmichael.

Just imported from London, in the Good-Intent, Capt. Reddick, and to be sold by the Subscriber, in Williamsburg,

A LARGE Assortment of Drugs and Medicines, viz.——Verdigrease, Quickfilver, Allom, Antimony, Flour and Roll Brimstone, Borax, Sandiver, Spelter, white and yellow Arsnick, Balsam Tolu, Peru and Capivi, best Ruffia and New-England Castor, white Wax, Cremor Tartar, Jesuits Bark, Spanish Flies, Senna, Vermilion, Camomile Flowers, Colocynth, Scammony, French and Pearl Barley, red and white Lead, Mercury, common and flakey Manna, Opium, Oyl of Turpentine, Aqua Regia, China and Sarsaparilla Roots, fine Turky Rhubarb, Ipecacuana, Jallap, yellow and black Rofin, Epsom's and Glauber's Salts, Liquorice, Spermaceti, Tartar-Emetick, Crucibles, black Lead Pots, Lunar Caustick, Smelling-Bottles, Saffron, Tamarinds, Gold Leaf, Dutch Metal, Hartshorn Shavings, Essence of Lemons and Bergamet, Currans, Sallad and Barbers Oyl, Spices of all Sorts, white and brown Sugar-Candy, Barley Sugar, Almond Comfits, Carraway Comfits, Sugar Plumbs, candied Eryngo, candied Ginger, candied Angelica, candied Nutmegs, Almonds, Frances's Female strengthening Elixir, Bateman's and Stoughton's Drops, Daffy's and Squire's Elixir, Anderson's and Lockyer's Pills, Annodyne Necklaces, British Rock-Oyl, Turlington's Balsam, best Durham Flour of Muftard, Greenough's Tincture for the Gums and Teeth, Do. for the Toothake, Tooth Brushes, Eaton's Styptick, James's Fever-Powders, Saltpetre, Citron, Anchovies, Capers, Olives, Pruffian Blue, &c.

William Pasteur.

Advertisement in the *Virginia Gazette.*
Nov. 30, 1759
Hugh Mercer's Apothecary shop, Fredericksburg, Va.
Courtesy, Mrs. Louise W. Carmichael.

The Poor and the Afflicted

Courtesy, Stokes Collection, The New York Public Library.

A view of the House of Employment, Alms-House, Pennsylvania Hospital, and part of the City of Philadelphia. Engraved by J. Hulett after a drawing by Nicholas Garrison. 1767. The House of Employment was built in 1767. The hospital was first opened in 1756

Philadelphia was the medical center of America. Benjamin Rush, John Redman, William Shippen, John Morgan, Abraham Chovet, Thomas Cadwalader, and John Kearsley, Sr., were all great doctors.

Benjamin Rush, M. D. After a
portrait by Thomas Sully

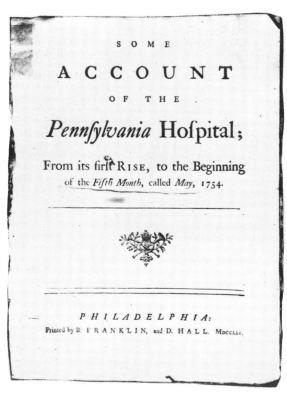

SOME

ACCOUNT

OF THE

Pennsylvania Hospital;

From its first RISE, to the Beginning
of the *Fifth Month*, called *May*, 1754.

PHILADELPHIA:
Printed by B. FRANKLIN, and D. HALL. MDCCLIV.

PHILADELPHIA, *July* 16.
Extract of a Letter from Chester, in Pennsylvania, July 13, 1752.
"On Thursday last a Person that went by the Name of Charles Hamilton came here, and offered to Sale at several Houses in Town sundry Medicines for different Disorders; pretending he was brought up to the Business of a Doctor and Surgeon, under one Doctor GREEN, a noted Mountebank in England; and that he embarked on Board a Brigantine, at Topsham, in England, last Fall, for Philadelphia, one Robinson Commander, but was cast away the latter End of January on the Coast of North-Carolina; and that he had travelled from thence through Virginia and Maryland, and has a Pass signed by some Magistrates in Virginia and Maryland, and one in Newcastle County: But it being suspected that the Doctor was a Woman in Mens Cloaths, was taken up, examined, and found to be a Woman; and confessed that she had used that Disguise for several Years. She is very bold, and can give no good Account of herself; says she is about Twenty-eight Years of Age, though she seems to be about Forty. She wears a blue Camblet Coat, with Silver Twist Buttons, too large for her. She is detained in Prison here, 'til we see whether any Body appears against her, if not she will be discharged. She says now her Name is Charlotte Hamilton."

Item from *Virginia Gazette*, Aug. 28, 1752

Runaway Slaves

After 1750 Negro slavery became more and more of an economic problem. Agriculture, particularly in the South, was based largely on this cheap labor. Many New England families owned Negro servants and apprentices. Both in the North and the South the Negro was regarded as property, and was bought and sold at public auction. Often slaves attempted to run away and the newspapers of the day were filled with advertisements offering rewards for their apprehension.

Virginia, ff.

By the Honourable ROBERT DINWIDDIE, Efq; His Majefty's Lieutenant Governor, and Commander in Chief, of the Colony and Dominion of *Virginia* :

To all Sheriffs, Conftables, and other His Majefty's Liege People, to whom thefe Prefents fhall come. Greeting.

WHEREAS *Dick*, a Negroe Man Slave, belonging to *Tarftall Hack*, of the County of *Northumberland*, in the Night of the third of *July* laft paft, entered the Dwelling Houfe of his faid Mafter, and grievoufly wounding him with a Broad-Ax, in the left Shoulder and Arm, with an Intent to murder his faid Mafter, and hath fince fled from Juftice : The faid *Dick* is a well-fet, artful, and cunning Fellow, about forty Years of Age, five Feet feven or eight Inches high, broad Shoulders, large Hips, a fmall Waift, Bow Leggs, and flat Feet, his Teeth very open before, has fome grey Hairs in his Head and Beard, and feveral Scars on his Head ; he underftands going by Water, Shoe-making, Carpenters Work, and Sawing.

THESE are therefore in His Majefty's Name, to command and require all Sheriffs, Conftables, and other His Majefty's Liege People, within this Colony, to make diligent Search and Purfuit, by Way of Hue and Cry, within their feveral Counties and Precincts, after the faid *Dick* ; and him having found, to apprehend and carry before the next Juftice of the Peace, that he may be dealt with according to Law. And I do defire the Governors of the neighbouring Colonies and Provinces, to be affifting in bringing the faid *Dick* to Juftice.

GIVEN under my Hand, and the Seal of the Colony, at Williamfburg, this 21ft Day of Auguft, One Thoufand Seven Hundred and Fifty Two, in the Twenty Sixth Year of the Reign of our Sovereign Lord King GEORGE the Second.

ROBERT DINWIDDIE.

N. B. The faid *Dick* is outlawed, and a Reward of Three Piftoles is to be given to any Perfon that fhall apprehend him in this Colony, and if taken in any other Colony the Reward is Five Piftoles.

TO BE SOLD on board the Ship *Bance-Yland*, on tuefday the 6th of *May* next, at *Afhley-Ferry* ; a choice cargo of about 250 fine healthy

NEGROES,

juft arrived from the Windward & Rice Coaft. —The utmoft care has already been taken, and fhall be continued, to keep them free from the leaft danger of being infected with the SMALL-POX, no boat having been on board, and all other communication with people from *Charles-Town* prevented.

Auftin, Laurens, & Appleby.

N. B. Full one Half of the above Negroes have had the SMALL-POX in their own Country.

Courtesy, The Library of Congress, Washington, D. C. ca. 1763.

Slave auction

August 14, 17 2.

RAN from the Subfcriber, at *Hampton*, Two Negroe Men, one named *Boatfwain*, a lufty Fellow, he has had the Small-pox, and has been mark'd on the Temple ; had on a brown Linen Shirt, wide Trowfers, and blue Fearnothing Waftecoat. The other named *George*, a very black, fhort, well-fet Fellow ; had on a white Shirt, black Plufh Breeches, and a blue Fearnothing Waftecoat. Whoever fecures and conveys them to me, at *Sarah*'s Creek, in *Gloucefter* County, fhall have a Piftole Reward for each, befides what the Law allows, paid by

2   *John Briggs.*

March 20, 1752.

RAN away from the Subfcriber, living in *Prince George* County, about a Fortnight ago, a lufty well-fet *Virginia*-born Negroe Man Slave, named *Vulin* ; he is a fmooth-tongued cunning Fellow, and it's probable will endeavour to impofe on People, by pretending to be what he is not ; and it's not unlikely will change his Name ; he is between 39 and 40 Years of Age, about 5 Feet 10 Inches high, and had 66 when he went away, an Oznabrigs Shirt, a Cotton Waiftcoat and Breeches, dy'd Yellow, and a Pair of Breeches not dy'd. Whoever will take up and fecure him, fo that I may have him again, fhall have Two Piftoles if taken up on the South Side of *James* River, if in *Carolina*, or the North Side of *James* River, Three Piftoles Reward, befides what the Law allows, paid by

William Broadnax.

Courtesy, Historic American Buildings Survey, Washington, D. C.

Slave quarters, "Hampton", Towson vicinity, Maryland

Work All Day Long

Negroes were brought from the sugar fields and cotton plantations of the West Indies.

Sugar plantation   *Pomet A Compleat History of Druggs. 1725.*

Cotton   Diderot and D'Alembert *Encyclopedie.*
Recueil des planches. 1762-72.

Tobacco   Courtesy, Mr. George Arents, New York.

Negro Poet

Some Negroes were given a liberal education. Phillis Wheatley the poet is a shining example.

Courtesy, The New York Public Library.

POEMS

ON

VARIOUS SUBJECTS,

RELIGIOUS AND MORAL.

BY

PHILLIS WHEATLEY,

NEGRO SERVANT to Mr. JOHN WHEATLEY,
of BOSTON, in NEW ENGLAND.

LONDON:
Printed for A. BELL, Bookseller, Aldgate; and sold by
Messrs. COX and BERRY, King-Street, BOSTON.
MDCCLXXIII.

Children

The pleasures and hardships of childhood in the colonial era were largely dependent upon circumstances of birth and environment. The wealthier families gave their children expensive toys and beautiful clothing; the poorer families gave their children homemade toys and garments, and, all too often, exacted long hours of labor from them. Many became apprentices to hard taskmasters at a tender age. They matured rapidly. In conformity to the traditions of gentility which then prevailed all children were taught good manners. Disrespect to one's elders brought quick punishment.

Courtesy, Essex Institute, Salem, Mass.

Sarah (Northey) King and her daughter.
Artist unknown

Courtesy, Maryland Historical Society, and Frick Art Reference Library, New York.

Eleanor Darnall (later Mrs. Daniel Carroll).
Portrait by J. E. Kühn

Courtesy, Mr. Ledlie Irwin Laughlin, Princeton, N. J.

Pewter nursing bottles, Colonial Period

Courtesy, The Bowdoin College Museum of Fine Arts, Brunswick, Me.

James Bowdoin III and his sister Elizabeth as children. ca. 1760.
Portrait by Joseph Blackburn

Toys

Kitchen toys. Probably New
York. 18th Century

Courtesy, The Metropolitan Museum of Art,
New York.

Below Jointed wooden dolls.
18th Century. The center doll is
of later date. The noses of the
18th Century dolls were carved,
not painted

Courtesy, Doll Museum, Wenham, Mass.

Dolls

Courtesy, Museum of the City of New York

"Abigail Van Rensselaer." Wax doll.
ca. 1760

Grave doll. 18th Cen-
tury. When children died
their dolls were put in a
glass-covered box and
placed on the grave

Courtesy, Museum of the City of New York

Young Dreamer

Courtesy, Museum of Fine Arts, Boston.

Henry Pelham. Portrait by John Singleton Copley

Little Goody Twoshoes

Courtesy, Plimpton Collection, Columbia University Library, New York.

Pages from *The History of Little Goody Twoshoes*, 1787

Reading, Writing, And Arithmetic

Page from Thomas Dilworth's *A New Guide to the English Tongue*. 1770

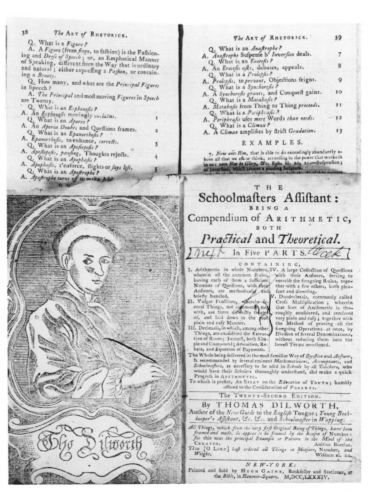

Selections from Dilworth's *Schoolmaster's Assistant*, 1784

Courtesy, Plimpton Collection, Columbia University Library, New York.

The House That Jack Built

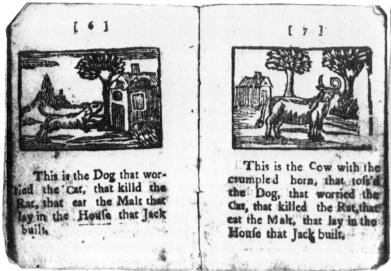

[6]

This is the Dog that wor-
ried the Cat, that killd the
Rat, that eat the Malt that
lay in the House that Jack
built.

[7]

This is the Cow with the
crumpled horn, that toss'd
the Dog, that worried the
Cat, that killed the Rat, that
eat the Malt, that lay in the
House that Jack built.

Courtesy, Plimpton Collection, Columbia University Library, New York.

Pages from *The House That Jack Built.* 1790

Juſt imported in the Captains
Shoals and Miller from London, and in the Grace,
Capt. Neallin, from Briſtol; a choice aſſortment of
EUROPEAN AND INDIA GOODS, ſuitable
for the ſeaſon, to be ſold cheap, by ASPINWALL
and DOUGHTY, at their ſtore next door to Col.
DePeyſter's, Treaſurer. Alſo Globe Lamps.

On Monday the 3d of December,
Inſt. the Revd. JOHN LEWIS MAYOR, begun
to teach French, Latin and Greek. Attendance
will be given from two to five o'clock in the afternoon, and from ſix to eight in the evening, ſaturday
excepted. Mr. Mayor is to be ſpoke with at Mrs.
Faviere's, near the Long-Bridge.

AT the Houſe formerly *Thomas Chalkley's*
in *Latitia* Court, near *Blackhorſe* Alley, are Taught
WRITING, ARITHMETICK, with the
true Grounds of the FRENCH TONGUE,
at *Twenty Shillings* per Quarter, by
THOMAS BALL.

P. S. For the more ſpeedy Inſtruction of his Scholars,
he has calculated the following Tables, *viz.* 1. A Table
for knowing the Genders of Nouns by their Terminations.
2. A Table for the Forming of Tenſes. 3. A Table of
all the irregular Verbs. 4. A Table repreſenting the
Terminations of the ſimple Tenſes of Verbs. Which Tables, together with a nice Explanation of all the *French
Particles* (now in the Preſs) will be of great Uſe to thoſe
who have a Deſire to learn a Language ſo neceſſary and
polite.

N. B. His Wife teaches Writing and French. Likewiſe Singing, Playing on the Spinet, Dancing, and all ſorts
of Needle-Work are taught by his Siſter lately arrived from
London.

Reading, writing, and arithme-
tick in all its parts, vulgar and decimal, logarith-
metical and inſtrumental; geometry, trigonometry,
plain and ſpherical; ſurveying, gauging and dialing,
aſtronomy, the projection of the ſphere upon the plan
of any circle, with the calculation and projection of
the eclipſes of the luminaries: Alſo navigation, as
plain, mercator, and great circle ſailing, by all the
various ways heretofore taught, *viz.* geomatrically,
logarithmetically, tabulary, or inſtrumentally; alſo
by a new and compleat method, without the help
of books, tables, ſcales, or mathematical inſtru-
ments: Alſo merchants accounts are carefully taught
at the corner houſe, near the *Quaker Meeting,* in
Crown-Street, (near Oſwego-Market) where young
men inclin'd to learn, may be boarded, and where
gentlemen may have any ſort of writing authentically
drawn, by   *JOHN NATHAN HUTCHINS.*

Advertising for pupils

Fraktur

Among the Pennsylvania Germans the art of
penmanship was highly developed, and certificates were decorated with what is known
as the fraktur method.

Courtesy, Philadelphia Museum of Art, Philadelphia.

Birth certificate, Pennsylvania. 1784.
Fraktur

School House

Nathan Hale School. New London, Conn.
Etching by James H. Fincken

Courtesy, Colonial Society of America.

The Almanack

The most widely read publications in all the colonies next to the Holy Bible were the almanacs. Farmers planted their crops according to the phases of the moon as recorded in the "almanack." Great faith was placed in the prognostications of these cheap publications. Interesting reading matter was placed in many of them, following the example of *Poor Robin*, a facetious English almanac. Court sessions, distances between towns, currency rates, and other facts were also given. In 1752 the New Style calendar was adopted, causing much confusion in dates. Conservatives clung to Old Style.

Stable. Woodlands. Philadelphia. 18th Century

Courtesy, Essex Institute, Salem, Mass.

Courtesy, The New York Public Library.

Pages from *Father Abraham's Almanack.* 1759

Courtesy, Essex Institute, Salem, Mass.

Barn. Osborne Place, Peabody, Mass. 18th Century

Conestoga Wagon

The Pennsylvania Germans developed a peculiar type of wagon adapted to transporting heavy loads long distances. They called this freight carrier the Conestoga Wagon.

Courtesy, Baltimore and Ohio Railroad.

Conestoga wagon

Conestoga wagons carried this equipment.

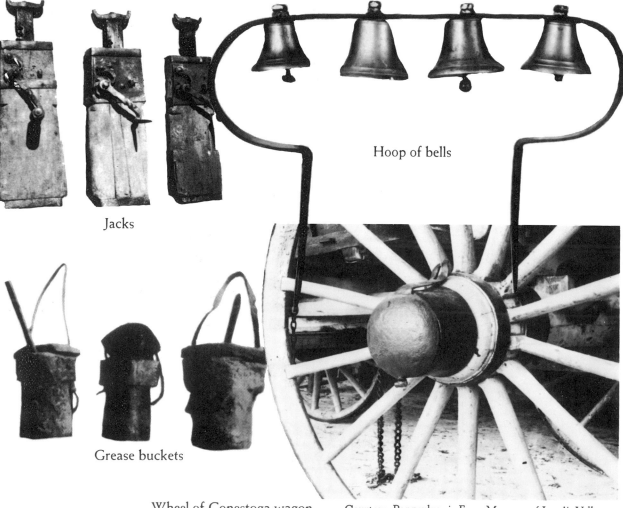

Jacks

Hoop of bells

Grease buckets

Wheel of Conestoga wagon   *Courtesy,* Pennsylvania Farm Museum of Landis Valley,
Lancaster Co., Pa.

Other Vehicles

Farm wagon. Tyngsboro, Mass. ca. 1750-1800

Buggy. New Hampshire. ca. 1780

Left Ox cart. Engraved from an original
painting by G. Harvey

French coach belonging
to James Beekman of
New York. ca. 1770.
Note the coat of arms
on the panel

Trade Unions

Labor was becoming self-conscious and societies were being organized for protection and improvement.

ARTICLES AND REGULATIONS

OF — THE

FRIENDLY SOCIETY — OF TRADESMEN,

HOUSE CARPENTERS, — In the City of *New-York*,

Made and agreed upon the 10th Day of *March*, in the Year of our LORD, 1767,

For the USES and CONSIDERATIONS herein after mentioned.

Courtesy, Broadside Collection, The New York Public Library.

The house carpenters of New York form a society

Carpenters at work

Diderot and D'Alembert *Encyclopedie.*
Recueil des planches. 1762-72.

The Graphic Arts

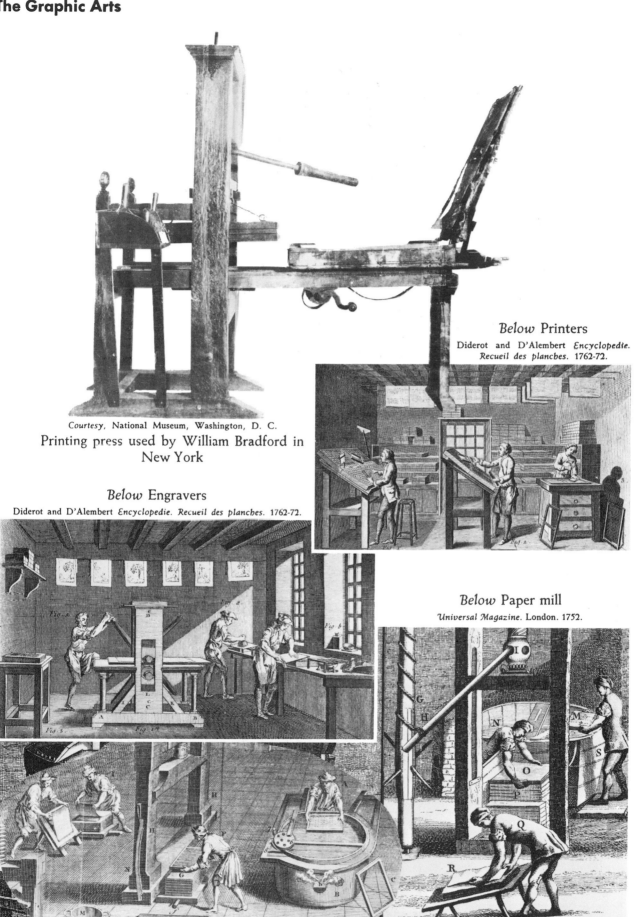

Courtesy, National Museum, Washington, D. C.

Printing press used by William Bradford in New York

Below Printers

Diderot and D'Alembert *Encyclopedie. Recueil des planches.* 1762-72.

Below Engravers

Diderot and D'Alembert *Encyclopedie. Recueil des planches.* 1762-72.

Below Paper mill

Universal Magazine. London. 1752.

Woodcuts

Newspaper illustration was extremely crude. A few small woodcuts were used in the advertising columns. The same ones were repeated over and over.

Courtesy, Tapley Salem Imprints (1927).

Electricity

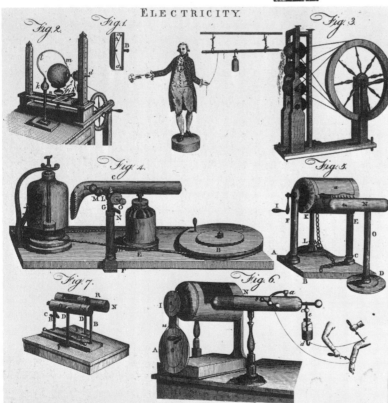

Benjamin Franklin and other scientists were experimenting with the Leyden jar and other electrical apparatus, but the powers of this newly-discovered phenomenon were but dimly recognized.

Left Electrical apparatus
Encyclopedia. Philadelphia. 1798.

Stonecutter's Art

The artists who cut inscriptions on tombstones were kept busy. Some of them became very proficient.

Courtesy, Essex Institute, Salem, Mass.
Gravestone. Charter Street Burying Ground, Salem, Mass.

The Bible In Iron

Courtesy, Bucks County Historical Society, Doylestown, Pa.
Stove plate made in Pennsylvania. Biblical subjects were popular

Left Pennsylvania German tombstone
Courtesy, Landis Valley Museum, Landis Valley, Pa.

Native Born Artists

Many leading American artists went to London to further their art studies—a few, such as Benjamin West and John Singleton Copley, remained there to take their place alongside the leading British painters. West even became the president of the Royal Academy in 1792, holding this distinguished honor until 1820.

Courtesy, Metropolitan Museum of Art, New York.

The American School. Painting by Matthew Pratt. 1765. This shows Benjamin West's studio in London. West is shown standing at the left correcting a drawing held by Matthew Pratt

Courtesy, Carolina Art Association, Charleston, S. C.

Portrait of Thomas Middleton, by Benjamin West

Courtesy, The Cleveland Museum of Art, Cleveland, Ohio.

Nathaniel Hurd, the Silversmith. Portrait by John Singleton Copley

Architecture

The first settlers built their houses themselves. As wealth increased professional architects were paid to make designs for mansions and public buildings.

Courtesy, Yale University Art Gallery.

William Buckland, architect. Portrait by Charles Willson Peale

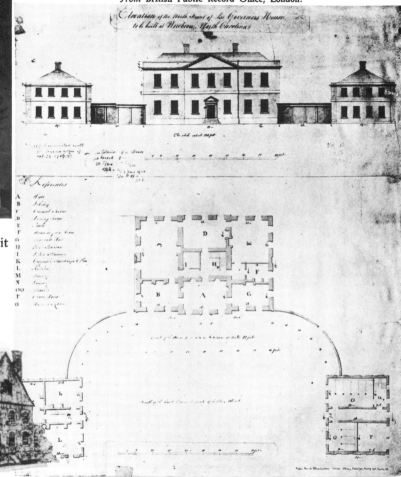

Below Plan of the palace of Gov. William Tryon of N. C., by John Hawks. 1767

From British Public Record Office, London.

Courtesy, Connecticut Magazine.

State House, New Haven, Conn. 1763

Wansey *The Journal of an Excursion to the United States of North America.* 1796.

State House. Philadelphia. Designed by Andrew Hamilton and John Kearsley

Fort Duquesne

We shall now turn to the military affairs of the American colonies. The final struggle between France and England for possession of America was set off by a clash for control of what is now Pittsburgh. The French had built Fort Duquesne at that strategic site.

The Crown Collection in the British Museum.
Left Fort Duquesne

Below Blockhouse of Fort Duquesne

Courtesy, The Stokes Collection, The New York Public Library.
View of Pittsburgh. Drawn by V. Collot or his companion Joseph Warin. 1796

Braddock's Expedition

In 1755, General Edward Braddock marched towards Fort Duquesne with a large force of British and provincial troops, but was defeated, and lost his own life in the battle. His insistence on arranging his troops in close formation instead of dispersing them among the trees in Indian fashion, cost him the victory. George Washington, a young Virginia surveyor, who knew Indian tactics as well as the terrain, had pleaded with Braddock to alter his strategy, but to no avail. Washington barely escaped with his own life in the disaster that followed.

Courtesy, New York State Library.

Surveying instruments of George Washington. Now owned by the New York State Library, Albany

Courtesy, The Valentine Museum, Richmond, Va.

Field desk of Virginia Walnut said to have been used in Braddock's campaign

Birthplace of George Washington, Bridges Creek, Westmoreland County, Va. Currier & Ives lithograph

The Ohio Country

The rich land of the Ohio Valley was the ultimate object of the British penetration. Traders had established posts in this country, but as long as the French were at Fort Duquesne the English settlements were jeopardized. In 1758 Brigadier-General John Forbes, and Colonel Henry Bouquet, who was second in command, captured Fort Duquesne. Forbes had advanced westward from Bedford, Pa., building Forbes Road through the wilderness as he went and studding it with blockhouses.

Fort Loudon

The capture of Fort Duquesne was partly offset by the loss of Fort Loudon on the Little Tennessee River to the disgruntled Cherokee Indians in 1760.

Colonel Bouquet in conference with the Indians. After a painting by Benjamin West

Vignette by F. O. C. Darley

Courtesy, Harvard University Library.

Plan of Fort Loudon by William Gerard De Brahm, the engineer who constructed it

Right Judd's Friend, or Outacite, Creek Indian. Sketch by Sir Joshua Reynolds, made in 1762 when Outacite was taken to London by Lieutenant Henry Timberlake

The Indians were divided in their loyalties, some fighting on the English side and some on the French. Sir William Johnson of New York Province won the lasting friendship of the Six Nations by acting as their agent and benefactor. His marriage to an Indian girl proved that his affection was genuine. He negotiated treaties for them and served as their military leader during the French and Indian wars.

Johnson Hall, Johnstown, N. Y. Residence of Sir William Johnson

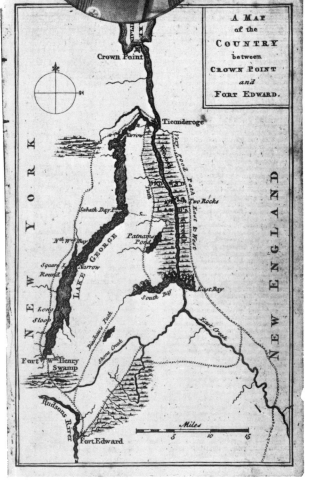

Left Portrait of Sir William Johnson

King Hendrick, Mohawk Sachem and friend of Sir William Johnson. He was regarded as the greatest Indian of his time. He was killed in the Battle of Lake George in Johnson's attempt to capture Crown Point in 1755

Friends or Foes?

The Mask of the Twisted Face

According to Indian legend an imposter was struck on the side of his face by a moving mountain when he dared to challenge the power of the creator.

Left Mask of the Twisted Face. Mohawk
Courtesy, Museum of the American Indian, Heye Foundation,
New York City.

The spirit of the Indian still haunts the hills and valleys of the white man.

Right Doctor mask. Seneca
Courtesy, Museum of the American Indian,
Heye Foundation, New York City.

By the Honorable
JOHN PENN, Esquire,

Lieutenant Governor and Commander in Chief of the Province of *Pennsylvania* and Counties of *New-Castle*, *Kent* and *Sussex* on DELAWARE.

To all to whom these Presents shall come, or may concern; Greeting:

Wᴴᴇʀᴇᴀꜱ   prayed my
Licence to trade with the Nations or Tribes of Indians, with whom his Majesty is connected, and who live under his protection; and   given security to observe such Regulations as his Majesty shall at any Time think fit, by himself, or by his Commissaries to be appointed for that Purpose, to order and direct for the Benefit of the Trade with the said Indians; and not to trade or traffick with; or vend, sell, or dispose, of any Goods, Wares or Merchandizes of any Kind whatever, to any Indian or Indians within the Country of any the Indian Nations aforesaid, beyond the Settlements of the Inhabitants, except at
the Forts or Posts which are already, or shall hereafter be established by his Majesty, and garrisoned by his Troops. I Do ᴛʜᴇʀᴇꜰᴏʀᴇ hereby authorize and impower the said
                        to trade with the said Nations or Tribes of Indians for the Space of one Year from the date hereof. This Licence to be void, and the Security forfeited in Case the said
                        shall refuse or neglect to observe such regulations as aforesaid.

GIVEN *under my Hand, and Seal at Arms, at* PHILADELPHIA, *the*
Day of   176 In the   Year of the Reign of Our Sovereign Lord
GᴇᴏʀGᴇ *the Third, by the Grace of* GOD, *of* GʀᴇᴀᴛBʀɪᴛᴀɪɴ, Fʀᴀɴᴄᴇ, *and* Iʀᴇʟᴀɴᴅ, Kɪɴɢ.
Defender of the Faith, and so forth.

By His Hᴏɴᴏᴜʀ's Command,

Licence to trade with the Indians

Rogers' Rangers

Major Robert Rogers and his Rangers terrified the French and Indians with their daring raids, and their method of attack was based on the Indian tactics of camouflage and ambush rather than on the traditional British open formations which cost so many lives. Rogers married Elizabeth Brown, a Portsmouth, N. H., belle, wrote a play on the Indian chief Pontiac, and, embittered over the government's lack of recognition of his talents, turned traitor during the American Revolution.

Major Robert Rogers

Elizabeth Browne (Mrs. Robert Rogers). Portrait by Joseph Blackburn

Left Powder horn used in the French and Indian wars. It belonged to Michael B. Goldthwaite. Dated Oct. 2, 1756, at Fort William Henry

Courtesy, Maine Historical Society, Portland, Me.

All Gentlemen Volunteers, and Others.

THAT have a Mind to serve his Majesty King GEORGE the Second, for a limited Time, in the Independant Companies of Rangers now in *Nova-Scotia*, may apply to Lieutenant *Alexander Callender*, at Mr. *Jonas Leonard's*, at the Sign of the *Lamb* at the South End of *Boston*, where they shall be kindly entertained, enter into present Pay, and have good Quarters, and when they join their respective Companies at *Hallifax*, shall be compleatly cloathed in blue Broad-Cloth, receive Arms, Accoutrements, Provisions, and all other Things necessary for a Gentleman Ranger: And for their further Encouragement, his Excellency Governor CORNWALLIS has by Proclamation lately published, promised a Reward of *Five Hundred Pounds*, old Tenor, for every *Indian* Scalp or Prisoner brought in, which Sum will be immediately paid by the Treasurer of the Province, upon the Scalp or Prisoner being produc'd.

N. B. Lieutenant *Callender* has obtained Leave from His Honour the Lieutenant Governor, to beat up for Rangers in any Part of this Province. *Boston*, September 8. 1750.

JUST PUBLISHED,
(And sold opposite the Prison in Queen-Street;)

*T*Rue RELIGION delineated ; Or, EXPERIMENTAL RELIGION as distinguished from FORMALITY on the one Hand, and ENTHUSIASM on the other, set in a Scriptural and Rational Light.

PONTEACH:

OR THE

Savages of America.

A

TRAGEDY.

LONDON:

Printed for the Author ; and Sold by J. MILLAN, opposite the Admiralty, Whitehall.

M.DCC.LXVI.
[Price 2 s. 6 d.]

Title-page of a play written by Major Robert Rogers

Excerpt from *Boston Weekly News Letter.*
Oct. 4, 1750

Residents of New England villages gathered at the taverns and churches to hear the latest news from soldiers home on furlough.

Hanson *History of the Old Towns of Norridgewock and Canaan.* 1849.

Oosoola, Me. A typical New England village

Whitefield *The Homes of Our Forefathers.* 1880-86.

Blockhouse. Winslow, Me.

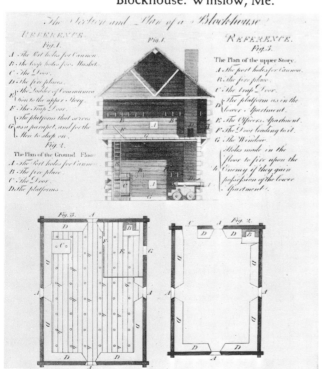

Marion J. Bradshaw *The Maine Land.* 1941.

First Congregational Church, Kennebunkport, Me. Built 1764

Left Plan of an American block house

Anburey *Travels Through America.* 1789.

Fort Oswego on Lake Ontario was the key to the Great Lakes. The British strongly fortified it and built their ships there.

A South View of OSWEGO, *on Lake Ontario, in North America.*

Fort Oswego. Note the shipbuilding going on
London Magazine. May 1760.

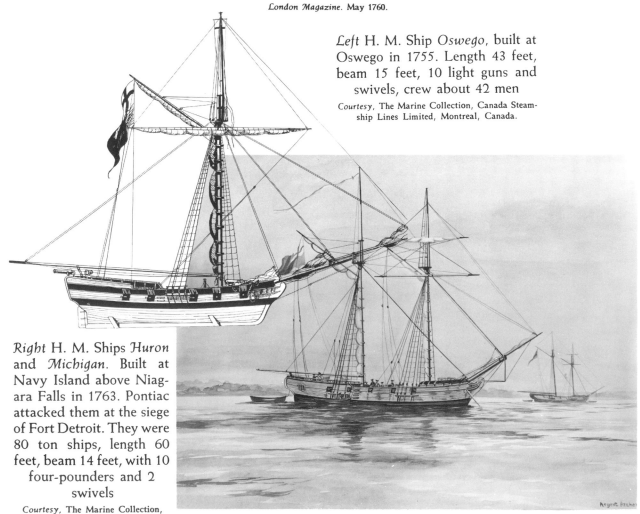

Left H. M. Ship *Oswego*, built at Oswego in 1755. Length 43 feet, beam 15 feet, 10 light guns and swivels, crew about 42 men

Courtesy, The Marine Collection, Canada Steamship Lines Limited, Montreal, Canada.

Right H. M. Ships *Huron* and *Michigan*. Built at Navy Island above Niagara Falls in 1763. Pontiac attacked them at the siege of Fort Detroit. They were 80 ton ships, length 60 feet, beam 14 feet, with 10 four-pounders and 2 swivels

Courtesy, The Marine Collection, Canada Steamship Lines Limited, Montreal, Canada.

Courtesy, The Marine Collection, Canada Steamship Lines Limited, Montreal, Canada.

The French fleet, Lake Ontario. 1757. Shows *L'Huron*, *La Marquise de Vaudreuil*, and other vessels.

Left Whaleboats used in 1758 by Col. Bradstreet's expedition to Fort Frontenac. They were brought up the Mohawk River from the Hudson, portaged over the Great Carrying Place to Lake Oneida, and then down the Onondaga River to Fort Oswego. Note the howitzers and shields. The boats were 35 feet long. Bradstreet used about 200 of them in this expedition

Courtesy, The Marine Collection, Canada Steamship Lines Limited, Montreal, Canada.

Ticonderoga. Note the whaleboat and howitzer

The Crown Collection in the British Museum.

Quebec

The stronghold of the French was at Quebec. It was an almost impregnable fortress. Here we see the French troops being reviewed at Quebec.

Reviewing troops at Quebec. Water color by an unknown artist, probably a soldier stationed there around 1750

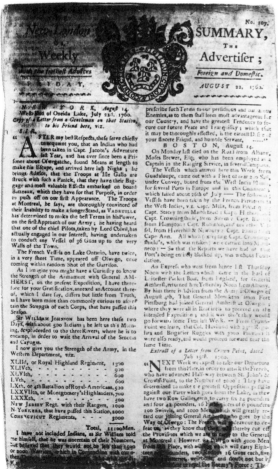

Account of the military and naval engagements of 1760

Plan of Fort Erie. Built by John Montresor

Stamp Act

In 1765 Great Britain passed the Stamp Act. It amounted to taxation without representation. From one end of the American colonies to the other the issue was hotly debated, and the unpopular measure was repealed in 1766.

Sorrow

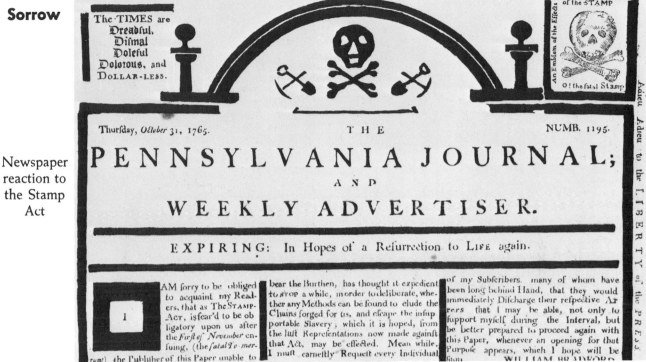

Newspaper reaction to the Stamp Act

England Take Heed!

Peters *A General History of Connecticut.* 1829.

Unpopular Tories were hanged in effigy at Lebanon, Conn.

Right Announcement of the repeal of the Stamp Act

Courtesy, The New York Public Library.

Joy

Glorious News.

BOSTON, Friday 11 o'Clock, 16th *May* 1766.
THIS Inftant arrived here the Brig Harrifon, belonging to *John Hancock*, Efq; Captain *Shubael Coffin*, in 6 Weeks and 2 Days from LONDON, with important News, as follows.

From the LONDON GAZETTE.

Weftminfter, March 18th, 1766.

THIS day his Majefty came to the Houfe of Peers, and being in his royal robes feated on the throne with the ufual folemnity, Sir Francis Molineux, Gentleman Ufher of the Black Rod, was fent with a Meffage from his Majefty to the Houfe of Commons, commanding their attendance in the Houfe of Peers. The Commons being come thither accordingly, his Majefty was pleafed to give his royal affent to

An ACT to REPEAL an Act made in the laft Seffion of Parliament, intituled, an Act for granting and applying certain Stamp-Duties and other Duties in the Britifh Colonies and Plantations in America, towards further defraying the expences of defending, protecting and fecuring the fame, and for amending fuch parts of the feveral Acts of Parliament relating to the trade and revenues of the faid Colonies and Plantations, as direct the manner of determining and recovering the penalties and forfeitures therein mentioned.

Alfo ten public bills, and feventeen private ones.

Yefterday there was a meeting of the principal Merchants concerned in the American trade, at the King's Arms tavern in Cornhill, to confider of an Addrefs to his Majefty on the beneficial Repeal of the late Stamp-Act.

Yefterday morning about eleven o'clock a great number of North American Merchants went in their coaches from the King's Arms tavern in Cornhill to the Houfe of Peers, to pay their duty to his Majefty, and to exprefs their fatisfaction at his figning the Bill for Repealing the American Stamp-Act; there was upwards of fifty coaches in the proceffion.

Laft night the faid gentlemen difpatched an exprefs for Falmouth, with fifteen copies of the Act for repealing the Stamp-Act, to be forwarded immediately for New York.

Orders are given for feveral merchantmen in the river to proceed to fea immediately on their refpective voyages to North America, fome of whom have been cleared out fince the firft of November laft.

Yefterday meffengers were difpatched to Birmingham, Sheffield, Manchefter, and all the great manufacturing towns in England, with an account of the final decifion of an auguft affembly relating to the Stamp-Act.

10

THE AMERICAN REVOLUTION

Courtesy, Essex Institute, Salem, Mass.

Boy's shoe. Period of the American Revolution

The boy who wore this shoe lived in stirring times. Great issues were at stake. He was old enough to listen attentively to his elders who quoted the words of James Otis:

"Taxation without Representation
is Tyranny"

These words would be repeated by generations yet unborn.

James Otis. Portrait after Joseph Blackburn. 1755

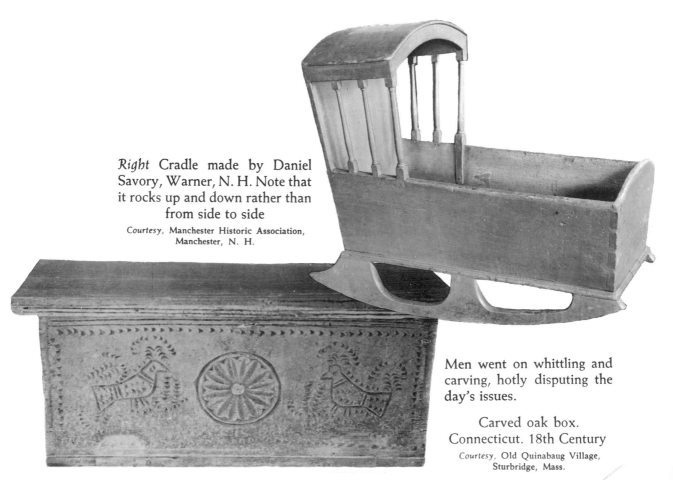

Right Cradle made by Daniel Savory, Warner, N. H. Note that it rocks up and down rather than from side to side

Courtesy, Manchester Historic Association, Manchester, N. H.

Men went on whittling and carving, hotly disputing the day's issues.

Carved oak box.
Connecticut. 18th Century

Courtesy, Old Quinabaug Village, Sturbridge, Mass.

Working—Waiting

A cocked hat of the period is seen at the *right*. Spanning the page is a forged iron balance scale made by H. Jackson in Connecticut and dated 1770. At the *bottom* is a reconstruction of the blacksmith shop of Elkanah Deane, Williamsburg, Va., 1772.

Hat, *Courtesy*, New Hampshire Historical Society, Concord, N. H.; scale, *Courtesy*, Old Sturbridge Village, Sturbridge, Mass.

Courtesy, Colonial Williamsburg, Inc., Williamsburg, Va.

Danger Signal

Courtesy, The New-York Historical Society, New York.

Statue of William Pitt after British soldiers had mutilated it.

Wise statesmen in England, particularly Edmund Burke and William Pitt, foresaw the danger of armed rebellion in America if unjust taxes continued to be imposed.

Pitt's views were so esteemed in America that the people of New York erected a statue to him, which the British soldiers mutilated when they captured the city, during the American Revolution. The Americans had previously melted down the statue of George III, in New York, and made it into bullets.

Courtesy, The New-York Historical Society, New York.

Americans demolishing the Statue of George III. Woodcut by Alexander Anderson

William Pitt

"Master of the Puppets"

In Boston, Samuel Adams expressed the voice of the patriots. He dared to speak of democracy, even to haughty Thomas Hutchinson, Governor of Massachusetts. Hutchinson referred to Adams as "Master of the Puppets".

Courtesy, Museum of Fine Arts. Boston.

Samuel Adams. Portrait by John Singleton Copley.

Freedom of Speech and Assembly

Patriots delivered democratic speeches in Faneuil Hall in Boston, at town meetings, or at the Liberty Tree. Almost every American town had a Liberty Tree, under which patriots gathered to organize and protest.

"BY UNITING WE STAND, BY DIVIDING WE FALL".

Thus wrote John Dickinson of Pennsylvania.

Cartoon by Benjamin Franklin. 1754. This was often reprinted in colonial newspapers until 1789.

John Dickinson. Portrait by Charles Willson Peale

Benjamin Franklin was sent to London to safeguard American rights. For exposing damaging correspondence by Gov. Hutchinson of Massachusetts, he was rebuked by the Privy Council and deprived of his post as Post-Master-General.

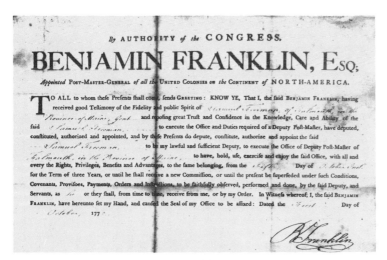

Courtesy, The Maine Historical Society, Portland, Me.
Post-master's appointment signed by Benjamin Franklin

Trumbull M'Fingal. 1795 edition. The town meeting caricatured here shows a tense scene between Tories and Patriots

More Troops Arrived In Boston

Courtesy, Stokes Collection, The New York Public Library.

Engraving by Paul Revere. 1770. Date depicted 1768

Courtesy, Stokes Collection, The New York Public Library.

British troops quartered on Boston Common. Water color by Christian Remick. 1768. The house at the right is the elegant mansion of the wealthy merchant and patriot, John Hancock

The Boston Massacre

On March 5, 1770, occurred the Boston Massacre. One snowy night a few civilians taunted and assaulted a British sentry. Owing to a misunderstanding of an order, the British troops, hurriedly called out, fired on the small crowd, killing three and wounding eight, two of whom died from their wounds. Feeling ran high, and Paul Revere made his lurid engraving, which fanned the flames of emotion to an even higher pitch. This old print is a classic example of propaganda.

Right The Boston Massacre. Engraved by Paul Revere. 1770. The State House is shown in the background. This incident was celebrated in poems, sermons, and orations, year after year, on the anniversary of the so-called massacre

Title-page of an oration by Joseph Warren, commemorating the Boston Massacre

Two leading patriots, Josiah Quincy and John Adams, through a sense of duty, defended the British officers responsible for the incident, and they were acquitted, but the die was cast. Blood had been shed.

Birthplace of John Adams. Braintree, Mass.

Whitefield, *The Homes of Our Forefathers.* 1880-1886.

The Regulators

In North Carolina the extravagances and abuses of Governor Tryon were exasperating the tax-ridden citizens into open revolt. An organization called The Regulators marched into the courtroom at Hillsborough, N. C., and demanded redress for wrongs. Troops were called out to punish The Regulators, and at the Battle of Alamance, May 16, 1771, they were dispersed, but shots had been fired against the representatives of the British Crown.

Scene of the Battle of Alamance. Drawn by
Benson J. Lossing

Execution of James Pugh, one of The
Regulators. Commemorative tablet

Left Tryon's Palace. New Bern,
N. C. Designed by John Hawks
Lossing *Pictorial Field Book of the Revolution.*
1852.

In Williamsburg, Va., the Royal Governor entertained his Tory guests as usual, and the actions of the rabble at Boston and at the Battle of Alamance were strongly censured. Loyal British subjects should stand firm against these upstart agitators and "democrats".

Supper Room. Governor's Palace. Williamsburg, Va.
Courtesy, Colonial Williamsburg, Inc. Photo by Richard Garrison.

The Boston Tea Party

On the night of December 16, 1773, occurred the Boston Tea Party. The British had imposed a tax on this popular commodity, and remembering the Stamp Act, the Americans were in no mood to pay what they regarded as an insolent levy, and meetings were held under the Liberty Trees in Boston, Philadelphia, Charleston, New York and other American cities. British ships were warned not to unload their cargoes of tea. A party of patriots disguised as Indians boarded an English vessel at Griffin's Wharf in Boston and dumped 342 chests of tea into the harbor.

Courtesy, The New-York Historical Society, New York.

The Boston Tea Party. English caricature. 1774

Lettsom's The Natural History of the Tea-tree. 1799.

Bohea Tea Plant

Brethren, and Fellow Citizens!

YOU may depend, that those odious Miscreants and detestable Tools to Ministry and Governor, the TEA CONSIGNEES, (those Traitors to their Country, Butchers, who have done, and are doing every Thing to Murder and destroy all that shall stand in the Way of their private Interest,) are determined to come and reside again in the Town of Boston.

I therefore give you this early Notice, that you may hold yourselves in Readiness, on the shortest Notice, to give them such a Reception, as such vile Ingrates deserve. JOYCE, jun.
(Chairman of the Committee for Tarring and Feathering

☞ If any Person should be so hardy as to Tear this down, they may expect my severest Resentment. J   un.

Courtesy, The Colonial Society of Massachusetts, Boston.

The Boston Tea Party. A Handbill

Courtesy, Metropolitan Museum of Art, New York.

Silver teapot by Paul Revere

"Give Me Liberty or Give Me Death"

On March 20, 1775, Patrick Henry arose before a body of patriots assembled in St. John's Church in Richmond, Va., and in reply to British acts of tyranny shouted: "Give me liberty or give me death!" The effect was electrical. Virginia stood ready to stand by courageous Massachusetts if armed rebellion should come.

Duyckinck *National Portrait Gallery*. 1862.
Patrick Henry

Courtesy, Valentine Museum, Richmond, Va.
St. John's Church. Richmond, Va.

Right Walnut table belonging to Patrick Henry
Courtesy, The Valentine Museum, Richmond, Va.

Left The churchyard of St. John's Church, Richmond, Va.
Courtesy, Valentine Museum, Richmond, Va., and the Metropolitan Museum of Art, New York.

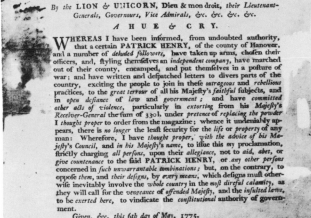

By the LION & UNICORN, Dieu & mon droit, their Lieutenant-
Generals, Governours, Vice Admirals, &c. &c. &c. &c.

A HUE & CRY.

WHEREAS I have been informed, from undoubted authority,
that a certain PATRICK HENRY, of the county of Hanover,
and a number of *deluded followers,* have taken up arms, chosen their
officers, and, styling themselves an *independent company,* have marched
out of their county, encamped, and put themselves in a posture of
war; and have written and despatched letters to divers parts of the
country, exciting the people to join in these *outrageous* and *rebellious*
practices, to the *great terrour* of all his Majesty's *faithful* subjects, and
in *open defiance of law and government;* and have committed
other acts of violence, particularly in *extorting* from his Majesty's
Receiver-General the sum of 330l. under *pretence of replacing the powder*
I thought proper to order from the magazine; whence it undeniably appears, there is *no longer* the least security for the *life* or *property* of any
man: Wherefore, I have *thought proper,* with the advice of his Majesty's Council, and *in his Majesty's name,* to issue this my proclamation,
strictly charging all persons, upon their allegiance, not to aid, abet, or
give countenance to the said PATRICK HENRY, or *any other persons*
concerned in *such unwarrantable combinations;* but, on the contrary, to
oppose them, and their designs, by *every means,* which designs must otherwise inevitably involve the *whole country in the most direful calamity,* as
they will call for the *vengeance of offended Majesty,* and the *insulted laws,*
to be *exerted here,* to vindicate the *constitutional* authority of government.

Given, &c. this 6th day of May, 1775.

D * * * *

G * * d * * * the P * * * *

Courtesy, The Library of Congress.

A Hue and Cry for Patrick Henry. 1775. This was
a bold parody on the official proclamation issued by
Governor Dunmore and reveals the temper of the
times

Courtesy, Landis Valley Museum, Landis Valley, Pa.
Colonial lanterns

Courtesy, Colonial Williamsburg, Inc. Photo by Richard Garrison.
Apollo Room. Raleigh Tavern. Williamsburg, Va.
When the Governor of Virginia angrily dissolved the
House of Burgesses, the patriots reassembled in the
Apollo Room of the Raleigh Tavern and made defiant
speeches

"The British Are Coming!"

Committees of Public Safety were organized throughout the colonies. Minute-men were trained for emer-
gencies. In Massachusetts, Paul Revere, William Dawes,
Samuel Prescott and others, who were in close touch
with Samuel Adams, John Hancock, and Joseph Warren, were instructed to keep their eye on the movements
of the British troops in Boston. If they marched out of
town for a surprise attack, lanterns should flash signal
lights and couriers were to ride to Lexington and Concord to rouse the countryside to arms. The British crept
out of Boston on the night of April 18, 1775, and Paul
Revere and his aides carried out their well-rehearsed
orders. A skirmish was fought at Lexington on the
morning of April 19, and the Revolutionary War
was on.

An Impartial History of the War in America.
1780.
American Rifleman

The Battle of Lexington

The Battle of Lexington. April 19, 1775. Engraving by Amos Doolittle

The British troops overwhelmed the few provincials at Lexington and marched to Concord where later in the day they were defeated and sent reeling back towards Boston.

The Battle of Concord

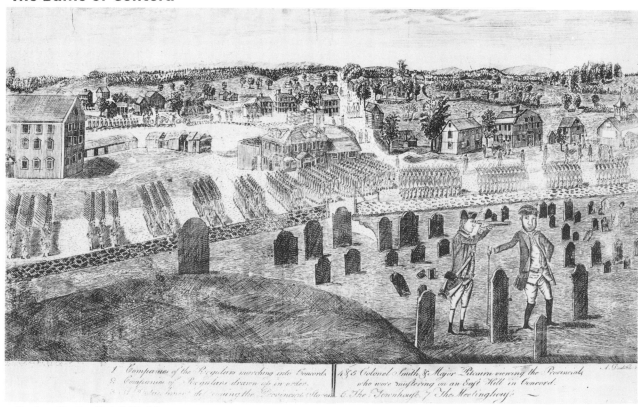

British troops entering Concord, Mass. Engraving by Amos Doolittle

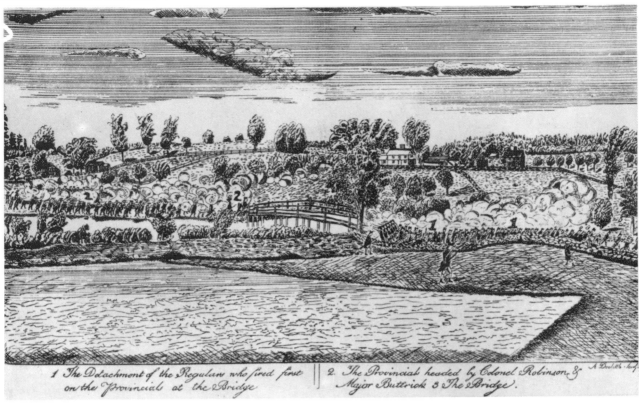

1 The Detachment of the Regulars who fired first on the Provincials at the Bridge 2. The Provincials headed by Colonel Robinson & Major Buttrick 3 The Bridge.

A Doolittle Sculp

Courtesy, The New York Public Library.

Battle at North Bridge, Concord. April 19, 1775. Engraving by Amos Doolittle

1.Americanischer Scharffschütz oder Jäger (Rifleman 2.regulaire Infanterie von Pensilvanien.

Colonial Uniforms
Sprengel *Allgemeines Historisches Taschenbuch.* 1784.

1.General Washington's reitende Leibgarde. 2.die independent Company. Chef General Washington.

British sentry. American Revolution. Print published by Rudolph Ackermann, London

Dorchester Heights

Subsequently the British occupied Dorchester Heights, overlooking Boston; and the Americans occupied Breed's Hill, which rose above Charlestown.

Dorchester Heights. A drawing by Archibald Robertson, Lt. General, Royal Engineers. 1776

View of Boston. A drawing by Archibald Robertson, Lt. General, Royal Engineers. 1776

Bunker Hill

On June 17, 1775, occurred the battle of Breed's Hill, though Bunker Hill, slightly north-ward, gave its name to the battle. The British troops marched up the hill in close formation, and the withering fire of the provincials cut them down like blades of grass. It was the worst casualty the British army had suffered, but when the Americans ran out of ammunition the British were able to occupy the hill.

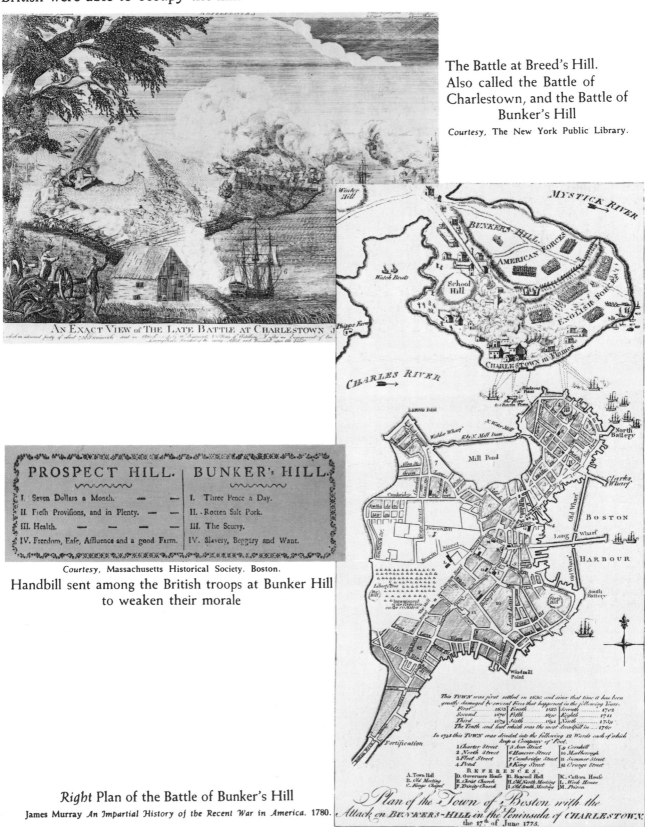

AN EXACT VIEW of THE LATE BATTLE AT CHARLESTOWN

The Battle at Breed's Hill.
Also called the Battle of
Charlestown, and the Battle of
Bunker's Hill

Courtesy, The New York Public Library.

PROSPECT HILL.	BUNKER'S HILL.
I. Seven Dollars a Month.	I. Three Pence a Day.
II. Fresh Provisions, and in Plenty.	II. Rotten Salt Pork.
III. Health.	III. The Scurvy.
IV. Freedom, Ease, Affluence and a good Farm.	IV. Slavery, Beggary and Want.

Courtesy, Massachusetts Historical Society. Boston.
Handbill sent among the British troops at Bunker Hill
to weaken their morale

Right Plan of the Battle of Bunker's Hill

James Murray *An Impartial History of the Recent War in America.* 1780.

Plan of the Town of Boston with the
Attack on BUNKERS-HILL in the Peninsula of CHARLESTOWN
the 17th of June 1775.

George Washington Takes Command

On July 3, 1775, George Washington took command of the Continental Army under an elm tree in Cambridge, Mass., near the campus of Harvard College.

George Washington. Portrait by Charles Willson Peale

Washington Elm. Cambridge, Mass.

View of Harvard College. Engraved by Paul Revere, 1768

Courtesy, The Essex Institute, Salem, Mass.

Loubat *The Medallic History of the United States.* v. 2. 1878.
Medal celebrating George Washington and the siege of Boston. Designed by Pierre Simon Duvivier. This was the first medal voted by Congress

Holden Chapel. Harvard College

"Keep Your Powder Dry"

The army which Washington had at his command was poorly trained, poorly equipped, and poorly paid. He needed cannon, and he needed gunpowder. Ethan Allen and his Green Mountain Boys, in concert with Benedict Arnold and his Connecticut troops, surprised the garrison at Fort Ticonderoga and hauled the captured cannon through the Green Mountains by ox teams, bringing them safely to the outskirts of Boston.

Powder magazine. North Attleboro, Mass. Built 1768

Courtesy, Colonial Williamsburg, Inc. Photo by Richard Garrison.
Powder magazine. Williamsburg, Va. Built ca. 1714

Courtesy, Charleston Museum, Charleston, S. C.
Powder magazine. Charleston, S. C. Built 1703

Courtesy, Essex Institute, Salem, Mass.
Powder house. Marblehead, Mass. Built 1755

Guns and Rifles

Bullet moulds

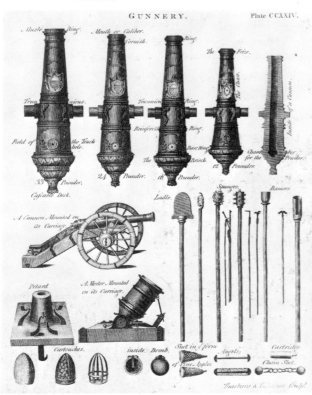

Gunnery. *Encyclopedia*, Philadelphia. 1798

Silver ornaments for rifle stocks. Made by German
gunsmiths in Pennsylvania

Left Revolutionary pistols

"Kentucky Rifles"

The Pennsylvania Germans made these long-barreled weapons which helped win
the American Revolution. They were adapted to American tactics and terrain. The
British could not cope with the deadly accuracy of the "Kentucky Rifles".

Loyalists

British officers found a welcome in the homes of the Loyalists, those men and women in America faithful to the Crown. John Adams always said that at least one-third of the population did not want independence, and that another third did not care one way or the other. This pro-British sentiment threatened at times to sabotage the war efforts of General Washington. Money and goods he needed for his tattered army were carried out of the country by the Loyalists, in connivance with the British fleet.

Courtesy, Harvard University.

Isaac Royall and family of Massachusetts. By Robert Feke. Royall was a Loyalist

Left Gov. John Wentworth of New Hampshire

Courtesy, The New York Public Library.
Portrait by John Singleton Copley.

Lady Frances Wentworth. Wife of Governor John Wentworth of New Hampshire. Portrait by John Singleton Copley

Courtesy, The New York Public Library.

Some of the Loyalists, or Tories, were tarred and feathered by excited mobs. Many lesser indignities were perpetrated.

Engravings by E. Tisdale in the first illustrated edition of John Trumbull's *M'Fingal*, a burlesque on the Loyalists

Courtesy, The New-York Historical Society, New York.

Army button worn by the New York volunteers, a Loyalist unit

Courtesy, Essex Institute, Salem, Mass.

Colonel Benjamin Pickman, Loyalist, of Massachusetts

Photographed by Pach Bros.

Cadwallader Colden, Loyalist Governor of New York. Portrait by Matthew Pratt. 1772

By the KING,

A PROCLAMATION,

For suppressing Rebellion and Sedition.

GEORGE R.

WHEREAS many of Our Subjects in divers Parts of Our Colonies and Plantations in *North America*, misled by dangerous and ill-designing Men, and forgetting the Allegiance which they owe to the Power that has protected and sustained them, after various disorderly Acts committed in Disturbance of the Publick Peace, to the Obstruction of lawful Commerce, and to the Oppression of Our loyal Subjects carrying on the same, have at length proceeded to an open and avowed Rebellion, by arraying themselves in hostile Manner to withstand the

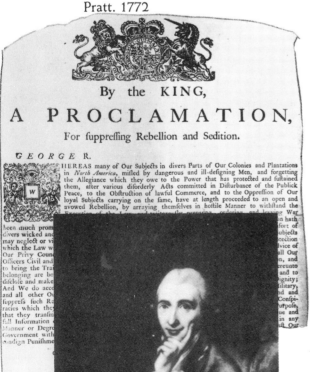

TEUCRO DUCE NIL DESPERANDOM.

First Battalion of PENNSYLVANIA LOYALISTS, commanded by His Excellency Sir WILLIAM HOWE, K.B.

ALL INTREPID ABLE-BODIED

HEROES,

WHO are willing to serve His MAJESTY KING GEORGE the Third, in Defence of their Country, Laws and Constitution, against the arbitrary Usurpations of a tyrannical Congress, have now not only an Opportunity of manifesting their Spirit, by assisting in reducing to Obedience their too-long deluded Countrymen, but also of acquiring the polite Accomplishments of a Soldier, by serving only two Years, or during the present Rebellion in America.

Such spirited Fellows, who are willing to engage, will be rewarded at the End of the War, besides their Laurels, with 50 Acres of Land, where every gallant Hero may retire, and enjoy his Bottle and Lass.

Each Volunteer will receive, as a Bounty, FIVE DOLLARS, besides Arms, Cloathing and Accoutrements, and every other Requisite proper to accommodate a Gentleman Soldier, by applying to Lieutenant Colonel ALLEN, or at Captain KEARNY's Rendezvous, at PATRICK TONRY's, three Doors above Market-street, in Second-street.

Courtesy, The New York Public Library.

Broadside. Philadelphia. 1777

Left The King appeals to all loyal subjects

"THESE ARE THE TIMES THAT TRY MEN'S SOULS" wrote Thomas Paine, whose fiery appeals to the Patriots offset the Tory satire of Jonathan Odell and Joseph Stansbury.

Left Thomas Paine. Portrait by Charles Willson Peale

Declaration of Independence

In 1776 the Continental Congress assembled in Philadelphia to prosecute the war and to make a public declaration of principles. From this Congress came the memorable document known as "*The Unanimous Declaration of the Thirteen United States of America*," popularly known as *The Declaration of Independence*.

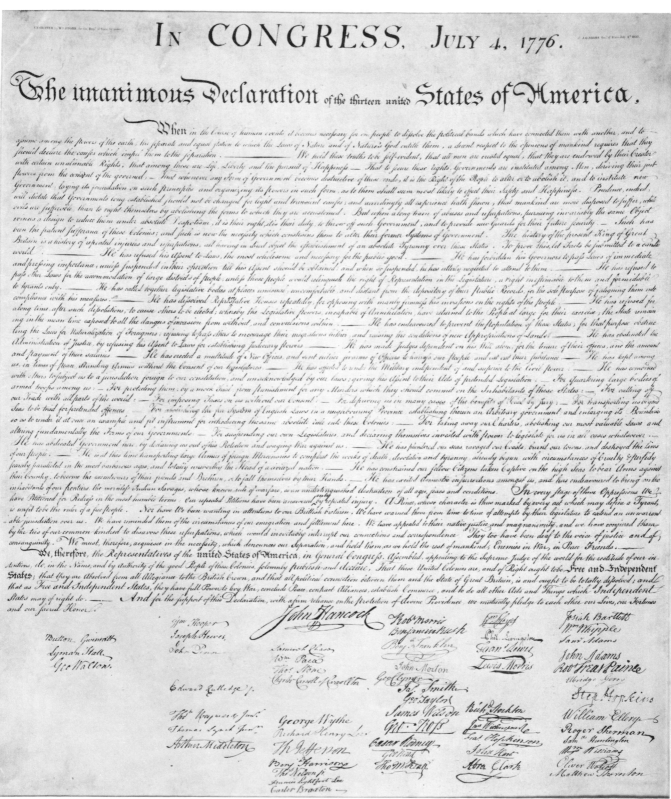

The Declaration of Independence. The original draft was written by Thomas Jefferson

Some of the Signers

These were the men whose faith and foresight created a model of government which was, and is, the hope of mankind.

Benjamin Franklin. Pennsylvania
From Portrait by Charles Willson Peale.

Francis Hopkinson. New Jersey
From Portrait by Robert Edge Pine.

Thomas Jefferson. Virginia
Bust by Houdon.

Charles Carroll of Carrollton.
Maryland
From Portrait by Chester Harding.

John Hancock. Massachusetts
From Portrait by John Singleton Copley.

Philip Livingston. New York

Elbridge Gerry. Massachusetts
Portrait by J. Bogle.

Some of the Signers

George Read. Delaware
From Portrait by Robert Edge Pine.

John Adams. Massachusetts
Portrait by John Singleton Copley

Richard Henry Lee. Virginia
Portrait by Charles Willson Peale.

Joseph Hewes. North Carolina
Courtesy, Independence
National Historical Park, Philadelphia.

William Hooper. North Carolina
From Portrait by John Trumbull.

Stephen Hopkins. Rhode Island.
Portrait after John Trumbull

Oliver Wolcott. Connecticut
Courtesy, Independence
National Historical Park, Philadelphia.

Some of the Signers

Josiah Bartlett. New Hampshire
From a drawing in Emmet Collection,
New York Public Library

Lyman Hall. Georgia
From a drawing in Emmet Collection.

Matthew Thornton. New
Hampshire
From a drawing in Emmet Collection.

Roger Sherman. Connecticut
Portrait by Ralph Earl.
Courtesy, Yale University Art Gallery

Samuel Chase. Maryland
Portrait by Charles Willson Peale.
Courtesy, Frick Art Reference Library.

John Witherspoon. New Jersey
Portrait by Charles Willson Peale.
Courtesy, Independence
National Historical Park, Philadelphia.

Arthur Middleton. South Carolina
From Portrait by Benjamin West.

Independence Hall

In the State House in Philadelphia *The Declaration of Independence* was adopted on July 2, 1776, although July 4 is the traditional date of its annual celebration. On July 8, the document was publicly read, and the Liberty Bell may have pealed forth the good news from the State House, although the steeple was so rickety at that time that the ringing of the bell was considered unsafe.

The State House, Philadelphia;
an engraving from the *Columbian Magazine*

Liberty Bell. Now in Independence Hall. It was cracked and silenced on Washington's Birthday in 1846. Its Biblical inscription reads: "Proclaim Liberty throughout all the land unto the inhabitants thereof." It weighs over 2080 pounds

South door of Independence Hall
Courtesy, Essex Institute, Salem, Mass.

Wanted: Soldiers and Sailors

As the war dragged on without decisive results many soldiers returned to their farms and shops when their terms of enlistment expired. A few deserted. Proper food, clothing, and medical attention could not be furnished the troops because of the breakdown in the supply system. Bad roads delayed transportation. The Continental Congress was too new to be thoroughly trained in the act of prosecuting a costly war. The manpower problem was acute. Criticism of General Washington's conduct of the war began to be heard.

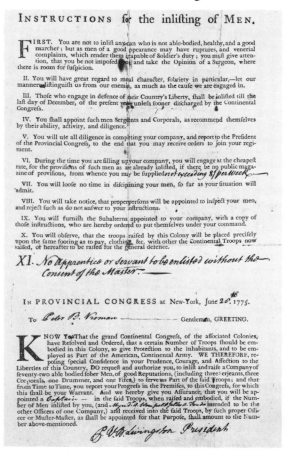

Army recruiting notice.
Courtesy, New-York Historical Society

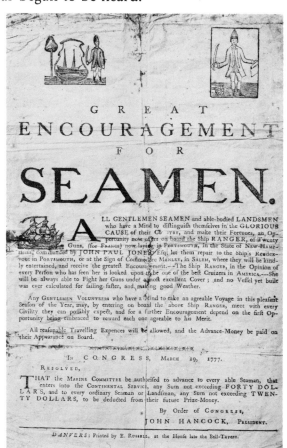

Navy recruiting poster

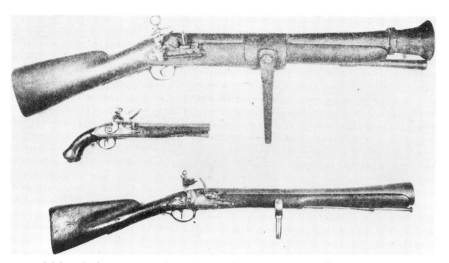

Naval blunderbuss—swivels and pistol. J. B. Cone Collection
Courtesy, Essex Institute, Salem, Mass.

Money Was Scarce

It took money to wage war, and there was little to be had. Coin was almost non-existent, and Congress sanctioned paper money. The colonial currency, and that issued by the separate states, served as models.

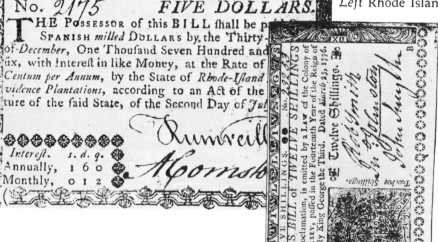

Courtesy, Maryland Historical Society.
Maryland indented bill. 1774

Courtesy, The New-York Historical Society, New York.
Ten shilling note issued by the Colony of New York. Feb. 16, 1771. Note the warning to counterfeiters

Left Rhode Island bill. 1780

Courtesy, The Collection of George R. D. Schieffelin.
Twelve shilling note. New Jersey. 1776

Left Currency table published in the New York *Pocket Almanac*. 1774

"Not Worth a Continental"

Anburey *Travels Through America.* 1789.

Robert Morris
Financier of the American Revolution

From a portrait by Ed. Savage.

Continental currency. 1779

Dickeson *American Numismatical Manual.* 1859.

Tokens issued in America during the American Revolution

Courtesy, Maryland Historical Society.

Chalmers and Barry Coins minted in Maryland in 1783. Chalmers was an Annapolis goldsmith

The War In New York

When the British troops evacuated Boston, General Washington went to New York to prepare for the attack that was almost sure to come. In July, 1776, the British landed on Staten Island, and within a few weeks had pushed Washington's army out of Long Island, and out of Manhattan Island. On Nov. 16th they captured Fort Washington on the Hudson River. General Washington had no choice but to retire to New Jersey.

The attack on Fort Washington. 1776. Drawn on the spot by Thomas Davies, a Captain of Artillery. The Morris House appears at the top of the hill to the left. Hessian troops made up the bulk of the attacking force

Left Ruins of Trinity Church. New York City. Date depicted ca. 1780. Almost five hundred buildings were burned Sept. 21, 1776, and the patriots blamed the British for it

Courtesy, The New York Public Library.

Right Roger Morris House. New York City. Now called the Jumel Mansion, which served as Washington's headquarters in Sept. 1776

Valentine's Manual. 1854.

Blockade

Simultaneously with the landing in New York, the British fleet struck a blow at Fort Sullivan, at Charleston, S. C. The war was spreading. The British plan was to blockade the American ports.

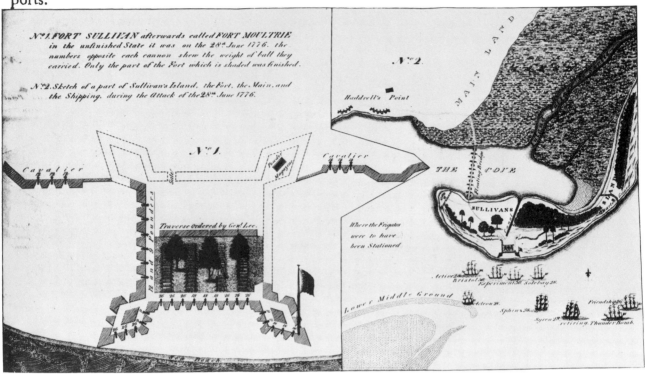

John Drayton *Memoirs of the American Revolution*. 1821.

Plan of Fort Sullivan. 1776

Some of the best early views of American ports were made by the excellent artists accompanying the British fleet in the Revolutionary War.

Courtesy, National Park Service.

View inside ship museum, Yorktown, Va., showing replica of a gun deck of a British frigate

Atlantic Neptune. 1781.

Portsmouth, New Hampshire. 1777

Hope . . .

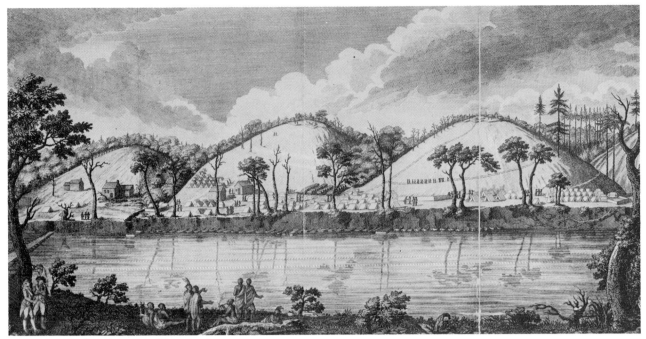

Anburey *Travels Through America.* 1789.

View of General Burgoyne's camp on the Hudson River. 1777

And Fate

Anburey *Travels Through America.* 1789.

Remnant of Burgoyne's Army interned at Charlottesville, Va.

Southern Heroes

Courtesy, Carolina Art Association, Charleston, S. C.
The Battle of Eutaw Springs was fought around this tavern. Water color by Charles Fraser. 1800

General Francis Marion, whose bold forays against the British lines of communication earned him the soubriquet of the "Swamp Fox". He participated in the Battle of Eutaw Springs

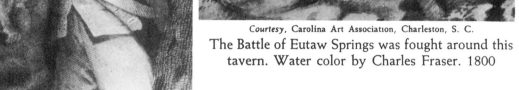

Above Brigadier-General Daniel Morgan, in buckskin uniform. He was the hero of the Battle of Cowpens (S. C.) Jan. 17, 1781

Left Brigadier-General Lachlan McIntosh, who was in the siege of Savannah, and the defense of Charleston

Portraits from Herring and Longacre *National Portrait Gallery of Distinguished Americans*. 1836.

British army buttons
found on the battle-
grounds of the Amer-
ican Revolution

Courtesy, The New-York
Historical Society, New York.

Right Portrait of Colonel Marinus
Willet, by Ralph Earl, showing the
type of officer's uniform worn by the
Americans

Courtesy, Metropolitan Museum of Art, New York.

J. Milbert *Itineraire Pittoresque du fleuve Hudson.* 1829. v. 3.

Haverstraw, New York. This shows the Hudson River scenery much as it appeared in George Washing
ton's times. He had to transport his army across this river when he evacuated Westchester County

"Yankee Doodle"

The song the American troops sang as they went forth into battle was *Yankee Doodle*. Originally composed by the British to poke fun at the green provincial troops, this lively ballad was adopted by the American patriots during the American Revolution, some years after its first appearance, the exact date of which is a subject of controversy. The American soldier has always marched to humorous ditties.

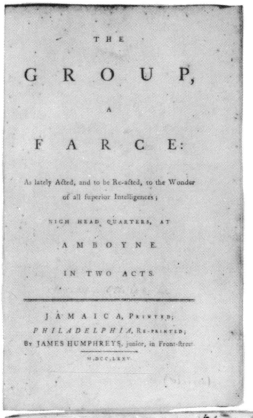

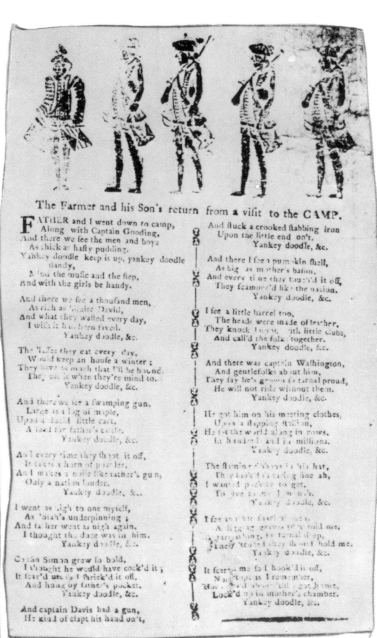

Left Title-page of *The Group*, a patriotic play by Mercy Warren. 1775

Courtesy, New York Public Library.

Two versions of the ballad *Yankee Doodle*

Out of the American Revolution emerged a school of native playwrights, including Mercy Warren, and the real beginnings of American drama. Mercy Warren's brother, James Otis, was a gifted orator, and her husband, James Warren, was an American general.

At the Delaware

After retiring from New York, General Washington moved his army to New Jersey and then to Pennsylvania. He recrossed the Delaware River to strike two hard blows at Trenton, Dec. 26, 1776, and Princeton, Jan. 3, 1777.

Courtesy, Metropolitan Museum of Art, New York. Washington Crossing the Delaware. Painting by Emanuel Leutze

While neither contemporary nor authentic, this picture has, through its long popularity, established itself as the symbol of Washington's great exploit.

He conscripted all the ferrymen up and down the Delaware to facilitate the moving of his men and supplies across the river. Here we see a typical ferry with its pontoon approach.

Columbian Magazine. August, 1787.
Gray's Ferry. Schuylkill River. Pa.

Philadelphia

Sir William Howe, who commanded the troops that took New York, entered Philadelphia in triumph, after defeating the Continental Army at the Brandywine, Sept. 11, 1777. This British victory was offset by American victories at Oriskany, New York, and Bennington, Vermont, followed by the capture of Burgoyne's army, but Washington's own army was condemned to face a hard winter at Valley Forge.

An Impartial History of the War in America.
1780.

Sir William Howe

Duyckinck National Portrait Gallery.
1862-67.

General John Stark, Hero of
Battle of Bennington

Left General John Stark's powder horn

Courtesy, Manchester Historic Association, Manchester, N. H.

Rationing

Courtesy, The New York Public Library.

Rationing notice issued by Sir William
Howe. Philadelphia. 1777

From *Godey's Lady's Book*, 1844.

Chew Mansion. Germantown, Pa.

In Enemy Hands

There were many Tory Loyalists in Philadelphia, and the British officers went to assemblies and to the theatre. Wartime Philadelphia was gay and fashionable. Howe and his aides were entertained at country estates in the environs of the city.

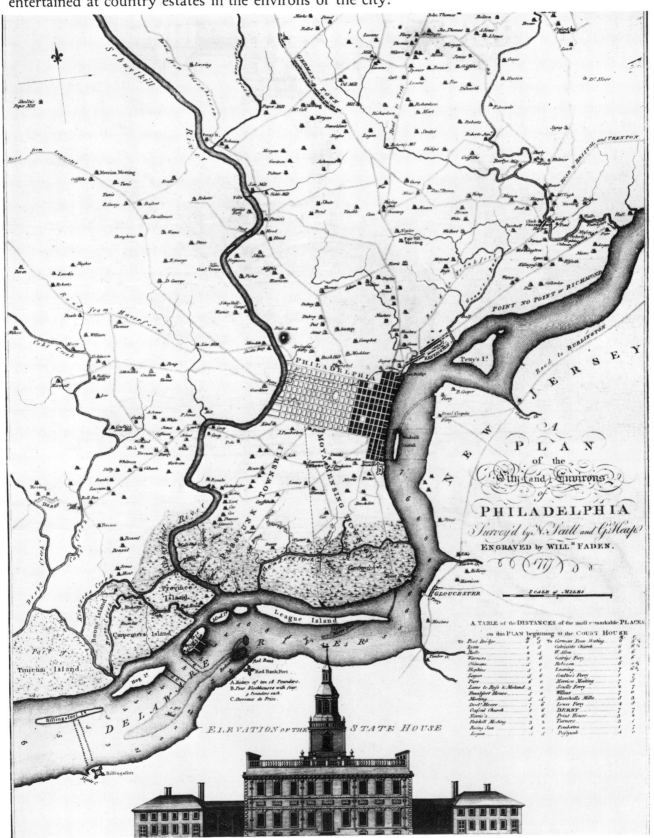

Plan of the City and Environs of Philadelphia. Engraved by William Faden.
1777. Note the fine drawing of the State House

The Mischianza

Major John Andre designed stage settings for a spectacular *fête champêtre* and military pageant at "Walnut Grove", the Wharton family estate, in honor of Sir William Howe, May 18, 1778. One London firm sold £12,000 worth of laces, silks and other finery for the entertainment. Later Andre was captured by the Americans in New York State and hanged, being charged with plotting with Benedict Arnold for the betrayal of West Point.

Ticket and invitation to the Mischianza (or Meschianza)

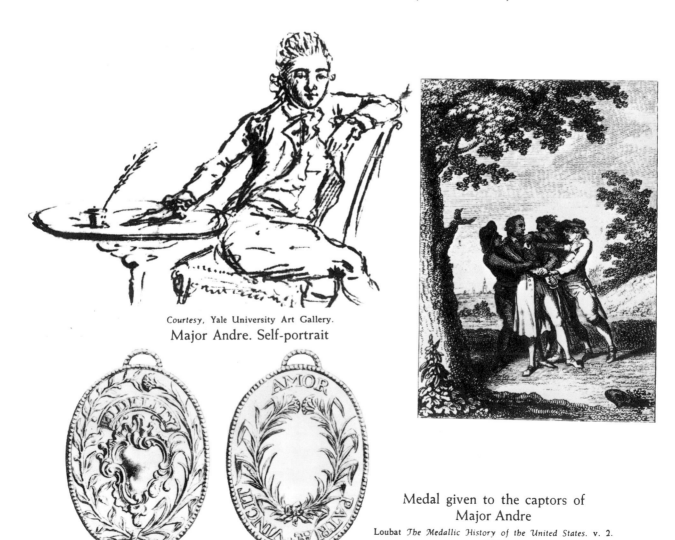

Courtesy, Yale University Art Gallery.
Major Andre. Self-portrait

Medal given to the captors of
Major Andre

Loubat *The Medallic History of the United States.* v. 2.
1878.

Traitor

Benedict Arnold performed brilliant feats, including a classic march to Quebec through the Maine wilderness, and held the respect of his leader George Washington, but Congress was so tardy in its recognition of his valuable services that he became embittered. While in command at Philadelphia he fell in love with Peggy Shippen, the darling of Philadelphia society, and enthroned her at Mt. Pleasant after their marriage. He soon fell into debt, received further rebukes from Congress, and finally turned traitor.

Benedict Arnold

Peggy Shippen (Mrs. Benedict Arnold) and child. Portrait by Daniel Gardner

Courtesy, Pennsylvania Historical Society, Phila.

Courtesy, Philadelphia Museum of Art. Philadelphia.

Room from Mt. Pleasant. Philadelphia

West Point
A. Constitution Island; B. Chain stretched across the Hudson River to prevent the passage of British ships; C. Fort Clinton. After a view in the *New York Magazine*

The Robinson House across the River from West Point. Benedict Arnold established his headquarters here. He was having breakfast with George Washington in this house when news of the capture of Andre reached him

Christ Church In Philadelphia

Both the British and the Americans attended service at Christ Church, begun in 1727 by the architect John Kearsley, one of the designers of Independence Hall. Benjamin Franklin's pew, along with George Washington's, is still pointed out. Franklin lies buried in its churchyard.

Photo by Frank Cousins. *Courtesy*, Essex Institute, Salem, Mass.

Interior of Christ Church. Philadelphia

Photo by Frank Cousins.

Pulpit of Christ Church. Installed 1770

Life Went On

Philadelphians found time to read the latest book on horsemanship, and to attend balls and plays.

Philip Astley *The Modern Riding-Master*
Philadelphia, 1776

Right Costume of the period of the American
Revolution

Courtesy, Metropolitan Museum of Art, New York.

Valley Forge

While the British were enjoying the comforts and pleasures of Philadelphia, Washington's tattered army was half-starved and half-frozen at bleak Valley Forge. It was America's darkest hour.

Courtesy, Valley Forge Park Commission.

Washington's Headquarters at Valley Forge

Right Washington's food problem

Courtesy, Pennsylvania Historical Society.

By His EXCELLENCY

GEORGE WASHINGTON, Esquire,

GENERAL and COMMANDER in CHIEF of the Forces
of the UNITED STATES of AMERICA.

BY Virtue of the Power and Direction to Me especially given, I hereby enjoin and require all Persons residing within seventy Miles of my Head Quarters to thresh one Half of their Grain by the 1st Day of February, and the other Half by the 1st Day of March next ensuing, on Pain, in Case of Failure of having all that shall remain in Sheaves after the Period above mentioned, seized by the Commissaries and Quarter-Masters of the Army, and paid for as Straw

GIVEN *under my Hand, at Head Quarters, near the Valley Forge, in Philadelphia County,* this 20th *Day of December,* 1777.

G. WASHINGTON.

By His Excellency's Command,

ROBERT H. HARRISON, Sec'y.

LANCASTER: Printed by JOHN DUNLAP.

Left Camp bedstead used by George Washington at Valley Forge

Courtesy, The New-York Historical Society, New York.

Right Military kit said to have been used by Colonel Nicholas Fish during the Revolutionary War. The fork and spoon are hinged. No such elegance was found at Valley Forge

Courtesy, The New-York Historical Society, New York.

Help From Abroad

A military genius from Germany, Baron Von Steuben, came to Valley Forge and was appalled at what he saw. He took over the military training of the Continental Army and instructed them in the arts of war. He made disciplined soldiers from raw recruits. The Polish patriot, Thaddeus Kosciusko, and the young French hero, the Marquis de LaFayette, also came to help America win freedom. LaFayette brought troops.

Baron Von Steuben
Portrait by Charles Willson Peale. 1780

Left Thaddeus Kosciusko

Sprengel *Allgemeines Historisches Taschenbuch.*
1784.

French troops landing at Newport, R. I.

LaFayette. Portrait by Charles Willson Peale

French Troops

The sight of these gaily uniformed French troops heartened the weary Americans. It was the beginning of a lasting friendship between the two countries.

Courtesy, Vinkhuizen Collection. The New York Public Library.

French soldier. 1779   French soldier. 1772

Diderot and D'Alembert Encyclopedie. Recueil des Planches. 1762-72.

French soldiers

The American Navy

With the aid of the French fleet, the American Navy more than held its own, and the iron ring of the blockade was broken. The greatest naval hero of the war was John Paul Jones.

Courtesy, The New-York Historical Society, New York.

Commodore Esek Hopkins. Commander in Chief of the American fleet. Mezzotint published in London by Thomas Hart. 1776

John Paul Jones. Engraving by Moreau the Younger. 1780. Jones, in the *Bon Homme Richard*, won an epic naval battle for the *Serapis*, Sept. 23, 1779

Naval Button. American Revolution

Courtesy, The New-York Historical Society, New York.

Courtesy, Essex Institute, Salem, Mass.
A "Cohorn" Used in the main-top

Pine-tree flag of an American cruiser. 1776. It had a green tree on a white bunting. On the reverse was the motto "Appeal to Heaven". Note the liberty cap on the flag pole

What Sailors Had To Know

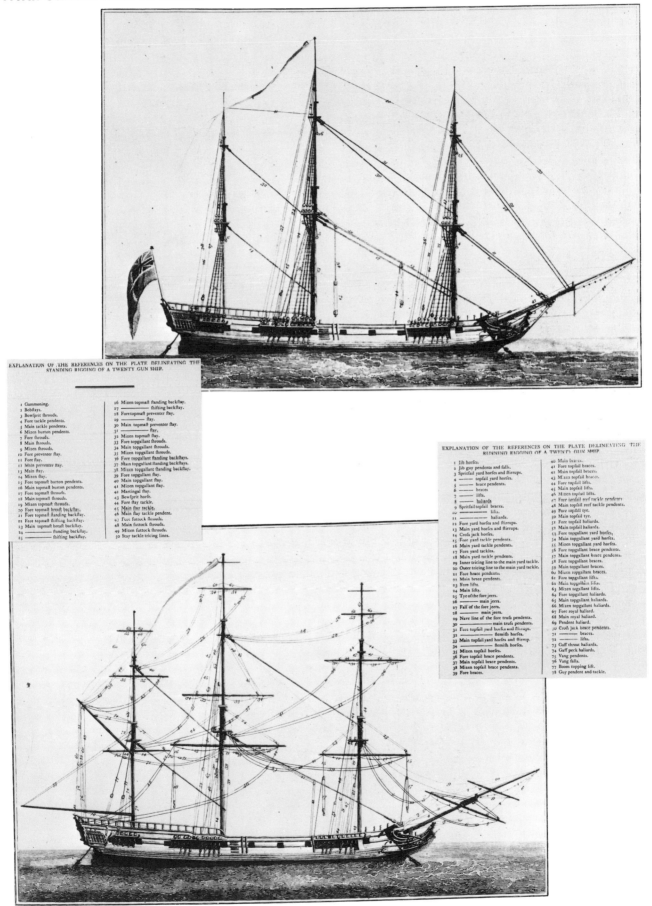

Illustrations from Steel, *The Elements and Practice of Rigging and Seamanship.* 1794

What Sailors Had To Know

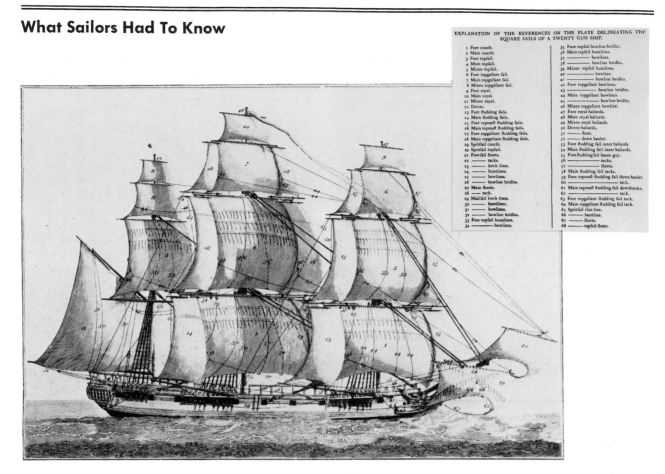

EXPLANATION OF THE REFERENCES ON THE PLATE DELINEATING THE SQUARE SAILS OF A TWENTY GUN SHIP.

1 Fore courfe.		35 Fore topfail bowline bridles.	
2 Main courfe.		36 Main topfail buntlines.	
3 Fore topfail.		37 ———— bowlines.	
4 Main topfail.		38 ———— bowline bridles.	
5 Mizen topfail.		39 Mizen topfail buntlines.	
6 Fore topgallant fail.		40 ———— bowline.	
7 Main topgallant fail.		41 ———— bowline bridles.	
8 Mizen topgallant fail.		42 Fore topgallant buntlines.	
9 Fore royal.		43 ———— bowline bridles.	
10 Main royal.		44 Main topgallant bowlines.	
11 Mizen royal.		45 ———— bowline bridles.	
12 Driver.		46 Mizen topgallant bowline.	
13 Fore studding fails.		47 Fore royal haliards.	
14 Main studding fails.		48 Main royal haliards.	
15 Fore topmast studding fails.		49 Mizen royal haliards.	
16 Main topmast studding fails.		50 Driver haliards.	
17 Fore topgallant studding fails.		51 ———— fheet.	
18 Main topgallant studding fails.		52 ———— down hauler.	
19 Spritfail courfe.		53 Fore studding fail inner haliards.	
20 Spritfail topfail.		54 Main studding fail inner haliards.	
21 Fore fail fheets.		55 Fore studding fail boom guy.	
22 ———— tacks.		56 ———— tacks.	
23 ———— leech lines.		57 ———— fheets.	
24 ———— buntlines.		58 Main studding fail tacks.	
25 ———— bowlines.		59 Fore topmast studding fail down hauler.	
26 ———— bowline bridles.		60 ———— tack.	
27 Main fail fheets.		61 Main topmast studding fail downhauler.	
28 ———— tack.		62 ———— tack.	
29 Mail fail leech lines.		63 Fore topgallant studding fail tack.	
30 ———— buntlines.		64 Main topgallant studding fail tack.	
31 ———— bowlines.		65 Spritfail clue line.	
32 ———— bowline bridles.		66 ———— buntline.	
33 Fore topfail buntlines.		67 ———— fheets.	
34 ———— bowlines.		68 ———— topfail fheets.	

EXPLANATION OF THE REFERENCES ON THE PLATE DELINEATING THE FORE-AND-AFT SAILS OF A TWENTY GUN SHIP.

1 Jib.		36 Main topmast flayfail fheets.	
2 Fore topmast flayfail.		37 Middle flayfail flay.	
3 Fore flayfail.		38 ———— haliards.	
4 Main flayfail.		39 ———— down hauler.	
5 Main topmast flayfail.		40 ———— tacks.	
6 Middle flayfail.		41 ———— fheets.	
7 Main topgallant flayfail.		42 ———— tricing line.	
8 Mizen flayfail.		43 Main topgallant flayfail flay.	
9 Mizen topmast flayfail.		44 ———— haliards.	
10 Mizen topmast flayfail.		45 ———— down hauler.	
11 Mizen.		46 ———— tacks.	
12 Jib downhauler.		47 ———— fheets.	
13 ———— haliards.		48 Mizen flay.	
14 ———— fheets.		49 ———— flayfail haliards.	
15 ———— flay.		50 ———— down hauler.	
16 ———— outhauler.		51 ———— brails.	
17 ———— inhauler.		52 ———— tacks.	
18 Fore topmast flay.		53 ———— fheets.	
19 Fore topmast flayfail downhauler.		54 Mizen topmast flay.	
20 ———— haliards.		55 ———— flayfail haliards.	
21 ———— fheets.		56 ———— down hauler.	
22 ———— outhauler.		57 ———— tacks.	
23 Fore preventer flay.		58 ———— fheets.	
24 Fore flayfail haliards.		59 Mizen topgallant flay.	
25 ———— downhauler.		60 ———— flayfail haliards.	
26 ———— fheets.		61 ———— down hauler.	
27 Main flayfail flay.		62 ———— tacks.	
28 ———— haliards.		63 ———— fheets.	
29 ———— downhauler.		64 Tack of the mizen courfe.	
30 ———— fheets.		65 Sheet of the mizen courfe.	
31 Main topmast preventer flay.		66 Throat brails	
32 ———— flayfail haliards.		67 Middle brails } of the mizen courfe.	
33 ———— down hauler.		68 Peek brails	
34 ———— brails.		69 Fancy line.	
35 ———— tacks.			

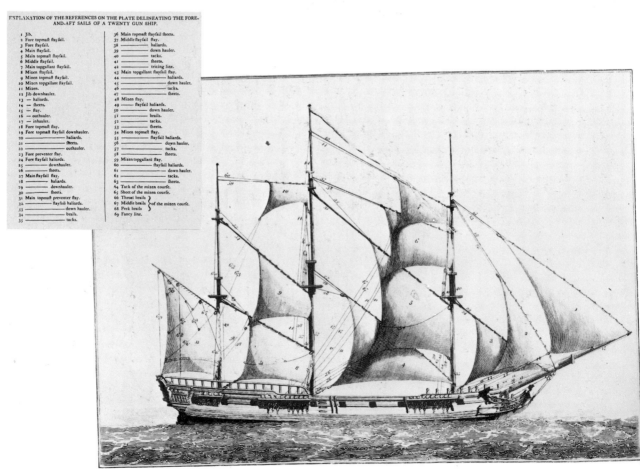

Illustrations from Steel, *The Elements and Practice of Rigging and Seamanship.* 1794

Human Suffering

Many American and British soldiers were kept in filthy prisons, and those who were wounded on the battlefield received very little medical attention owing to the lack of doctors and surgeons. Amputations were crude and painful.

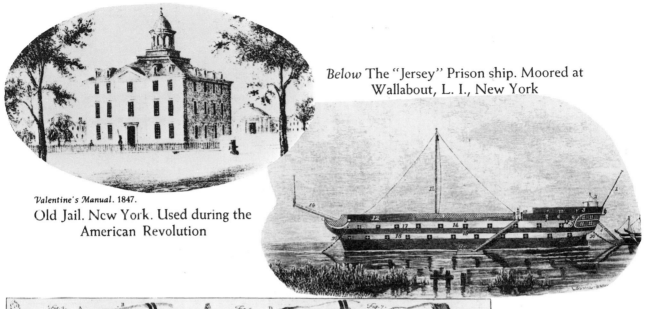

Valentine's Manual. 1847.
Old Jail. New York. Used during the American Revolution

Below The "Jersey" Prison ship. Moored at Wallabout, L. I., New York

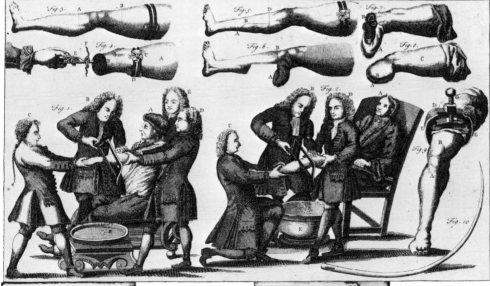

Heister *General System of Surgery.* 1743
Courtesy, New York Academy of Medicine, New York.

Below Illustrations from Benjamin Bell's *A System of Surgery.* 1791
Courtesy, New York Academy of Medicine, New York.

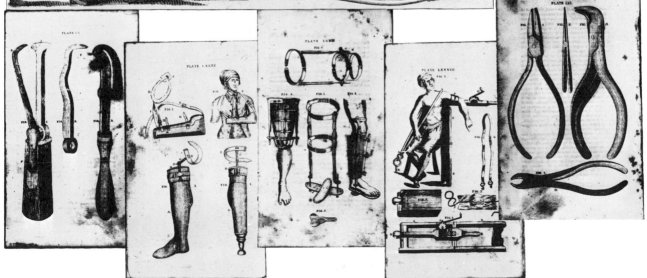

Yorktown

The Battle of Yorktown, fought not far from Jamestown, Va., where the first English settlement in America was founded in 1607, practically brought the Revolutionary War to a close. George Washington, the hero of the long struggle, returned to private life at his home in Mount Vernon, after taking leave of his officers at Fraunces Tavern in New York.

Illumination.

COLONEL TILGHMAN, Aid de Camp to his Excellency General WASHINGTON, having brought official acounts of the SURRENDER of Lord Cornwallis, and the Garrifons of York and Gloucefter, thofe Citizens who chufe to ILLUMINATE on the GLORIOUS OCCASION, will do it this evening at Six, and extinguifh their lights at Nine o'clock.

Decorum and harmony are earneftly recommended to every Citizen, and a general difcountenance to the leaft appearance of riot.

Oftober 24, 1781.

Courtesy, Colonial Society of America.

Fraunces Tavern. New York. Etching by Robert Shaw

Mount Vernon

Left View of Mount Vernon, Home of George Washington

Weld *Travels through the States of North America.* 1799.

Right View of Mount Vernon. Engraved by Francis Jukes after a drawing by Alexander Robertson. 1800. Date depicted 1799

Courtesy, Stokes Collection. The New York Public Library.

The Society of the Cincinnati

To perpetuate the friendships made on the field of battle, Washington and his officers formed the Society of the Cincinnati in 1783. Its social traditions have always been maintained.

Badge of the Cincinnati

Headquarters of Baron Von Steuben, Verplanck House, Fishkill, N. Y., where the Society of the Cincinnati was founded

Courtesy, Colonial Society of America

The United States Seal

Flag of the Society of the Cincinnati. The American eagle is a prominent feature

From a drawing by L. F. Grant, in Thomas *The Society of the Cincinnati.*
Published by G. P. Putnam's Sons

The first United States Seal. 1782. Designed by William Barton and Charles Thomson

The "Stars and Stripes"

The American flag, the "Stars and Stripes", dates officially from June 14, 1777, and was a marine flag in the beginning, being so used by John Paul Jones. The story that Betsy Ross made the first "Stars and Stripes" is only one of many flag myths. There were numerous variations in the design of this flag, and many claimants for the honor of first displaying it.

Courtesy, The Easton Public Library, Easton, Pa.
The Easton Flag. An early version of the "Stars and Stripes"

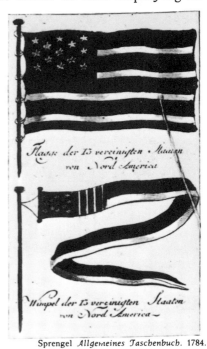

Sprengel Allgemeines Taschenbuch. 1784.
The "Stars and Stripes". The top stripe is red, the next blue, and the next white on a blue field

The American Eagle Was Beginning to Scream

Catesby The Natural History of Carolina. 1754.
The American Eagle

The eagle became the symbol of American independence and began to appear on seals, trade marks, and as a decorative motif in the arts and crafts.

Woodcut by Alexander Anderson

Left The eagle motif in furniture

Peace . . .

War-weary patriots emptied their powder horns and went back to field and shop.

Courtesy, New Hampshire Historical Society, Concord, N. H.

Powder horn of John Calfe

American primitive painting. Artist unknown. Found near Lancaster, Pa.

Courtesy, Mr. Harry Stone. New York City.

They put away their uniforms with the new buttons which bore the letters U.S.A.

Pride . . .

Army button. American Revolution

Courtesy, The New-York Historical Society, New York.

They hung their rifles over the mantel piece.

And Hope

Across a peaceful land the church bells pealed a message of hope

First Parish meeting house. Portland, Me. 1740. The bell was added in 1758, the steeple in 1761

Willis, *The History of Portland.* 1833.

Birth of a Nation

The unexploited natural resources of the United States awaited the pioneer. Free men poured from the Eastern seaboard, crossed the mountain barriers and swarmed into the Ohio and Mississippi valleys, poured through the Cumberland Gap and along the Wilderness Road into Tennessee and Kentucky.

Picturesque America. 1872-74.

The Cumberland Gap

Men like Daniel Boone and Simon Kenton were the trail-blazers of empire. They saw great herds of buffalo.

Courtesy, The Filson Club,
Louisville, Ky.

Daniel Boone

Courtesy, The Filson Club,
Louisville, Ky.

Simon Kenton

Catesby The Natural History
of Carolina. 1754.

Rivers . . .

Men of Connecticut crossed the Housatonic and the Hudson and pushed towards Ohio.

Picturesque America. 1872-74.

The Housatonic River

And Roads

Christopher Colles published his *The Roads of the United States*, in response to the demands of a travel-minded generation.

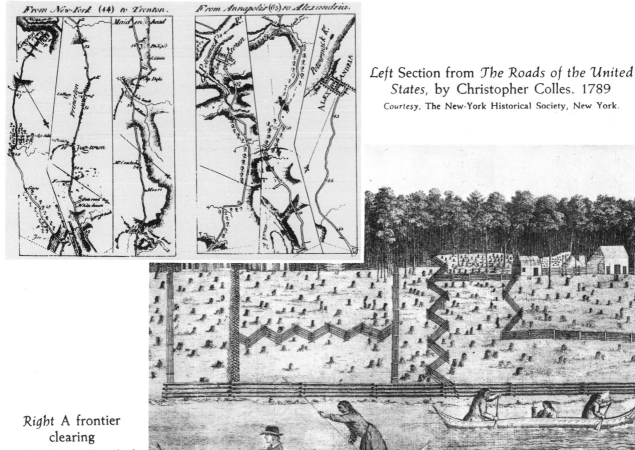

Left Section from *The Roads of the United States*, by Christopher Colles. 1789

Courtesy, The New-York Historical Society, New York.

Right A frontier clearing

Campbell *Travels Through the Interior Inhabited Parts of North America.* 1793.

On the March

Through Pennsylvania lumbered the Conestoga wagons, the freight trains of the era.

Conestoga Wagon. Drawing by F. O. C. Darley

Covered Wagon. A banknote engraving

Marylanders headed westward

Courtesy, Maryland Historical Society, Baltimore, Md.

New towns sprang up on the frontier.

Wilderness settlement

Basil Hall *Forty Sketches made with the Camera Lucida in North America.* 1829.

Westward Ho!

From Niagara Falls to far south of the Natural Bridge, America was on the march, pushing ever westward.

Weld *Travels Through the United States of North America.* 1799.

Niagara Falls

The Natural Bridge, Virginia

Towns of Destiny

Courtesy, The Stokes Collection, The New York Public Library.

Detroit, Michigan. 1794

Courtesy, The Stokes Collection, The New York Public Library.

Baltimore, Md.

INDEX

A

Abbey, the, Chestertown, Md., 316

Adams, John, birthplace at Braintree, Mass., 363; Portrait, 379

Adams, Samuel, portrait by John Singleton Copley, 360

Adolphus, Gustavus, globe dedicated to him by William Jansson, 1617, 162

Advertisements:
Barber, 18th century, 306
Horse racing, 1763, 325
Land: Maryland, colonial, 177; Pennsylvania, colonial, 230; Virginia, 1609, 19
Liquor, 18th century, 325
Medicine, general, 1759, 331
Rangers, recruiting volunteers, 1750, 352
Reading, writing and arithmetic, 18th century, 338
Slaves: runaway, 18th century, 333; unclaimed, 1759, 288
Tailor, 18th century, 310
Theaters: 1752, 327; 1753, 327
See also Broadsides; Posters; Proclamations; Signs

Adz, 17th century, 29

Agricultural implements, Plows: wooden, Pennsylvania, colonial, 242

Agriculture, See Agricultural Implements; Almanacs; Chickens; Corn; Cotton; Farms; Mules; Oxen; Rice; Sugar; Tobacco

Alamance, Battle of, 364

Albany, N. Y., Old Dutch Church, model of, 155; first St. Peter's Church, 1714-15, 255; Van Rensselaer Manor House, 18th century, 315; See also Orange, Fort

Alden, John, House, Duxbury, Mass., 48

Allegheny River, at Pittsburgh, Pa., 347

Allerton (or Cobb) House, Kingston, Mass., 48

Allyn House, Plymouth, Mass., 48

Almanacs, Danforth's 1647, 93; Father Abraham's 1759, 339; Poor Richard's, 285

"Almodington," Almodington, Maryland, c. 1750, 316

Alsop, George, early Maryland poet, portrait of, 195

Ambler House, ruins of, Jamestown, Va., 24

America, discovery of, 1; map of, sixteenth century, 2

Amish, See Mennonite

Amory, John, portrait of, by Copley, 1768, 297

Amsterdam, Holland, weigh house in and map of, 141; view of surrounding country, 17th century, 143; West India House, 17th century, 137

Amusements, See Books; Cards; Dance; Drama; Music; Sports

Ancient and Honourable Artillery Company, facsimile of original charter and first flag used by, Boston, Mass., 110

Anderson, Alexander, woodcut of attack on Indian House at Deerfield Massacre, 269; woodcut of Americans demolishing statue of George III, 360; woodcut showing eagle motif, 406

André, Major John, capture by Americans, medal given to his captors, self-portrait, 394

Andros, Governor Edmond, broadside warning to him by people of Boston, 1689, 131

Animal life, Plymouth Colony, 43; See also specific name of animal

Annapolis, Md., houses in, Brice House, 1740, 317; Jonas Green House, c. 1680, 183; Old Treasury, c. 1690, 183; Paca House, 1763, 317; Sands House, c. 1680, 183; Aunt Lucy Smith's cook shop, 17th century, 183

Anne Arundel County, Md., Cedar Park, c. 1700, 185

Apollo Room, Raleigh Tavern, Williamsburg, Va., 367

Apothecaries' Hall, Charleston, S. C., colonial, 210

Apothecary shops, model of, 18th century, restoration of Hugh Mercer's, Fredericksburg Va. (interior and exterior), 18th century, 331

Apprentices, form of indenture for, 18th century, 285

Aptucxet, Plymouth Colony's first trading post, 48

Archer Lane, Boston, England, old house in, 80

Architecture, Moravian type, Michael Braun Rock House, 1766, 216; State House, New Haven, Conn., 1763, Governor's Palace, North Carolina, 1767, State House, Philadelphia, Pa., 18th century, 346; See also Attics; Barns; Blockhouses; Capitols; Churches; Colleges and Universities; Houses; Interiors; Log Buildings; Markets; Mills; Prisons; Public Buildings, by cities; Schools; Stables; Taverns

Arithmetick, by Isaac Greenwood, page from, 1729, 285

Army, See Battles; French and Indian War; Revolutionary War; Uniforms

Army button with "U. S. A.," American Revolution, 407

Arnold, Benedict, portrait of, portrait of wife and child, view of room in his house, Mt. Pleasant and his headquarters, the Robinson House, 395

Arnold, Eleazer House (interior), Lincoln, R. I., 85-86

Artillery, See Cannon; Firearms

Arundel, Anne, wife of Cecilius Calvert, portrait of, 190

Ashley River, as seen from Middleton Place, South Carolina, 203

Astrolabe, Champlain's, 34

415

Asylums, Bethesda Orphanage, near Savannah, Ga., 18th century, 227

Attics, 17th century, New England, 85

Axes, 17th century, found in Maine, 64; stone, Indian, New Hampshire, 68; colonial, 75

B

Baby bottles, colonial, pewter, 335

Bacon's Castle, Jamestown, Va., 24

Badger, Joseph, portrait of Rev. Jonathan Edwards, 273; portrait of Mrs. Jonathan Edwards, 274

Ballad, "Barren Allen," as sung in mountains of North Carolina, 218

Ballou, Ider, meeting house, Cumberland, R. I., early 18th century, 102

Balls, the Mischianza, ticket and invitation to, 1778, 395

Baltimore, Md., aquatint based on sketch by John Moale in 1752, 295; Mount Clare, 1754, 317; view of, c. 1805, 411

Baltimore County, Md., Old Gunpowder Meeting 17th century, 194

Bancker, Adrian, silver casters by, 291

Baptisms, Rev. Robert Jordan's Baptismal basin, 17th century, New England, 63; Moravian, Colonial, 239; Lutheran christening, 1799, 275

Baptist Churches; Elder Ballou meeting house, Cumberland, R. I., 102; See also Churches

Barbados, 17th century map of, 197

"Barbara Allen," ballad sung in mountain of North Carolina, 218

Barber Shops, 17th century, 120

Barbers, Dutch, 17th century, 144

Barns, tobacco, Calvert County, Md., 188; St. Mary's City, Md., 17th century, 190; with hex decorations, Pennsylvania, 242; log, Pennsylvania, 243; at Osborne Place, Peabody, Mass., 18th century, 339

Barrels, meat packing, 17th century, 145; for shipping goods, 1670, 160; c. 1775, 188; c. 1736, 214; meat in 18th century, 243; making of, by coopers in 18th century, 284

Barrington, Fort, Georgia, plan of, by William Gerard de Brahm, 224

Bartlett, Josiah, portrait of, 380

Bartram, John, copper plate believed to have been made by, 289

Baskets, used by bricklayers, 17th century, 23; vegetable, c. 1640, 90 and 92; bread, 18th century, 245

Bath, N.C., St. Thomas Church, 1734, 211

Bathing, Finnish Bath, c. 1802, 164

Bay Psalm Book, title-page of, 124

Bayberry plant, 118

Beacon, as used on Beacon Hill, Boston, in 17th century, 75

Bears, in early North Carolina, 212

Beaver, 18th century conception of animal and its hut, 66

Bedroom Furniture, See Furniture

Beekman mansion, New York City, N. Y., 313

"Bellarmine" jug, 17th century, 28

Bells, belonging to Father Rasle, 270; used on Conestoga wagon, 18th century, 340; Liberty Bell, Philadelphia, Pa., 381

Berkeley, Bishop George, home of, in Middletown, R. I., 286

Berks County, Pa., barn decorations, 242

Bethesda Orphanage, near Savannah, Ga., 18th century, 227

Bethlehem, Pa., 18th century engraving of, 238

Bethlehem Islands, in Lehigh River, 239

Betty Lamps, See Lamps

Bible, marginal notes from one belonging to Pilgrims, 45; title-page of Genevan, used by Pilgrims, 50; Genevan version, 1606, 124; page from Genevan version, 1611, 127; pages from John Speed's Genealogy of the Bible, 85

Billiards, as played in 18th century, 326

Billop House, Staten Island, New York, 158

Birch trees, winter, New England, 91

Birth Certificates, Caleb Lippincott, 1772, 325; Pennsylvania, decorated, fraktur method, 1784, 338

"Black Beard" (Captain Teach), the pirate, portrait of, and proclamation offering reward for capture of, 214

Blackburn, Joseph, portrait of Margaret Sylvester Chesebrough, 1754, 307; portrait of Theodore Atkinson, Jr., 310; portrait of James Bowdoin III and his sister Elizabeth, 335; portrait of Mrs. Robert Rogers, 352; portrait of James Otis, 1755, 358

Blacksmith, Shops, 17th century, 76; Dutch 17th century, 144; Elkanah Deane, Williamsburg, Va., 1772, 359

Blackstone, William, grave of, 103

Blackwater Presbyterian Church, between Frankford and Ocean View, Del., 173

Blessing of the Bay, Winthrop's boat, 111

Blockhouses, New England, 17th century, 108 and 109; Swedish, Naaman's Delaware 17th century, 163; 18th century, 270; at Ford Duquesne, 347; at Winslow, Maine, colonial, plan of an American block house, 18th century, 353

Bloomfield, Maine, early view of, 257

Boats:
Canoes: Indian dugout, found in Great Dismal Swamp, N. C., 215; Indian dugout, c. 1585, 7
Whaleboats: used at Ticonderoga in French and Indian War, 355
See also Ships

Bogardus farm, Dutch, near New Amsterdam, 143

Bogle, J., portrait of Elbridge Gerry, 378

Bolzius, John Martin, portrait of, 221

Bonnets, See Costume, Women; Item: Hats

Bookbinding, trade card of Andrew Barclay, bookbinder, 18th century, 287

Bookplates, Stephen Cleveland, 18th century, 297; James Logan, Philadelphia, Pa., 18th century, 287; Parish Library, Maryland, colonial, 193; Thomas Prince, 18th century, 281

Books:
Alsop, George, A Character of the Province of Maryland, 1666, 195
Astley, Philip, The Modern Riding-Master, 1776, 396
Bay Psalm Book, 1640, 124
Best Sellers of the 1600's, 122
Book of Psalmes, pages from 1618, 60
Book of Psalms, the Whole, 1606, 127
Bray, Thomas, An Essay Towards Promoting All Neces-

sary and Useful Knowledge, 1697, 193

Colles, Christopher, The Roads of the United States, 409

Cook, Ebenezer, Sot-Weed Factor, 1708, 191

Declaration of the Reasons and Motives for the Present Appearing in Arms of their Majesties Protestant Subjects in the Province of Maryland, 1689, 194

Dilworth, Thomas, A New Guide to the English Tongue, 1770, 337

Edwards, Jonathan, Sinners in the Hands of an Angry God, 274

Goody Twoshoes, The History of Little, 1787, 337

Greenwood, Isaac, Arithmetick, 285

Horn-Book, 17th century, 121

House That Jack Built, The, 1790, 338

Illuminated Manuscript, by Sisters of Ephrata Cloister, 277

Massachusetts Primer, 286

New England Primer, 1690, 122; enlarged, 1736, 286

Nova Britannia, title-page of, 1609, 19

Ward, Samuel, Woe to Drunkards, 1622, 122

Warren, Joseph, Boston Massacre Oration, title-page of, 363

Weems, Mason Locke, Life of William Penn, 1822, 230

Wheatley, Phillis, Poems on Various Subjects, Religious and Moral, 1773, 334

Wigglesworth, Michael, The Day of Doom, 1673, 122

Boone, Daniel, portrait, 408

Bootjack, Pennsylvania, colonial, 248

Boots, See Costume, Men; Item: Boots

Boston, England, St. Botolph's Church, John Cotton's Old Vicarage, 74; "The Old Three Tuns," Old house in Archer Lane, 80

Boston, Mass. (Listed Chronologically)

Beacon on Beacon Hill, colonial, 75

Benjamin Franklin's birthplace, 17th century, 80

Province House, c. 1676, 134

Burgis-Johnston Plan, c. 1728, 256

Carwitham, view of, 1731-36, 256

Faneuil Hall, 18th century, 283

Liberty Tree, 361

British troops arriving, 1768, engraving by Paul Revere, 362

View by Archibald Robertson, 1776, 370

Boston Massacre, engraving by Paul Revere, 1770, oration by Joseph Warren in commemoration of, title-page from, 363

Boston Tea Party, an English caricature, a handbill warning the tea consignees, 365

Bottles, found at Jamestown, 27; Dutch cruet bottles, colonial, 145; traded to Indians for furs, 223; glass by Stiegel, colonial, 321; See also Baby Bottles

Bouquet, Colonel Henry, in conference with the Indians, 349

Bowdoin, James, and sister Elizabeth, portrait by Joseph Blackburn, 335

Bowdoin, William, portrait of, by Robert Feke, 268

Bowler, Metcalf, House, Portsmouth, N. H., 314

Bowling, See Sports: Bowling

Bowls, steatite, Indian, New Hampshire, 68; See also Silver

Bowne House, Flushing, Long Island, 161

Bowyer, William, Governor Endecott's sundial, made by, 72

Boxes, carved oak, 18th century, 358; strong box belonging to Father Rasle, 18th century, 270

Boylston, Thomas, Mr. and Mrs., portraits by John Singleton Copley, 305

"Brabants," plantation home near Charleston, S. C., 202

Bradford, Major John, House, Kingston, Mass., 49

Bradford, Governor William, record of marriage to Dorothy May, 40; autograph of, 42; christening mitts and shirts of, 60

Bradford, William, printing press of, 343

Bradstreet, Anne, home of, 135

Bradstreet, Simon, portrait of, 135

Braintree, Mass., birthplace of John Adams, 363

Braun, Michael, Rock House, near Salisbury, Rowan County, N. C., 216

Bray, Thomas, An Essay Towards Promoting All Necessary and Useful Knowledge, excerpts from, 193

Brazier, silver, by Johann de Nye, colonial, 290

Bread, making of, Pennsylvania, colonial, 245

Bread basket, Pennsylvania, colonial, 245

Brent, Margaret, record of her request to vote in Maryland in 1639, 195

Breughel, Peter, (the Elder), allegorical drawing of meat packing, 145; paintings of Kermiss of Hoboken and Kermiss of St. George, 150; painting of children at play, 151

Brewster, William, autograph of, 42

Brice House, Annapolis, Md., 1740, 317

Bricks, 17th century method of making and laying, 23, 148

Bridgehampton, L. I., N. Y., windmill, 107

Bridgeport, Conn., Silliman House, 18th century, 259

Bridges, North Bridge, Concord, Mass., 1775, 369

Bridges Creek, Westmoreland County, Va., birthplace of George Washington, 348

Bristol, England, wharfs at, 35

British Foot Guards, in exercises from British Manual of Arms, 280

British troops, in colonies, 1768, 362; Boston Massacre, 1770, 363; See also Revolutionary War; War of 1812

Broadsides, from people of Connecticut to Governor Adros, 1689, 131; lamenting the death of old tenor (currency) in Massachusetts, 1750, 282; poems on three counterfeiters being put in pillory, 1767, 328; account of Salem tragedy in which ten people lost their lives while sailing, 329; to raise troops for King George III, 1777, 376

Brockway House (interior), Hamburg, Conn., 100

Brooklyn, N. Y. Vechte-Cortelyou House at Gowanus, 1699, 142; Schenck House, Canarsie Park, 147

Browne, Abraham, Jr., House, Watertown, Mass., 78; interior, 89

Browne, Moses, portrait of, 297

Bruton Parish Church, Williamsburg, Va., 279

Buckets, sap, used by Puritans, 90; meat packing, 17th century, 145; fire, c. 1785, 330; grease, Conestoga wagon, 18th century, 340

Buckland, William, portrait by Charles Willson Peale, 346

Buckle, shoe, 17th century, 27

Buckskin suit, colonial North Carolina, 215

Buffalo, c. 1754, 408

Building, See Carpenters, etc.

Buildings, See Houses; Churches; Public Buildings, listings under names of large cities

Bullet Moulds, colonial, 374

Bullfinch, Charles, adds third story to Faneuil Hall, Boston, Mass., 1805, 283

Bunker's Hill, battle of, view of the battle; a plan of the battle; handbill sent to British troops to lower their morale, 371

Bunks, Swedish, colonial, 167

Burgis–Johnston plan of Boston, c. 1728, 256

Burgis, William, engraving of Harvard College in 1726, 134

Burgoyne, General John, remnant of his Army interned at Charlottesville, Va., 387

Burials, See Cemeteries; Tombstones

Burl utensils, as used by Pilgrims, 17th century, 89

Burlington, N. J., octagonal church, 174; Revell House, 1685, 175

Burt, Benjamin, silver porringer by, 290

Burt, John, silver chafing dish by, 319

Butchering tools and utensils, used in colonial Pennsylvania, 244

Butter Molds, colonial, 119; Pennsylvania Germans, colonial, 246; Pennsylvania German with tulip design, 247

Buttons, 18th century sample cards, 267; Army button worn by New York volunteers, 376; worn during American Revolution by British soldiers, 389; naval, American Revolution, 400; Army, American Revolution, 407

Byrd, Evelyn, portrait of, 263

Byrd, William, lottery ticket of, 327

Byrd, William II, "Westover," his home, 266

C

Cabinet-maker, 17th century, 118

Cabot, Joseph, house of, Salem, Mass., 264

Cabot, Sebastian, portrait of, 34

Calfe, John, powder horn belonging to, 407

Calvert, Cecilius, second Lord Baltimore, portrait of, 176

Calvert, Charles, portrait as a child, by Gustavus Hesselius, 170

Calvert, George, first Lord Baltimore, portrait of, 176

Calvert, Leonard, Governor of Maryland, portrait of, 176

Calvert County, Md., tobacco barns, colonial, 188; room from Eltonhead Manor, c. 1720, 262

Cambridge, Mass., Washington Elm, 372

Camp meetings, in the woods, 274

Campaigns, military, See French and Indian Wars; Revolutionary War

Campion, Miss, with horn-book, portrait, 121

Candles and Candlesticks, snuffer used at Jamestown, 17th century, 27; molds, 17th century, 82; manufacture from bayberries, colonial, 118; dipping reel, Pennsylvania, colonial, 244; molds, Pennsylvania, colonial, 244

Cannon, (Listed Chronologically):
Fort Carolina, Florida, c. 1564, 4
17th century, 13
Port Royal, Bay of Fundy, c. 1609, 35
Rensselarerwyck Manor, 17th century, 156
18th century, 374
British frigate, 18th century, 386

Cannon stove, designed by Baron Stiegel, 324

Canoes, See Boats

Cape Anne, settlement, founding in 1625, 72

Cape Cod, sand dunes as seen by Pilgrims, 42

Cape Fear, N. C., Orton Plantation, 1725, 215

Capen, Parson, House (interior), Topsfield, Mass., 88; (exterior), 133

Capitols:
State:
Connecticut, State House, New Haven, 1763, 346
Pennsylvania, State House, Philadelphia, Pa., 18th century, 381; 1777, 393; c. 1794, 346
Virginia, Williamsburg, 18th century, 253, 289

Cards, from London, 18th century, 328

Carlisle, Pa., view, 18th century, 251

Carolina, map of, sixteenth century, 5

Caroline, Fort, sixteenth century, 4

Carpenter, Esther (Gerrish), portrait of, 306

Carpenter, J. B., portrait of Millard Fillmore, 392

Carpenters, 17th century, 22, tools, 17th century, 76 and 77; building Church, early 18th century, 125; articles and regulations of trade union in New York City, 1767, 342

Carriages, (Listed Chronologically):
Mennonite buggy, 18th century, 276
New Hampshire buggy, c. 1780, 341

Carroll, Charles, portrait by Chester Harding, 378

Cartier, Jacques, portrait of, 34

Cartoons, "Join, or Die," by Benjamin Franklin, 361; Boston Tea Party, English caricature, 1774, 365

Carwitham view of Boston, Mass., c. 1731-36, 256

Castello Plan of New Amsterdam, 140

Catesby, Mark, prints of sassafras and ginseng, 1754, 16; print of skunk, 1754, 43; print of bayberry, 1754, 118; print of rice plant, 1754, 204; print of rattlesnake, 1754, 212

Cato's Tavern, Boston Post Road, early 18th century, 271

Cecil County, Md., charcoal-burner's hut, 192

Cedar Park, Anne Arundel County, Md., 184

Cedar Plank House, Hancock's Bridge, N. J., 175

Cemeteries, Jamestown Island, 30; Burial hill at Plymouth, Mass., 60

Ceremonies, See Indian, Dances; Weddings

Certificates, fireman's New York, 1787, 330

Chafing dish, silver, by John Burt, Boston, colonial, 319

Chairs, See Furniture

Chair mender, colonial, 249

Chamber of Commerce, meeting place of first in New York, Great Seal of Chamber of Commerce of the State of New York, 303

Champlain, Samuel de, battle with Iroquois Indians, 1609, 137; portrait of, 34

Charcoal-burner's hut, Cecil County, Md., colonial, 192

Charles City County, Va., "Westover," 1726, 266

Charleston, S. C. (Listed Chronologically):
"Medway," 1686, 202
"Brabants," 18th century, 202
Rose Hill Plantation, 18th century, 202
Powder magazine, 1703, 373
Fenwick Hall, 1730, 202
"Hampton," 1735, 201
View by Roberts, 1739, 198
St. Philip's Church, c. 1739, 199
Drayton Hall (interior), 1740, 262; (exterior), 1740, 265

Plan of the city by W. G. DeBrahm, c. 1760, St. Michael's Church, 1752, 200

Middleton Place, 1755, 203

Indigo processing, c. 1750, 209

Apothecaries' Hall, c. 1750, 210

Pringle House, 18th century, Gibbes House, 18th century, 317

Charlestown, Battle of, *See* Bunker's Hill, Battle of

Charlotte, N. C., McIntyre Log Cabin, c. 1726, 216

Chase, Samuel, portrait by Charles Willson Peale, 380

Chasuble, Father Marquette's, 1618, 178

Cheese, making of, Pennsylvania, colonial, 245

Cheese press, 17th century, 85

Chemistry, symbols, list of, 18th century, 331

Cheney, Benjamin, tall clock by, 323

Chesebrough, Margaret Sylvester, portrait by Joseph Blackburn, 1754, 307

Chester, Pa., Penn's landing, 229; Caleb Pusey House, c. 1718, Old Assembly House and Penn's Landing Place, Town Hall, 1724, 232; Penn's Meeting House, early 18th century, 234; St. Paul's Church, 1703, 235

Chestertown, Md., room from "The Abbey," 18th century, 316

Chests, *See* Furniture

Chew Mansion, Germantown, Pa., 392

Chickens, raising and marketing, 17th century, 92

Children:
  Moravian Love-Feast, c. 1757, 239
  18th century, 335
  See also Costume; Portraits; Schools; Toys

China, table service, colonial, Monteith Lowescroft, colonial, 320

China Trade, ship Grand Turk and Chinese plate belonging to Elias Hasket Derby, c. 1781, 299

Christ Church, Philadelphia, Pa., view of interior and pulpit, 396

Christenings, *See* Baptisms

Churches (Listed Chronologically, by states):
  Connecticut, Meeting House at Hartford, Conn., 98, First meeting house in New Haven, Conn., 17th century, 105

  Delaware, Swedish Lutheran, Wilmington, 17th century, 171; Blackwater Presbyterian Church, between Frankford and Ocean View, Friends Meeting House, Wilmington, Episcopal, New Castle, colonial, 173; First Presbyterian Meeting House, Wilmington, 18th century, 275

  Maine, First Congregational Church, Kennebunkport, 1764, 353; First Parish meeting house, Portland, 18th century, 408

  Maryland, St. Luke's (Old Wye), Wye Mills, c. 1700, 193; Old Gunpowder Meeting, Baltimore County, Trinity Church, Dorchester County, 17th century, 194

  Massachusetts, Second Meeting House, Plymouth, 59; used by Roger Williams, Salem, Mass., 74; "Old Ship" Meeting House, Hingham, 17th century, 125; First Church, Boston, Mass., silver communion cup given by John Winthrop, 126; St. Peter's, Salem, 18th century, St. Michael's, Marblehead, 18th century, 279

  New Jersey, octagonal Quaker Church, Burlington, colonial, 174

  New York, Old Dutch, Albany, model of, 155; New Dutch Church, New York City, 1731, 255; Old Dutch, Shawangunk, 17th century, Sleepy Hollow, Tarrytown, 17th century, Old Stone, Jamaica, L. I., 17th century, First Reformed (Dutch), Jamaica, L. I., 18th century, 158; St. Peter's, Albany (first one), colonial, 255; ruins of Trinity Church, after fire, ern views, Friends' Meeting House, Haverford, colo-New York City, 1776, 385

  North Carolina, St. Thomas, Bath, colonial, 211; St. Paul's, Edenton, colonial, 211

  Pennsylvania, Gloria Dei, Swedish Lutheran, 18th century, Philadelphia, 171, 172; Old Assembly House, Chester, 234; St. David's, Radnor, colonial and mod-nial, St. Paul's, Chester, colonial, Friends' Meeting House, Merion, colonial and modern, 235; Meeting Houses, Pennsylvania Quakers, 237; Lutheran, Trappe, early and modern views, 241; Old Lutheran, York, 241; Ephrata Cloister, near Lancaster, Pa., 250, 277; Christ Church, Philadelphia, two interior views, 18th century, 396

  Rhode Island, Elder Ballou meeting house, Cumberland, early 18th century, 102; synagogue similar to Trouro Synagogue in Newport, 18th century, 278

  South Carolina, St. Philip's, Charleston, colonial, 199; St. Michael's, colonial, St. James', Goose Creek, colonial, 200

  Virginia, Old Brick Church, Isle of Wight County, old church at Jamestown, 25; Bruton Parish, Williamsburg, 18th century, 279; St. John's, two views, Richmond, 366

Churns, 17th century, 54

Cider press, Pennsylvania, colonial, 242

Cincinnati, Society of the, 405

Claggett, William, tall clock by, 323

Claiborne, William (of Kent Island), Portrait of, 190

Clam rake, 17th century, 92

Clapp, Captain, tavern of, 326

Clark House, Stratford, Conn., 100

Cleveland, Stephen, bookplate of, 297

Clinton, Fort, West Point, N. Y., 395

Clocks (Listed Chronologically):
  Chamber clock, Parson Capen House, Topsfield, Mass., colonial, 88
  Swedish, colonial, 168
  By John Goddard, Newport, R. I., c. 1770, 322
  By William Claggett, 18th century, by Benjamin Cheney, Hartford, Conn., 18th century, face by Hyram Faris, Annapolis, Md., 18th century, label of Aaron Willard, Boston, Mass., 18th century, 323
  First Congregational Church, Kennebunk, Me., 353
  First Parish meeting house, Portland, Me., 407
  See also Watches

Cloth, *See* Textiles

Clothes, *See* Costume

Coaches, James Beekman's, New York City, c. 1770, 341

Cod Fishing, *See* Fishing, Cod

Coddington House, Newport, R. I., 17th cenury, 102

Coffee House, London, 17th century, 42

Cohorn, used in main-top of American Ships, Revolutionary War, 400

Coiffures, Women: 18th century, 306; *See also* Hair Dressing; Portraits

Coins, *See* Money
Colden, Cadwallader, portrait by Matthew Pratt, 1772, 376
Colleges and Universities:
  Brown, view of, 1793, 296
  Columbia, view, 18th century, list of graduates from, 1758-1774, 296
  Harvard, engraving by William Burgis, 1726, 134; view of 1795, 328; engraving by Paul Revere, 1768, view of Holden Chapel, 372
  Princeton, view of, 1764, 296
  William and Mary, Wren Building, 30; copper plate showing Brafferton Hall, Wren Building, President's House, c. 1740, 289
  Yale, Elihu Yale, portrait of, first building at, 268; portrait of Ezra Stiles, president, 307
Colles, Christopher, *The Roads of the United States*, section from, 409
Collin, Rev. Nicholas, Swedish Lutheran minister, portrait of, 172
Collot, Victor, drawing of Pittsburgh, 1796, 347
Columbia University, *See* Colleges and Universities
Columbus, Christopher, woodcut depicting discovery of America, 1; discovery of America, 3
Communion Cup, silver, given by John Winthrop, 126
Concord, Mass., British troops entering, 1775, 368; battle at North Bridge, engraving by Amos Doolittle, 369
Conestoga Wagons, *See* Wagons, covered
Coney, John, silver cup by, 290; Monteith bowl by, 292
Congregational Churches, *See* Churches
Congress, United States, first medal voted by, 372
Connecticut Charter, 1662, 131
Connecticut Colony, 97-101
Connecticut River, 98
Cook, Ebenezer, author of *Sot-Weed Factor*, 1708, 191
Cookie cutters, Pennsylvania German, 246
Cooking, use of brick oven in chimney by Puritans, 87; Pennsylvania German, colonial, 244; *See also* Kitchen Utensils; Kitchens
Cooper, Peter, painting of Philadelphia, Pa., 1718-20, 256
Cooper's tools, colonial, 118
Copley, John Singleton, portraits by:
  Adams, John, 379
  Adams, Samuel, 360
  Amory, John, 1768, 297
  Boylston, Mr. & Mrs. Thomas, 305
  Hancock, John, 378
  Hurd, Nathaniel, 345
  Pelham, Henry, 337
  Skinner, Miss, 306
  Wentworth, Lady Frances, and Governor John, 375
  Winslow, Mr. and Mrs. Isaac, 305
Corn:
  Grinding, by Indians, 57
  Planting, by Indians, 1590, 46
Cornwaley's Crosse, Manor of, St. Mary's County, Md., 180
Costume:
  Children:
    Pilgrim children, 17th century, 59
    Dutch, 17th century, 152
  Children, (Listed by item)

Christening mitts, 17th century, 60
Shoes, wooden, New Amsterdam, c. 1658, 152; boy's shoe, 18th century, 358
Men:
  Virginia, c. 1630, 26
  Doublet, c. 1630, 84
  Massachusetts, Pilgrims, 17th century, 59
  Shoe buckle, 17th century, 27
  Snowshoes, 17th century, 65
  Puritan cloak and stockings, 17th century, 84
  Hat, slipper and doublet, 1639, 186
  Boots, 1639, 187
  Gentleman, London, England, c. 1650, 84
  Maryland planter, 17th century, 193
  Colonial frontiersman, c. 1720, 257
  Buckskin, North Carolina, c. 1725, 215
  Frontiersman (by F. O. C. Darley), c. 1740, 349
  Hunter, Canadian, c. 1753, 65
  Velvet suit worn by Dr. John Peter Le Mayeur, c. 1760, 310
  Cocked hat, c. 1772, 359
  Frontiersmen, c. 1794, 410
  Signers of the *Declaration of Independence*, 378-380
Men, (Listed by Item):
  Boots, 1639, 187
  Buckle, shoe, Jamestown, 17th century, 27
  Buckskin, North Carolina, c. 1725, 215
  Cloaks, Puritan, 17th century, 84
  Doublets, c. 1630, 84; 1639, 186
  Hats, cocked, three cornered, 1639, 186; cocked, colonial, 359
  Shoes, Snowshoes, 17th century, 65
  Slippers, 1639, 186
  Stockings, Puritan, 17th century, 84
  Suits, velvet, Dr. John P. Le Mayeur's, c. 1760, 310
Men, (Listed by function):
  Amish, Pennsylvania, 276
  Frontiersmen, c. 1720, 257; c. 1740, 349; c. 1794, 410
  Hunter, Canadian, c. 1753, 65
  Planter, Maryland, 17th century, 193
  Quakers, Pennsylvania, 237
Women:
  Virginia, 17th century, 26
  Massachusetts, 17th century, 53-54, 59
  Snowshoes, 17th century, 65
  English dresses, 17th century, 87
  Pattens, 17th century, 90
  Housewives, 17th century, 92
  Massachusetts, Puritan, 17th century, 123
  Household dresses, Dutch, 17th century, 145-46
  Dutch, 17th century, 154
  Swedish, Delaware, 17th century, 164
  Quaker bonnet, linen mittens, silk reticule, facsimile of Quaker dress, c. 1703, 236
  Dress, 1719, 267
  Shoes, slipper, 1730, 267
  Dress, c. 1775, 308
  Dress, c. 1776, 396
  Pocketbooks, 18th century, 308
  Costume doll, "Mehetable Hodges," 18th century, and buttons, New England, 18th century, 267
Women (Listed by item):

Buttons, New England, 18th century, 267
Costume doll, "Mehetable Hodges," 18th century, 267
Dresses, English, 17th century, 87; Dutch, household, 17th century, 145-6; Quaker, facsimile of, colonial, 236; wedding dress, 1719, 267; c. 1776, 396
Handbags, silk, colonial, 236; embroidered crewel-work, 18th century, 308
Hats, Quaker bonnet, silk, 236
Mittens, linen, 236
Patterns, 17th century, 90
Shoes, snowshoes, 17th century, 65; 1730, 267
Women (Listed by function):
  Amish, Pennsylvania, 276
  Housewives, 17th century, 92
  Quakers, Pennsylvania, 237
  See also Coiffures; Fans; Indians, Costumes; Portraits; Uniforms
Cotton, Baling, 18th century, 334
Cotton, Rev. John, Portrait of, 73; residence and vicarage of, England, 74
Counterfeiting, "'Tis death to," 383
Counting House, Philadelphia, 18th century, 301
"Country House," foundations of, 24
Court House, See under name of town of county
Covered Wagon, See Wagon, covered
Cowles House, detail from, Farmington, Conn., 99
Craddock House, Medford, Mass., 109
Cradles, See Furniture
Crafts, See Burl; China; Embroidery; Glass; Needlepoint; Pennsylvania German; Quilts; Textiles; Silver
Creamers, See Silver
Creek, See Indians, Creek
Crime, counterfeiting and punishment for, 1767, 328; See also Prisons; Punishments
"Croaton," word left on doorpost by Roanoke settlers, 9
Cross, William, silver nutmeg grater by, 292
Crown Point, map of, 350
Cruet bottles, Dutch, 17th century, 145
Cuffs, See Costume, Men: Item
Cumberland, R. I., Elder Ballou meeting house, interior and exterior view, 102
Cumberland Gap, view of, 408
Cupboards, See Furniture
Curls, See Coiffures
Curling irons, 18th century, 306
Currency, See Money
Currier & Ives, lithograph, Birthplace of George Washington, Westmoreland County, Va., 348
Curtis Creek Furnace, Anne Arundel County, Md., 192
Cushion cover, Dutch, 17th century, 146
Cutchogue, L. I., The Old House, 17th century, 78; The Old House (stairway), 86
Cuyp, Albert, painting of the Pilgrims embarking at Delftshaven, 40
Cypress, Northampton County, N. C., 215

D

Dagger hilt, Jamestown, 27
Dairying, See Milk Maid

Dalarna, Sweden, room in a 17th century house, 167
Dance, The, Negro, 19th century, 208; See also Balls
Danforth, Samuel, Almanack, used by Puritans, 93
Danvers, Mass., Rebecca Nurse House, 1678, 128; stairways in "The Lindens," 1745, 260; Judge Samuel Horton's privy, 18th century, 318
Darby Creek Log House, Pennsylvania, 168
Darley, F. O. C., Engraving of Indian attacking a hunter, 213; vignette of frontier man and woman caring for wounded soldier, 257; drawing of Indians taking captives, 269; drawing of camp meeting, 274; vignette of a hunter, 349; drawing of a Conestoga Wagon, 410
Darnall, Eleanor, portrait by J. E. Kuhn, 335
Davenport, Rev. John, signature of, 105; Puritan minister in New Haven, portrait of, 124
Davies, Thomas, sketch of attack on Fort Washington, 1776, 385
Dawkins, H., engraving of College of New Jersey (Princeton University), 1764, 296
Day of Doom, The, by Michael Wigglesworth (pages from), 1673, 122
Dean, Nathan, privy of, 318
Deane, Elkanah, blacksmith shop of, 359
De Brahm, William Gerard, plans of Charleston, S. C., and Fort Johnson, 200; estimate of cost of operating rice plantation, c. 1750, 206; plan of Ebenezer, Ga., 222; plan of Fort Barrington, Ga., 224; plan of Fort Loudon, 349
DeBries House, East Greenbush, N. Y., 148
DeBry, Theodore, engraving of Jacques Le Moyne's drawings of Fort Carolina, 1592, 4; engraving of John White's map of Roanoc, 1590, 5; engraving of Indians making a dugout, 1590, 7; engraving of Indian massacre in Virginia, 1590, 22
Declaration of Independence, reproduction of the original, 377; portrait of some of the signers, 378-80; place of its adoption and the Liberty Bell, 381
Declaration of the Reasons and Motives for the Present Appearing in Arms of their Majesties Protestant Subjects in the Province of Maryland, 1689, page from, 194
Dederick House, Kingston, N. Y., 157
Dedham, Mass., Fairbanks House, c. 1636, 133
Deer, engraving by Sartain, 43
Deerfield, Mass., Sheldon House, 18th century, 258; Frary House, 18th century, 264
Deerfield Massacre, 1704, 269
Delaware, See Indians
Delaware River, Penn landing at Chester, Pa., 229; Washington crossing the, 391
Delftshaven, Holland, port of embarkation of one group of Pilgrims, 40
Delftware plate, Dutch, 17th century, 147
de Nys, Johann, silver brazier by, 290
De Passe, Simon, portrait of Pocahontas by, 14
DePeyster Boy, one of children of Abraham DePeyster, Jr., New York, portrait of, 154
Derby, Elias Hasket, portrait by James Frothingham, wharf of, Salem, Mass., 298; porcelain plate made for, tea house, ship Grand Turk, 299; bill he paid for having ship figureheads carved, 300
Desk box, American oak, 17th century, 126
Desks, See Furniture

Detroit, Mich., view, 1794, 411

Dickinson, John, portrait by Charles Willson Peale, 361

Dickinson, Samuel, House, Kingston-upon-Hull, Kent County, Del., 173

Dilworth, Thomas, *A New Guide to the English Tongue*, page from 1770, 337

Dining rooms, *See* Furniture; Interiors

Dippers, gourd, colonial, 320

Dishes, *See* China; Silver; Tableware

Dish ring, silver, by Myer Myers, colonial, 292

Dixwell, John, Regicide, map showing grave of, signature of, 130

Docks, *See* Piers

Doctors, *See* Medicine

Dogs:

Pets, Miss Campion's dog, 1661, 121; Abraham De Peyster, Jr.'s, 17th century, 154; Eleanor Darnall's, c. 1760, 335; dog running by Conestoga Wagon, 18th century, 410

Dolls, *See* Toys: Dolls

Dolson, T., 18th century view of merchant's counting house, published by, 301

Doolittle, Amos, engraving of British troops entering Concord, Mass., 1775, engraving of Battle of Lexington, 1775, 368; engraving of battle at North Bridge, Concord, Mass., 369

Doorways, Dutch, colonial from, Thors, 149; colonial, 258; Mt. Pleasant, Philadelphia, Pa., 18th century, 312

Dorchester County, Md., Trinity Church, c. 1680, 194

Dorchester Heights, Boston, Mass., drawing by Archibald Robertson, 1776, 370

Dough troughs, Pennsylvania, colonial, 245

Doughoregan Manor, Howard County, Md., 265

Dove, the, 176

Dover, N. H., William Damme Garrison House, c. 1698, 108

Drain Board, stone, 17th century, 54

Drama:

Playbill for Otway's "The Orphan," 1750, and "Beau in the Sudds," earliest American playbill, 327

Advertising "The Merchant of Venice," Virginia, 1752, 327

Advertising Anthony Joseph Dugee's act on the slack wire, 1753, 327

"The Group," by Mercy Warren, title-page of, 1775, 390

Draw Knives, colonial, 76

Drayton Hall, Ashley River, S. C., 262, 265

Drinking, sermon by Samuel Ward, Title-page of, 1622, 122; ads for sale of rum, wine, and brandy, 18th century, 325

Drinking vessels, Swedish, colonial, 166

Drowne, Shem, weathervane by him on Province House in Boston, Mass., 134

Drums, 17th century, 13

Ducks, canvas back, Maryland, colonial, 191

Duquesne, Fort, Pittsburgh, Pa., plan of, and blockhouse at, 347

Dutch, on Hudson and Delaware, 136-160

Dutch boy, 17th century, 152

Dutch Church, Albany, N. Y., 155; First Reformed Church, Jamaica, L. I., 158

Dutch faces, 154

Dutch houses, 17th century, 142, 148, 159

Dutch landscape, 17th century, 143

Dutch Oven, *See* Kitchen Utensils

Dutch West India Company, and New Amsterdam, 138-9; model of New Amsterdam, 1660, 140; Patroons, 156

Duvivier, Pierre Simon, George Washington medal designed by, 372

Duxbury, Mass., John Alden House, 1653, Standish House, 17th century, 48

Duyckinck, Mrs. Gerret, portrait by her husband, 154

E

Eagle (symbol), United States Seal, 1782, 405; woodcut with eagle, c. 1800, mirror frame with eagle, c. 1800, picture of eagle, 1754, 406

Earl, Ralph, portraits of Mr. and Mrs. Benjamin Tallmadge and children, 304; portrait of Roger Sherman, 380; portrait of Colonel Marinus Willet, 389

East New Market, Md., meat house at "Old House of the Hinges," 18th century, 318

East Taunton, Mass., Nathan Dean's privy, 18th century, 318

Easter Liturgy, Moravian, Pennsylvania, colonial, 240

Eastman, Seth, painting of an Indian sugar camp, c. 1850, 46

Easty, Mary, petition in witchcraft case, c. 1692, 128

Eaton, Theophilus, House of, New Haven, Conn., signature of, 105

Ebenezer, Ga., plan by William Gerard DeBrahm, 222

Edenton, N. C., St. Paul's Church, 1736, 211

Edwards, Rev. Jonathan, portrait of, home of, 273; title-page of sermon at Enfield, Mass., 1741, 274

Edwards, Mrs. Jonathan, portrait of, 274

Electricity, apparatus, 18th century, 344

Eliot, Bernard, Mr. and Mrs., portraits of, by Jeremiah Theus, 304

Eliot, John, preaching to the Indians, 194

Elm Tree, Wethersfield, Conn., 98

Eltonhead, Manor, Calvert County, Md., 262

Embroidery, sampler by Mary Hollingworth, 17th century, 61; c. 1740, 292; crewelwork, lady's pocketbook, and pocketbook made by Eliza Willard, 18th century, 308

Embroidery Frame, 18th century, 309

Emigration westward, at close of Revolutionary War, 410

Endecott, John, sundial of, 72; chair of, 84; sword of, 95; portrait of, 72

Ephrata Cloister, mill at, colonial, 250; near Lancaster, Pa., 277

Erie, Fort, on Niagara River, plan of, as built by John Montresor, 356

Escritoire, *See* Furniture

Esopus Landing, Hudson River, 157

Essay Towards Promoting All Necessary and Useful Knowledge, by Thomas Bray, pages from, 1697, 193

Eutaw Springs, battle of, 388

Everard, Gilles, author of *Panacea*, 20

Exeter, N. H., Gilman Garrison House, c. 1650, 108

F

Factories, *See* Interiors: Factories

Faden, William, plan of city of Philadelphia, Pa., 1777, 393

Fairbanks House, Dedham, Mass., 133

Fairfield, Conn., Ogden House (interior and exterior), 106

Fairs, Dutch Kermis, colonial, 150

Faithorne, William, engraving of Augustine Herman's map of Virginia and Maryland, 1673, 189

Falls:

Jones' Falls, near Baltimore, Md., c. 1820, 195

Niagara, c. 1799, 411

Sawkill River, c. 1830, 232

Faneuil Hall, 1805, 283

Fans, English, colonial, 263

Faris, Hyram, clock face by, 323

Faris, William, design for a teapot, 291

Farmers, Dutch, 17th century, 144

Farmer's Almanack, The, See Books

Farming, vegetables and herbs grown by Puritans, 93; Puritans, 98; *See also*, Agriculture; Agricultural Implements; Farmers; Gardens; names of specific commodities

Farmington, Conn., Gleason House, detail from, detail from a demolished house, detail from Older Cowles House, 99; Whitman House, c. 1660, 100

Farms:

Bogardus, Dutch, near New Amsterdam, 143

Swedish, colonial, Finnish, model of, colonial, 169

Quaker, colonial, 237

18th century, Pennsylvania, 242

Fashion, *See* Costume

Father Abraham's Almanack, title-page of, 1759, 339

Feke, Robert, portrait of William Bowdoin, 1748, 268; portrait of Isaac Royall and family, 375

Fences:

Brick, Middleton Place, S. C., 203

Ornamental iron, Charles City County, Va., 18th century, 266; Charleston, S. C., 18th century, 317

Picket, Salem, Mass., 133; New York, 255; Princeton, N. J., 1764, 296

Post and rail, near Wilmington, Del., 18th century, 169; Lancaster, Pa., 1796, 251; New York, 1731, 255

Snake, South Carolina, 18th century, 202; South Carolina, c. 1829, 206; near Lancaster, Pa., 18th century, 271; frontier settlement, 18th century, 409

Stockade, Fort William and Mary, Piscataqua River, 17th century, 70

Stone, Kingston, Mass., 17th century, 49; Wilmington, Del., 1740, 275; Concord, Mass., 1775, 368

Stone and picket, Harvard College, 1795, 328

Fenner House, Johnston, R. I., 102

Fenwick Hall, Stono River, near Charleston, S. C., 1730, 202

Fenwick, Lady, grave of, Saybrook, Conn., 101

Ferries:

New York City, list of rates on New York to "Island of Nassau" Ferry, c. 1733, 272

Philadelphia Ferry, 18th century, 272

Gray's Ferry, Schuylkill River, Pa., 391

Finance:

Stabilizing of Massachusetts currency by Great Britain after siege of Louisburg, 282

Robert Morris, financier, 384

Types of money in use during American Revolution, 384

Fincken, James H., etching of Nathan Hale School, New London, Conn., 338

Finley, Samuel, President of College of New Jersey (Princeton), portrait of, 275

Finns, social life of, 164

Fire buckets, 1784-1789, 330

Fire engines, New Hampshire, colonial, Salem, N. C., 1784, 330

Fire, equipment for fighting, 17th century, 112; 17th century Dutch, 153

Fire scoop, colonial, 86

Fire Screen, *See* Furniture

Firearms:

Guns, swivels, colonial, 382

Muskets, matchlock, 17th century, 95, 96; Swedish, 17th century, 163; 17th century, 187; details of, colonial, 214

Pistols, Revolutionary War period, 374; c. 1775, 374; colonial, 382

Rifles, "Kentucky," c. 1775, silver ornaments for rifle stocks, c. 1775, 374

Firemen, Certificate, New York, 1787, 330

Fireplaces:

Harlow House, Plymouth, Mass., 17th century, 52

Ogden House, Fairfield, Conn., colonial, 106

Dutch, colonial, 149

Swedish, colonial, 168

Tudor Hall, St. Mary's County, Md., 183

Charleston kitchen, colonial, 203

New England, 18th century, 314

Maryland, 18th century, 316

Apollo Room, Raleigh Tavern, Williamsburg, Va., 18th century, 367

Kitchen, colonial, 407

Fish, Colonel Nicholas, mess kit, Revolutionary War, 397

Fish, fishing stages, salting down cod, 33; women cleaning, 17th century, 92

Fishing, by Indians at Roanoke settlement, 7; for cod on Grand Banks, 17th century, 31

Fishkill, N. Y., Verplanck House, 18th century, 405

Fiskdale, Mass., Shumway House, c. 1740, 259

Flags:

American, Easton Flag, early version of stars and stripes, 406

Cross of St. George, used by Ancient and Honourable Artillery Company, c. 1638, 110

Siege of Louisberg, flag carried at, 1744-45, 280

Society of the Cincinnati, 1783, 405

Flax brake, colonial, 116-117

Flax, skeins of, 117

Flax wheel, 17th century, 53

Florida, French in, 4; map of, sixteenth century, 5

Flushing, N. Y., Bowne House, 1661, George Fox preaching to Quakers, c. 1671, 161

"Folly," The, St. Mary's County, Md., 184

Footstools, *See* Furniture: Stools

Foot stove, 17th century, 123

Foot washing, practiced by Amish and Moravian sects, 276

Foster, John, wood engraving of Rev. Richard Mather, 73

Fouache, J. B., silver soup tureen and pair of vegetable dishes by, 320

Fowls, *See* Chickens

Fox, George, Quaker leader, portrait of, preaching to Quakers, Flushing, Long Island, 161

Fox Hunting, *See* Hunting

Fox, red, 257

Foyers, entrance hall, Drayton Hall, Ashley River, S. C., 18th century, 262; Mt. Pleasant, Fairmount Park, Philadelphia, Pa., 18th century, 312

Fraktur, Pennsylvania German, 18th century, 338

France, ships used during French and Indian wars, 355; troops being reviewed at Quebec, c. 1750, 356; troops landing, Newport, R. I., Revolutionary War, 398; soldiers sent to aid in American Revolution, 399

Franklin, Benjamin, supposed birthplace of, Boston, Mass., 80; *Poor Richard's Almanack,* printing press used by, 285; stove designed by, 324; imprint: *Some Account of the Pennsylvania Hospital,* title-page of, 1754, 332; "Join, or Die" cartoon, by him, 1754, post-master's appointment, signed by him, 361; portrait by Charles Willson Peale, 378

Franklin Stove, 324

Frary House, Deerfield, Mass., 264

Fraser, Charles, water color of scene near Charleston, S. C., 1801, 201; water color of "Brabants," near Charleston, S. C., 202; water color of tavern around which Battle of Eutaw Springs was fought, 388

Fraunces Tavern, New York City, etching by Robert Shaw, 404

Freake, Mrs. Elizabeth Clarke, and baby Mary, portrait of, 87

Frederica, Del., smokehouse at "Mordington," Frederica vicinity, 18th century, 318

Frederica, Ga., plan of fortifications at, 224

Fredericksburg, Va., Hugh Mercer's Apothecary shop, c. 1763, 331

French, *See* France

French and Indian Wars, 347-356

Friends Meeting Houses, Haverford, Pa., Merion, Pa., 235; Wilmington, Del., 173

Frigate, *See* Ships: Naval

Frontier, clearing, 18th century, 409

Frothingham, James, portrait of Elias Hasket Derby, 298

Frows and frow clubs, colonial, 77

Fur Trade:
  Furrier, 17th century, 118
  Selling in Holland, 17th century, 137
  Traders at New Amsterdam, 138
  Bottles traded to Indians in exchange for furs, 223
  Price list of skins, 1767, 311

Furnace Creek, Md., Curtis Creek Furnace, 192

Furnaces:
  Curtis Creek Furnace, Anne Arundel County, Md., colonial, 192
  Nassawango Furnace, near Snow Hill, Worcester County, Md., colonial, 192
  Outdoor, Pennsylvania, colonial, 243

Furniture (Listed by items):
  Beds, Thomas Hart House, Ipswich, Mass., c. 1640, 81; Shaw House, Hampton, N. H., 17th century, 82;

  Swedish, colonial, 167; Millbach, Lebanon County, Pa., 18th century, 216; Governor's Palace, Williamsburg, Va., 18th century, 263; Green room, Beekman mansion, New York City, 18th century, 313; camp bedstead used by Washington, 397

  Chairs (Listed Chronologically):
    Three-legged or Boffet chair, 16th century, 83
    Carved oak wainscot, early 17th century, Elder Brewster's, early 17th century, Carver, early 17th century, Mather high chair, early 17th century, 51
    Turned slat-back chair, 17th century, 52
    Cane seat and back, 17th century, 69
    Turned slat-back, 17th century, wainscott, c. 1600, 84
    Carver, and slat-back, colonial, 88
    Bannister-back, colonial, 89
    Dutch, colonial, 148-9
    Kubbstol, primitive Swedish chair, colonial, 166
    Swedish, colonial, 167-8
    Dutch, cyma curves, colonial, and slat-back, New England, colonial, 259
    Pennsylvania German, 18th century, 261
    Eltonhead Manor, Calvert County, Md., c. 1720, and cane chairs, Henry Sewall House, Secretary, Md., 1720, 262
    Side Chairs, bed chamber, Governor's Palace, Williamsburg, Va., 18th century, 263
    Side Chairs, Metcalf Bowler House, Portsmouth, N. H., 18th century, and highbacked armchairs, Samuel Wentworth house, Portsmouth, N. H., 18th century, 314
    Side Chairs, Van Rensselaer Manor House, Albany, N. Y., 18th century, 315
    Side Chairs, Daphne Room, Raleigh Tavern, Williamsburg, Va., colonial, and upholstered wing, Almodington, Md., c. 1750, 316
    Side, and armchairs, Mt. Pleasant, Philadelphia, Pa., 18th century, 395

  Chests, Spanish treasure, 16th century, 3; linen, Virginia, 17th century, 29; linen, New England, 17th century, 55; Thomas Hart House, Ipswich, Mass., c. 1640, 81; hand carved oak, New England, 17th century, 83; Swedish, 17th century, 165; dower, by Christian Setzer, 1785, Pennsylvania German, 247; of drawers, New England, c. 1740, 259

  Clocks, *See* Clocks

  Cradles, Peregrine White's, 50; doll's, early New Hampshire, 69; Massachusetts, c. 1640, 81; Parson Capen House, Topsfield, Mass., colonial, 88; Swedish, 17th century, 166; by Daniel Savory, Warner, N. H., colonial, 358

  Cupboards, pine, Pennsylvania German, 247; built-in, Newington, Conn., c. 1735, 259

  Desks, said to have been used on Braddock's campaign of 1755, 348

  Escritoire, block-front, 1760-70, 323

  Highboy, c. 1760, 322

  Kas, Dutch, 17th century, 149, 152

  Lamps, *See* Lighting

  Linen press, Dutch, 17th century, 146

  Lowboys, by John Goddard, Newport, R. I., c. 1760, style of William Savery, Philadelphia, Pa., c. 1750, 322

  Mangle, Swedish, colonial, 166

Mirrors, wall, Mt. Pleasant, Philadelphia, Pa., c. 1750, 312; wall, Daphne Room, Raleigh Tavern, Williamsburg, Va., 18th century, 316; over mantel, Almodington, Maryland, c. 1750, 316

Press cupboards, used by Pilgrims, 50; colonial, 88

Secretary, by John Goddard, Newport, R. I., c. 1770, 322

Settles, pine, colonial, 88; Pennsylvania colonial, 248

Stools, three-legged Swedish, colonial, 164; foot stool, Lancaster County, Pa., colonial, 249

Stoves, See Stoves

Tables (Listed Chronologically):
  Trestle, colonial, and folding, 17th century, 55
  Bed, Shaw House, Hampton, N. H., 17th century, 82
  Dining room, Schenck House, Brooklyn, N. Y., colonial, 147
  Dutch, colonial, 148-9
  Scandinavian, 17th century, 166
  Dining room, Swedish, colonial, 167
  Dining room, Letitia Street House, Philadelphia, Pa., 233
  Dining room, Shumway House, Fiskdale, Mass., 18th century, and butterfly, 18th century, 259
  Trestle, dining room, and occasional, Pennsylvania German, Millbach, Lebanon County, Pa., 18th century, 261
  Gate-legged, Henry Sewall House, Secretary, Md., 1720, 262
  Bed chamber, Governor's Palace, Williamsburg, Va., colonial, 263
  Gate-legged, Samuel Wentworth House, Portsmouth, N. H., 18th century, 314
  Side Table, claw-foot, Van Rensselaer Manor House, Albany, N. Y., 18th century, 315
  See also Interiors

Furniture label, of William Savery, 323

Furniture manufacture, 17th century, 118

G

Galloway, Richard, Cedar Park, Md., built by him, c. 1700, 185

Games, See Cards; Sports

Gaols, See Prisons

Gardner, Daniel, portrait of Peggy Shippen and child, 395

Garrison, Nicholas, drawing of Philadelphia, Pa., 1767, 332

Garrison Houses, See Block Houses

Garrison House (home of T. D. Garrison), Dover, N. H., 108

Genealogy of the Bible, John Speed's, 85

George III, king of England, Americans demolishing his statue, 360

Georgia, Trustees receiving the Indians, 1734, 219

Georgia Gazette, See Periodicals: Newspapers

Germantown, Pa., birthplace of David Rittenhouse, Paper-mill Run, 250; Chew Mansion, 18th century, 392

Gerrish, Abigail, and her grandmother, portraits of, by John Greenwood, c. 1750, 268

Gerry, Elbridge, portrait by J. Bogle, 378

Gibbes House, Charleston, S. C., 317

Gibbs, James, designs for church clock towers from A Book of Artichtecture, 1726, 199

Gibbs, Robert, portrait of, 121

Gilman Garrison House, detail from, Exeter, N. H., 108

Ginseng, Virginia, 16

Glass, glassmaking, 17th century, 18; glassmakers at work, 18th century, 321; objects made by Stiegel, colonial, 321

Gleason House, Farmington, Conn., detail from, 99

Globe, engraved by William Jansson and dedicated to Gustavus Adolphus, 1617, 162

Gloria Dei, Swedish Lutheran Church, 171, 172

Goddard, John, lowboy by, secretary by, tall clock by, 322

Goffe, William, Regicide, signature of, 130

Gold Coins, See Money: Coins

Goldthwaite, Michael B., powder horn of, 1756, 352

Goose Creek, S. C., St. James' Church, 1711, 200

Gordon, Peter, view of Savannah, Ga., 1734, 220

Gorton House, Providence, R. I., 17th century, 102

Gourd dipper, colonial, 320

Governor's Castle, St. Mary's City, Md., artifacts found at, 183; a reconstruction of it, 1639, 185

Governor's Palace, rooms from, Williamsburg, Va., 263

Gowanus, L. I., N. Y., "Old Stone House" at, 142

Graeme Park, Pa., Gov. Keith House, 1721, 265

Graham, Morris, house of, Pine Plains, N. Y., 148

Grand Banks, fishing boats on, 31

Grant, Alexander, House, Salem, N. J., 174

Gravestones, See Cemeteries; Tombstones

Graveyards, See Cemeteries

Gray's Ferry, Schuylkill River, Pa., 18th century view, 391

Grease Buckets, used in Conestoga Wagon, 18th century, 340

"Great Awakening," c. 1740, 273

Great Pond, Acadia National Park, Mount Desert, Maine, 66

Great Smoky Mountains, N. C., 218

Green, Jonas, House, Annapolis, Md., 183

Greenwood, John, drawing of Yale College, 1749, 286; portrait of Abigail Gerrish and her grandmother, c. 1750, 268

Grigg, Williams, silver tongs by, 319

Grist mills, as used in mountains, 218

"Group, The," a play by Mercy Warren, title-page of, 1775, 390

Guilford, Conn., Caldwell House, detail from, Hyland-Wildman House, detail from, 99; Whitefield House, c. 1640, 100

Guilden (coin), 1698, United Provinces, 153

H

Habre de Venture, Port Tobacco, Charles County, Md., 316

Hackensack, N. J., Terheun House, c. 1670, 175

Hairdressing, Pumpkin haircut, Connecticut, 17th century, Barber shop, 17th century, 120; Dutch barber, 17th century, 144; advertisement by haircutter, 306; See also Coiffures

Hale, Nathan, School, New London, Conn., Colonial, 338

Half Moon, model of the, 136

Hall, Basil, Wilderness settlement, sketch of, c. 1829, 410; view of a Georgia log cabin, c. 1829, 221

Hall, Lyman, portrait of, 380

Hamburg, Conn., Brockway House (stairway), 100

Hamilton, Andrew, architect of State House in Philadelphia, 346

Hammersley, Thomas, silver marrow spoon by, 319

Hampton, home of the Horry family, near Charleston, S. C., 201

Hampton, N. H., Shaw House (bedroom), 82

Hancock, John, home on Boston Common, 362; portrait by John Singleton Copley, 378

Hancock House, Hancock's Bridge, N. J., 175

Hancock-Clarke House (Interior), Lexington, Mass., 85

Hancock's Bridge, N. J., Hancock House, 17th century, Cedar Plank House, 17th century, 175

Handbills, Warning to tea consignees, Boston, Mass., 365

Harding, Chester, portrait of Charles Carroll, 378

Hardware:
    Hinges: found at Jamestown, 26
    Locks: barn, Colonial Pennsylvania, 243

Harlow House (interior), Plymouth, Mass., 52, 54

Harness, See Carriages; Coaches; Wagons

Hart, Thomas, House (interior), Ipswich, Mass., c. 1640, 49, 81

Hartford, Conn., Rev. Thomas Hooker's House, Meeting House, 98

Harvard University, See Colleges and Universities

Harveys Neck, Perquimans County, N. C., early 18th century, 216

Hasbrouck, Benjamin, House, High Falls, New York, fireplace from, Colonial, 149

Hatchels, Colonial, 116, 117

Hatchets, hewing, Colonial, 75

Hats, See Costume; Uniforms

Hatteras beach, shipwreck on, 9

Hatters, preparing wool for felt, at work, 18th century, 311; block and mallet, 17th century, 113

Haverford, Pa., Friends Meeting House, 1700, 235

Haverstraw, N. Y., view of, c. 1825, 389

Hawkins, John, coat-of-arms with slave as crest, 20

Hawks, John, Governor Tryon's palace at New Bern, N. C., designed by him, 364

Heap, George, View of Philadelphia, c. 1750, 293; View of Philadelphia Ferry, c. 1750, 272

Heathcote, Caleb, Mayor of New York City, 1711-13, portrait of, 268

Heating, See Fireplaces; Stoves

Helmet, Swedish, 17th century, 163

Hemp, drawing fibers, c. 1756, heckling, c. 1756, plant, 116; rope made from, c. 1762, 116, 284

Hempstead House, New London, Conn., 100

Hendrick, King, Mohawk Sachem, portrait of, 350

Henniker, N. H., Ocean-Born-Mary House (brick oven), 87

Henry, Patrick, "Give Me Liberty or Give Me Death," church where he made this speech, his walnut table, his portrait, 366; parody broadside of Governor Dunmore's proclamation against him, 367

Herbs, Colonial, 17th century, 58, 93

Herrman, Augustine, Map of Va., and Md., 1760, portrait of, 1673, 189

Hesselius, Gustavus, Portrait of Charles Calvert as a child, portrait of Tishcohan, Delaware chief, 1735, 170; painting of Lappawinsoe, Delaware chief, 1735, 231

Hewes, Joseph, portrait by L. C. Tiffany, 379

Hexerei, used by Pennsylvania Germans on barns, 242

Heywood, Charles, Rose Hill Plantation, home of, 202

Hicks, Edward, primitive painting of Quaker Farm, 237

Highboy, See Furniture

Hill, J., engraving after Shaw of Jones' Falls near Baltimore, 195

Hinges, See Hardware

Hingham, Mass., tide mill, c. 1643, 119; "Old Ship," Meeting House, 1681, 125

Hobbs, Abigail, indictment against, in witchcraft case, 128

Hobby-horse, Colonial Pennsylvania, 249

Hogarth, William, drawing of stocks, 18th century, 129

Holidays, See Celebrations

Hollister House, South Glastonbury, Conn., detail from, 99

Holm, Thomas C., engravings of Indians in New Sweden, 162

Holme, Thomas, plan of Philadelphia, Pa., 229

Holmesburg, Pa., Red Lion Inn, 1730, 272

Holy Bible, Genevan version, page from, 1606, 124

Hooker, Rev. Thomas, house of, Hartford, Conn., 98

Hooper, William, engraving after portrait by John Trumbull, 379

Hopkins, Commodore Esek, portrait, published by Thomas Hart, 400

Hopkins, John, The Whole Book of Psalmes, 1606, page from, 127

Hopkins, Stephen, portrait by Robert Edge Pine, 379

Hopkinson, Francis, trade card of, 303; portrait by Robert Edge Pine, 378

Horn-Book, 121

Horse, See Stables

Horse saddles, 18th century, 271

Horton, Samuel, privy of, 318

Hospitals, Philadelphia, Pa., Some Account of (title-page), 1754 and view, 332

Houdon, bust of Thomas Jefferson, 378

Housatonic River, view on, 409

House That Jack Built, pages from, 1790, 338

Houses, Exterior (Listed by approximate date of building):
    Allerton or Cobb House, Kingston, Mass., c. 1640, 48
    McIntire Garrison House, York, Me., c. 1640, 109
    Whipple House, Ipswich, Mass., c. 1640, 79
    Whitfield House or Old Stone House, Guilford, Conn., 1640, 100
    Iron Works House, Saugus, Mass., 1643, 79
    Jenkins Garrison House, York, Me., c. 1650, 106
    Scotch-Boardman House, Saugus, Mass., c. 1651, 78
    John Alden House, Duxbury, Mass., 1653, 48
    Jacquett House, Long Hook Farm, Del., c. 1660, 173
    Rensselaerswyck Manor, New York, c. 1660, 156
    Whitman House, Farmington, Conn., c. 1660, 100
    Bowne House, Flushing, Long Island, New York, 1661, 161
    House of Seven Gables, Salem, Mass., 1662, 133
    Abraham Browne, Jr., House, Watertown, Mass., c. 1663, 78
    Terheun House, Hackensack, N. J., c. 1670, 175

Craddock House, Medford, Mass., 1677-80, 109
Vaughn, Portsmouth, N. H., c. 1670, 69
Rebecca Nurse House, Danvers, Mass., 1678, 128
Jonas Green House, Annapolis, Md., c. 1680, 183
Sands House, Annapolis, Md., c. 1680, 183
Parson Capen House, Topsfield, Mass., 1683, 133
John Ward House, Salem, Mass., 1684, 78
Revell House, Burlington, N. J., 1685, 175
John Van Arrsens' plantation, Medway, South Carolina, c. 1686, 202
Tile House (Dutch), Newcastle, Del., Colonial, 1687, 159
Manor of Cornwaley's Crosse, St. Mary's County, Md., c. 1690, 182
William Damme Garrison House, Dover, N. H., c. 1698, 108
House occupied by William Penn, Philadelphia, Pa., 1699-1700, 234
Allyn House, Plymouth, Mass., 17th century, 48
Eleazer Arnold House, Lincoln, R. I., 17th century, 86
Bacon's Castle, Jamestown, Va., 17th century, 24
Benjamin Franklin, possible birthplace, Boston, Mass., 17th century, 80
Billop House, Staten Island, New York, 17th century, 158
Major John Bradford House, Kingston, Mass., 17th century, 49
Bradstreet House, North Andover, Mass., 17th century, 135
Clark House, Stratford, Conn., 17th century, 100
Coddington House, Newport, R. I., 17th century, 102
Country House (Foundation), Jamestown, Va., 17th century, 24
DeBries, East Greenbush, N. Y., 17th century, 148
Dederick House, Kingston, N. Y., 17th century, 157
Theophilus Eaton House, New Haven, Conn., 17th century, 105
Fairbanks House, Dedham, Mass., 17th century, 133
Fenner House, Johnston, R. I., 17th century, 102
Gorton House, Providence, R. I., 17th century, 102
Greenspring House, near Jamestown, Va., 17th century, 25
Hempstead House, New London, Conn., 17th century, 100
Rev. Thomas Hooker's House, Hartford, Conn., 17th century, 98
Howland House, Plymouth, Mass., 17th century, 49
Indian House, Deerfield, Mass., 17th century, 269
Leonard House, Raynham, Mass., 17th century, 79
Letitia Street House, Philadelphia, Pa., 17th century, 233
Lynde House, Melrose, Mass., 17th century, 79
"Melrose" slave quarters, Wedgefield vicinity, S. C., 17th century, 208
Morris Graham, Pine Plains, N. Y., 17th century, 148
Norwalk, Conn., 17th century, 106
Ogden House, Fairfield, Conn., 17th century, 106
The Old House, Cutchogue, Long Island, N. Y., 17th century, 78
Old Calvert Mansion, Mount Airy, Prince George's County, Md., 17th century, 184
Old Dutch Cottage, Beaver Street, New Amsterdam, 17th century, 142
Old Dutch House, Broad Street, New Amsterdam, 17th century, 142
Old Dutch House, Pearl Street, New Amsterdam, 17th century, 142
Roger Mowry's "Ordinaire," Providence, R. I., 17th century, 103
Pierce-Little House, Newberry, Mass., 17th century, 79
Caleb Pusey House, near Chester, Pa., 17th century, 232
Sayre House, Southampton, L. I., 17th century, 107
Schenck House, Brooklyn, N. Y., 17th century, 147
Standish House, Duxbury, Mass., 17th century, 48
Stidham House, Wilmington, Del., 17th century, 173
Sutton House, Ipswich, Mass., 17th century, 79
Swedish House, Wilmington, Del., 17th century, 162
Adam Thoroughgood, Jamestown, Va., 17th century, 24
Vechte-Cortelyou House, Brooklyn, N. Y., 17th century, 142
Williams House, Providence, R. I., 17th century, 101
John Adams, birthplace, Braintree, Mass., Colonial, 363
Bartram House, Philadelphia, Pa., Colonial, 256
Samuel Dickinson House, Kingston-upon-Hull, Kent County, Del., Colonial, 173
Jonathan Edwards, home, Northampton, Mass., Colonial, 273
"Folly" House, St. Mary's County, Md., Colonial, 184
Frary House, Deerfield, Mass., Colonial, 264
Leigh House, Freehold, St. Mary's City, Md., Colonial, 180
"Long Lane Farm," St. Mary's County, Md., Colonial, 184
Orton Plantation, Cape Fear, N. C., Colonial, 215
David Rittenhouse, birthplace at Papermill Run, Germantown, Pa., Colonial, 250
Aunt Lucy Smith's Cook Shop, Annapolis, Md., Colonial, 183
Cedar Park House, Anne Arundel County, Md., c. 1700, 184
Tillinghast Mansion, Providence, R. I., c. 1710, 264
Moll Pitcher House, Marblehead, Mass., c. 1720, 260
"Westover," north front, Charles City County, Va., 1726, 266
Doughoregan Manor, Howard County, Md., 1727, 265
Fenwick Hall, Stono River, near Charleston, S. C., c. 1730, 202
Stratford, Westmoreland County, Va., c. 1730, 266
Hampton, near Charleston, S. C., 1735, 201
Middleton Place, near Charleston, S. C., 1738, 203
Brice House, Annapolis, Md., 1740, 317
Drayton Hall, Ashley River, S. C., c. 1740, 265
Mount Vernon, Va., George Washington's House, 1743, 404
Joseph Cabot House, Salem, Mass., 1748, 264
Van Courtlandt Mansion, New York, N. Y., 1748, 264
Mount Clare, Baltimore, Md., 1754, 317
Gov. Benning Wentworth House, Little Harbor, N. H., 1755, 314
Paca House, Annapolis, Md., 1763, 317
John Hancock's Mansion, Boston, Mass., 1768, 362
Beekman Mansion, New York, N. Y., 18th century, 313
George Berkeley House, Middletown, R. I., 18th century, 286
"Brabants," near Charleston, S. C., 18th century, 202

Michael Braun Rock House, near Salisbury, N. C., 18th century, 216

Bridges Creek, birthplace of George Washington, Westmoreland County, Va., 18th century, 348

Chew Mansion, Germantown, Pa., 18th century, 392

Gibbes House, Charleston, S. C., 18th century, 317

Alexander Grant House, Salem, N. J., early 18th century, 174

"Hampton," slave quarters, Towson vicinity, Maryland, 18th century, 333

Hancock House, Hancock's Bridge, N. J., 18th century, 175

Johnson Hall, Johnstown, N. Y., 18th century, 350

Governor Keith House, Graeme Park, Pa., early 18th century, 265

King House, Newport, R. I., early 18th century, 259

Roger Morris' House, New York, N. Y., 18th century, 385

Mt. Pleasant, Fairmount Park, Philadelphia, Pa., 18th century, 312

Newbold-White House, Harveys Neck, N. C., early 18th century, 216

Abel Nickolson House, Salem County, N. J., early 18th century, 265

Philipse Manor, Yonkers, N. Y., 18th century, 307

Pringle House, Charleston, S. C., 18th century, 317

Robinson House, West Point, N. Y., 18th century, 395

Rose Hill Plantation, home of Charles Heyward, S. C., 18th century, 202

Silliman House, Bridgeport, Conn., 18th century, 259

Adam Spach House, Winston-Salem, N. C., 18th century, 217

Gov. Trumbull's House, Lebanon, Conn., 18th century, 305

Gov. Tryon's palace at New Bern, N. C., 18th century, 364

Plan of Gov. Tryon's palace, N. C., 18th century, 346

Washington's headquarters, at Valley Forge, 18th century, 397

Conrad Weiser, home near Womelsdorf, Pa., 18th century, 276

Houses, Exterior (Listed alphabetically, by name):

Adams, John, birthplace, Braintree, Mass., Colonial, 363

Alden, John, House, Duxbury, Mass., 1653, 48

Allerton or Cobb House, Kingston, Mass., c. 1640, 48

Allyn House, Plymouth, Mass., 17th century, 48

Arnold, Eleazer, House, Lincoln, R. I., 17th century, 85, 86

Bacon's Castle, Jamestown, Va., 17th century, 24

Beekman Mansion, New York, N. Y., 18th century, 313

Berkeley's George, House, Middletown, R. I., 18th century, 286

Billop House, Staten Is., N. Y., 17th century, 158

Bowne House, Flushing, L. I., N. Y., 1661, 161

Brabants, plantation near Charleston, S. C., Colonial, 202

Bradford, Major John, House, Kingston, Mass., 17th century, 49

Bradstreet House, North Andover, Mass., 17th century, 135

Braun, Michael, Rock House, near Salisbury, N. C., 18th century, 216

Brice House, Annapolis, Md., 1740, 317

Browne, Abraham, Jr., home in Watertown, Mass., c. 1663, 78

Cabot, John, House, Salem, Mass., 1748, 264

Calvert, Old, Mansion, Mount Airy, Md., 17th century, 184

Capen, Parson, House, Topsfield, Mass., 1683, 133

Cedar Park House, Anne Arundel County, Md., c. 1700, 184

Chew Mansion, Germantown, Pa., 18th century, 392

Clark House, Stratford, Conn., 17th century, 100

Coddington House, Newport, R. I., 17th century, 102

Cornwaley's Crosse, Manor of, St. Mary's County, Md., c. 1690, 180

Country House, Jamestown, Va. (foundation), 17th century, 24

Craddock House, Medford, Mass., 1677-80, 109

Damme, William, Garrison House, Dover, N. H., c. 1698, 108

Dederick House, Kingston, N. Y., 17th century, 157

Dickinson, Samuel, House, Kingston-upon-Hull, Md., Colonial, 173

Doughoregan Manor, Howard County, Md., 1727, 265

Drayton Hall, Ashley River, S. C., c. 1740, 265

Eaton, Theophilus, House, New Haven, Conn., 17th century, 105

Edwards, Jonathan, Home of, Northampton, Mass., Colonial, 273

Fairbanks House, Dedham, Mass., 17th century, 133

Fenner House, Johnston, R. I., 17th century, 102

Fenwick Hall, Stono River near Charleston, S. C., c. 1730, 202

Folly House, St. Mary's County, Md., Colonial, 184

Frary House, Deerfield, Mass., Colonial, 264

Gibbes House, Charleston, S. C., 18th century, 317

Gorton House, Providence, R. I., 17th century, 102

Grant, Alexander, House, Salem, N. J., early 18th century, 174

Green, Jones, House, Annapolis, Md., c. 1680, 183

Greenspring, near Jamestown, Va., 17th century, 25

Hampton, near Charleston, S. C., Colonial, 201

Hampton, slave quarters, Towson vicinity, Md., 18th century, 333

Hancock House, Hancock's Bridge, N. J., 18th century, 175

Hancock's, John, Mansion, Boston, Mass., 1768, 362

Hempstead House, New London, Conn., 17th century, 100

Hooker's, Rev. Thomas, house, Hartford, Conn., 17th century, 98

Howland House, Plymouth, Mass., 17th century, 49

Indian House, Deerfield, Mass., 17th century, 269

Iron Works House, Saugus, Mass., 1643, 79

Jacquett House, Long Hook Farm, Del., c. 1660, 173

Jenkins Garrison House, York, Me., c. 1650, 109

Johnson Hall, Johnstown, N. Y., 18th century, 350

Keith, Governor, House, Graeme Park, Pa., early 18th century, 265

King House, Newport, R. I., early 18th century, 259

Leigh House, St. Mary's City, Md., Colonial, 180

Leonard House, Raynham, Mass., 17th century, 79

Letitia Street House, Philadelphia, Pa., 17th century, 233

Long Lane Farm, St. Mary's County, Md., Colonial, 184

Lynde House, Melrose, Mass., 17th century, 79

McIntire Garrison House, York, Me., c. 1640, 109

Medway, plantation built by John Van Arrsens, c. 1686, 202

Melrose, slave quarters, Wedgefield vicinity, S. C., 17th century, 208

Middleton Place, near Charleston, S. C., colonial, 203

Morris', Roger, house, New York, N. Y., 18th century, 385

Mount Clare, Baltimore, Md., 1754, 317

Mount Pleasant, Fairmount Park, Philadelphia, Pa., 18th century, 312

Mount Vernon, Va., George Washington's house, 404

Newbold-White House, Harveys Neck, N. C., early 18th century, 216

Nickolson, Abel, House, Salem County, N. J., early 18th century, 265

Nurse, Rebecca, House, Danvers, Mass., 1678, 128

Ogden House, Fairfield, Conn., 17th century, 106

Old House, The, Cutchogue, L. I., N. Y., 17th century, 78

Ordinarie, Roger Mowry's, Providence, R. I., 17th century, 103

Orton Plantation, Cape Fear, N. C., Colonial, 215

Paca House, Annapolis, Md., 1763, 317

Philipse Manor, Yonkers, N. Y., 18th century, 307

Pierce-Little House, Newbury, Mass., 17th century, 79

Pitcher, Moll, House, Marblehead, Mass., c. 1720, 260

Pringle House, Charleston, S. C., 18th century, 317

Pusey, Caleb, House, near Chester, Pa., colonial, 232

Rensselaerswyck Manor, New York, c. 1660, 156

Revell House, Burlington, N. J., 1685, 175

Rittenhouse, David, Germantown, Pa., Colonial, 250

Robinson House, West Point, N. Y., 18th century, 395

Rose Hill Plantation, home of Charles Heyward, S. C., 18th century, 202

Sands House, Annapolis, Md., c. 1680, 183

Sayre House, Southampton, L. I., 17th century, 107

Schenck House, Brooklyn, N. Y., 17th century, 147

Scotch-Boardman House, Saugus, Mass., c. 1651, 78

Seven Gables, House of, Salem, Mass., 1663, 133

Silliman House, Bridgeport, Conn., Colonial, 259

Smith's, Aunt Lucy, cook shop, Annapolis, Md., Colonial, 183

Spach, Adam, House, near Winston-Salem, N. C., 18th century, 217

Standish House, Duxbury, Mass., 17th century, 48

Stidham House, Wilmington, Del., 17th century, 173

Stratford, Westmoreland County, Va., c. 1730, 266

Sutton House, Ipswich, Mass., 17th Century, 79

Taylor House, Westport, Conn., c. 1690, 106

Terheun House, Hackensack, N. J., c. 1670, 175

Thoroughgood, Adam, Jamestown, Va., 17th century, 24

Tillinghast Mansion, Providence, R. I., c. 1710, 264

Trumbull's, Gov., house, Lebanon, Conn., 18th century, 305

Tryon's, Gov., palace at New Bern, N. C., 18th century, 346, 364

Valley Forge, Washington's headquarters at, 18th century, 397

Van Courtlandt Mansion, New York, N. Y., 1748, 264

Vaughn House, Portsmouth, N. H., c. 1670, 69

Vechte-Courtelyou House, Brooklyn, N. Y., 17th century, 142

Ward, John, House, Salem, Mass., 1684, 78

Weiser, Conrad, near Womelsdorf, Pa., Colonial, 276

Wentworth, Gov. Benning, House, Little Harbor, N. H., 1755, 314

Whipple House, Ipswich, Mass., c. 1640, 79

Whitfield House, or Old Stone House, Guilford, Conn., c. 1640, 100

Whitman House, Farmington, Conn., c. 1660, 100

Williams House, Providence, R. I., 17th century, 101

Houses, Interior, (Listed by approximate date of building):

Thomas Hart House, Ipswich, Mass., c. 1640, 49, 81

Abraham Browne, Jr., House, Watertown, Mass., c. 1663, 89

Parson Capen House, Topsfield, Mass., 1683, 88

Hancock-Clarke House, Lexington, Mass., 1698, 85

Eleazer Arnold House, Lincoln, R. I., 17th century, 85

Brockway House, Hamburg, Conn., 17th century, 100

Connecticut House, details from, 17th century, 99

Harlow House, Plymouth, Mass., 17th century, 52, 54

Letitia Street House of William Penn, Philadelphia, Pa., 17th century, 233

Ocean-Born-Mary House, Henniker, N. H., 17th century, 87

Ogden House, Fairfield, Conn., 17th century, 106

The Old House (stairway), Cutchogue, L. I., N. Y., 17th century, 86

Plymouth houses, Plymouth, Mass., 17th century, 52

Schenck House, Brooklyn, N. Y., 17th century, 147

Shaw House, Hampton, N. H., 17th century, 82

West Boxford, Mass., 17th century, 118

Cedar Plank House, Hancock's Bridge, N. J., Colonial, 175

Benjamin Hasbrouck House (fireplace), High Falls, N. Y., Colonial, 149

New England House, Colonial, 114

Sheldon House (doorway), Deerfield, Mass., Colonial, 258

Stephen Thors House (Dutch door), New Hackensack, N. Y., Colonial, 149

Warner House (doorway), Portsmouth, N. H., Colonial, 258

Eltonhead Manor, Calvert County, Md., c. 1720, 262

Stenton House, Logan Park, Philadelphia, Pa., c. 1721, 258

Orne House, Marblehead, Mass., c. 1730, 260

Newington, Conn., c. 1735, 259

Drayton Hall, Ashley River, S. C., c. 1740, 262

Shumway House, Fiskdale, Mass., c. 1740, 259

The Lindens, Danvers, Mass., 1745, 260

Almodington, Md., c. 1750, 316

Jeremiah Lee Mansion, Marblehead, Mass., 1768, 315

The Abbey, Chestertown, Md., 18th century, 316

Beekman Mansion, New York, N. Y., 18th century, 313

Habre de Venture, Port Tobacco, Charles County, Md., 18th century, 316

Metcalf Bowler House, Portsmouth, N. H., 18th century, 314

Milbach House, Lebanon County, Pa., 18th century, 261

Mount Pleasant, Philadelphia, Pa., 18th century, 312, 395

Henry Sewell House, Secretary, Md., early 18th century, 262

Van Rensselaer Manor House, Albany, N. Y., 18th century, 315

Samuel Wentworth House, Portsmouth, N. H., 18th century, 314

West Boxford, Mass., early 18th century, 260

Williamsburg, Va., Governor's Palace, 18th century, 263, 264

Houses, *Interior*, (Listed alphabetically, by name):

Abbey, The, Chestertown, Md., 18th century, 316

Almodington, c. 1750, 316

Arnold, Eleazer, House, Lincoln, R. I., 17th century, 85

Beekman Mansion, New York, N. Y., 18th century, 313

Bowler, Metcalf House, Portsmouth, N. H., 18th century, 314

Brockway House, Hamburg, Conn., 17th century, 100

Browne, Abraham, Jr., House, Watertown, Mass., c. 1663, 89

Capen, Parson, House. Topsfield, Mass., 1683, 88

Cedar Plank House, Hancock's Bridge, N. J., Colonial, 175

Drayton Hall, Ashley River, S. C., c. 1740, 262

Eltonhead Manor, Calvert County, Md., c. 1720, 262

Governor's Castle (reconstruction), St. Mary's City, Md., 17th century, 185

Governor's Palace, Williamsburg, Va., 18th century, colonial, 263, 364

Habre de Venture, Port Tobacco, Charles County, Md., 18th century, 316

Hancock-Clarke House, Lexington, Mass., c. 1698, 85

Harlow House, Plymouth, Mass., 17th century, 52, 54

Hart, Thomas, House, Ipswich, Mass., c. 1640, 49, 81

Hasbrouck, Benjamin, House, High Falls, N. Y., Colonial, 149

Lee, Jeremiah, Mansion, Marblehead, Mass., 1768, 315

Letitia Street House of William Penn, Philadelphia, Pa., 17th century, 233

Lindens, the, Danvers, Mass., 1745, 260

Millbach House, Lebanon County, Pa., 18th century, 261

Mount Pleasant, Philadelphia, Pa., 18th century, 312, 395

Ocean-Born-Mary House, Henniker, N. H., 17th century, 87

Ogden House, Fairfield, Conn., 17th century, 106

Old House, The, Cutchogue, L. I., N. Y., 17th century, 86

Old Three Tuns, The, Boston, England, 17th century, 80

Orne House, Marblehead, Mass., c. 1730, 260

Schenck House, Brooklyn, N. Y., 17th century, 147

Sewell, Henry, House, Secretary, Md., 18th century, 262

Shaw House, Hampton, N. H., 17th century, 82

Sheldon House (doorway), Deerfield, Mass., Colonial, 258

Shumway House, Fiskdale, Mass., c. 1740, 259

Stenton House (doorway), Logan Park, Philadelphia, Pa., c. 1721, 258

Thors, Stephen House (Dutch door), New Hackensack, N. Y., Colonial, 149

Van Rensselaer Manor House, Albany, N. Y., 18th century, 315

Warner House (doorway), Portsmouth, N. H., Colonial, 258

Wentworth, Samuel, House, Portsmouth, N. H., 18th century, 314

Houses, foreign prototypes:

English:

Boston, Old Three Tuns, 17th century, 80

Boston, Old houses, 17th century, 80

Compared with American, 17th century, 182

Swedish:

Dalarna, Sweden, Colonial, 167, 168

Houses, *See also* Architecture; Indians: Houses; Log Buildings

Howard County, Md., Doughoregan Manor, 1727, 265

Howe, Sir William, portrait of; rationing notice issued by him, 392

Howland House, Plymouth, Mass., 49

Hudson and Delaware settlements, map of, 1651, 159

Hudson, Henry, on the Hudson River and model of his ship, 136

Hudson River, at New Amsterdam, c. 1643, 138; Bogardus farm, c. 1679, 143; at Fort Washington, 1776, 385; General Burgoyne's Camp, 1777, 387; aquatint view, 1802, 136; at Haverstraw, N. Y., c. 1825, 389; Esopus Landing, c. 1850, 157

Hunting, Fox, 1772, 325

Hurd, Jacob, silver tray by, and silver teapot by, 291

Hurd, Nathaniel, portrait by John Singleton Copley, 18th century, 345

Huron, The (British), 354

L'Huron (French), 355

Hyland-Wildman House, Guilford, Conn., detail, 99

Hymn Books: Ainsworth's *The Book of Psalmes*, pages from, 60

Hyssop, raised by Puritans, 93

I

Illuminated manuscript, made at Ephrata Cloister, 277

Independence Hall, Philadelphia, Pa.: photograph of South door; the Liberty Bell, 381; engraving, 1777, 393

Indian House, Deerfield, Mass., c. 1700, 269

Indian Rock, Narragansett, R. I., 101

Indians, (Listed by subjects):

Battles:

Champlain defeats Iroquois, 1609, 137

Virginia Massacre, 1622, 22

Pequots, 1637, 104

Taking captives, drawing by F. O. C. Darley, 269

Attack on Indian House, Deerfield Massacre, 269

Corn, planting, 46; pounding with mortar and pestle, 57

Costume:

Carolina Indians, Roanoke Island, 16th century, 6, 7

Cherokee, 213

Councils, trustees of Georgia receiving Indians, 1734, 219; with General Bouquet, 1758, 349

Dances: Carolina Indians, ceremonial dance on Roanoke Island, 6

Dances: Miramichi, 35
Fishing, Va., c. 1585, 7
Houses, Bark, 57
Hunting, Miramichi killing a moose, 35
Making maple sugar, 46
Massacres, 1622, 22; Champlain's, of Iroquois, 1609, 137
Religion, Miramichi Indians taught by priests, 35; John
    Eliot preaching, 94; blessing by Father White, 177;
    Moravians baptizing, 217; *see also* Indians: Dances
Scalping victims, 213
Trade, price list of goods, 1703, 270; license to trade
    with Indians, 18th century, 351
Trade list, goods given by Penn in exchange for land,
    230
Treaties with, by Penn at Shackamaxon, 230
Villages, 57; at Roanoke Island, c. 1585, 6-7
Wampum, as used in 17th cetury, 19, 46
Indians (Listed alphabetically, by tribes):
    California, welcoming Drake, 1579, 8
    Cherokee, costume, 213
    Creek, Tomo-Chi-Chi and Creek House, c. 1830, 222;
        Outacite, 1762, 349
    Delaware, Tishcohan portrait of, c. 1735, 170; in New
        Sweden, c. 1640, 162
    Iroquois, massacre of, by Champlain, 1609, 137
    Kiowa, encampment, 1820, 200
    Miramichi, 35
    Mohawk, portrait of King Hendrick, Sachem, 350; mask
        of the Twisted Face, 351
    Niantic, Sachem Ninigret, 103
    Pequots, defeat of, 1637, 104
    Seneca, doctor mask, 351
    Wampanoags, Zerviah G. Mitchell, descendant, 57; King
        Philip, engraving by Paul Revere, 108
Indigo, being cultivated and processed by slaves, plant,
    processing on plantation near Charleston, S. C., 209
Industries, *See* Cotton; Fishing; Glass; Indigo; Lumbering;
    Printing; Textiles; Tobacco; Wool, etc.
Inkstand, Colonial, 132
Inns, *See* Taverns
Insignia, *See* Uniforms
Interiors:
    Apothecaries, Hall, Charleston, S. C., 17th century, 210;
        Hugh Mercer's Shop, Fredericksburg, Va., 1763, shop,
        18th century, 331
    Attic, Hancock-Clarke House, Lexington, Mass., c. 1698,
        85
    Barber Shop, Dutch, 17th century, 144
    Bedrooms, Thomas Hart House, Ipswich, Mass., c. 1640,
        81; Shaw House, Hampton, N. H., 17th century, 82;
        Dutch, 17th century, 144; Millbach, Lebanon County,
        Pa., 1752, 261; Governor's Palace, Williamsburg, Va.,
        1720, 263; Mt. Pleasant, 18th century, 312; Green
        room, Beekman Mansion, 18th century, 313
    Churches, Elder Ballou Meeting House, Cumberland,
        R. I., 102; Christ Church, Philadelphia, 18th cen-
        tury, 396; Gloria Dei, 17th century, 172; Old Gun-
        powder Meeting, Baltimore County, Md., 194; St.
        James's Church, Goose Creek, S. C., 1711, 200; Jew-
        ish Synagogue, 1733-4, 278; Moravian Church, c.
        1757, 239; Old Brick Church, Isle of Wight County,

1887, 25; Quaker Meeting House, 18th century, 234
Dining Rooms, Thomas Hart House, Ipswich, Mass., c.
    1640, 49; Schenck House, Canarsie Park, Brooklyn,
    17th century, 147; Letitia Street House, Philadelphia,
    Pa., 17th century, 233; Daphne Room, Raleigh Tav-
    ern, Williamsburg, Va., c. 1750, 316; Millbach,
    Lebanon County, Pa., 1752, 261; Supper room, Gov-
    ernor's Palace, Williamsburg, Va., 18th century, 364
Domestic room, 17th century, 117
Dutch, New Amsterdam, 17th century, 147, 149
Factories, cheese, 18th century, 245; hat, 18th century,
    311
Finnish bath, c. 1802, home, c. 1802, 164
Halls, Millbach, Lebanon County, Pa., 1752, 261; en-
    trance, Drayton Hall, Ashley River, S. C., 1740, 262;
    Mt. Pleasant, 18th century, 312; stairway, Jeremiah
    Lee Mansion, 18th century, 315; section of great
    hall, Van Rensselaer Manor House, Albany, N. Y.,
    18th century, 315
Harlow House, Plymouth, Mass., 17th century, 54
Kitchens, Harlow House, Plymouth, Mass., 17th cen-
    tury, 52; Ocean-Born-Mary House, Henniker, N. H.,
    17th century, 87; Parson Capen House, Topsfield,
    Mass., 17th century, New England Colonial, 88;
    Abraham Browne, Jr., House, Watertown, Mass., c.
    1663, 89; Dutch, 17th century, 145; Abbot's Glaston-
    bury Abbey, Somersetshire, England, 174; Charles-
    ton, S. C., colonial, 203; Pennsylvania German, York,
    Pa., 1800, 244; Governor's Palace, Williamsburg, Va.,
    18th century, 263; Oakland, S. C., 18th century, 318;
    Colonial, 407
Living rooms, West Boxford, Mass., c. 1675-1704, 118;
    model of one in New Amsterdam house, Colonial,
    147; Swedish, Colonial, 168; Letitia Street House,
    Philadelphia, Pa., 17th century, 233; room from
    Newington, Conn., 18th century, 259; Shumway
    House, Fiskdale, Mass., c. 1740, 259; room from
    West Boxford, Mass., c. 1725, Orne House, Marble-
    head, Mass., 18th century, 260; Eltonhead Manor,
    Calver County, Md., c. 1720, Henry Sewall House,
    Secretary, Md., 1720, 262; Blue Room, Beekman Man-
    sion, 18th century, 313; Metcalf Bowler House, Ports-
    mouth, N. H., 1765, Samuel Wentworth House, Ports-
    mouth, N. H., 1761, 314; The Abbey, Chestertown,
    Md., 18th century, Almodington, Md., c. 1750, Habre
    de Venture, Port Tobacco, Charles County, Md., 18th
    century, 316
Mills, Tide, Hingham, Mass., 1643, 119; paper, 18th
    century, 343
New Amsterdam, 17th century, 147-149
Ogden House, Fairfield, Conn., 17th century, 106
Plants:
    Engraving, 18th century, 343
    Hemp dressing, c. 1756, 116
    Printing, 18th century, 343
Prisons, debtor's cell, gaol at Williamsburg, Va., c.
    1701, 288
Quaker Synod, 18th century, 237
Stairways, *See* Stairways
Stores:
    Cabinet-maker's, 17th century, 118

Furriers, 17th century, 118
Hat shop, c. 1765, 311
Shoemaker's, 1762, 310
Tailor shop, Dutch, 17th century, 144, 146; c. 1762, 310
Weaving shop, 17th century, 115
Swedish rooms, 17th century, 167, 168
Taverns, billiards, 1776, 326; Apollo Room, Raleigh Tavern, Williamsburg, Va., 1775, 367; 18th century, 326
Williamsburg, Va., House of Burgesses, c. 1750, 289
Work room, Tanners', c. 1760, 117
Inventory, of Justinian Snowe, Md., 1639, 186, 187
Ipswich, Mass., Thomas Hart House, c. 1640, 49; bedroom, 81; Whipple House, c. 1640, Sutton House, 17th century, 79
Iron:
Bog, 22
Furnaces, Colonial Md., 192
Objects, fire scoop, 17th century, 86; furnaces, See Furnaces; hinges, 17th century, 26; Kitchen utensils, See Kitchen Utensils; Liberty Bell, Philadelphia, Pa., 381; Machinery, See Machinery; forged iron balance scale, 1770, 359; See also Stoves
Ironworks house, Saugus, Mass., 79
Isle of Shoals, N. H., 67

J

Jack planes, Colonial, 77
Jacks, as used on Conestoga Wagon, 18th century, 340
Jackson, H., forged iron scale by, 359
Jacquett House, Long Hook Farm, Del., 1660, 173
Jails, See Prisons
Jamaica, Long Island, Old Stone Church at, 158
James River, Jamestown, Va., 12
Jamestown, Va., site of, 12; arrival of English at, type of houses at, 13; remains of State House at, 23; remains of houses at, 24; church at, 25; window casement and hardware found at, costume of ladies and gentlemen, 26; household objects used at, 27; pottery and jugs found at, 28; spoons, knives and forks from, 29; Travis graveyard at, 30
Jansson, William, globe engraved by, 1617, 162
Jefferson, Thomas, and the Declaration of Independence, 377; portrait of a bust by Houdon, 378
Jenkins Garrison, House, York, Me., 109
Jew's harp, from Jamestown, 27
Johnson, Fort, Charleston, S. C., William Gerard De Brahm's plan of it, c. 1760, 200
Johnson, Joshua, painting of Mrs. John Moale and granddaughter, c. 1800, 295
Johnson, Sir William, relations with Indians, home at Johnstown, N. Y., portrait, 350
Johnson Hall, Johnstown, N. Y., 350
Johnston, R. I., Fenner House, 17th century, 102
Johnston, Thomas, engraving of Yale College, 1749, 286
Johnstown, N. Y., Johnson Hall, 18th century, 350
"Join, or Die" cartoon, by Benjamin Franklin, 361
Jones, John Paul, portrait from an engraving by Moreau the younger, 400
Jones, Rebecca, Quaker preacher, relics of, 236
Jones' Falls, near Baltimore, Md., Colonial, 195
Jordan, Rev. Robert, baptismal basin of, 63
Journalism, See Periodicals: Newspapers
Judd's Friend (or Outacite), Creek Indian, sketch by Sir Joshua Reynolds, 1762, 349
Judges, Cave, New Haven, Conn., 130
Jug, 17th century, one from Jamestown and one from New England, 28; earthenware, N. H., Colonial, 68
Jukes, Francis, engraving of Mount Vernon, 1800, 404

K

Kas, See Furniture: Kas
Kearsley, John, as architect of State House, Philadelphia, Pa., 346; Christ Church, Philadelphia, Pa., of which he was architect, 396
Keith, Gov., house of, Graeme Park, Pa., 265
Kelpius, Johannes, founder of The Woman of the Wilderness sect, 240
Kennebec River, map showing Sagadahoc settlement, at mouth, c. 1607, 36
Kennebunkport, Me., First Congregational Church, 1764, 353
Kensington, Pa., Penn's treaty with Indians, 1682, 230
Kenton, Simon, portrait of, 408
Kentucky Rifles, 18th century, 374
Kermiss, Dutch fair, 17th century, 150
Kettles, iron, used in kitchen, York, Pa., 1800, 244; brass, used in Colonial Va., 266
Key found at Jamestown, 26
King, Sarah (Northey), portrait of her and her daughter, 335
King House, Newport, R. I., 259
King's College, New York, See Columbia University
Kingston, Mass., Allerton or Cobb House, c. 1640, 48; Major John Bradford House, 17th century, 49
Kingston, N. Y., plan of, Dederick House, 157
Kingston-upon-Hull, Kent County, Del., Samuel Dickinson House, 17th century, 173
Kiowas, See Indians: Kiowa
Kitchens, See Interiors, Kitchens
Kitchen utensils:
Burl utensils, as used by Pilgrims, 17th century, 56, 89
Butter molds, Pennsylvania German, Colonial, 119; 18th century, 246
Colonial New England, exhibit, 88
Cookie cutters, Pennsylvania German, 18th century, 246
Dutch oven, as used by Pilgrims, 56; in Charleston Kitchen, Colonial, 203; as used by Pennsylvania Germans, Colonial, 248
Kettles, Indians making maple sugar in, c. 1723, 46; used in Ocean-Born-Mary House, Henniker, N. H., Colonial, 87; used in York, Pa., 1800, 244; used in Virginia, 18th century, 266
Knives and forks, used in Jamestown, 17th century, 29; cleaner, Colonial Pennsylvania, 248
Muffin irons, Pennsylvania German, Colonial, 248
Pots, Colonial, 87; iron, belonging to Captain Myles

Standish, 50; belonging to Rebecca Jones, 18th century Quaker, 236

Skillet, belonging to Rebecca Jones, 18th century Quaker, 236

Spice Mill, Colonial, 119

Knives, draw, 17th century, 76

Kosciusko, Thaddeus, portrait, 398

Kruisdaalder (cross dollar), 1655, Brabant, Philip IV of Spain, 153

Kuhn, J. E., portrait of Eleanor Darnall, 335

L

Labor Unions, Colonial, 342

Ladders, House building, early 18th century, 77; building church, early 18th century, 125

Lafayette, Marquis de, portrait by Charles Willson Peale, 398

Lamps:
Betty, 17th century Puritan, 81
Flemish, 17th century, 149

Lancaster, Pa., 18th century view of, 251; Old Spread Eagle Inn, 18th century, 271

Landis' Store, Pennsylvania Colonial, 243

Lantern, Colonial, 367

Lappawinsoe, Delaware chief, painted by Gustavus Hesselius, 231

Latrobe, Benjamin, drawing of Gov. William Berkeley's mansion, 25

Leather, making of, in Colonial times, 117

Lebanon County, Pa., rooms from Millbach, 1752, 261

Lebanon, Conn., Gov. Trumbull's house and war office, 18th century, 305; Tories hung in effigy, c. 1770, 357

Lee, Jeremiah, Mansion (interior), Marblehead, Mass., 315

Lee, Richard Henry, portrait by Charles Willson Peale, 379

Lee, Robert E., Birthplace, 266

Lee, Thomas, home "Stratford," Westmoreland County, Va., 266

LeHigh River, Pa., 231; Bethlehem Islands in, 239

Leigh House, St. Mary's Hill, Freehold, Md., 180

Leisure, See Amusements

Le Moyne, Jacques, drawings of Fort Caroline, 1592, 4

Leonard House, Raynham, Mass., 79

Le Roux, Charles, silver salt cellars by, 319; silver tankard by, 320

Letelier, John, silver teaset by, 215

Letitia Street House, home of William Penn, Philadelphia, Pa., 233

Letters, 17th century, 132

Leutze, Emanuel, painting of Washington crossing the Delaware, 391

Leverett, John, Governor of Massachusetts Bay Colony, portrait, 94

Lexington, battle of, engraving by Amos Doolittle, 368

Lexington, Mass., Hancock-Clarke House (attic), c. 1698, 85

Leyden, Holland, map of, Dutch home of Pilgrims, 39

Liberty Bell, Philadelphia, Pa., 381

Libraries, Newport, R. I., Redwood, 1748, 287

Library Company, Philadelphia, Pa., excerpt from the Minutes of, 287

License, to trade with Indians, 18th century, 351

Lighting:
Candles, snuffer used at Jamestown, 17th century, 27
Rush light holders, 17th century, 52; lights, 17th century Puritan, 81
Betty lamps, 17th century Puritan, 81
Candle molds, 17th century Puritan, 82
Candles, manufactured from bayberries, Colonial, 118
Lamp, Flemish, 17th century, 149
Chandelier, Dutch, 17th century, 149
Candles, dipping reel, Colonial Pennsylvania, 244
Candle molds, Colonial Pennsylvania, 244
Lanterns, Colonial, 367

Lincoln, R. I., Eleazer Arnold House (attic), c. 1681, 85, 86

Lindens, The, Danvers, Mass., 260

Linen Press, See Furniture: Linen Press

Lippincott, Caleb, birth certificate of, 325

Little Goody Twoshoes, pages from, 1787, 337

Little Harbor, N. H., Gov. Benning Wentworth House, 1755, 314

Living rooms, See Interiors: Living rooms

Livingston, Philip, portrait, 378

Locke, John, portrait, and his Fundamental Constitutions of Carolina, 196

Locks, barn, 243

Log Buildings:
McIntyre Log Cabin, near Charlotte, Mecklenberg County, N. C., c. 1726, 216
Log House at Winston-Salem, N. C., c. 1766, 217
Darby Creek House, Pa., Colonial, 168
Cabins, Swedish, Colonial, 168
Two cabins, Pa., Colonial, 231
Barn, Pa., Colonial, Landis' Store, Pa., 243
Georgia Cabin, c. 1829, 221
Creek Indian House, c. 1835, 222

Logging, See Lumbering

Logan, James, bookplate of, 287

Lolonois, François, pirate, portrait, 160

London, showing Tower where William Penn was imprisoned, 288

Long Hook Farm, Del., Jacquet House, c. 1660, 173

Long horn, Swedish, Colonial, 169

Long Lane Farm, St. Mary's County, Md., 184

Lonsdale, R. I., William Blackstone's grave, 103

Looking glasses, See Furniture: Mirrors

Loom, 17th century, 54; Colonial, 115

Lords Proprietors of the Province of Carolina, signature of, and Great Seal of, 197

Lossing, Benson J., drawing of scene of Battle of Alamance, 364

Lotteries, tickets belonging to William Byrd, 1767, and George Washington, 1768, 327

Louisburg, on Cape Breton Island, view, and expedition, 1744-45, 280, 281

Lovelace, Gov., letter to Gov. Winthrop, 132

Lowboys, See Furniture

Loyalists in American Revolution, See Tories

Ludlow, Roger, letter urging westward expansion of Massachusetts Bay colony, 97

Lumbering:
Sawmills, 18th century, 270
Timber area, New Hampshire, map, 17th century, 67
Tools, axes and hatchets used in, 75
Lutherans, immigration to Georgia, 221; church at Trappe, Pa., 241; Heinrich Melchior Muhlenberg, founder of churches and schools, and sketch of christening, 275
Lynde House, Melrose, Mass., 79

M

Mail, *See* Postal Service
Maine, early settlements, 64-66
Manchester, N. H., Steatite Indian bowl found at, 68
Mangle, *See* Furniture: Mangle
Manhattan Island, 1626, 138
Maps:
America, 16th century map of, 2
Amsterdam, Holland, 17th century, 141
Battle of Bunker's Hill, plan, 1775, 371
Carolina and Florida Rivers, John White's map, c. 1585, 5
Charleston, S. C., Wm. Gerard De Brahm's plan, c. 1760, 200
Crown Point and Fort Edward, map of country between, 18th century, 350
Ebenezer, Ga., Wm. Gerard De Brahm's plan of, 18th century, 222
English colonies in North America, c. 1700, 252
Fort Barrington, Ga., by Wm. Gerard De Brahm, Colonial, 224
Fort Erie, Colonial, 356
Fort Johnson, Wm. Gerard De Brahm's plan for, Charleston, S. C., c. 1760, 200
Fort Loudon, plan of, by Wm. Gerard De Brahm, 18th century, 349
Fort Sullivan, plan of, 1776, 386
Frederica, Ga., map showing fortifications, Colonial, 224
Hudson and Delaware, settlements, map by Virginia Farrer, 1651, 159
Island of Barbados, 17th century, 197
Kingston, N. Y., plan of, 17th century, 157
Leyden, Holland, Dutch home of Pilgrims, 39
New Amsterdam during Dutch possession, 159
New England, John Smith's map of, 37
New England, map of, 1675, 135
New Hampshire timber area for use of Royal Navy, 17th century, 67
New Haven, Conn., 1641, 105
New York City, 1742-44, 254
Philadelphia, Plan of, by Thomas Holme, 17th century, 229; plan of City and Environs by William Faden, 1777, 393
Port Royal (Nova Scotia), c. 1609, 35
Roanoke Island, by John White, 1590, 5
Saco, Maine, fort at, 17th century, 66
Sagadahoc, Maine, c. 1607, 36
St. Augustine, Fla., 17th century, 4
St. Croix Island, Champlain's colony at, c. 1613, 34
Savannah County, Ga., 18th century, 220
Schenectady, N. Y., 17th century, 157

Scrooby, England, showing home of Pilgrims, 38
South Carolina, Herman Moll's, showing names of early settlers, 198
Strawberry Bank and New Hampshire, 17th century, 70-71
Virginia, by John Smith, 17th century, 14
Virginia and Maryland, by Augustin Herrman, 1670, 189
Williamsburg, Va., with location of each building, 1782, 253
Marblehead, Mass.:
Orne House, c. 1730, 260
Moll Pitcher House, c. 1720, 260
Powder House, 1755, 373
St. Michaels Church, 1714, 279
Jeremiah Lee Mansion, 1768, 315
Marion, General Francis, portrait of, 388
Markets, Dutch, 17th century, 144
Marquette, Father, chasuble of, 178
Maryland, 176-95; map, by Augustine Herrman in 1670, 189
Maryland, *See also* Annapolis; Houses: Interiors; St. Mary's City; St. Mary's County
Maryland Gazette, The, See Periodicals: Newspapers
Marzipan moulds for festival cookies, Pa., Colonial, 246
Masks, from Jamestown, 29; worn by 17th century Puritan women, 123; Indian mask of the twisted face, and Indian doctor mask, 351
Mason and Dixon Line, establishment of, and marker from, 295
Massachusetts Bay Colony, Charter of, 73
Massacres, *See* Indians: Massacres
Mathematics, Rule of Three, used in 18th century, 285
Mather, Rev. Cotton, portrait of, 113
Mather, Rev. Richard, wood engraving of, by John Foster, 73
Mayflower, model of, 41
Mayflower Compact, 42
McIntire, Samuel, ship figurehead carved by, 300
McIntire Garrison House, York, Me., 109
McIntosh, Brigadier-General Lachlan, portrait of, 388
McIntyre Log Cabin, near Charlotte, Mecklenberg County, N. C., 216
Meat:
Barrel, Colonial Pa., 243
Butchering tools and utensils used in Colonial Pa., 244
House, "Old House of the Hinges," East New Market, Md., 18th century, 318
Medals:
First voted by Congress, 372
George Washington and siege of Boston, in celebration of, 372
To captors of Major Andre, 394
Medford, Mass., Peter Tufts House (or Old Fort or Craddock House), 1677-80, 109
Medicine:
17th century, 120
Surgery, ear, nose and throat operations, and amputations, c. 1674, 120
Dentist, Dutch, 17th century, 144
Ad, 1759, 331
18th century methods of surgery and instruments used, 403

See also Apothecary Shops; Hospitals

Medway, plantation home built by Jan Van Arrsens, S. C., 202

Meeting houses, *See* Churches: Pennsylvania

Melrose, Mass., Lynde House, 17th century, 79

Mennonites, buggy, Amish couple, foot washing ritual, 276

Mercer, Hugh, pencil drawing by Trumbull, 331

Mercury, The, See Periodicals: Newspapers

Merion, Pa., Friends Meeting House, Colonial and modern view, 235

Mess kit, used by Colonel Nicholas Fish during Revolutionary War, 397

Methodism, brought to Georgia by Rev. George Whitefield, 273

Michigan, The, 354

Middleton, Arthur, portrait by Benjamin West, 380

Middleton, R. I., Home of George Berkeley, 18th century, 286

Middleton, Thomas, portrait by Benjamin West, 345

Middleton Place, near Charleston, S. C., and view of Ashley River from Middleton Place, 203

Militia, Massachusetts Bay Colony, 94-96

Milk pail, wooden, Swedish, Colonial, 165

Milkmaid, 17th century, 119

Millbach, Lebanon County, house, Pa., 261

Miller, Lewis, watercolor pictures by:
Lutheran Church (old one), York, Pa., service in, 1800, 241
Lutheran Schoolhouse, York, Pa., 1805, 241
Woman baking bread, and a woman frying potatoes, York, Pa., 1800, 244
Lutheran Church (old one), christening in, York, Pa., 1799, 275

Mills:
Paper, interior, 18th century, 343
Saw Mills:
Long Island, N. Y., Colonial, 107
18th century, 270
Tan bark, New Hampshire, Colonial, 117
Water:
New London, Conn., built by John Winthrop, c. 1650, 100
Tide operated, built, c. 1643, 119
Mountain grist mill, 218
Cresheim Creek, Pa., colonial, 250
Ephrata Cloister, Ephrata, Pa., Colonial, 250
Wind:
Cape Cod, Colonial, 57
Bridgehampton, Long Island, Colonial, 107
Mechanism of a windmill, 119, 143
New Amsterdam, c. 1679, 142
Holland, c. 1690, 143

Millstone, Pa., Colonial, 250

Mirrors, *See* Furniture

Mischianza, ticket and invitation to, 394

Mitchell, Zerviah G., descendant of Massasoit, portrait of, 57

Mittens, *See* Costume

Moale, John, sketch of Baltimore, Md., 1752, 295

Moale, Mrs. John, portrait of, with granddaughter, painted by Joshua Johnson, Negro artist, c. 1800, 295

Modern Riding-Master, The, by Philip Astley, 1776, 396

Mohawk, *See* Indians, Mohawk

Moll, Herman, map showing names of early settlers in South Carolina, 1715, 198

Money:
Coins:
Elizabethan, showing a ship, 5
Double Crown, James I Period, found at Jamestown, 19
Seventeenth Century, from Castine Hoard, 63
Leewen Daalder (Lion dollar), Netherlands, 1641, 63
Louis XIII, Ecu blanc, 1652, 63
Pine tree shilling, Mass., 1652, 63
Philip IV, 8 Reales, Lima, Peru, 1659, 63
Charles II, 8 Reales, Bolivia, 1678, 63
Pine tree shillings, c. 1652, 126
Kruisdaalder (cross dollar), 1655, 153
Gulden, United Provinces, Gelderland and Zeeland, 1698, 153
Pistole, or two escudos, Charles II of Spain, 1655-1700, 153
Seventeenth century, found at Richmond's Island, 63
Algiers, Muhammad IV, 1648-1687, 160
Morroco Filali Sherifs Ismail, 1672-1727, 160
Coin from Fez, 1681, 160
Rosa Americana penny, 1723, 282
George II shilling, 1758, 303
Eight Reales, 1767, 303
Chalmers, and Barry, sixpence, 1783, threepence, 1783, one shilling, 1783, 384
Paper:
Promissory note, New Hampshire, 1734, 282
Two pence, Mass., 1744, 282
Six pence, Mass., 1744, 282
Ten shilling note, New York, 1771, 383
Maryland indented eight dollar bill, 1774, 383
Twelve shilling note, N. J., 1776, 383
Continental currency, 1779, 384
Rhode Island five dollar bill, 1780, 383
Tokens, issued during American Revolution, 384
Wampum, as used by the Indians in the 17th century, 19; as used by Indians in time of Pilgrims, 46
See also, Counterfeiting

Monhegan Island, Me., 64

Monongahela River, at Pittsburgh, Pa., 347

Monsters, 1

Monteith bowl, by John Coney, Colonial, 292

Monteith, Lowestoft, Colonial, 320

Montresor, John, and building of Fort Erie, 356

Moore House, Windsor, Conn., detail from, 99

Moravians, houses built by in North Carolina, baptizing of Indians, teaching of Christianity rites to Negroes, 217; being married in group ceremony, 238; Children's Love Feast, 239; christening, 239; Easter liturgy of, Colonial, Pa., 240; *See also* Mennonites

Mordington, smokehouse at, 318

Moreau the younger, engraving of John Paul Jones, 400

Morgan, Brigadier-General Daniel, portrait of, 388

Morgan, John, pirate, portrait of, 160

Morris, Lewis, Governor of New Jersey, portrait by John Watson, 175

Morris, Robert, portrait by Edward Savage, 384

Morris, Roger, house in New York City, 385

Mortar, 18th century, 374
Mortar and pestle, Colonial, 89
Mount Airy, Prince George's County, Md., old Calvert mansion, 184
Mount Clare, Baltimore, Md., 317
Mount Pleasant, Fairmount Park, Philadelphia, Pa., 312; room in, 395
Mount Vernon, Va., two views, 404
Mountaineer, in front of his cabin, 410
Mouse traps, Colonial Pennsylvania, 249; Dutch, 17th century, 149
Mowry, Roger, "Ordinarie" (house) of, Providence, R. I., 103
Muffin irons, Colonial Pennsylvania, 248
Mugs, See Silver
Muhlenberg, Heinrich Melchior, portrait of, 275
Mulberry, in Virginia, 17
Mules, Boots used on, in rice fields, 204
Music:
    Instruments:
        17th century, 94
        First pipe organ built in America, 240
    Printed:
        Bay Psalm Book, The, used by Puritans, 124
        Book of Psalmes, The, hymn book used by Pilgrims, 60
        Hymn book printed at Ephrata Cloister, 277
        New England Church music, 1721, 279
        Yankee Doodle, as sung by troops in American Revolution, 390
    Recreation:
        Finns singing, Colonial, 164
        Moravian Easter liturgy, 240
Musketeer, 17th century, 47
Muskets, Swedish, 17th century, 163
Myers, Myer, silver tankard made for Livingston family, 278; silver dish ring by, 292

N

Naaman's, Del., Swedish block house, c. 1654, 163
Narragansett, R. I., view of Indian Rock, 101
Nassawango Furnace, near Snow Hill, Worcester County, Md., 192
Natural Bridge, Va., view of, 411
Navigation, quadrants as used by navigators in Colonial times, 301
Navy:
    Recruiting poster used during American Revolution, 382
    Pine-tree flag of an American cruiser, 1776, 400
    "Cohorn," American Revolution, 400
    Naval Button, American Revolution, 400
    John Paul Jones, portrait, 400
    Commodore Esek Hopkins, Commander-in-Chief during American Revolution, 400
    Ships, what sailors had to know at the time of the Revolution, 401
    See also Boats; Ships; Uniforms
Navy Yards, See Shipyards; Shipbuilding
Needlepoint, picture worked by Sarah Warren, Mass., 1748, 309
Negroes:
    Houses in Guinea, 20
    Joshua Johnson, 18th century Negro Artist, 295
    Phillis Wheatley, Negro poetess, 1773, 334
    See also Slavery
New Amsterdam:
    Early views, 138
    Model of, 140
    Stadhuys, 1679, 141
    Old Dutch houses, 17th century, 142
    Bogardus farm, c. 1679, 143
    Dutch interiors, 17th century, 148
    Map of, during Dutch possession, 159
New Bern, N. C., Tryon's Palace, 18th century, 364
New Castle, Del., Old Dutch House, 17th century, and tile house, 17th century, 159; Episcopal Church, 1704, 173
New Dutch Church, New York City, finished, 1731, 255
New England:
    John Smith's map of, 37
    View of coast, 72
    Map of, 1675, 135
New England Company, organizes government at Salem, 72
New England Primer, 122
New Guide to the English Tongue, A, by Thomas Dilworth, 1770, 337
New Hampshire, 17th century, 67-71
New Haven, Conn.:
    Theophilus Eaton House, 105
    First Meeting House in, 105
    Plan of, in 1641, 105
    West Rock near, 106, 130
    Plan of City, showing grave of John Dixwell, regicide, 130
    Yale College, 1749, 286
    State House, 1763, 346
New Haven, Colony, 105-6
New Jersey, founding of, and life in Colonial times, 174, 175
New London, Conn., mill built by John Winthrop the Younger, 100; Hempstead House, 1643, 100; Nathan Hale School, 18th century, 338
New Netherland, 136-160
New Plymouth, See Plymouth
New York, N. Y.:
    Beekman mansion, 18th century, 313
    Fraunces Tavern, 18th century, 404
    King's College, Columbia University, 18th century, 296
    Morris, Roger, house, 18th century, 385
    New Dutch Church, 1731, 255
    Old Jail, 18th century, 403
    Royal Exchange, 1754, 303
    Trinity Church, c. 1780, 385
    Van Courtlandt Mansion, 1748, 264
    Views, 1746, 255
    See also Maps; New Amsterdam
Newark, New Jersey, early view of, 174
Newbold-White House, Harveys Neck, Perquimans County, N. C., 216
Newbury, Mass., Pierce-Little House, 79
Newington, Conn., room in 18th century house, 259

Newport, R. I., Coddington House, 1641, 102; Old tower, 103; King House, c. 1710, 259; Redwood Library, c. 1748, 287; French troops landing during Revolutionary War, 398

Newport Mercury, See Periodicals: Newspapers

Newspapers, *See* Periodicals: Newspapers; Printing

Niagara Falls, view of, c. 1799, 411

Nickelson, Abel, House of, Salem County, N. J., 265

Night watchman, Colonial times, 255

Ninigret, Sachem, a Niantic Indian, 103

North Andover, Mass., Bradstreet House, 135

North Attleboro, Mass., powder magazine, 1768, 373

Northampton, Mass., home of Jonathan Edwards, 273

Northampton County, cypress swamp, N. C., 215

Notes, *See* Money

Nova Britannia, title-page of, 19

Nurse, Rebecca, House, Danvers, Mass., 128

Nursing Bottles, pewter, Colonial, 335

Nutmeg grater, silver, by William Cross, Colonial, 292

O

Oakland, kitchen at, 318

Ocean-Born-Mary House, Henniker, N. H., 87

Ogden House, Fairfield, Conn., 106

Ohio River, Pittsburgh, Pa., 347

Old Brick Church, Isle of Wight County, Va., 25

Old Fort, Peter Tufts House, Medford, Mass., 109

Old Gunpowder Meeting, Baltimore County, Md., 194

Old House, The, Cutchogue, Long Island, N. Y., 78, 86

Old House of the Hinges, meat House, 318

Old Man of the Mountain, rock formation in White Mountains, 69

Old Newbury, Mass., Poore's Tavern, c. 1650, 109

Old Ship Meeting House, Hingham, Mass., 125

Old Stone Fort at Windsor, Conn., 17th century, 98

Old Stone House or Whitfield House, Guilford, Conn., 100

Old Swedes, Swedish Lutheran Church, Wilmington, Del., 171

Old Tenor, Ode on the Death of, 282

Old Three Tuns, The, Boston, England, 80

Old Treasury, Annapolis, Md., 183

Onion Field, Wethersfield, Conn., Colonial, 98

Onkelbag, Gerrit, silver, cups by, 145

Oosoola, Me., Colonial view of, 353

Orange, Fort, Layout of, 155

Ordnance, 18th century, 374

Orne House, Marblehead, Mass., 260

Orphans, Orphanage, Bethesda, near Savannah, Ga., 18th century, 227

Orton Plantation, Cape Fear, N. C., 215

Osborne Place, Peabody, Mass., 18th century, 339

Oswego, Fort, 18th century view of, 354

Oswego, H.M. Ship, 1755, 354

Otis, James, portrait by Joseph Blackburn, 1755, 358

Otis, Jonathan, top of silver caster by, 319

Outacite, *See* Judd's Friend

Oven, outdoor baking, used in early Pa., 244; Dutch, Colonial Pa., 248

Oxen:

  Teams, 17th century, and present day, 90

  Carts, two-wheeled, Port Tobacco, Charles County, Md., Colonial, 192

  Crossing stream, from painting by G. Harvery, 341

  Pulling covered wagon, Colonial, 410

P

Paca House, Annapolis, Md., 317

Packing, Meat, Dutch, drawn by Peter Breughel the Elder, 17th century, 145

Paine, Thomas, portrait by Charles Willson Peale, 376; *See also* Books

Paneling:

  Shaw House, bedroom, Hampton, N. H., 17th century, 82

  Cedar Plank House, Hancock's Bridge, N. J., Colonial, 175

  New England, Colonial, 259

  18th century, 262

  Governor's Palace, Williamsburg, Va., 18th century, 263

  18th century, 313-16

  Apollo Room, Raleigh Tavern, Williamsburg, Va., 18th century, 367

Paper, Mill, 18th century, 343

Paper Money, *See* Money

Paradisi in Sole, plates from, by John Parkinson, 93

Parks, Boston, Mass., Common, 1768, 362

Parlors, *See* Interiors: Living rooms

Patroons, Dutch West India Company's publication listing rights of, 156

Patten, wooden, 17th century, 90

Peabody, Mass., ancient oak tree, 58; Osborne Place, barn, 18th century, 339

Peake, James, engraving of 18th century Pennsylvania farm, 242

Peale, Charles Willson, portraits by:

  William Buckland, 346

  John Dickinson, 361

  George Washington, 372

  Thomas Paine, 376

  Benjamin Franklin, 378

  Richard Henry Lee, 379

  Samuel Chase, 380

  John Witherspoon, 380

  Marquis de Lafayette, 398

  Baron Von Steuben, 1780, 398

Pelham, Henry, portrait by John Singleton Copley, 337

Pemaquid, Me., ancient pavings, 64

Penn, John, his license to trade with the Indians, 351

Penn, William:

  Two portraits of, 228

  Tower where imprisoned, 228

  Landing at Chester, 229

  Landing at Philadelphia, 229

  Treaty with the Indians (painting by Benjamin West), 1682, 230

  The Life of William Penn, by Mason Locke Weems, excerpt from, 230

  His Letitia Street House, Philadelphia, Pa., 233

Slate roof house occupied in Philadelphia, 1699-1700, 234
Meeting House of, Chester, Pa., 234
Doll brought to Pennsylvania by him, 234
Pennsylvania Germans:
242-249
Doors, stairways and furniture, 18th century, 261
Birth certificate decorated in fraktur, 1784, 338
Use of Conestoga Wagon, 340
Tombstone made by, 18th century, 344
Rifle stock ornaments made by, and "Kentucky Rifles" made by, 374
See also Miller, Lewis
Pennsylvania Hospital:
Account of its beginning, printed by B. Franklin and D. Hall, 1754, 332
View of, 1767, 332
Pennyroyal, raised by the Puritans, 93
Pensacola, Fla., 18th century view of, 226
Pepperell, Sir William, painting by John Smibert, and Louisburg Expedition, 280
Pequots, See Indians: Pequot
Periodicals:
Newspapers:
Boston, Mass., Boston Weekly News Letter, ad from, 352
Georgia Gazette, excerpt from, 1763, 294
Maryland Gazette, front page for, Dec. 17, 1728, 288
Newport, R. I.:
Newport Mercury, 1758, 294
Savannah, Ga.:
Georgia Gazette, 1763, 294
Williamsburg, Va.:
Virginia Gazette, article from, Aug. 28, 1752, 332; front page from, 1752, 294; shipping notices from, 297
Perkins, George, watercolor of St. Peter's Church, Salem, Mass., 1733, 279
Persimmon, in Virginia, 17
Petard, 18th century, 374
Pets, See Dogs
Pewter:
Nursing bottles, Colonial, 335
Plates, Colonial, 89
Porringers, Colonial, 89
Spoons, "Chuckatuck," 17th century, 29
Philadelphia, Pa.:
Christ Church, 18th century, 396
Gloria Dei, c. 1700, 171-2
Letitia Street House, 1682-83, 233
Mount Pleasant, Fairmount Park, 18th century, 312
Pennsylvania Hospital, 1767, 332
Slate Roof House, 1699-1700, 234
State House, c. 1794, 346; c. 1778, 381; engraved by William Faden, 1777, 393
Stenton, doorway from, Logan Park, c. 1721, 258
Views, Peter Cooper's painting of, 1718-20, 256; by George Heap, colonial, 293; engraving by J. Hulett from drawing by Nicholas Garrison, 1767, 332
Woodlands' stable, 18th century, 339
See also Maps; Penn, William
Philip, "King," Indian Chief, engraving by Paul Revere,

108
Philipse, Mr. and Mrs. Philip, portraits by John Wollaston, 307
Philipse Manor, Yonkers, N. Y., 307
Pickman, Colonel Benjamin, portrait of, 376
Pieces of Eight (Eight Reales), used in 18th century, 303
Pierce-Little House, Newbury, Mass., 79
Piers:
Delftshaven, Holland, 17th century, 40
Salem, Mass., Derby's Wharf, 18th century, 298
Virginia, as found in colonial Virginia and Maryland, 188
Pike, use of, 17th century 47
Pilgrims, embarking at Delftshaven, Holland, 40; first view of America, 42; first homes, 44; marginal notes in Bible, 45; first trading post of, 48; Bible used by, 50; houses and furniture, 54; wooden dishes and utensils of, 56; costume of, 59; burial hill at Plymouth, Mass., 60; hymns sung by, 60; costume of, 60; dolls and samplers made by, 61; See also Plymouth Colony
"Pilgrims Going to Church," painting by Boughton, 59
Pillories, See Punishments
Pine, Robert Edge, portrait of Francis Hopkinson, 378; portrait of George Read, 379; portrait of a group of men including Stephen Hopkins, 379
Pine-tree flag, used on American ships, 1776, 400
Pine tree shilling, 63, 126
Pipe organ, first built in America, 240
Pipes, clay, found at Jamestown, 20
Pirates, 17th century, 160
Pistole (coin), Charles II of Spain, 1655-1700, 153
Pistols, See Firearms
Piscataqua River, at Fort William and Mary, 70-71
Pitcher, Moll, House, Marblehead, Mass., 260
Pitchers, cider, New Hampshire, colonial, 68; cream, silver one, by Paul Revere, colonial, 319
Pitt, William, portrait of, 360
Pittsburgh, View by Collot or his companion, Joseph Warin, 1796, 347; See also Duquesne, Fort
Plantations (Listed by subject, See below for listing by name)
Cotton, 18th century, 334
Indigo, 18th century, 209
Life on, as described in Sot-Weed Factor, 1708, 191; early 19th century, 208
Sugar, 18th century, 334
Tobacco, 18th century, 334
Plantations (Listed by Name):
Brabants, near Charleston, S. C., colonial, 202
Drayton Hall, Ashley River, S. C., 1740, 262, 265
Fenwick Hall, Stono River, near Charleston, S. C., 1730, 202
Hampton, near Charleston, S. C., 1735, 201
Hampton, slave quarters, Towson vicinity, Md., 333
Medway, S. C., colonial, 202
Melrose, Wedgefield vicinity, S. C., 208
Middleton Place, near Charleston, S. C., 1738, 203
Oakland, Kitchen of, South Carolina, 318
Orton, Cape Fear, N. C., 1725, 215
Rose Hill, S. C., Colonial, 202
Stratford, Westmoreland County, Va., 266
Tryon's Palace, New Bern, N. C., 18th century, 364

Westover, North front, Charles City County, Va., 266

Plates, *See* Tableware

Playbills, *See* Drama

Playing cards, advertising, 230

Plows, *See* Agricultural Implements

Plymouth, Mass., animal life at, 43; Allyn House, 17th century, 48; Howland House, 17th century, 52, 54; Peregrine White's pear tree, 58; Second Meeting House, 1683, 59; burial hill at, 60; High Street in, 62; Leyden Street in, 62; *See also* Pilgrims

Plymouth Rock, landing place of Pilgrims, 43

Pocahontas, portrait of, by Simon de Passe, 14; rescue of John Smith, 15

Pocketbooks, *See* Costume, Women, Item: Handbags

Poetry, by George Alsop, frontispiece of *A Character of the Province of Maryland*, 1666, 195; poem on taking of Louisburg, 1745, 281; by Phillis Wheatley, 1773, 334

Pollard, Anne, portrait, 123

Ponteach: or the Savages of America, play by Major Robert Rogers, 352

Pontiac, Chief, play about him by Robert Rogers, 352

Poor Richard's Almanack, by Benjamin Franklin, 1733, 285

Poore's Tavern, Old Newbury, Mass., 17th century, 109

Popple, Henry, detail from map by, 1733, 188

Porcelain, Chinese plate made for Elias Hasket Derby, 299

Porringers, *See* Pewter; Silver

Port Royal, Nova Scotia, map of, 1609, 35

Port Tobacco, Md., ox carts in, 192; room from Habre de Venture, 18th century, 316

Portland, Maine, first Parish meeting house, c. 1761, 107

Porto Bello, the fair of, 160

Portraits:

Adams, John, by Copley, 18th century, 379

Adams, Samuel, by Copley, 18th century, 360

Alsop, George, 17th century Maryland poet, 195

Amory, John, merchant of Boston, by Copley, 1768, 297

Arnold, Benedict, 18th century, 395

Arundel, Anne, wife of Cecilius Calvert, 190

Atkinson, Theodore, Jr., by Joseph Blackburn, 310

Bartlett, Josiah, 18th century, 380

Bolzius, John Martin, 18th century, 221

Boone, Daniel, 18th century, 408

Bowdoin, James III, and his sister Elizabeth, by Joseph Blackburn, c. 1760, 335

Bowdoin, William, by Robert Feke, 268

Boylston, Thomas, 18th century, by Copley, 305

Boylston, Mrs. Thomas, 18th century, by Copley, 305

Bradstreet, Simon, c. 1679, 135

Brown, Moses, Providence merchant, Colonial, 297

Buckland, William, 18th century, by Charles Willson Peale, 346

Byrd, Evelyn, 263

Cabot, Sebastian, 34

Calvert, Cecilius, second Lord Baltimore, 176

Calvert, Charles, by Gustavus Hesselius, 18th century, 170

Calvert, George, First Lord Baltimore, 176

Calvert, Leonard, Governor of Maryland, 176

Campion, Miss, Puritan Child, 121

Carpenter, Esther Gerrish, 18th century, 306

Carroll, Charles, 18th century, by Chester Harding, 378

Cartier, Jacques, 34

Champlain, Samuel de, 34

Chase, Samuel, by Charles Willson Peale, 18th century, 380

Cherokee Indian, 213

Chesebrough, Margaret Sylvester, 1754, 307

Claiborne, William, 17th century, 190

Colden, Cadwallader, by Matthew Pratt, 1772, 376

Collin, Rev. Nicholas, early Swedish Lutheran Minister, 172

Cotton, Rev. John, 73

Creek Indian, pencil sketch by John Trumbull, 222

Darnall, Eleanor, by J. E. Kuhn, 18th century, 335

Davenport, Rev. John, Puritan minister, 124

DePeyster boy, colonial, 154

Derby, Elias Hasket, by James Frothingham, colonial, 298

Dickinson, John, by Charles Willson Peale, 18th century, 361

Dutch boy, colonial, 152

Duyckinck, Mrs. Gerret, by her husband, colonial, 154

Edwards, Rev. Jonathan, 273

Edwards, Mrs. Jonathan, 274

Eliot, Bernard, by Jeremiah Theus, 18th century, 304

Eliot, Mrs. Bernard, by Jeremiah Theus, 18th century, 304

Endecott, John, 72

Finley, Samuel, engraved by John Sartain, 275

Fox, George, Quaker leader, colonial, 161

Franklin, Benjamin, by Charles Willson Peale, 18th century, 378

Freake, Mrs. Elizabeth Clarke and baby Mary, 17th century, 87

Gerrish, Abigail, and her grandmother, Abigail Holloway Gerrish, by John Greenwood, 268

Gerry, Elbridge, by J. Bogle, 18th century, 378

Gibbs, Robert, Puritan child, 121

Hall, Lyman, 18th century, 380

Hancock, by Copley, 378

Heathcote, Caleb, Mayor of New York City, 1711-13, 268

Hendrick, King, Mohawk Sachem, 18th century, 350

Henry, Patrick, 18th century, 366

Herrman, Augustine, 17th century map maker, 189

Hewes, Joseph, by L. C. Tiffany, 18th century, 379

Hooper, William, by John Trumbull, 379

Hopkins, Commodore Esek, published by Thomas Hart, 1776, 400

Hopkins, Stephen and a group of men, by Robert Edge Pine, 18th century, 379

Hopkinson, Francis, by Robert Edge Pine, 18th century, 378

Howe, Sir William, 18th century, 392

Hurd, Nathaniel, by Copley, 18th century, 345

Jefferson, Thomas, from a bust by Houdon, 18th century, 378

Johnson, Sir William, 18th century, 350

Jones, John Paul, from an engraving by Moreau the younger, 18th century, 400

Kelpius, Johannes, founder of sect "The Woman of the Wilderness," colonial, 240

Kenton, Simon, 18th century, 408

King, Sarah Northey and daughter, 18th century, 335

Kosciusko, Thaddeus, 18th century, 398

Lafayette, Marquis de, by Charles Willson Peale, 18th century, 398

Lappawinsoe, Delaware chief, by Gustavus Hesselius, 1735, 231

Lee, Richard Henry, by Charles Willson Peale, 379

Leverett, Governor of Massachusetts Bay Colony, 94

Livingston, Philip, 18th century, 378

Locke, John, author of *Fundamental Constitutions of Carolina*, 196

Lolonois, Francois, pirate, 17th century, 160

Marion, General Francis, 18th century, 388

Mather, Rev. Cotton, 113

Mather, Rev. Richard, wood engraving by John Foster, 73

McIntosh, Brig. Gen. Lachlan, 388

Mercer, Hugh, pencil drawing by John Trumbull, 18th century, 331

Middleton, Arthur, by Benjamin West, 18th century, 380

Middleton, Thomas, by Benjamin West, 18th century, 345

Mitchell, Zerviah G., 57

Moale, Mrs. John and granddaughter, by Joshua Johnson, c. 1800, 295

Morgan, Brig. Gen. Daniel, 18th century, 388

Morgan, John, pirate, 17th century, 160

Morris, Gov. Lewis, by John Watson, 1715, 175

Morris, Robert, by Edward Savage, 384

Ninigret, Sachem, A Niantic Indian of Rhode Island, 1637, 103

Oglethorpe, James, by Ravenet, 219

Otis, James, by Joseph Blackburn, 1755, 358

Paine, Thomas, by Charles Willson Peale, 376

Pelham, Henry, by Copley, 18th century, 337

Penn, William, colonial, 228

Pepperell, Sir William, by John Smibert, 18th century, 280

Philip, King, by Paul Revere, 108

Philipse, Mr. and Mrs. Philip, by John Wollaston, 18th century, 307

Pickman, Colonel Benjamin, 376

Pitt, William, 18th century, 360

Pocahontas, by Simon de Passe, 14

Pollard, Anne, Puritan lady, 123

Pratt, Matthew, painting by him showing himself and others in Benjamin West's Studio, 1765, 345

Printz, Johan, Governor of New Sweden, 163

Pynchon, William, 73

Quincy, John, Puritan child, 121

Raleigh, Sir Walter, 5

Read, George, by Robert Edge Pine, 18th century, 379

Rivera, Jacob Rodriguez, by Gilbert Stuart, 278

Rogers, Major Robert, 18th century, 352

Rogers, Mrs. Robert, by Joseph Blackburn, 18th century, 352

Royall, Isaac and Family, by Robert Feke, 18th century, 375

Rush, Benjamin, M. D., by Thomas Sully, 332

Rynders, Barent, Dutch merchant, colonial, 154

Rynders, Barent, Mrs., Colonial, 154

Schuyler, Peter, first mayor of Albany, Colonial, 154

Sewall, Judge Samuel, 113

Shaftesbury, Earl of, 196

Sherman, Roger, by Ralph Earl, 18th century, 380

Shippen, Peggy and child, by Daniel Gardner, 18th century, 395

Skinner, Miss, by Copley, 18th century, 306

Smith, John, 14

Stiles, Ezra, by Nathaniel Smibert, 18th century, 307

Stuyvesant, Peter, 139

Tallmadge, Benjamin and son, by Ralph Earl, 18th century, 304

Tallmadge, Benjamin, Mrs. and children, by Ralph Earl, 18th century, 304

Teach, Captain, pirate, 214

Thornton, Matthew, 18th century, 380

Tishcohan, Delaware chief, by Gustavus Hesselius, 18th century, 170

Tomo-Chi-Chi, Creek Indian chief, and his nephew, 18th century, 222

Trumbull, Gov. Jonathan, Jr., with his wife and eldest daughter, by John Trumbull, 18th century, 305

Tyng, Commodore Edward, c. 1744, 284

Van Rensselaer, Kiliaen, Dutch patroon, colonial, 156

Washington, George, by Charles Willson Peale, 18th century, 372

Wentworth, Lady Frances, by Copley, 18th century, 375

Wentworth, Gov. John, New Hampshire, 18th century, 375

Wesley, John, founder of Methodism, colonial, 227

West, Benjamin, in a group painting by Matthew Pratt, 1765, 345

Wheatley, Phillis, 1773, 334

Whitefield, Rev. George, 227, 273

Willet, Col. Marinus, by Ralph Earl, 18th century, 389

Winslow, Gov. Edward, 59

Winslow, Mr. and Mrs. Isaac, by Copley, 18th century, 305

Winthrop, John, 73

Witherspoon, John, by Charles Willson Peale, 380

Wolcott, Oliver, by John Trumbull, 379

Yale, Elihu, by Zeeman, 268

Portsmouth, N. H. (Listed Chronologically):

Vaughn House, c. 1670, 69

Samuel Wentworth House, c. 1671, 86

Warner House, 18th century, 258

Samuel Wentworth House, 1761, 314

Metcalf Bowler House, 1765, 314

View, 1777, 386

Postal Service:

Letter from Gov. Lovelace of New York to Gov. Winthrop of Conn., 1672, 132

Letter by John Winthrop the Younger, 1693, 132

Benjamin Franklin as postmaster general, and his signature on a postmaster's appointment, 361

Posters:

Recruiting, Army, late 18th century, 382

Navy, late 18th century, 382

Postmen, *See* Postal Service

Potatoes, in Virginia, 16

Potomac River, Mount Vernon, 404

Pots, *See* Kitchen Utensils

Pottery:

Objects; found at Jamestown, 28
Delftware plate, 17th century, 147
Moravian, Colonial, 238
Pennsylvania German, 247
Poultry, *See* Chickens
Powder horns, used in French and Indian wars, 352; used by General John Stark, 392; belonging to John Calfe, 1777, 407
Powder magazines, North Attleboro, Mass., 1768, Williamsburg, Va., 1714, Charleston, S. C., 1703, and Marblehead, Mass., 1755, 373
Pownall, Gov. Thomas, Sketch of Bethlehem, Pa., 1761, 238; sketch of an 18th century Pennsylvania farm, 242
Pratt, Matthew, painting of Benjamin West's London Studio, 1765, 345; portrait of Cadwallader Colden, 1772, 376
Presbyterian Meeting House, Wilmington, Del., 275
Press cupboards, *See* Furniture: Press cupboards
Presses, Printing, *See* Printing
Prices:
    Currency table, 1774, 383
    Ferry rates, New York to Island of Nassau, c. 1733, 272
Primitive painting, American, found near Lancaster, Pa., 407
Prince George's County, Md., Mount Airy, Calvert Mansion, c. 1680, 184
Prince, Thomas, bookplate of, handwriting of, and title-page of sermon by, 281
Princeton University, *See* Colleges and Universities: Princeton
Printing:
    Press used to print *The Bay Psalm Book*, 124
    Press used by Benjamin Franklin, 285
    Printers at work, 18th century, 343
    Press used by William Bradford in New York, 18th century, 343
    18th century woodcuts as newspaper illustrations, 344
    See also Books
Printz, Johan, Gov. of New Sweden, portrait of, 163; silver mug used by, 163
Prisoners of War, remnant of Burgoyne's army, Charlottesville, Va., 387; *Jersey*, prison ship, at Wallabout, L. I., N. Y., old jail, used during Revolution, New York, surgery and instruments used on prisoners during Revolution, 403
Prisons:
    New York City:
        Old jail, used as military prison during Revolution, 403
        Jersey, prison ship used during Revolution, 403
    Williamsburg, debtor's cell in public gaol, 288
    York, Me., Old gaol, 129
Privies, 18th century, 318; *See also* Plumbing
Proclamations:
    Gov. Wentworth concerning the looting of his Majesty's castle, N. H., 373
    King George III, to suppress rebellion in the colonies, 376
Programs, *See* Drama
Promissory note, *See* Money: Paper
Providence, R. I.:
    Williams House, 101

Gorton House, 17th century, 102
Roger Mowry's "Ordinarie," 1653, 103
Tillinghast Mansion, c. 1710, 264
Rhode Island College (Brown University), 1793, 296
Province House, Boston, Mass., 134
Public Buildings:
    Amsterdam, Holland, West India House, 137; weigh house, 17th century, 141
    Annapolis, Md., Old Treasury, 17th century, 183
    Boston, Mass., Faneuil Hall, 19th century, 283
    Chester, Pa., Town Hall, Colonial, 232
    New Amsterdam, Stadthuys, 1679, 141
    New York, N. Y., Royal Exchange, 1754, 303
    Newport, R. I., Redwood Library, 18th century, 287
    Philadelphia, Pa., Independence Hall, views, 381, 393
    See also Capitols; Churches
Pugh, James, tablet commemorating his execution, 364
Pulpit, Dutch, used in Church at Fort Orange, 155; field, used by George Whitefield, 273
"Pumpkin Head," type of hair cut, 17th century, 120
Punishments:
    Pillory:
        17th century, 38
        Charlestown, 1767, 328
    Scarlet Letter, c. 1690, 130
    Scolding bridle, c. 1692, 129
    Stocks, early 17th century, 13; c. 1692, 129
    Tarring and feathering, of Tories during Revolution, 375
    Whipping, 17th century, 38
    See also Crime; Prisons
Pupils, advertisements for, 18th century, 338
Puritans:
    First Homes of, 44, 72-135
    Early Homes and utensils of, 75
    Building of, and tools used by, 76-77
    Houses of, 78-80
    Typical house (interior), 81
    Furniture used by, 82-84
    Clothes worn by, 84
    Homes of, 85
    Costume of, 90
    Food used by, 92
    Use of Danforth's *Almanack*, 93
    Vegetables and herbs grown by, 93
    Use of matchlock muskets by militia, 95-96
    Churches and music, 18th century, 279
Pusey, Caleb, House, near Chester, Pa., 232
Putnam, Mrs. Ann, deposition in witchcraft case, 128
Pynchon, William, portrait of, 73

Q

Quadrants, as used by navigators in Colonial times, 301
Quaker synod, 237
Quakers, Life at Flushing, Long Island, 161; *See also* Churches: Pennsylvania
Quakeress preaching, 237
Quebec, French troops being reviewed in the city, c. 1750, 356
Quinabaug Village, Sturbridge, Mass., 134

Quincy, John, portrait of, 121
Quinnipiac River, New Haven founded at the mouth of, 105

R

Raccoon, as may have been seen in early North Carolina, 212
Racing, Advertisement for, 1763, 325
Radnor, Pa., St. David's Church, 18th century, 235
Rake, clam, 17th century, 92
Raleigh Colony, Indian life at, 6
Raleigh Tavern, Williamsburg, Va., 316, 326, 367
Rattlesnakes, 212
Raynham, Mass., Leonard House, 17th century, 79
Read, George, portrait by Robert Edge Pine, 379
Recreation, See Amusements
Red Lion Inn, near Holmesburg, Pa., 272
Redwood Library, Newport, R. I., 18th century, 287
Reels, colonial, for winding spun yarn, 115, 117
Regalia, Indian, See Indians: Costume
Religion:
    Baptisms, Rev. Robert Jordan's Baptismal basin, 17th century, 63
    Chasuble, Father Marquette's, 178
    Christenings, Moravian, colonial, 239; Lutheran, as sketched by Lewis Miller, 1799, 275
    See also Churches; Edwards, Jonathan; Ephrata Cloister; Indians: Religion; Various denominations
Remick, Christian, watercolor of British troops on Boston Common, 1768, 362
Rensselaerwyck Manor, 156
Revell House, Burlington, N. J., 175
Revere, Paul:
    Engravings, "King Philip," Indian Chief, 108; British troops arriving at Boston, 1768, 362; Boston Massacre, 1770, 363; Harvard College in 1768, 372
    Silver by, cream pitcher and sugar bowl, 319; teapot, 365
Revolutionary War, 367-404; propaganda, 371; financing, 383-84; prisoners of war, 387; demobilization, 404; See also under names of specific Battles; Ships; Tories; Uniforms
Reynolds, Sir Joshua, sketch of Judd's Friend (or Outacite), a Creek Indian, 1762, 349
Rhode Island College, See Colleges and Universities: Brown
Rice:
    Fields, South Carolina, colonial, 206
    Hoes and hook used in cultivating, 204
    Piggins used for, 205
    Plant of, 204
    Pounding of, by Negro women, 204
    Scales used for, 205
    Water machine, colonial, 206
    Winnowing from a plantation, 205; house, Hopsewee Plantation, South Sanhouse, Hopsewee Plantation, South Santee River, S. C., 205
Richmond, Va., St. John's Church, 18th century, 366
Richmond's Island, coins found there, 17th century, 63
Rifles, See Firearms

Rittenhouse, David, birthplace of, Germantown, Pa., 250
Rivera, Jacob Rodriguez, portrait by Gilbert Stuart, 278
Rivers, See under identifying name of each river
Roads of the United States, The, by Christopher Colles, 1789, 409
Roanoke Island, N. C., ancient grapevine at, 10; as it appears today, 9; map of, 5
Roberts, B., view of Charlestown, S. C., 1739, 198-99
Robertson, Alexander, drawing of Mount Vernon, 1799, 404
Robertson, Archibald, drawing of Boston, Mass., 1776, drawing of Dorchester Heights, Boston, Mass., 1776, 370
Robinson House, near West Point, N. Y., 395
Rogers, Major Robert, Ponteach, title-page of play written by, portrait of, recruiting broadside, 1750, 352
Rogers, Mrs. Robert, portrait by Joseph Blackburn, 352
Rolling pins, Pennsylvania, colonial, 245
Roofs, See Architecture; Houses
Rope, manufacture of, colonial, 116; manufacture of, in 18th century, 300; twisting of hemp, colonial, 284
Rope walk, colonial, 116
Rosa Americana penny, 1723, 282
Rose Hill Plantation, home of Charles Heyward, South Carolina, 202
Royal Exchange, New York, 1754, 303
Royall, Isaac and Family, painting by Robert Feke, 375
"Rule of Three," short-cut to calculation used in 18th century, 285
Rush, Benjamin, M. D., portrait by Thomas Sully, 332
Rush lights, See Lighting
Rush light holders, 17th century, 52
Rynders, Barent, Mr. and Mrs., portraits of, 154

S

Saco, Maine, fort at, 17th century, 66
Sagadahoc, Maine, map of, c. 1607, 36
Sagadahoc River, See Kennebec River
Sailmaking, colonial, 284
Sailors, See Seamen
Sails, diagrams of sails on two 20-gun ships, 1794, 402
St. Augustine, Fla., map of, 1671, 4; Spanish Governor's House, 225; view of Fort San Marco, 226
St. Botolph's Church, Boston, England, 74
St. Croix Island, map of Champlain's colony, c. 1613, 34
St. David's Church, Radnor, Pa., 235
St. James' Church, Goose Creek, S. C., 200
St. John's Church, Richmond, Va., 366
St. Johns River, Florida, Fort Carolina at mouth of river, 16th century, 4
St. Luke's Church, (Old Wye), Wye Mills, Md., 193
St. Mary's City, Governor's Castle, a reconstruction, 1639, 185; old barn, 17th century, 190
St. Mary's County, Md., Manor of Cornwaley's Crosse, c. 1690, 180; fireplace of "Tudor Hall," 17th century, artifacts found on the site of Governor's Castle, 183; The "Folly," 17th century, "Long Lane Farm," 17th century, 184; three-notch road, 192
St. Michael's Church, Charleston, S. C., 200
St. Michael's Church, Marblehead, Mass., 279
St. Paul's Church, Chester, Pa., 235

St. Paul's Church, Edenton, N. C., 211
St. Peter's Church, Albany, N. Y., 255
St. Peter's Church, Salem, Mass., 279
St. Phillip's Church, Charleston, S. C., 199
St. Thomas Church, Bath, N. C., 211
Salem, Mass.:
    Church used by Roger Williams, 74
    Reconstructed pioneer village at, 75
    John Ward House, 1684, 78
    House of Seven Gables, 1662, 133
    Charter Street Burying Ground, stone from, 1729, 134
    Joseph Cabot House, 1748, 264
    St. Peter's Church, 1733, 279
    Wharf, 18th century, 298
Salem, N. J., Alexander Grant House, 17th century, 174
Salem County, N. J., Abel Nickolson House, 1722, 265
Salem Doll, 267
Salisbury, N. C., Michael Bruan Rock House, 1766, 216
Salt, being obtained from marsh, colonial, 210
Salt Cellars, silver by Charles Le Roux, New York, colonial, 319
Salzburger Lutherans, first religious sect to emigrate to Georgia, 221
Sampler, by Mary Hollingworth, 17th century, Pilgrim, 61
San Marco, Fort, St. Augustine, Fla., view of, 226
Sandby, Paul, engraving of Bethlehem, Pa., 1761, 238
Sands House, Annapolis, Md., 183
Sap buckets, used by Puritans, 90
Sartain, John, engraving of Doughty's painting of deer, 1830, 43; engraving of William Penn, 220; engraved portrait of Samuel Finley, 275
Sassafras, Virginia, 17th century, 16
Saugus, Mass., "Scotch-Boardman House," 1651, 78; Iron works house, 1643, 79
Savage, Edward, portrait of Robert Morris, 384
Savannah, Ga., Peter Gordon's view, 1734, 220
Savannah County, Ga., 18th century, map of, 220
Savery, William, lowboy in style of, 322; furniture label of, 323
Savory, raised by Puritans, 93
Savory, Daniel, cradle by, 358
Sawkill River, falls of, as shown in early 19th century view, 232
Sawmill, 17th century, 17; 18th century, 270
Saws, 17th century, 76
Sayre House, Southampton, L. I., 107
Scales, wooden, 17th century, 54; rice, c. 1750, 205; forged iron balance scale, made by H. Jackson, 1770, 359
Scalping, scalps taken in battle, Indians scalping victims, 213
Scarlet Letter, The, by Nathaniel Hawthorne, 130
Scarlet Letter Law, 130
Schenck House, Brooklyn, N. Y., 147
Schenectady, N. Y., plan of, 157
School Primers, used by New England children, 18th century, 286
Schools:
    Country, Connecticut schoolhouse, colonial, 285
    Lutheran School, York, Pa., 1805, 241
    Nathan Hale School, New London, Conn., colonial, 338
Schuyler, Peter, first mayor of Albany, portrait of, 154
Schuyler, Major-General Philip, watch owned by, 306

Schuylkill River, Gray's Ferry, 391
Scissors grinder, 17th century, 113
Scolding Bridle, See Punishments
Scotch-Boardman House, Saugus, Mass., 78
Scrooby, England, Map showing English home of Pilgrims, 38
Sculpture, See Statuary
Seacoast, New England, 72
Seamen, agreement with master, 1758, 302
    See also Navy; Ships; Uniforms
Secretaries, See Furniture
Secretary, Md., living room, Henry Sewall House, 1720, 262
Seneca or snakeroot, raised by Puritans, 93
Senecas, See Indians, Seneca
Sermons, title-page of Woe to Drunkards, Samuel Ward, 1622, 122; title-page of, Sinners in the Hands of An Angry God, 1742, Jonathan Edwards, 274; title-page of, on victory at Louisburg, Thomas Prince, 1745, 281
Settles, See Furniture
Seven Gables, House of, Salem, Mass., 133
Sewall, Henry, living-room of, Secretary, Md., 262
Sewall, Judge Samuel, portrait of, 113
Shaftesbury, Earl of (Anthony Ashley Cooper), portrait of, 196
Shaving horse, and method of using, colonial, 76
Shaw, J., engraving from his painting of Jones' Falls near Baltimore, 195
Shaw, Robert, etching of Fraunces Tavern, New York City, 404; etching of spot where Swedes landed in Delaware, 162
Shaw House, Hampton, N. H., 82
Shawangunk, N. Y., old Dutch Church at, 158
Sheldon House, Deerfield, Mass., doorway of, 258
Sherman, Roger, portrait by Ralph Earl, 380
Shields, Thomas, silver tea set by, 215
Shillings, See Money
Shippen, Peggy, portrait, with her daughter, 395
Shipbuilding, 17th century, 18; 17th century, 111; by British at Fort Oswego, c. 1755, 354; See also Rope; Sailmaking; Shipyards
Shipping (Listed Chronologically):
    Wharfs at Bristol, England, 17th century, 35
    Cargo list of vessel bound for New England, in 1640, 67
    Virginia, early 18th century, 188
    Salem, Mass., 18th century, 298
    Bill, 1755, 301
Ship figureheads, c. 1791, 300
Ship riggings, diagrams of, two 20-gun ships, 1794, 401
Ships, Merchant (Listed Chronologically):
    Print of, 15th century, 1
    Galleons, 15th century, 3
    Type used by Raleigh, 16th century, 5
    16th century, 8
    17th century, 12
    Fishing vessels, 17th century, 31, 32
    Mayflower, the, 17th century, 41
    Blessing of the Bay, The, 1631, 111
    Whalers, 1631, 112
    Half Moon, The, Dutch, 17th century, 136
    Grand Turk, The, Used in the China trade, 1781, 299
    Pink, and Polacre, 18th century, 301

Brig, ketch, schooner, snow, bilander, 302
Great Lakes, ships used on, 1794, 411
Ships, Naval (Listed Chronologically):
 Warships, 16th century, 41
 Warships, 17th century, 111
 Great Lakes, used in French and Indian wars, 354
 French warships, Lake Ontario, 1757, 355
 British troop transports, Boston, Mass., 1768, 362
 Gun deck of British frigate, replica of, 18th century, 386
 H.M.S. Jersey, prison ship used during American Revolution, 403
 See also Boats and under name of specific ship
Shipyards, 18th century, 283
Shirts, *See* Costume, Men: Item
Shoemaking, 17th century, 113; 17th century Dutch wooden shoes, 153; shoemaker, 18th century, 310
Shoes, *See* Costume
Shoomac Park, Falls of the Schuylkill, 251
Shops, *See* Stores
Shovels, 17th century, made of white oak plank, 67
Shumway House, Fiskdale, Mass., 59
Sideboards, *See* Furniture
Signatures:
 Bradford, William, 40, 42
 Bradford, William, Mrs., 40
 Brewster, William, 42
 Davenport, John, 105
 Dixwell, John, 130
 Eaton, Theophilus, 105
 Franklin, Benjamin, 361
 Goff, William, 130
 May, Dorothy, 40
 Mayflower, Pilgrims', 42
 Standish, Myles, 42
 Whalley, Edward, 130
Signs (Listed Chronologically):
 Tavern sign, near Holmesburg, Pa., c. 1730, 272
 Blacksmith shop, Williamsburgh, Va., 1772, 359
 Tavern sign, near Lancaster, Pa., 18th century, 271
Silliman House, Bridgeport, Conn., 18th century, 259
Silver:
 Bowls, "Monteith," by John Coney, colonial, 292
 Brazier, by John de Nys, colonial, 290
 Casters, by Adrian Bancker, colonial, 291; caster top, by Jonathan Otis, Newport, R. I., colonial, 319
 Caudle Cup, by Gerrit Onkelbag, 17th century, 145
 Chafing dish, by John Burt, colonial, 319
 Communion cup, given by John Winthrop to the First Church, Boston, Mass., 126
 Cordial cup, by Gerrit Onkelbag, 17th century, 145
 Creamers, by John Letelier and Thomas Shields, Baltimore, Md., colonial, 215; by Paul Revere, colonial, 319
 Cup, by John Coney, Boston, Mass., colonial, 290
 Dish ring, by Myer Myers, colonial, 292
 Mugs, used by Johan Printz, 17th century, 163
 Nutmeg grater, by William Cross, colonial, 292
 Porringers, by Benjamin Burt, colonial, 290
 Rifle stock ornaments, colonial, 374
 Salt cellars, by Charles Le Roux, colonial, 319
 Soup tureen, by J. B. Fouache, colonial, 320
 Spoons, marrow, by Thomas Hammersley, colonial, 319; rat tail, and moulds, colonial, 320

 Sugar box, by Edward Winslow, colonial, 291
 Sugar urns, by John Letelier and Thomas Shields, Baltimore, Md., colonial, 215; by Paul Revere, colonial, 319
 Tankards, made for Livingston family by Myer Myers, 18th century, 278; by Edward Winslow, colonial, 290; by Peter Van Dyck, colonial, 291; by John Le Roux, colonial, 320
 Teapots, by Jacob Hurd, colonial, 291; by John Letelier and Thomas Shields, Baltimore, Md., colonial, 215; design for, by William Faris, Baltimore, Md., 291; by Paul Revere, 18th century, 365
 Teasets, by John Letelier and Thomas Shields, Baltimore, Md., colonial, 215
 Tongs, by William Grigg, colonial, 319
 Tray, by Jacob Hurd, colonial, 291
 Vegetable dishes, by J. B. Fouache, colonial, 320
Silver coins, *See* Money: Coins
Sink and drain board, wooden, colonial, Pennsylvania, 248
Sinners in the Hands of an Angry God, sermon preached by Jonathan Edwards in 1741, title-page of, 274
Skillet, colonial, 236
Skinner, Miss, portrait of, by Copley, 306
Skowhegan, Maine, early view of, 257
Skunk, 43
Slate Roof House, Philadelphia, Pa., occupied by William Penn, 1699-1700, 234
Slatington, LeHigh County, Pa., early view of, 257
Slavery (Listed Chronologically):
 Slave trader, 17th century, 160
 Slaves in rice fields, colonial, 206
 European trading center in Africa, 207
 Quarters at "Melrose," Wedgefield vicinity, S. C., 208
 Slaves on indigo plantation, South Carolina, 209
 Slaves instructed in Christianity by Moravians, 18th century, 217
 Advertisement offering unclaimed Negro for sale, 1759, 288
 Advertisement for sale of Negroes and runaway slaves, 18th century, 333
 Slave quarters, "Hampton," Towson vicinity, Maryland, 333
 Slaves working on sugar, cotton and tobacco plantations, 18th century, 334
 Portrait of Phillis Wheatley, Boston, Mass., 1773, 334
 Slaves dancing, early, 19th century, 208
Sleepy Hollow Church, Tarrytown, N. Y., 158
Sleighs, Swedish, 169
Slippers, *See* Costume
Sloops-of-War, *See* Ships, naval
Smibert, John, Faneuil Hall, Boston, Mass., designed by, 1740-42, 283; painting of Sir William Pepperell, 280
Smibert, Nathaniel, portrait of Ezra Stiles, president of Yale University, 307
Smith, Alice R. Huger, watercolor of Negroes winnowing rice, 205
Smith, Aunt Lucy's cook shop, Annapolis, Md., 183
Smith, John, adventures in Virginia, 15; map of New England, 1614, 37; map of Virginia, 1624, portrait of, 14
Smokehouse, "Mordington," Frederica vicinity, Delaware, 18th century, 318
Snowshoes, 17th century, 65

Somes Sound, Maine, site of French settlement, 1613, 37

Sot-Weed Factor, by Ebenezer Cook, two pages from, 191

Soup tureen, silver, by J. B. Fouache, colonial, 320

South Carolina, Herman Moll's map with names of early settlers, 198

South Glastonbury, Conn., Hollister House, detail from, 99

Southampton, L. I., N. Y., Sayre House, 107

Southold, L. I., N. Y., early view of the town, 107

Sovereign, *See* Money: Coins

Spach, Adam, House, near Winston-Salem, N. C., 1744, 217

Spanish coins, *See* Money: Coins

Spectacles, Benjamin Franklin's, 18th century, 378

Speed, John, author of *Genealogy of the Bible*, 85

Spice mill, colonial, 119

Spigot, from Jamestown, 27

Spinning wheels, Harlow House, Plymouth, Mass., 17th century, 53; single spindle, colonial, multiple spindle, colonial, 114; colonial, 117; *See also* Textiles

Spoons, "Chuckatuck" pewter, 17th century, 29; *See also* Kitchen utensils; Silver; spoons

Sports, Bowling, on the green, 17th century, 150; *See also* Fishing; Hunting

Spread Eagle Inn, near Lancaster, Pa., colonial, 271

Spur, found at Jamestown, 26

Squares and mitre squares, carpenter's, colonial, 77

Squirrel, flying, North Carolina, 212

Stables, Woodlands, Philadelphia, Pa., 18th century, 339

Stadthuys, shown on model of New Amsterdam, 1660, 140; as of 1679, 141

Stairways:
The Old House, Cutchogue, Long Island, N. Y., 17th century, 86; Samuel Wentworth House, Portsmouth, N. H., c. 1671, 86; Brockway House, Hamburg, Conn., 17th century, 100; The Lindens, Danvers, Mass., 1745, 260; Pennsylvania German, c. 1752, 261; Eltonhead Manor, Calvert County, Md., c. 1720, Drayton Hall, Ashley River, S. C., 1740, 262; Mt. Pleasant, Fairmount Park, Philadelphia, Pa., 18th century, 312; Jeremiah Lee Mansion, Marblehead, Mass., c. 1770, 315

Stamp Act, 357

Standish, Myles, signature of, 42

Standish House, Duxbury, Mass., 48

Stark, General John, portrait of, powder horn used by, 392

Staten Island, N. Y., Billop House, 17th century, 158

Statuary:
Statue of George III, New York City, demolished by Americans during the Revolution, 360
Statue of William Pitt, New York City, mutilated by British soldiers during Revolution, 360
Houdon's Bust of Thomas Jefferson, 378

Stenton, doorway of, Logan Park, Philadelphia, Pa., 258

Sternhold, Thomas, *The Whole Book of Psalmes*, page from, 1606, 127

Steuben, Baron von, portrait by Charles Willson Peale, 1780, 398

Stidham House, Wilmington, Del., 17th century, 173

Stiegel, William Henry ("Baron"), glassware made by, 321; type of stove designed by, 324

Stiles, Ezra, portrait of, by Smilbert, 307

Stockade, *See* Fences

Stockholm, Sweden, 17th century view of, 171

Stocks, *See* Punishments

Stools, *See* Furniture

Stores:
Apothecary shops, Charleston, S. C., colonial, 210; Fredericksburg, Va., colonial, 331
Cabinet-maker, 17th century, 118
General, Landis' store, 18th century, 243
Hat shop, 18th century, 311
Tailor shops, Dutch, 17th century, 144; 17th century, 146; 18th century, 310
Toy shop, 17th century Dutch, 152

Stove plates, Pennsylvania German, 18th century, 324, 344

Stoves:
Cannon stove, designed by "Baron" Stiegel, 18th century, 324
Foot stove, colonial, 123
Franklin stove, 18th century, 324
Lutheran Church, York, Pa., 1800, 241

Stratford, Westmoreland County, Va., 266

Stratford, Conn., Clark House, 100

Strawberry Bank, map showing early settlement at, 70-71

Strong Box, Father Rasle's, 270

Stuart, Gilbert, portrait of Jacob Rodriguez Rivera, 278

Sturbridge, Mass., model of Old Quinabaug Village, 134

Stuyvesant, Peter, portrait of, 139; house and orchard shown on model of New Amsterdam in 1660, 140

Sudbury, Mass., Wayside Inn, c. 1686, 109

Sugar, Indian sugar camp, time of Pilgrims, 46; sap buckets used by Puritans, 17th century, 90; plantation, West Indies, 18th century, 334

Sugar Box, silver, by Edward Winslow, 291

Sugar bowls, *See* Silver, Sugar urns

Suits, *See* Costume, Men

Sullivan, Fort, plan of, Charleston, S. C., 1776, 386

Sully, Thomas, engraving after his portrait of Benjamin Rush, M. D., 332

Surgery, *See* Medicine

Surveying instruments, George Washington's, 348

Susquehanna River, View, c. 1872, 251

Sutton House, Ipswich, Mass., 79

"Swamp Fox," General Francis Marion, portrait of, 388

Swedes, landing in Delaware, etching by Robert Shaw, 162; portrait of Johan Printz, 163; portrait of Gustavus Hesselius and wife, 170; Swedes Church, "Old" (Gloria Dei), Philadelphia, Pa., 1700, 171; portrait of Nicholas Collin, 172; Church, Wilmington, Del., 1699, 171

Swedish Block House, and arms, Delaware, 17th century, 163

Swedish furniture and room interiors, as used in New Sweden, 166-7

Swedish house, Wilmington, Del., 162

Swedish log cabin and American imitation, 168

Swedish wooden chests, 17th century, 165

Swords, Gov. John Endecott's, 95

System of Rhetoric, by John Sterling, page from, 1788, 337

T

Tables, *See* Furniture

Tableware:
   Chinese export porcelain plate, 18th century, 299
   Delftware plate, 17th century, 147
   Pewter plates, and porringers, colonial, 89
   Wooden dishes and tankards, used by Pilgrims, 17th century, 56
   See also Kitchen Utensils; Silver
Tailor's advertisement, New York, 1753, 310
Tallmadge, Benjamin and son, portrait of, by Ralph Earl, 304
Tallmadge, Mrs. Benjamin and two children, portrait by Ralph Earl, 304
Tan bark mill, New Hampshire, colonial, 117
Tankards, wooden, used by Pilgrims, 56; silver, made by Myer Myers, 278; silver, by Edward Winslow, Boston, Mass., colonial, 290; silver, by Peter Van Dyck, New York, colonial, 291; silver, by John Le Roux, New York, colonial, 320
Tanneries, tanners at work, 18th century, 117
Tarring and Feathering, *See* Punishments
Tarrytown, N. Y., Sleepy Hollow Church, 1699, 158
Taverns:
   Eutaw Springs, S. C., watercolor, c. 1800, 388
   Holmesburg, Pa., Red Lion Inn, 1730, 272
   Lancaster, Pa., Spread Eagle Inn, 18th century, 271
   New York, N. Y., Cato's Tavern, c. 1712, 271; Fraunces Tavern, 18th century, 404
   Old Newbury, Mass., Poore's Tavern, c. 1650, 109
   Sudbury, Mass., The Wayside Inn, c. 1686, 109
   Westfield, Mass., Captain Clapp's Tavern, doorway from, c. 1750, 326
   Williamsburg, Va., Raleigh Tavern, Daphne Room, 18th century, 316; taproom of, 326; Apollo Room, 18th century, 367
Tea house, of Elias Hasket Derby, Salem, Mass., 18th century, 299
Tea Plant, Bohea, 365
Teach, Captain, "Black Beard," the pirate, portrait of and proclamation offering reward for his capture, 214
Teapots, Pennsylvania, colonial, 236; *See also* Silver: Teapots
Teasets, *See* Silver: Teasets
Terheun House, Hackensack, N. J., 175
Text books, *See* Books
Textiles, Early American quilt, and two textiles of two-toned blue, 309; *See also* Weaving
Theus, Jeremiah, portrait of Bernard Eliot, 304; portrait of Mrs. Bernard Eliot, 304
Thomson, Charles, U. S. Seal designed by, 1782, 405
Thornton, Matthew, portrait of, 380
Thoroughgood, Adam, House, Jamestown, Va., 24
Thors, Stephen, House, Dutch door from, New Hackensack, N. Y., 149
Three-Notch Road, St. Mary's County, Md., 192
Thunder Hole, Mount Desert Island, 37
Ticonderoga, view in, 1757, 355
Tide Mill, Hingham, Mass., 17th century, 119
Tiffany, L. C., portrait of Joseph Hewes, 379
Tiles, delftware, used at Jamestown, 29
Tillinghast Mansion, Providence, R. I., 264
Tinker, as he appeared in colonial times, 249
Tisdale, Elkanah, engravings by:

Tories and Patriots at a town meeting, 361
   Torries Tarred and Feathered, 375
Tishcohan, Delaware chief, portrait of, 1735, 170
Tobacco:
   Clay pipes used at Jamestown, 20
   Shipping, Maryland and Virginia, c. 1775, 188
   Slaves working with, colonial, 334
   Barns used in Calvert County, Md., 19th century, 188
Toilets, Privies, 18th century, 318
Tombstones:
   Lady Fenwick's at Saybrook, 1645, 101
   18th century, Charter Street Burying Ground, Salem, Mass., 344
Tomo-Chi-Chi, Creek Indian Chief, and his nephew, portrait of, 222
Tongs, silver, by William Grigg, New York, colonial, 319
Tools:
   Adz, 17th century, 29
   Axes:
      Indian, stone, 68
      Felling, 17th century, 64
      Early colonial, various types, 75
      Carpentry, *See* Carpenters
   Hammers, 17th century, 186
   Hatchets, colonial, 75
   Knives, draw knives, 17th century, 76
   Pliers, 17th century, 186
   Saws, 17th century, 76
   Shaving horse, colonial, 76
   Shovel, white oak plank, 17th century, 67
   See also Agricultural implements; under name of specific trade
Topsfield, Mass., Parson Capen house, 1683, 133; interior, 88
Tories:
   Broadside to raise troops for the King, Philadelphia, 1777, 376
   Button worn by New York Loyalist volunteers, 376
   Colden Cadwallader, Loyalist Governor of New York, portrait, 376
   Hanging in effigy, Lebanon, Conn., 357
   Pickman, Colonel Benjamin, Massachusetts, Loyalist, portrait, 376
   Propaganda, 1776-77, 376
   Royall, Isaac, and family, 375
   Tarred and feathered by mobs, 375
   Town meeting, arguments with Patriots, 361
   Wentworth, Gov. John and Lady Frances, portraits, 375
Towel rollers, colonial, Pa., 245
Town meeting, Tories and Patriots arguing in, 361
Towson, Md., slave quarters at "Hampton," Towson vicinity, 18th century, 333
Toy shop, Dutch, 17th century, 152
Toys:
   Chair, Dutch, 17th century, 151
   Coach and horse, Dutch, 17th century, 151
   Dolls:
      Corn-husk, 17th century, 61
      Rag, 17th century, 61, 121
      Elizabethan, 121
      "Letitia Penn," 1699, 234
      Costume doll, 18th century, 267

Grave doll, 18th century, 336
Jointed wooden, 18th century, 336
Wax, c. 1760, 336
Kas, belonging to Dutch child, 152
Kitchen, 18th century, 336
Marbles, Dutch, 17th century, 151
Trade Card:
Bookbinder, Andrew Barclay, 18th century, 287
Cloth merchant, Francis Hopkinson, colonial, 303
Trading Posts, Plymouth Colony's first, 48
Transportation, *See* Boats; Carriages; Carts; Coaches; Oxen; Ships; Sleighs; Travel; Wagons
Trappe, Pa., Lutheran church in, early and modern views of, 241
Travel, 18th century, 271-2; *See also* Transportation
Travis graveyard at Jamestown Island, 30
Treaties, Indian, Penn's, at Shackamaxon, Pa., 1682, 230
Trees:
Birches, 36
Elm, Wethersfield, Conn., 98
Honey, N. C., 211
Indian fig, N. C., 211
Indian Nut, N. C., 211
Oak Peabody, Mass., 58
Oak, Wye Mills, Talbot County, Md., 190
Palmetto, 198, 211
Pear, Peregrine White's, 58
Sassafras, N. C., 211
Trenton, N. J., Washington crossing the Delaware, 1776, 391
Trinity Church, Dorchester County, Md., 194
Trinity Church, New York City, ruins after fire of 1776, 385
Trumbull, John:
Engraving after his portrait of William Hooper, 379
Pencil drawing of Hugh Mercer, 331
Portrait of Gov. Jonathan Trumbull, Jr., of Connecticut, with wife and eldest daughter, 305
Engraving after his portrait of Oliver Wolcott, 379
Trumbull, Gov. Jonathan, Jr., house and war office of, 305; portrait with wife and eldest daughter, 305
Trunk, colonial, 55; cowhide, colonial, 75
Tryon, Gov. William, plan of his palace, New Bern, N. C., 346; view of, 364
Tudor Hall, fireplace in, St. Mary's County, Md., 183
Tufts, Peter, House, Medford, Mass., 109
Tulip design, as used by Pennsylvania Germans, 247
Turner, making furniture, 17th century, 118
Tyng, Commodore Edward, portrait, 284

U

Underhill, Capt. John, manual of arms used by, 95; defeats Pequots in 1637, 104
Uniforms, Army:
British:
Musketeers, 17th century, 43, 47, 95-6
Foot Guards, 1746, 280
Sentry, American Revolution, 369
Officers, American Revolution, 392
Dutch:
Armor worn by pikemen, 17th century, 139
Soldier's, 17th century, 139
French:
Soldier's, 1608, 137
Soldier's in American Revolution, 399
Spanish, 16th century, 3
Swedish, helmet, 17th century, 163
United States (Continental):
Rifleman, American Revolution, 367
Soldier's, American Revolution, 369
Officer's, American Revolution, 388-9, 392, 395
Foreign general's, American Revolution, 398
Uniforms, Navy:
United States:
18th century:
Commodore Esek Hopkins, 1776, 400
John Paul Jones, 1780, 400
United States Army, *See* Army
United States Seal, first, 1782, 405
Universities, *See* Colleges and Universities
Utensils holder, embroidered, Quaker, colonial, 236

V

Valley Forge, Washington's headquarters, directions to farmers concerning grain, and camp bedstead used by him, 397
Van Courtlandt Mansion, New York City, 264
Van Dyck, Peter, silver tankard by, 291
Van Rensselaer, Kiliaen, Dutch patroon, portrait of, 156
Van Rensselaer Manor House, Albany, N. Y., 315
Vaughn House, Portsmouth, N. H., 69
Vechte-Cortelyou House, Brooklyn, N. Y., 142
Vegetable basket, 17th century, 90
Vegetable dishes, silver, by J. B. Fouache, colonial, 320
Vegetables, grown by Puritans, 93
Virginia, map of, by Augustine Herrman, 1670, 189
Virginia Colony, arrival of English at, 12; map of, by John Smith, 14; adventures of John Smith, 15; plants found at, 16, 17; sawmill and water wheel at, 17; glassmaking at, 18; money used at, 19
Virginia Company of Plymouth, map of its settlement at Sagadahoc, 36
Virginia Gazette, excerpt from, 1752, 294; shipping note from, colonial, 297
Von Steuben Baron, *See* Steuben

W

Wagons:
Covered:
Conestoga Wagon and equipment for, 18th century, 340, 410
Baltimore, c. 1802, 411
Farm, Tyngsboro, Mass., 1750-1800, 341
See also Carriages
Wallpaper, Jeremiah Lee Mansion, Marblehead, Mass.,

Van Rensselaer Manor House, Albany, N. Y., 18th century, 315; Daphne Room, Raleigh Tavern, Williamsburg, Va., 316

Wampum, *See* Indians, wampum

Ward, John, House, Salem, Mass., 78

Warming pan, 17th century, 123; colonial, 259

Warner House, Portsmouth, N. H., doorway of, 258

Warren, Joseph, Boston Massacre oration, title-page of, 1775, 363

Warren, Mercy, *The Group*, title-page of, 1775, 390

Wars, French and Indian Wars, 347-356; Revolutionary War, 358-407; Indian wars, *See* Indians, Wars; *See also* under individual listings of Wars and specific battles

Washington, Fort, New York, attack on, 1776, 385

Washington, George (Listed Chronologically):
  Birthplace at Bridges Creek, Westmoreland County, Va., 348
  Surveying instruments used by, 348
  Lottery ticket, signed by, 1768, 327
  Portrait by Charles Willson Peale, 372
  Headquarters, New York City, 1776, 385
  Crossing the Delaware, painting by Emanuel Leutze, 391
  Home, Mount Vernon, Va., views of, c. 1799, 404
  See also Valley Forge; Revolutionary War

Washington Elm, Cambridge, Mass., 372

Watches, chatelaine and watch, 18th century, 306; owned by General Philip Schuyler of New York, 18th century, 306

Waterfronts, *See* Piers

Water Wheels, 17th century, 17

Watertown, Mass., Abraham Browne, Jr., House, c. 1663, 78; Abraham Browne House kitchen, c. 1663, 89

Watson, John, portrait of Governor Lewis Morris, 1715, 175

Wayside Inn, Sudbury, Mass., 109

Weapons, *See* Cannons; Muskets

Weathervanes, by Shem Drowne, c. 1720, 134; from the Stadthuys in New Amsterdam, 141

Weaving, methods of, colonial, 53, 114-17

Weddings, Moravian group ceremony, c. 1750, 238

Wedgefield, S. C., slave quarters of "Melrose," Wedgefield vicinity, 208

Weiser, Conrad, portrait of and home near Womelsdorf, Pa., 276

Wentworth, Gov. Benning, House, Little Harbor, N. H., 314

Wentworth, Lady Frances, portrait by John Singleton Copley, 375

Wentworth, Gov. John, portrait, 375; proclamation concerning looting of his majesty's castle in province of New Hampshire, 373

Wentworth, Samuel, House, Portsmouth, N. H., 86, 314

Wesley, John, portrait of, 227

West, Benjamin, painting of Colonel Bouquet's conference with the Indians, 349; London Studio, painted by Matthew Pratt, 1765, 345; portrait of Arthur Middleton, 380; portrait of Thomas Middleton, 18th century, 345; painting of Penn's treaty with the Indians at Shackamaxon, 1682, 230

West Boxford, Mass., room in a house built, c. 1675-1704, 118; room in house, c. 1725, 260

West Point, N. Y., 18th century view, 395

West Rock, near New Haven, Conn., 106; hiding place of regicides, 130

Westfield, Mass., Captain Clapp's Tavern, c. 1750, 326

Westmoreland County, Va., Stratford, 1725-30, 266

"Westover," North front, Charles City County, Va., 266

Wethersfield, Conn., onion field, ancient elm tree, 98

Whalers, *See* Ships, Merchant

Whaling, 17th century, 112

Whalley, Edward, regicide, signature of, 130

Wharves, *See* Piers

Wheatley, Phillis, portrait of, and book of poems by, 334

Wheelwright's spoke shave, colonial, 118

Whipple House, Ipswich, Mass., 79

Whipping, *See* Punishments

Whiskers:
  Beards:
    Sir Walter Raleigh's, c. 1584, 5
    John Smith's, c. 1624, 14
    Samuel de Champlain's, c. 1613, 34
    Jacques Cartier's, c. 1540, 34
    Sebastian Cabot's, c. 1540, 34
    Musketeer's, 17th century, 47

White, Father, Jesuit priest, blesses the Indians, 177

White, John, watercolor of an English ship, 1585, 8; watercolors of Indian life in Virginia, c. 1585, 6, 7; map of rivers of Florida and Carolina, c. 1585, 5; map of Roanoc, c. 1585, 5

White, Peregrine, pear tree of, 58; cradle belonging to, 50

White Mountains (The Old Man of the Mountain), 69

Whitefield, Rev. George, portrait of, 227; portrait of and field pulpit used by, 273

Whitfield House or Old Stone House, Guilford, Conn., 100

Whitman House, Farmington, Conn., 100; detail from, 99

Whole Book of Psalmes, The, used by Puritans, 127

Wigwams, English type used at Plymouth, 44

Wilderness settlement, 410

Willard, Aaron, clock label by, 323

Willet, Colonel Marinus, portrait by Ralph Earl, 389

William and Mary College, *See* Colleges and Universities: William and Mary

William and Mary, Fort, on the Piscataqua River, 70-71

Williams, Roger, Church he used in Salem, Mass., 74

Williams House, Providence, R. I., 101

Williamsburg, Va.:
  Capitol at, restored, "Frenchman's map" of, 1782, 253
  Governor's Palace, bed chamber and kitchen, c. 1740, 263
  Bruton Parish Church, 1710-15, 279
  Debtor's cell in public gaol, built, c. 1701, 288
  The House of Burgesses, William and Mary College, the Capitol, the Wren Building and the Governor's Palace, all, c. 1740, 289
  Supper Room in the Governor's Palace, 18th century, 364
  Apollo Room in Raleigh Tavern, 18th century, 367
  Powder magazine built, c. 1714, 373
  See also Colleges and Universities: William and Mary College

Wilmington, Del. (Listed Chronologically):
  Swedish House, 17th century, 162
  Farm Land around, colonial, 169
  "Old Swedes" church, c. 1699, 171
  Friends Meeting House, 17th century, 173

Stidham House, 17th century, 173

First Presbyterian Meeting House, 1740, 275

Windmills, *See* Mills, Windmills

Windows, casement, at Jamestown, 26; casement, 17th century, Puritan, 82; *See also* Houses

Windsor, Conn., Old Stone Fort, 17th century, 98; Moore House, detail from, 99

Wine, jug found at Jamestown, 28; ads for sale of wine, rum and brandy, 18th century, 325

Winslow, Edward, silver tankard by, 290; silver sugar box by, 291

Winslow, Governor Edward, portrait of, 59

Winslow, Mr. and Mrs. Isaac, portraits by John Singleton Copley, 305

Winslow, Maine, Blockhouse, 18th century, 353

Winston-Salem, N. C., log house, 1766, Adam Spach House, 217

Winthrop, John, first governor under Charter of Massachusetts Bay Colony, portrait of, 73; Silver communion cup given by him to First Church, Boston, Mass., 126

Winthrop, John (the younger), mill at New London, Conn., built by, 100; letter by, 132

"Witch House," home of Rebecca Nurse, a supposed witch, 128

Witches, petition of Mary Easty, 128; indictment against Abigail Hobbs, 128; depositions of Mrs. Ann Putnam and Ann Putnam, Jr., 128; witch cicatrix, 127

Witherspoon, John, portrait by Charles Willson Peale, 380

Woe to Drunkards, 122

Wolcott, Oliver, portrait by John Trumbull, 379

Wollaston, John, portrait of, Mr. and Mrs. Philip Philipse, of Yonkers, N. Y., 307

Wolves, timber wolf, 13

Woman Suffrage, Margaret Brent's request to vote in

Maryland, 1639, 195

Womelsdorf, Pa., Conrad Weiser House, near Womelsdorf, 276

Women, *See* Coiffures; Costume; Portraits

Woodlands, Philadelphia, Pa., 18th century, 339

Wool, skeins of, 117; wool-cards, 17th century, 114

Wren, Sir Christopher, and William and Mary College, 30, 289

Wye Mills, Md., St. Luke's Church, "Old Wye," c. 1700, 193

Wye Oak, Wye Mills, Talbot County, Md., 190

Y

Yale, Elihu, portrait of, by Zeeman, 268

Yale University, *See* Colleges and Universities: Yale

Yankee Doodle, two broadside versions, 390

Yarn reels, 114-115

Yokes, oxen, *See* Oxen

Yonkers, N. Y., Philipse Manor, 18th century, 307

York, Maine, Jenkins Garrison House, 109; McIntire Garrison House, c. 1640, 109; Old gaol, colonial, 129

York, Pa., Old Lutheran Church, 1800, 241; Old Lutheran Church, a christening ceremony, 1799, 275; Lutheran school house, 1805, 241

Z

Zenger, Peter, proclamation by Gov. William Cosby offering reward for arrest of, 288